Tactics

Sakura Kinoshita × Kazuko Higashiyama

1

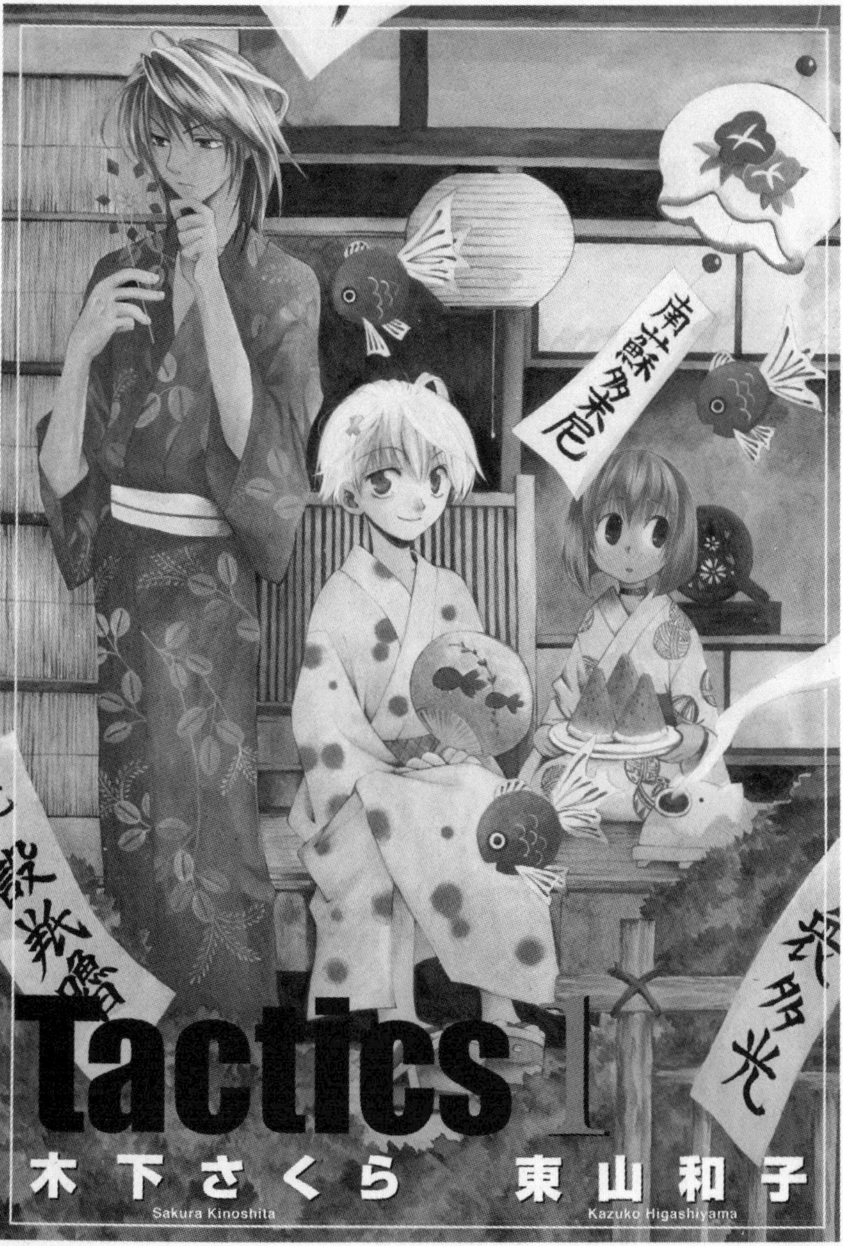
Tactics 1
木下さくら
Sakura Kinoshita
東山和子
Kazuko Higashiyama

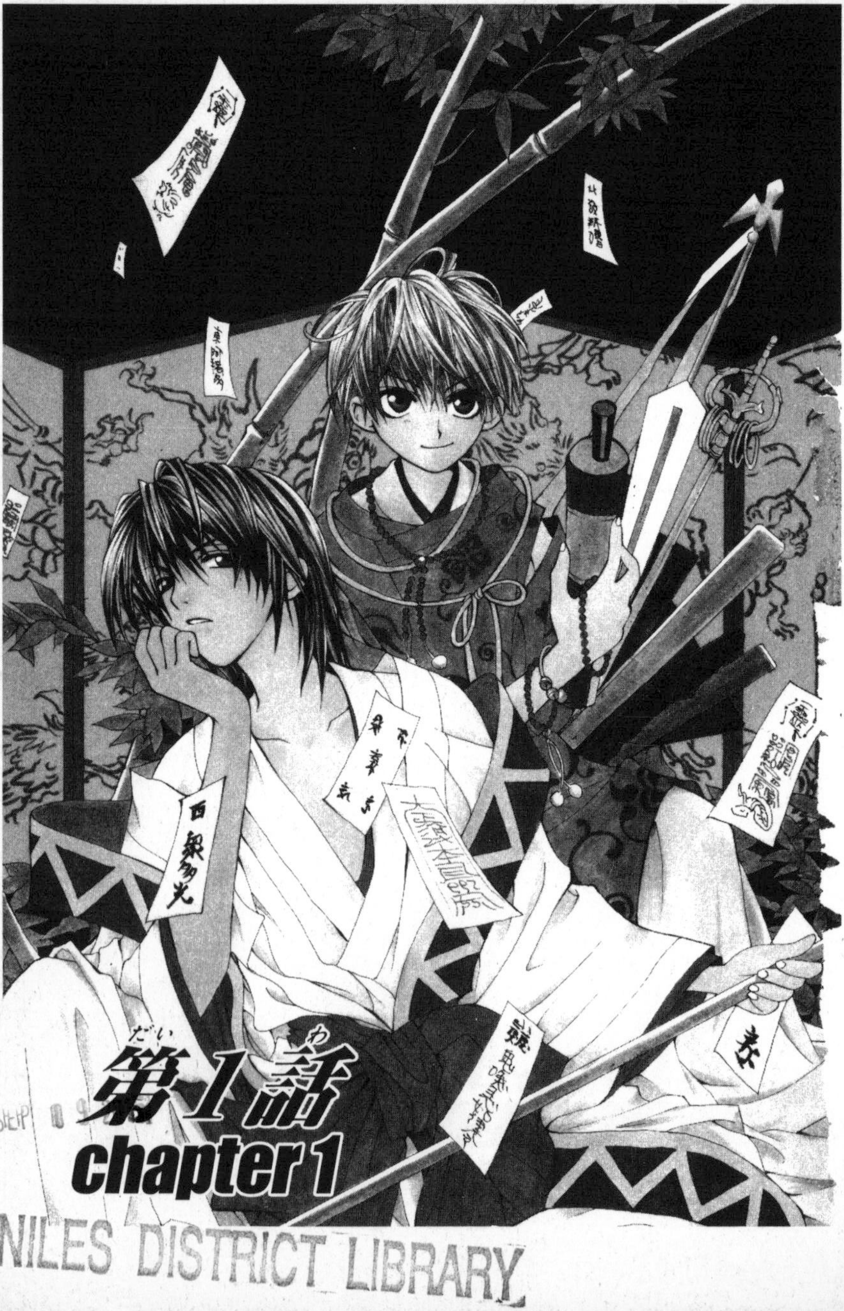
第1話
chapter 1

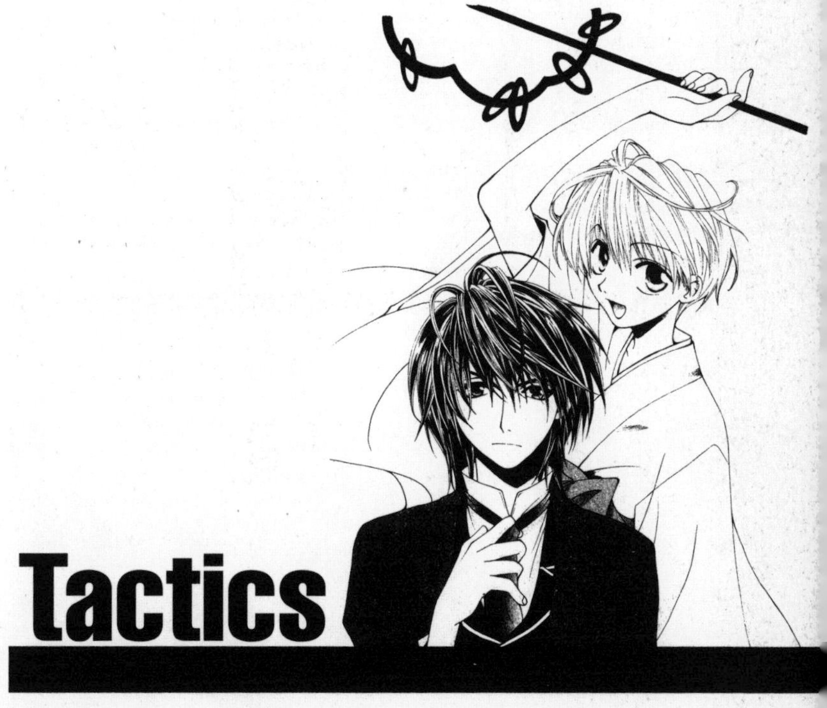

Tactics

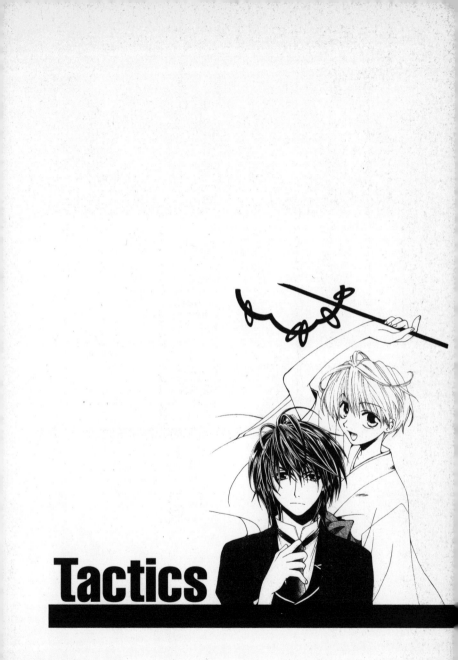

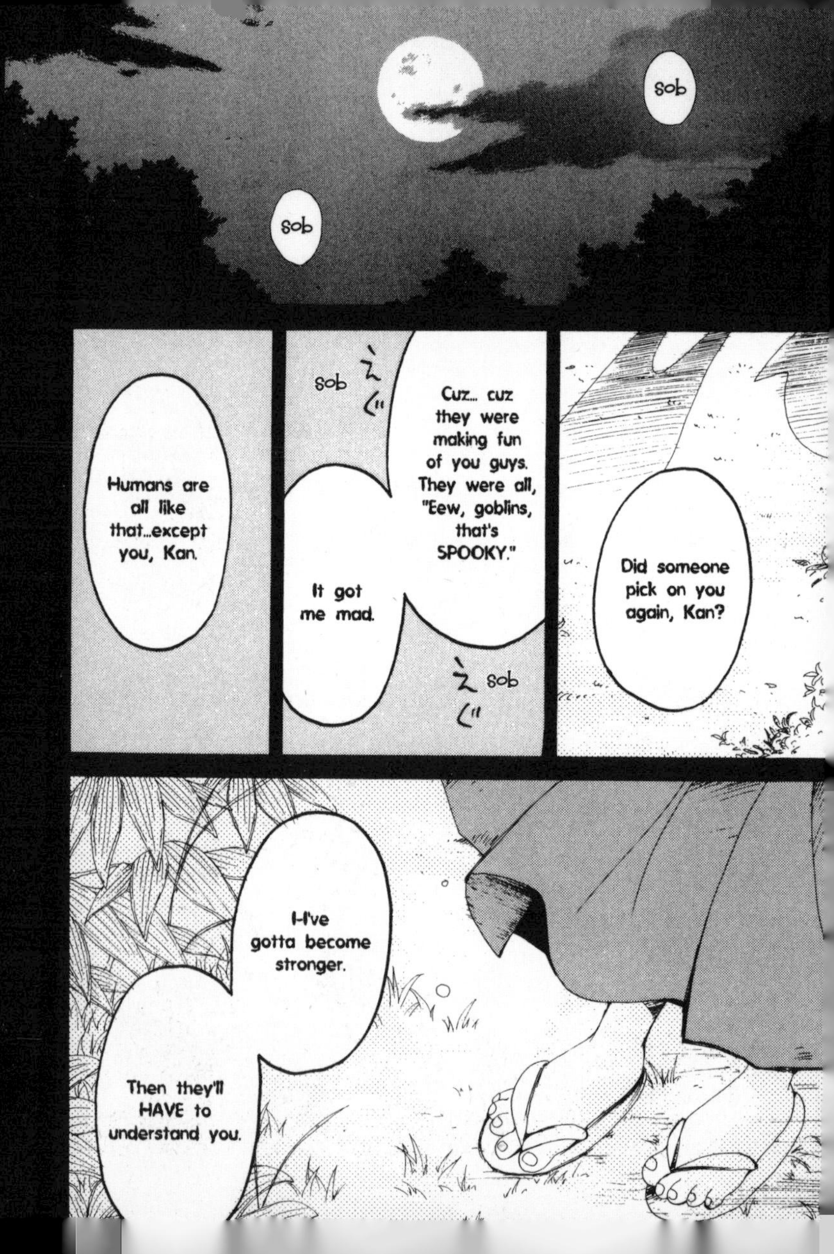
sob
sob
Did someone pick on you again, Kan?
えぐ
sob
Cuz... cuz they were making fun of you guys. They were all, "Eew, goblins, that's SPOOKY."
It got me mad.
えぐ
sob
Humans are all like that...except you, Kan.
I-I've gotta become stronger.
Then they'll HAVE to understand you.

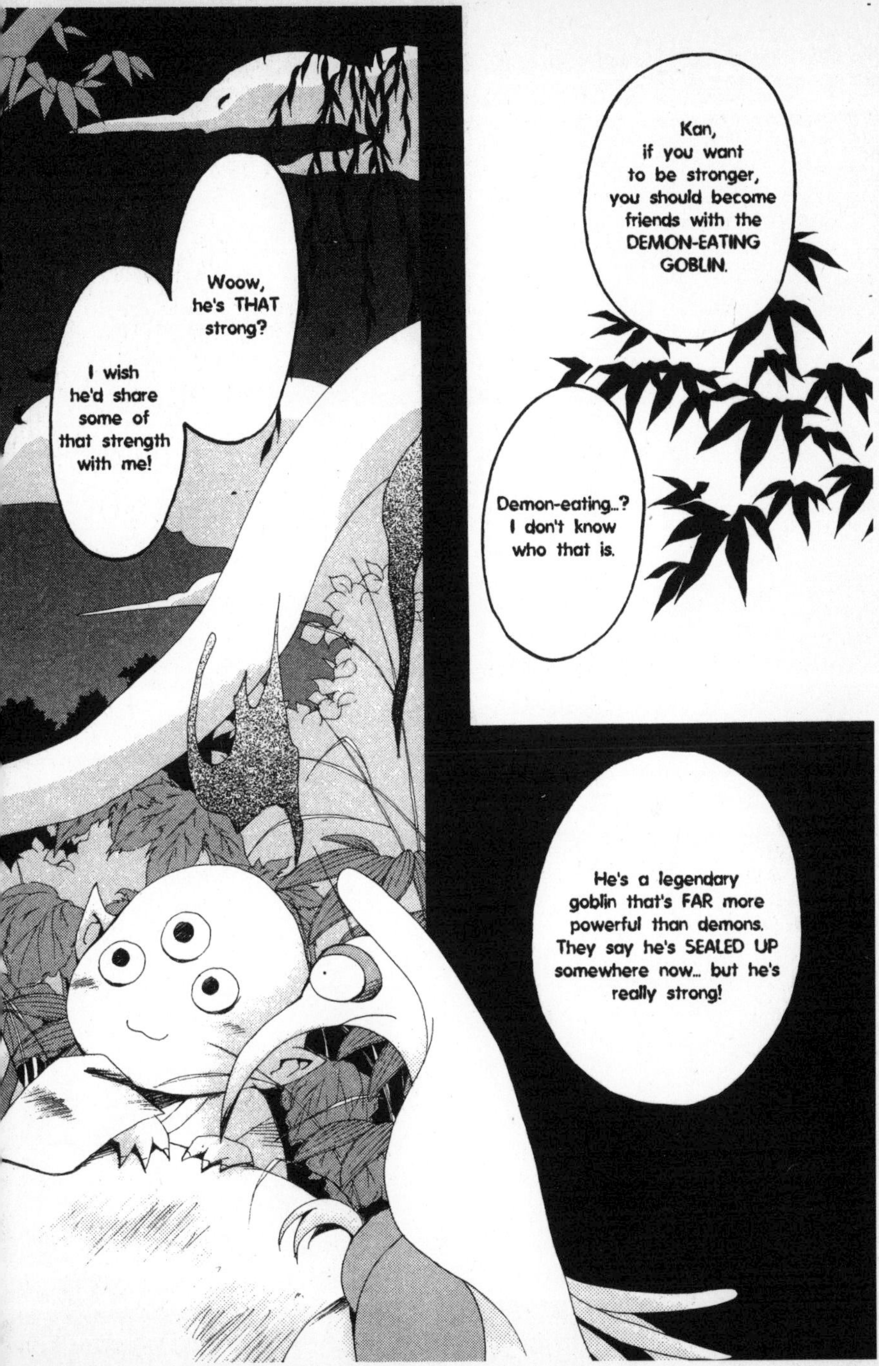
Kan, if you want to be stronger, you should become friends with the DEMON-EATING GOBLIN.
Demon-eating...? I don't know who that is.
He's a legendary goblin that's FAR more powerful than demons. They say he's SEALED UP somewhere now... but he's really strong!
Woow, he's THAT strong?
I wish he'd share some of that strength with me!

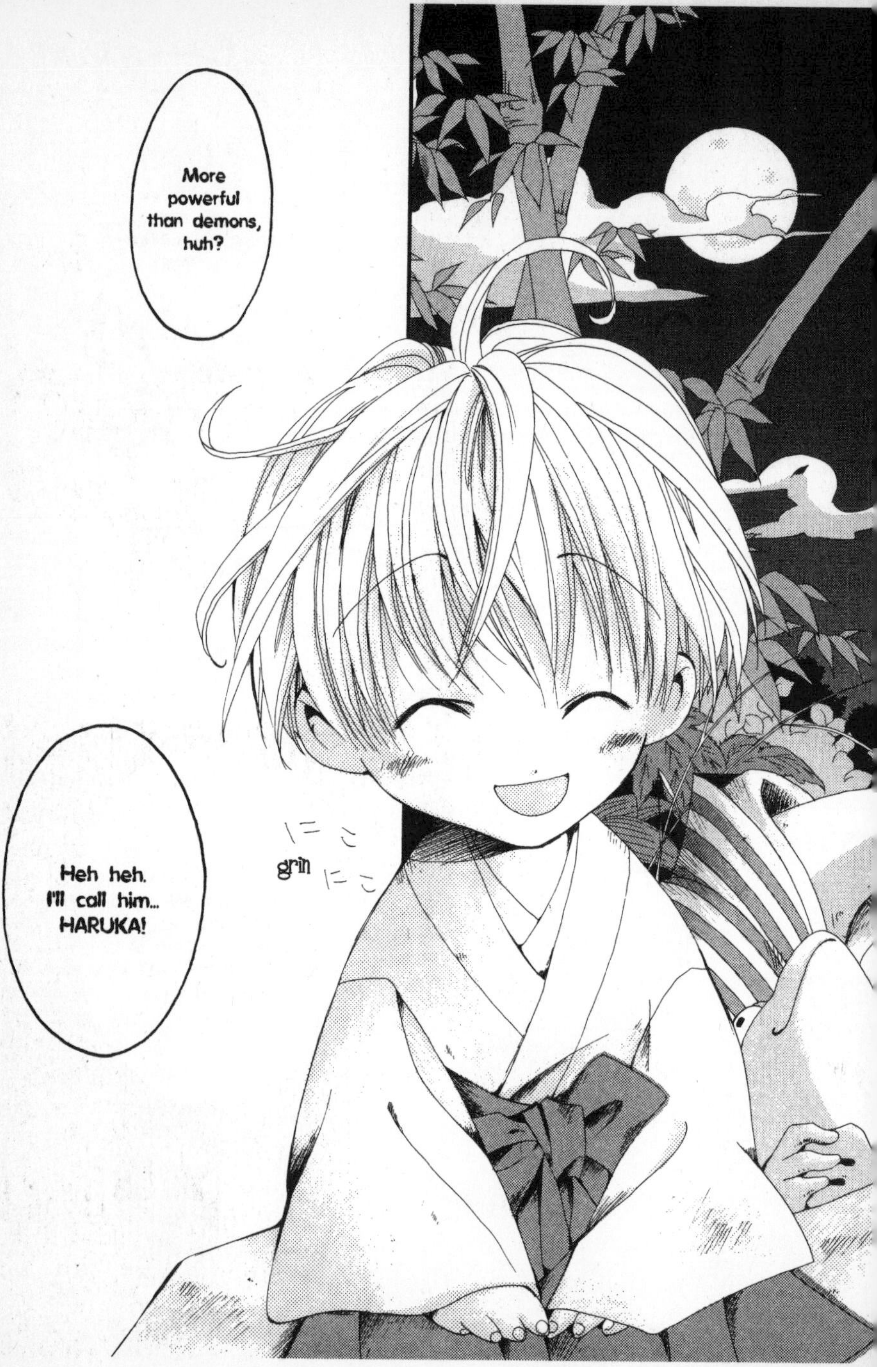
More powerful than demons, huh?
grin
Heh heh. I'll call him... HARUKA!

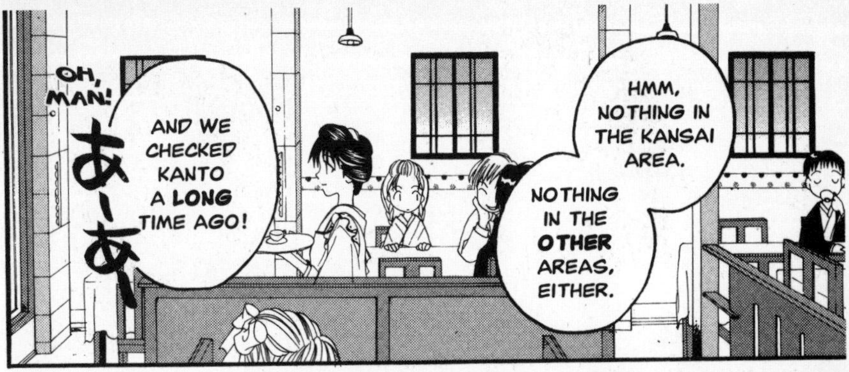
HMM, NOTHING IN THE KANSAI AREA.
NOTHING IN THE OTHER AREAS, EITHER.
AND WE CHECKED KANTO A LONG TIME AGO!
OH, MAN!
あ～あ

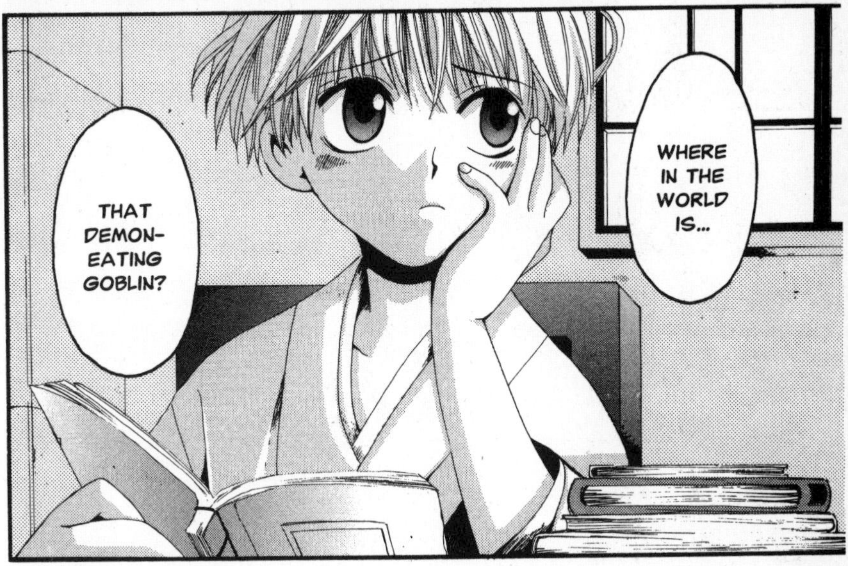
WHERE IN THE WORLD IS...
THAT DEMON-EATING GOBLIN?

I've been looking for him ever since that day—the legendary goblin, said to be the most POWERFUL of his kind.

He's supposed to be sealed up somewhere in this world…

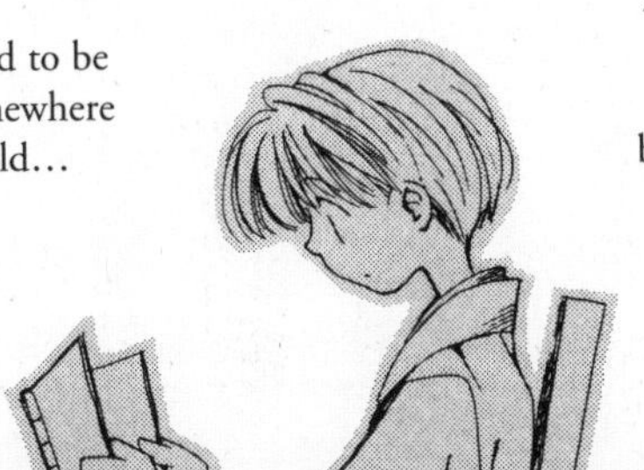

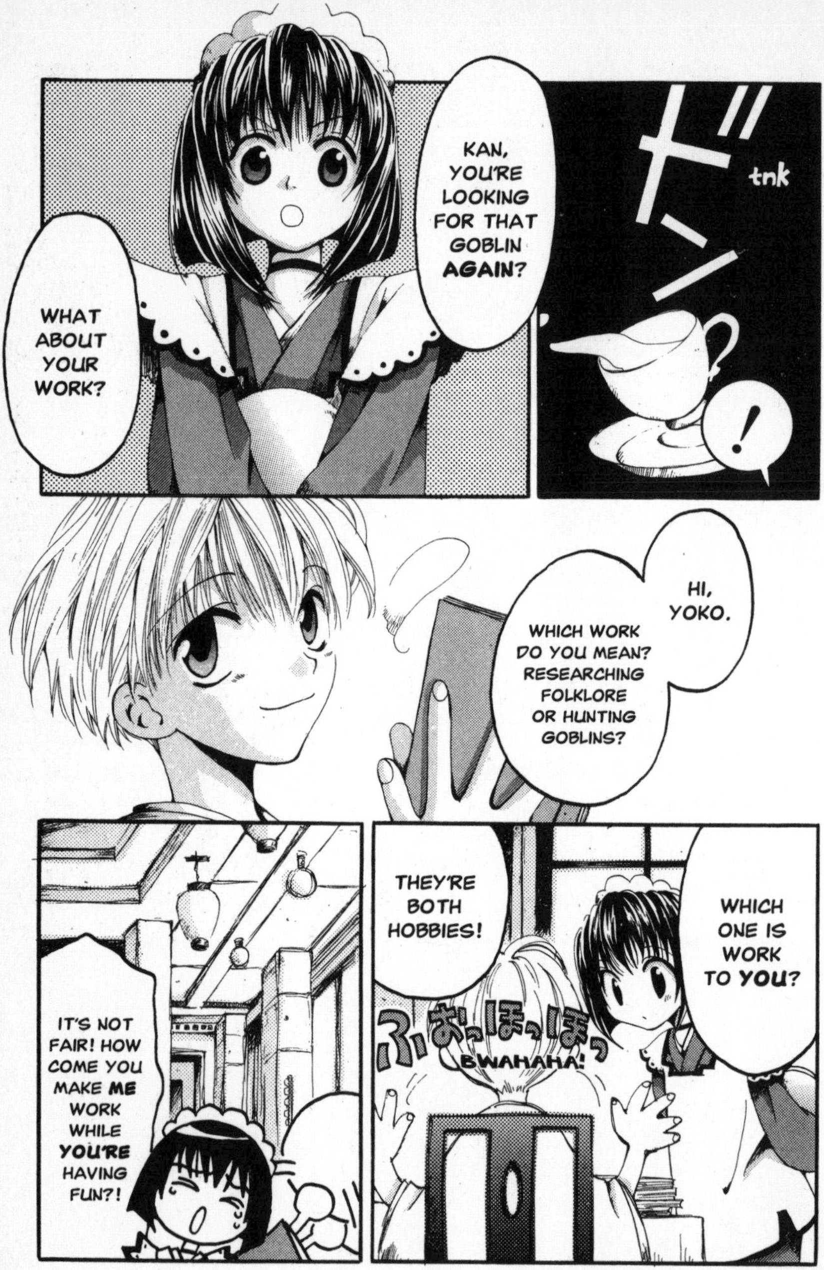
ドン
tnk
!
KAN, YOU'RE LOOKING FOR THAT GOBLIN **AGAIN**?
WHAT ABOUT YOUR WORK?
HI, YOKO.
WHICH WORK DO YOU MEAN? RESEARCHING FOLKLORE OR HUNTING GOBLINS?
WHICH ONE IS WORK TO **YOU**?
THEY'RE BOTH HOBBIES!
ふぉっほっほっ
BWAHAHA!
IT'S NOT FAIR! HOW COME YOU MAKE **ME** WORK WHILE **YOU'RE** HAVING FUN?!

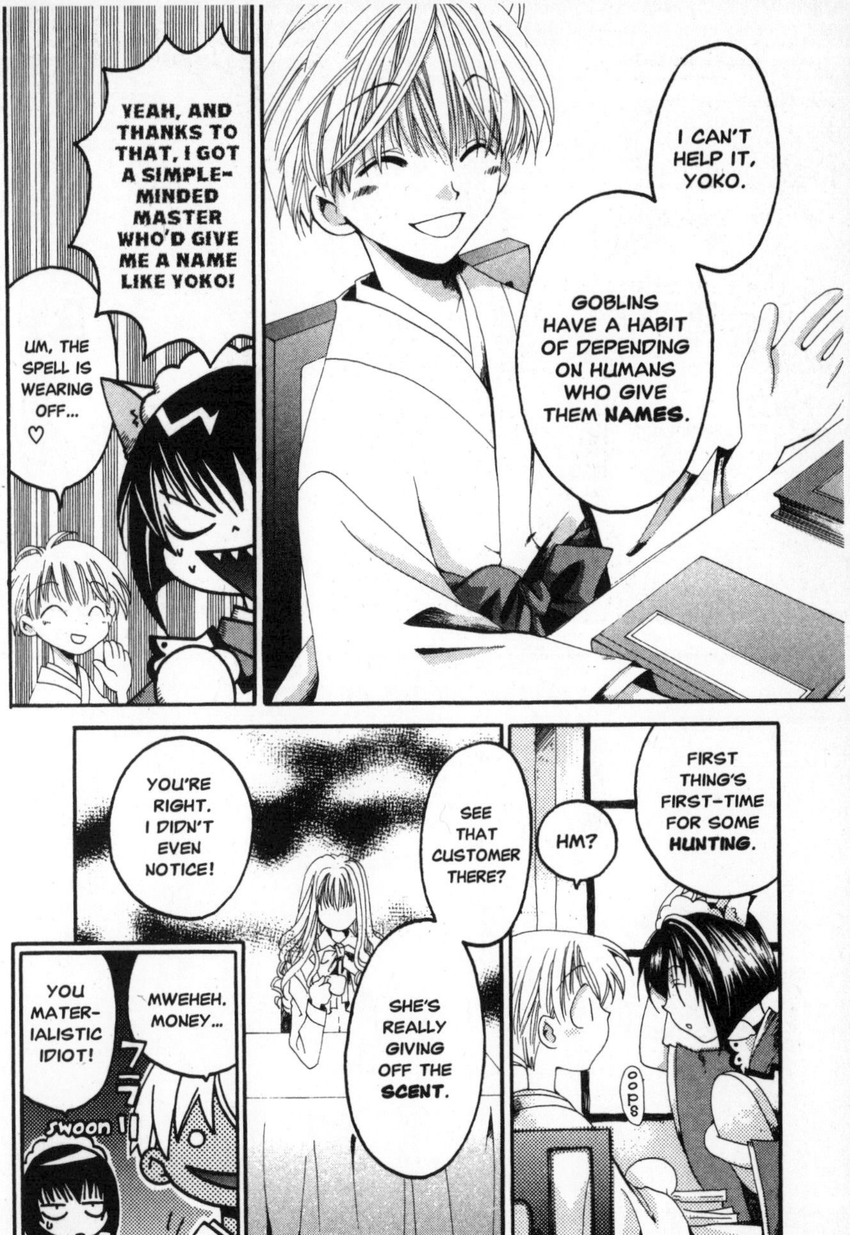
I CAN'T HELP IT, YOKO.
GOBLINS HAVE A HABIT OF DEPENDING ON HUMANS WHO GIVE THEM NAMES.
YEAH, AND THANKS TO THAT, I GOT A SIMPLE-MINDED MASTER WHO'D GIVE ME A NAME LIKE YOKO!
UM, THE SPELL IS WEARING OFF... ♡
FIRST THING'S FIRST–TIME FOR SOME HUNTING.
HM?
oops
SEE THAT CUSTOMER THERE?
SHE'S REALLY GIVING OFF THE SCENT.
YOU'RE RIGHT. I DIDN'T EVEN NOTICE!
MWEHEH. MONEY...
YOU MATERIALISTIC IDIOT!
swoon

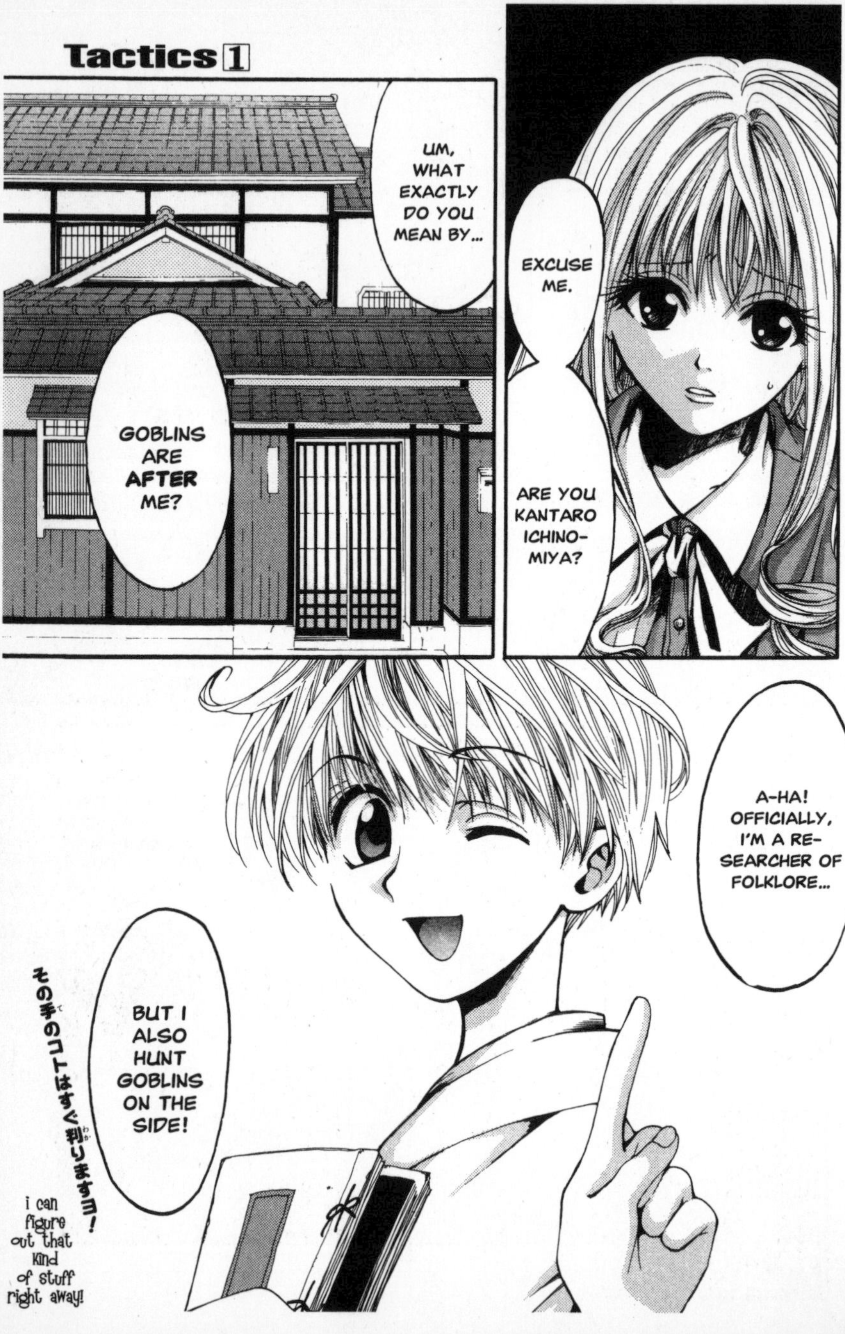
EXCUSE ME.
ARE YOU KANTARO ICHINO-MIYA?
UM, WHAT EXACTLY DO YOU MEAN BY...
GOBLINS ARE **AFTER** ME?
A-HA! OFFICIALLY, I'M A RE-SEARCHER OF FOLKLORE...
BUT I ALSO HUNT GOBLINS ON THE SIDE!
その手のコトはすぐ判りますヨ！
i can figure out that kind of stuff right away!

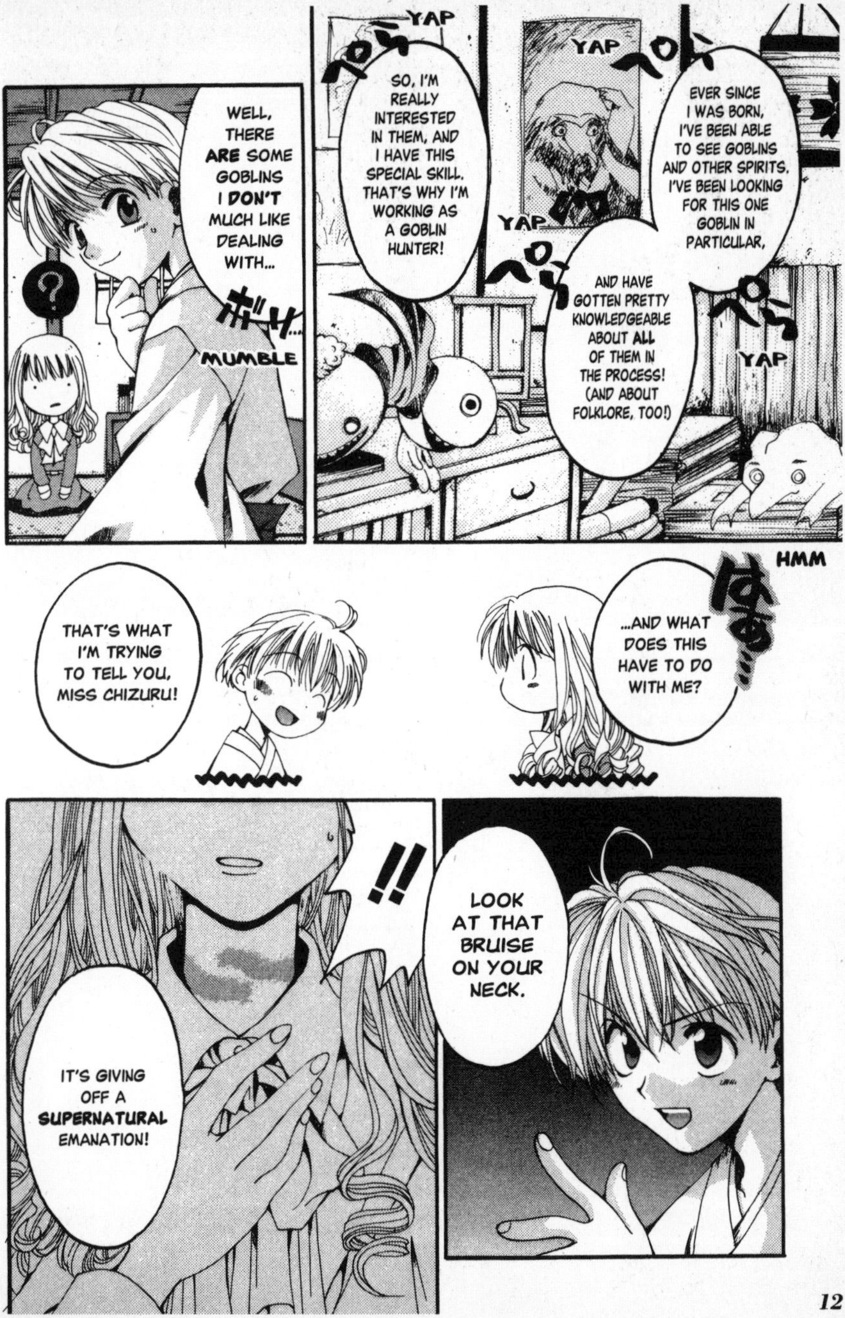
YAP
EVER SINCE I WAS BORN, I'VE BEEN ABLE TO SEE GOBLINS AND OTHER SPIRITS. I'VE BEEN LOOKING FOR THIS ONE GOBLIN IN PARTICULAR,
YAP
AND HAVE GOTTEN PRETTY KNOWLEDGEABLE ABOUT ALL OF THEM IN THE PROCESS! (AND ABOUT FOLKLORE, TOO!)
YAP
YAP
SO, I'M REALLY INTERESTED IN THEM, AND I HAVE THIS SPECIAL SKILL. THAT'S WHY I'M WORKING AS A GOBLIN HUNTER!
WELL, THERE ARE SOME GOBLINS I DON'T MUCH LIKE DEALING WITH...
MUMBLE
?
HMM
...AND WHAT DOES THIS HAVE TO DO WITH ME?
THAT'S WHAT I'M TRYING TO TELL YOU, MISS CHIZURU!
LOOK AT THAT BRUISE ON YOUR NECK.
!!
IT'S GIVING OFF A SUPERNATURAL EMANATION!

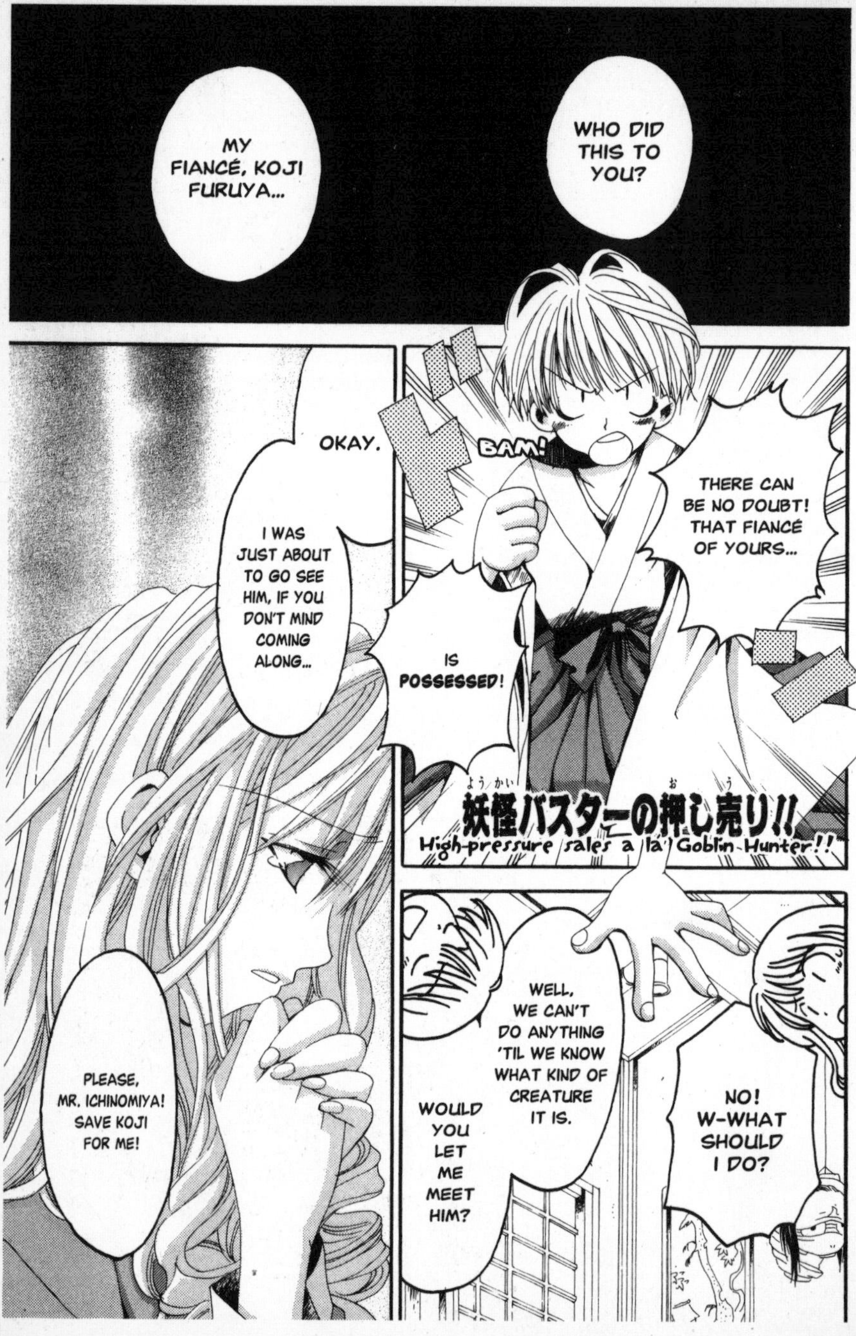
WHO DID THIS TO YOU?
MY FIANCÉ, KOJI FURUYA...
THERE CAN BE NO DOUBT! THAT FIANCÉ OF YOURS...
BAM!
IS POSSESSED!
妖怪バスターの押し売り!!
High-pressure sales a la Goblin Hunter!!
NO! W-WHAT SHOULD I DO?
WELL, WE CAN'T DO ANYTHING 'TIL WE KNOW WHAT KIND OF CREATURE IT IS.
WOULD YOU LET ME MEET HIM?
OKAY.
I WAS JUST ABOUT TO GO SEE HIM, IF YOU DON'T MIND COMING ALONG...
PLEASE, MR. ICHINOMIYA! SAVE KOJI FOR ME!

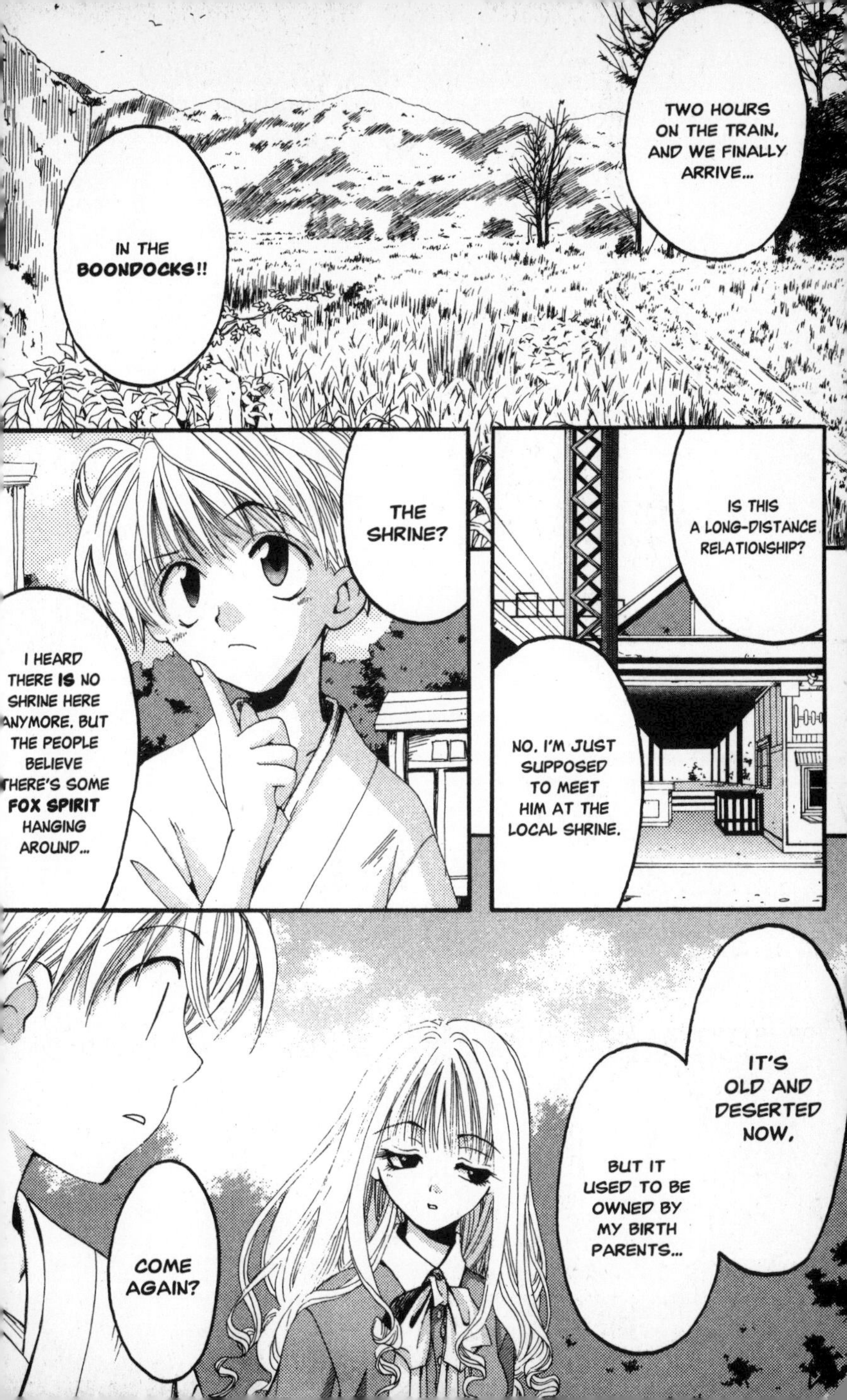
TWO HOURS ON THE TRAIN, AND WE FINALLY ARRIVE...
IN THE BOONDOCKS!!
IS THIS A LONG-DISTANCE RELATIONSHIP?
NO. I'M JUST SUPPOSED TO MEET HIM AT THE LOCAL SHRINE.
THE SHRINE?
I HEARD THERE IS NO SHRINE HERE ANYMORE. BUT THE PEOPLE BELIEVE THERE'S SOME FOX SPIRIT HANGING AROUND...
IT'S OLD AND DESERTED NOW,
BUT IT USED TO BE OWNED BY MY BIRTH PARENTS...
COME AGAIN?

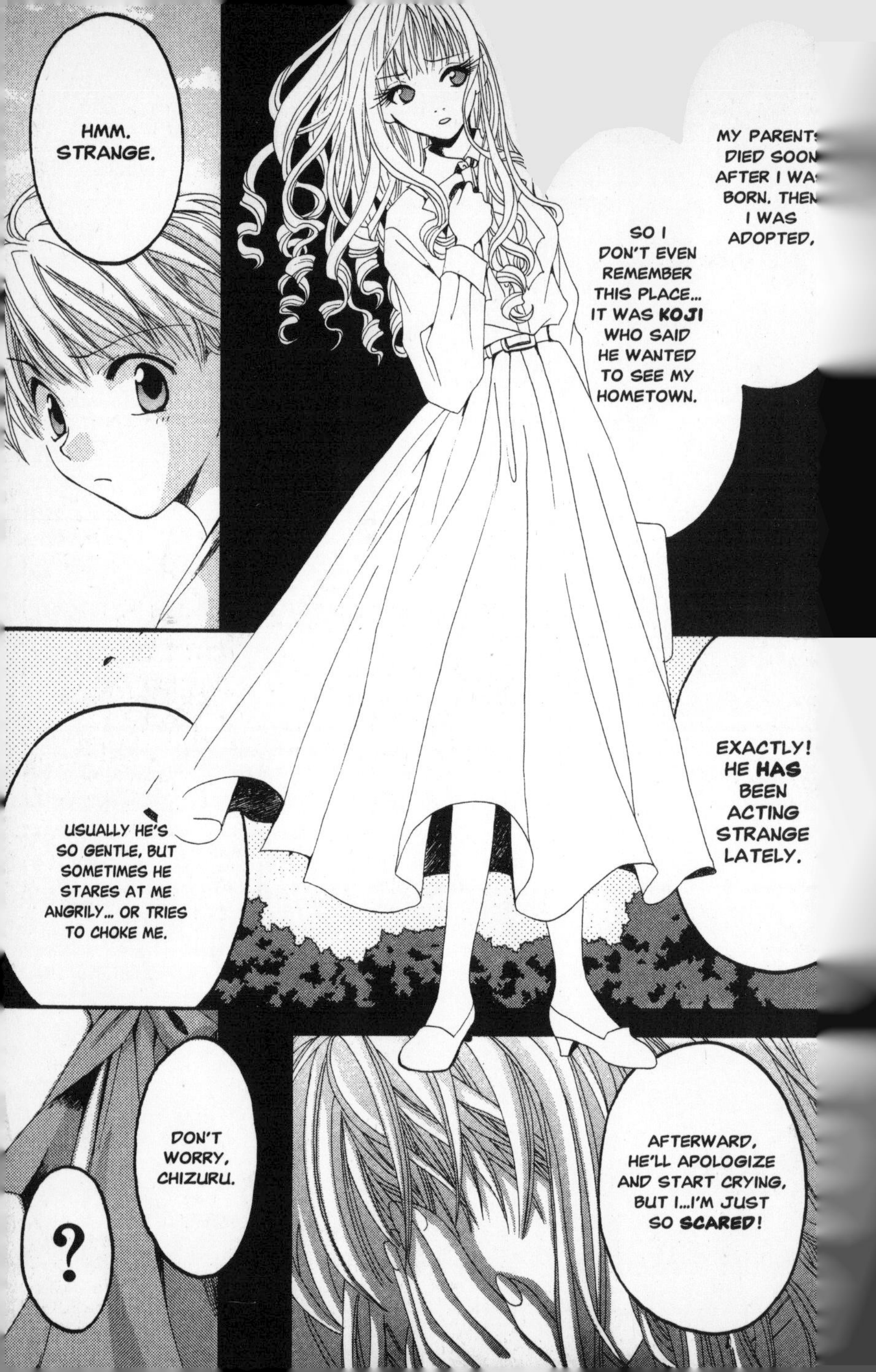
MY PARENTS DIED SOON AFTER I WAS BORN. THEN I WAS ADOPTED.
SO I DON'T EVEN REMEMBER THIS PLACE... IT WAS **KOJI** WHO SAID HE WANTED TO SEE MY HOMETOWN.
HMM. STRANGE.
EXACTLY! HE **HAS** BEEN ACTING STRANGE LATELY.
USUALLY HE'S SO GENTLE, BUT SOMETIMES HE STARES AT ME ANGRILY... OR TRIES TO CHOKE ME.
AFTERWARD, HE'LL APOLOGIZE AND START CRYING, BUT I...I'M JUST SO **SCARED**!
DON'T WORRY, CHIZURU.
?

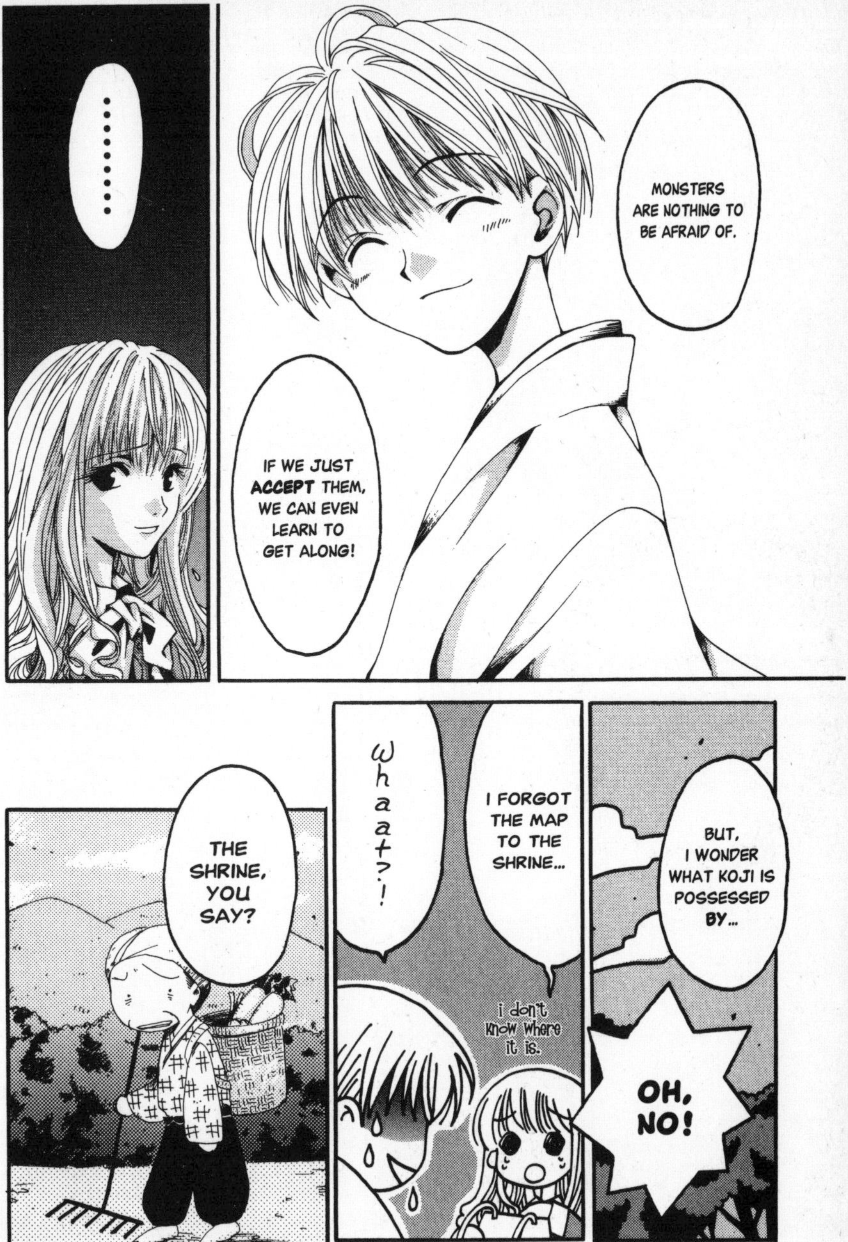
MONSTERS ARE NOTHING TO BE AFRAID OF.
IF WE JUST ACCEPT THEM, WE CAN EVEN LEARN TO GET ALONG!
....
BUT, I WONDER WHAT KOJI IS POSSESSED BY...
OH, NO!
I FORGOT THE MAP TO THE SHRINE...
Whaat?!
i don't know where it is.
THE SHRINE, YOU SAY?

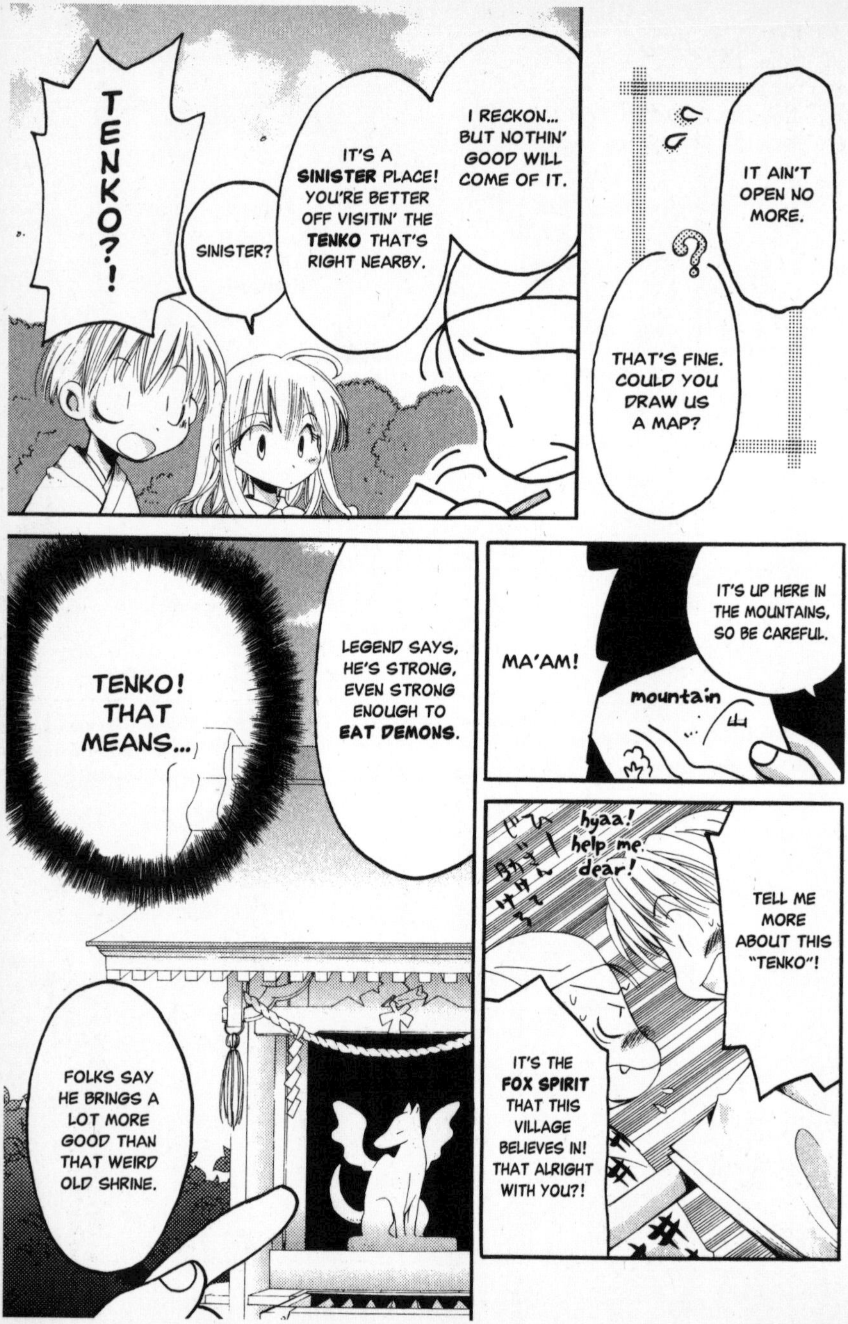
IT AIN'T OPEN NO MORE.
THAT'S FINE. COULD YOU DRAW US A MAP?
I RECKON... BUT NOTHIN' GOOD WILL COME OF IT.
IT'S A SINISTER PLACE! YOU'RE BETTER OFF VISITIN' THE TENKO THAT'S RIGHT NEARBY.
SINISTER?
TENKO?!
IT'S UP HERE IN THE MOUNTAINS, SO BE CAREFUL.
mountain
MA'AM!
TELL ME MORE ABOUT THIS "TENKO"!
hyaa! help me, dear!
IT'S THE FOX SPIRIT THAT THIS VILLAGE BELIEVES IN! THAT ALRIGHT WITH YOU?!
LEGEND SAYS, HE'S STRONG, EVEN STRONG ENOUGH TO EAT DEMONS.
TENKO! THAT MEANS...
FOLKS SAY HE BRINGS A LOT MORE GOOD THAN THAT WEIRD OLD SHRINE.

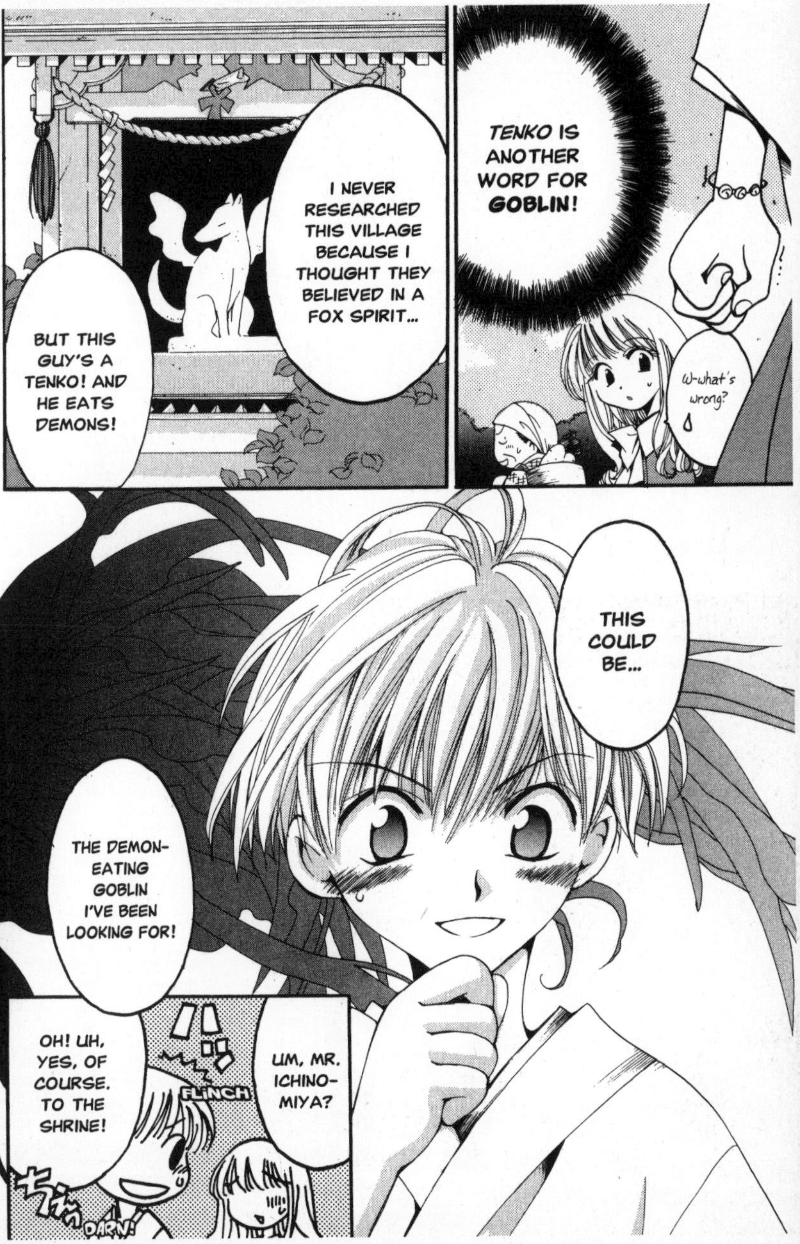
TENKO IS ANOTHER WORD FOR GOBLIN!
W-what's wrong?
I NEVER RESEARCHED THIS VILLAGE BECAUSE I THOUGHT THEY BELIEVED IN A FOX SPIRIT...
BUT THIS GUY'S A TENKO! AND HE EATS DEMONS!
THIS COULD BE...
THE DEMON-EATING GOBLIN I'VE BEEN LOOKING FOR!
UM, MR. ICHINO-MIYA?
FLINCH
OH! UH, YES, OF COURSE. TO THE SHRINE!
DARN!

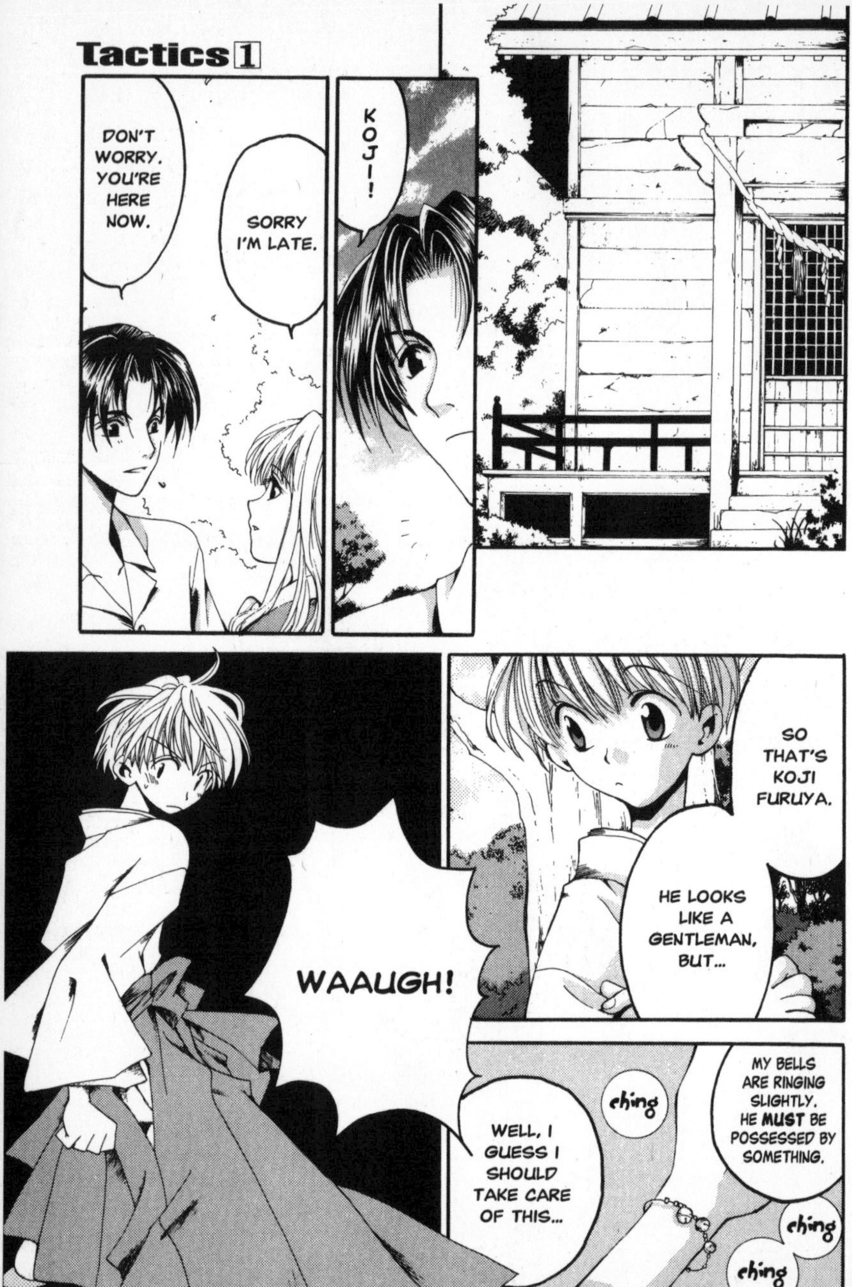
KOJI!
SORRY I'M LATE.
DON'T WORRY. YOU'RE HERE NOW.
SO THAT'S KOJI FURUYA.
HE LOOKS LIKE A GENTLEMAN, BUT...
MY BELLS ARE RINGING SLIGHTLY. HE MUST BE POSSESSED BY SOMETHING.
ching
WELL, I GUESS I SHOULD TAKE CARE OF THIS...
ching
ching
WAAUGH!

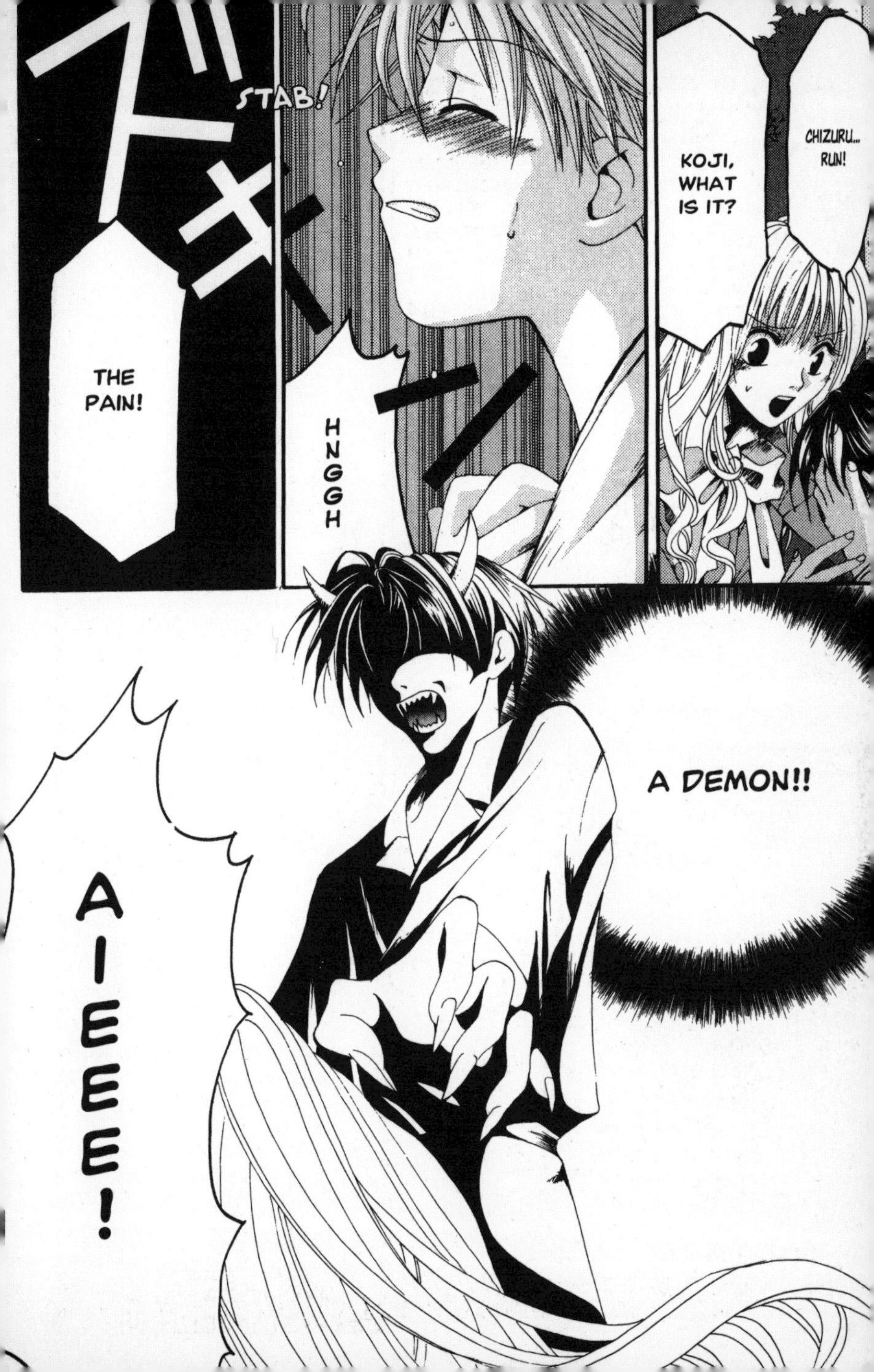
CHIZURU... RUN!
KOJI, WHAT IS IT?
STAB!
HNGGH
ズキ
THE PAIN!
A DEMON!!
AIEEE!

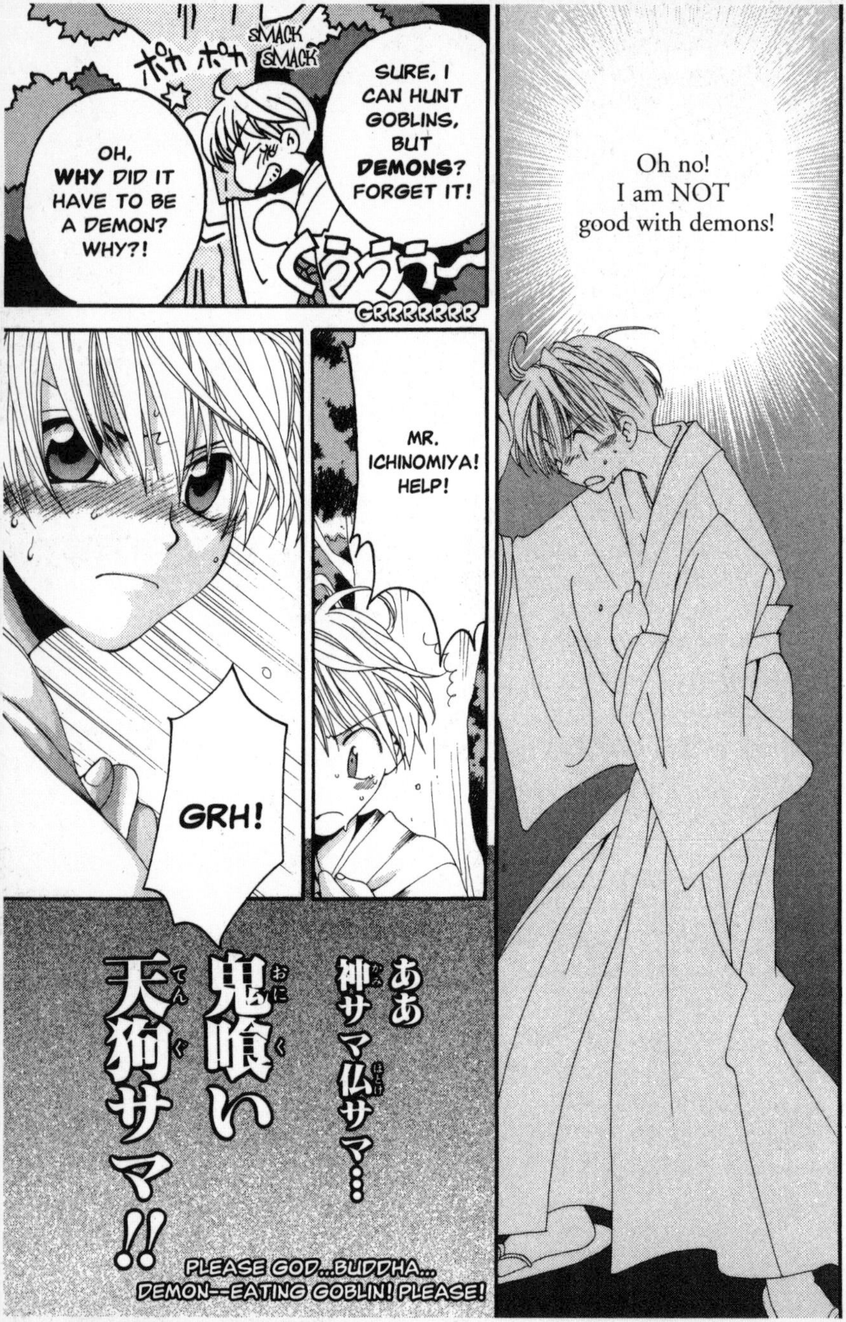
Oh no!
I am NOT
good with demons!
SURE, I CAN HUNT GOBLINS, BUT DEMONS? FORGET IT!
SMACK SMACK
OH, WHY DID IT HAVE TO BE A DEMON? WHY?!
GRRRRRRRR
MR. ICHINOMIYA! HELP!
GRH!
あぁ神サマ仏サマ…
鬼喰い天狗サマ!!
PLEASE GOD...BUDDHA...
DEMON--EATING GOBLIN! PLEASE!

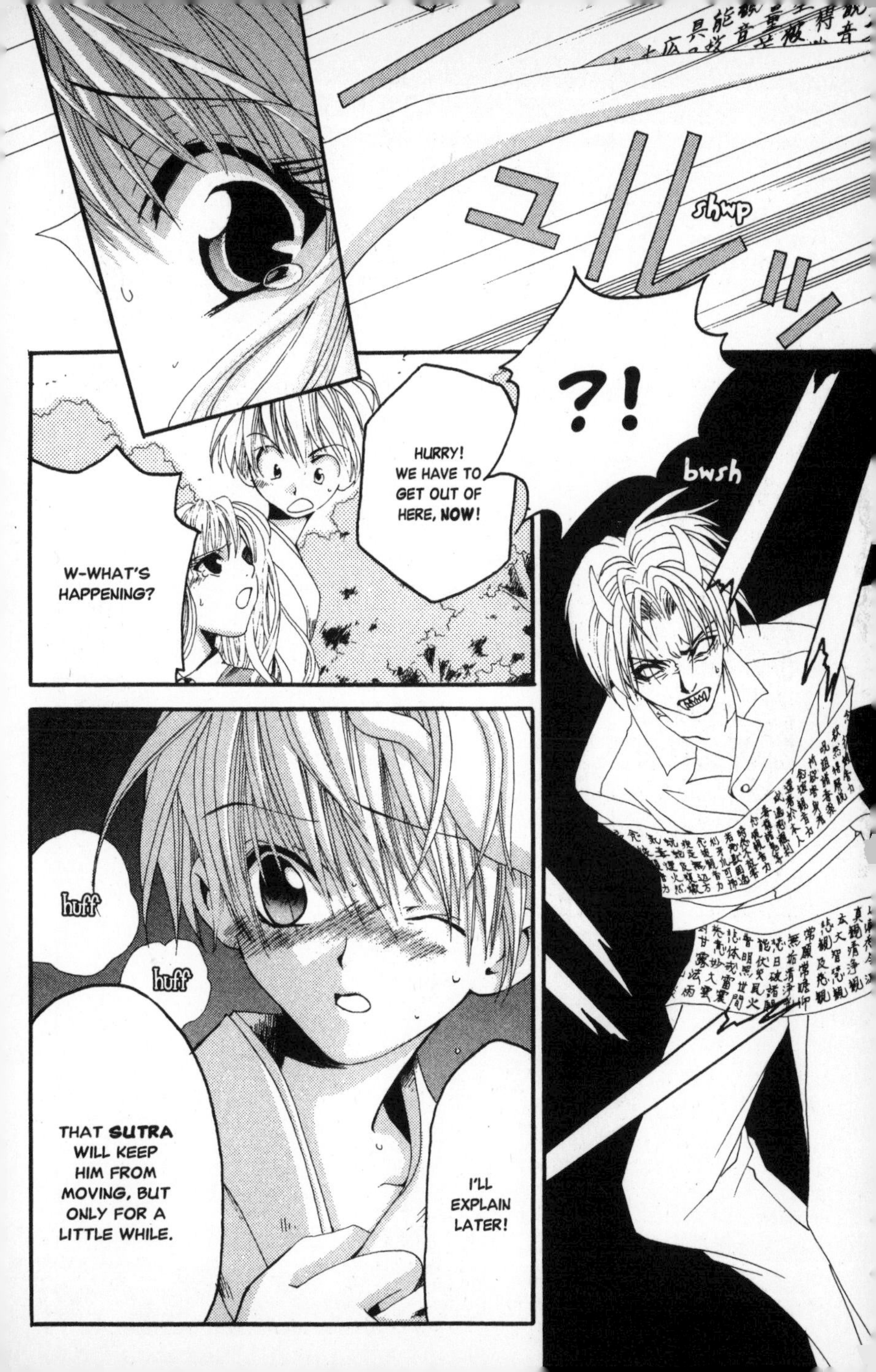
shwp
?!
bwsh
HURRY! WE HAVE TO GET OUT OF HERE, **NOW**!
W-WHAT'S HAPPENING?
huff
huff
THAT **SUTRA** WILL KEEP HIM FROM MOVING, BUT ONLY FOR A LITTLE WHILE.
I'LL EXPLAIN LATER!

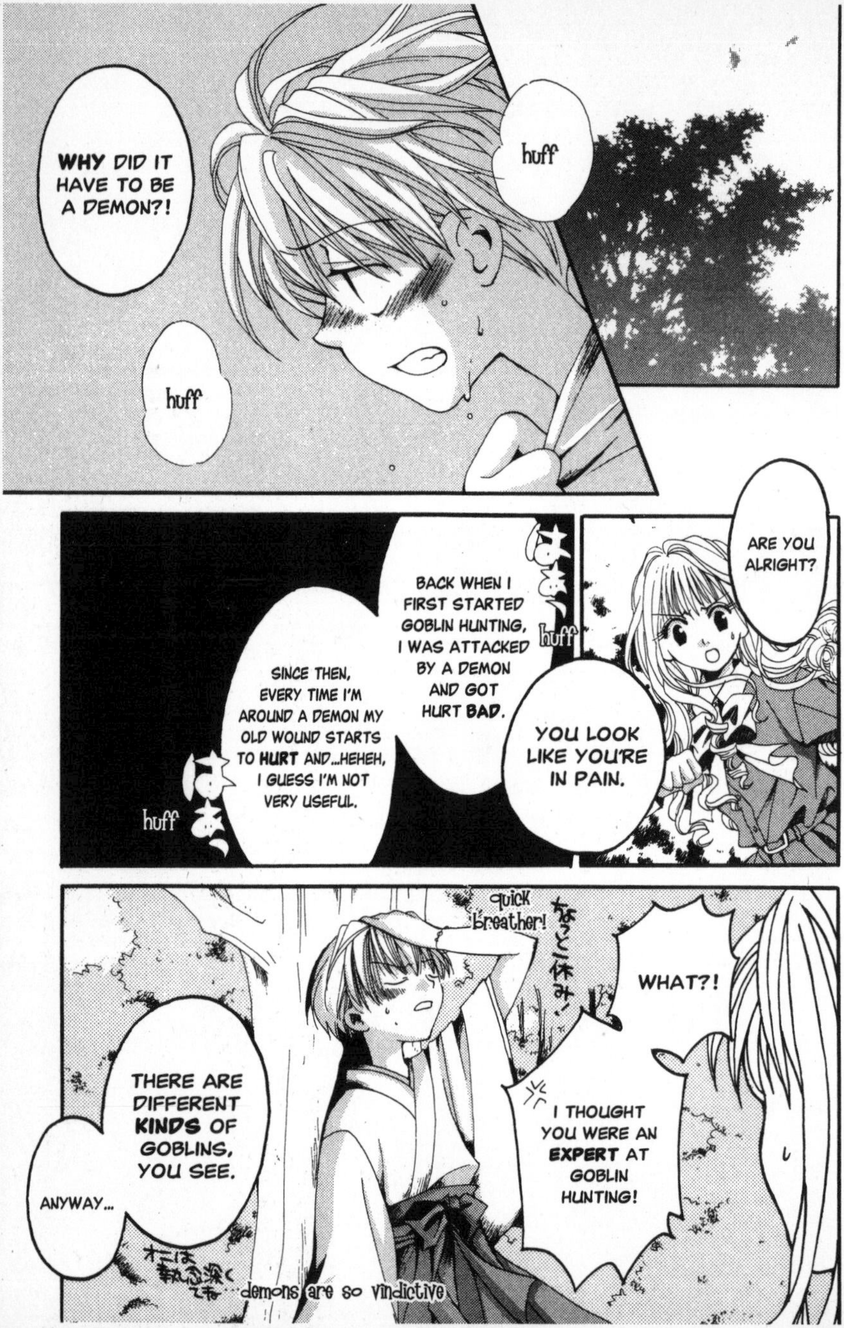

huff
WHY DID IT HAVE TO BE A DEMON?!
huff
ARE YOU ALRIGHT?
YOU LOOK LIKE YOU'RE IN PAIN.
はぁ
huff
BACK WHEN I FIRST STARTED GOBLIN HUNTING, I WAS ATTACKED BY A DEMON AND GOT HURT BAD.
SINCE THEN, EVERY TIME I'M AROUND A DEMON MY OLD WOUND STARTS TO HURT AND...HEHEH, I GUESS I'M NOT VERY USEFUL.
はぁ
huff
WHAT?!
I THOUGHT YOU WERE AN EXPERT AT GOBLIN HUNTING!
ちょっと休み!
quick breather!
THERE ARE DIFFERENT KINDS OF GOBLINS, YOU SEE.
ANYWAY...
オニは執念深くてね
demons are so vindictive

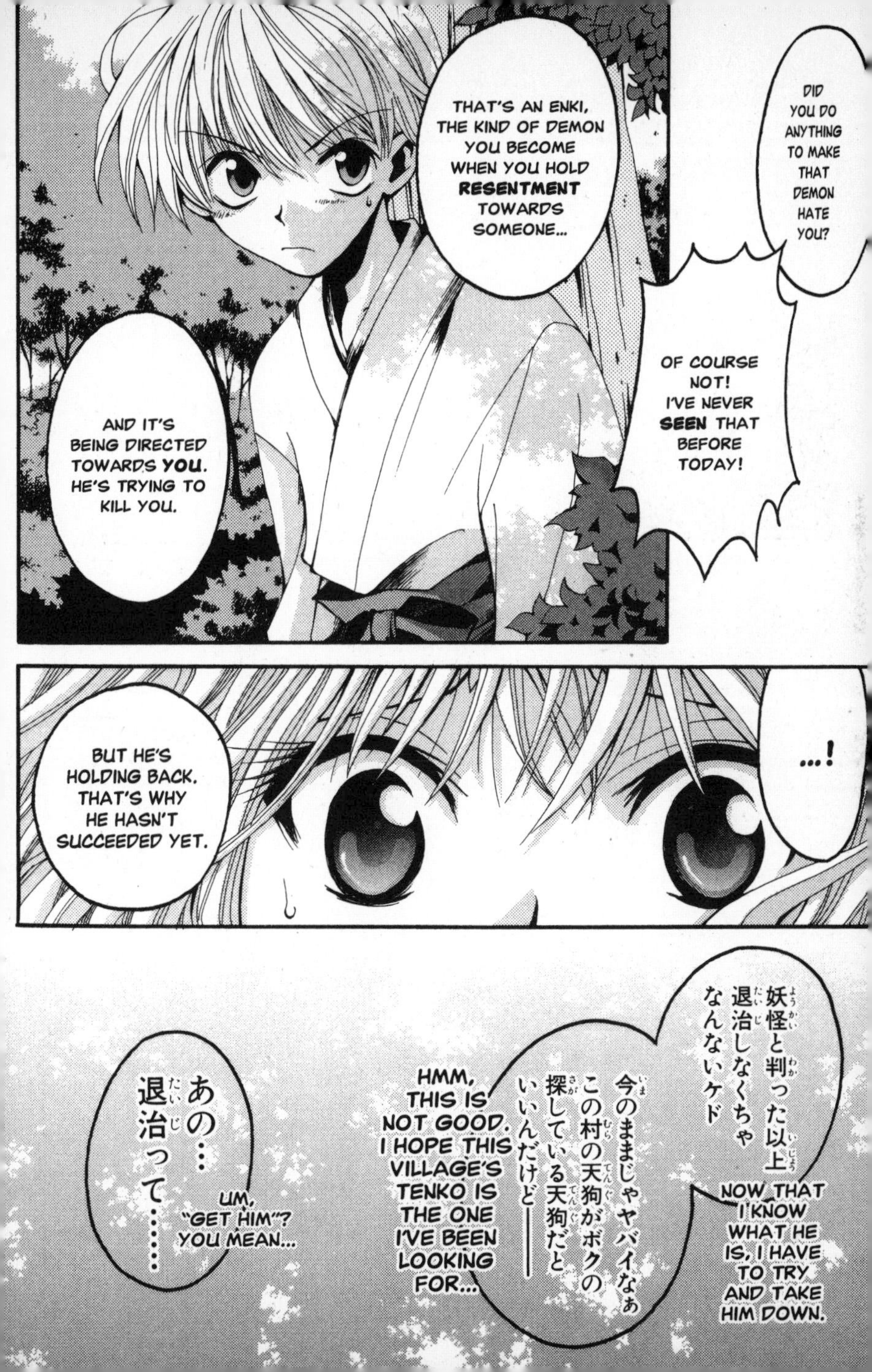
DID YOU DO ANYTHING TO MAKE THAT DEMON HATE YOU?
THAT'S AN ENKI, THE KIND OF DEMON YOU BECOME WHEN YOU HOLD **RESENTMENT** TOWARDS SOMEONE...
OF COURSE NOT! I'VE NEVER **SEEN** THAT BEFORE TODAY!
AND IT'S BEING DIRECTED TOWARDS **YOU**. HE'S TRYING TO KILL YOU.
...!
BUT HE'S HOLDING BACK. THAT'S WHY HE HASN'T SUCCEEDED YET.
妖怪と判った以上退治しなくちゃなんないケド
NOW THAT I KNOW WHAT HE IS, I HAVE TO TRY AND TAKE HIM DOWN.
今のままじゃヤバイなぁこの村の天狗がボクの探している天狗だといいんだけど――
HMM, THIS IS NOT GOOD. I HOPE THIS VILLAGE'S TENKO IS THE ONE I'VE BEEN LOOKING FOR...
あの…退治って……
UM, "GET HIM"? YOU MEAN...

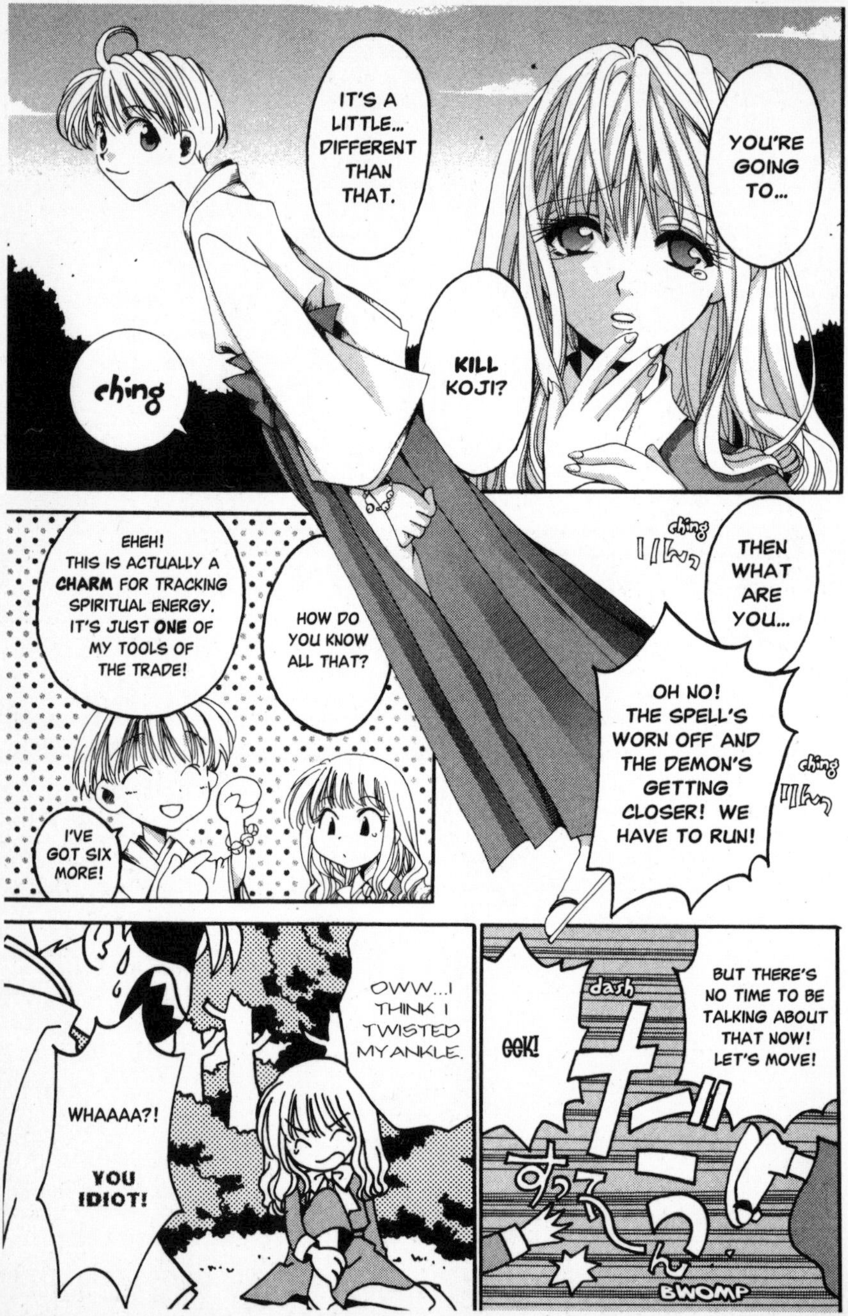
YOU'RE GOING TO...
KILL KOJI?
IT'S A LITTLE... DIFFERENT THAN THAT.
ching
ching
THEN WHAT ARE YOU...
OH NO! THE SPELL'S WORN OFF AND THE DEMON'S GETTING CLOSER! WE HAVE TO RUN!
ching
HOW DO YOU KNOW ALL THAT?
EHEH! THIS IS ACTUALLY A CHARM FOR TRACKING SPIRITUAL ENERGY. IT'S JUST ONE OF MY TOOLS OF THE TRADE!
I'VE GOT SIX MORE!
BUT THERE'S NO TIME TO BE TALKING ABOUT THAT NOW! LET'S MOVE!
dash
eek!
BWOMP
OWW...I THINK I TWISTED MY ANKLE.
WHAAAA?!
YOU IDIOT!

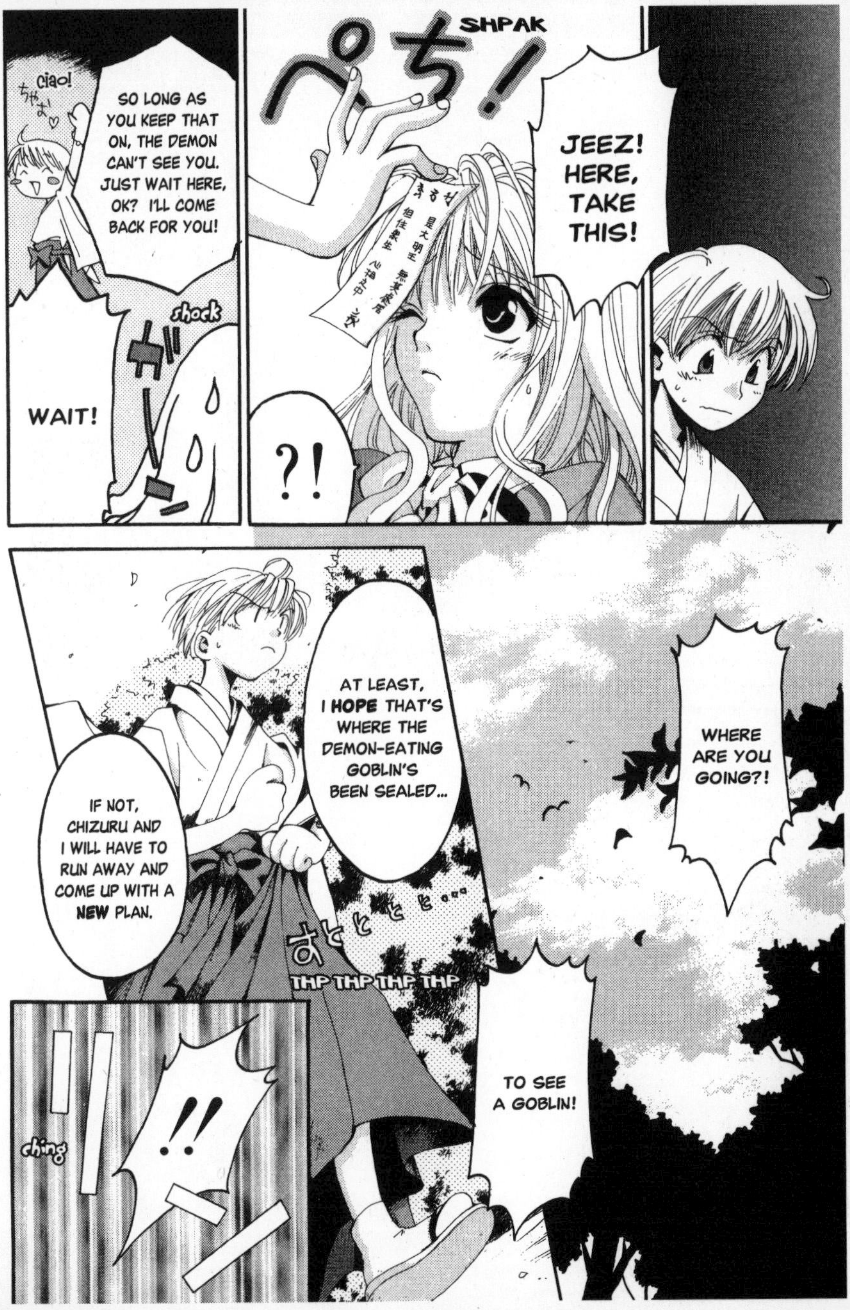
JEEZ! HERE, TAKE THIS!
ぺち！
SHPAK
?!
ciao!
SO LONG AS YOU KEEP THAT ON, THE DEMON CAN'T SEE YOU. JUST WAIT HERE, OK? I'LL COME BACK FOR YOU!
shock
WAIT!
WHERE ARE YOU GOING?!
TO SEE A GOBLIN!
AT LEAST, I HOPE THAT'S WHERE THE DEMON-EATING GOBLIN'S BEEN SEALED...
IF NOT, CHIZURU AND I WILL HAVE TO RUN AWAY AND COME UP WITH A NEW PLAN.
THP THP THP THP
!!
ching

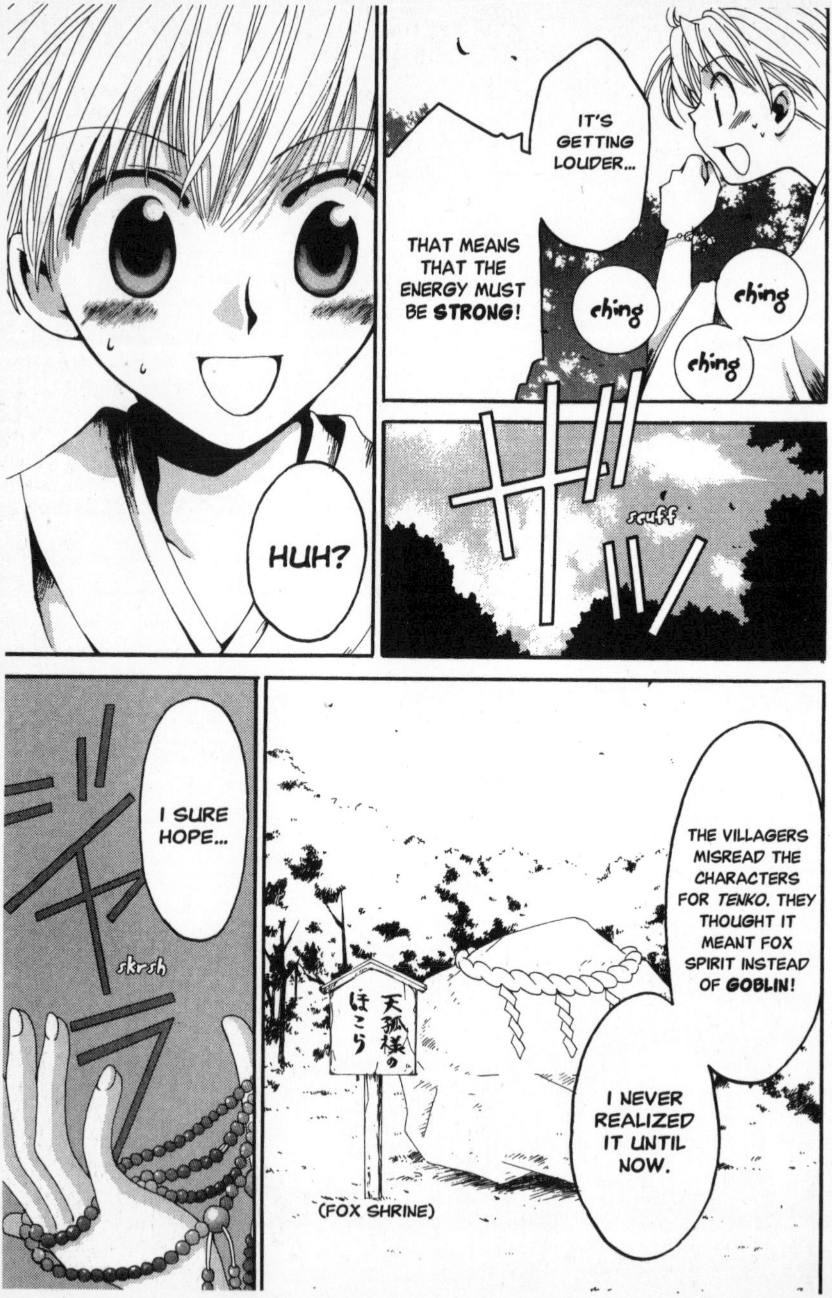
IT'S GETTING LOUDER...
THAT MEANS THAT THE ENERGY MUST BE **STRONG**!
ching
ching
ching
scuff
HUH?
THE VILLAGERS MISREAD THE CHARACTERS FOR *TENKO*. THEY THOUGHT IT MEANT FOX SPIRIT INSTEAD OF **GOBLIN**!
I NEVER REALIZED IT UNTIL NOW.
天狐様のほこら
(FOX SHRINE)
I SURE HOPE...
skrsh

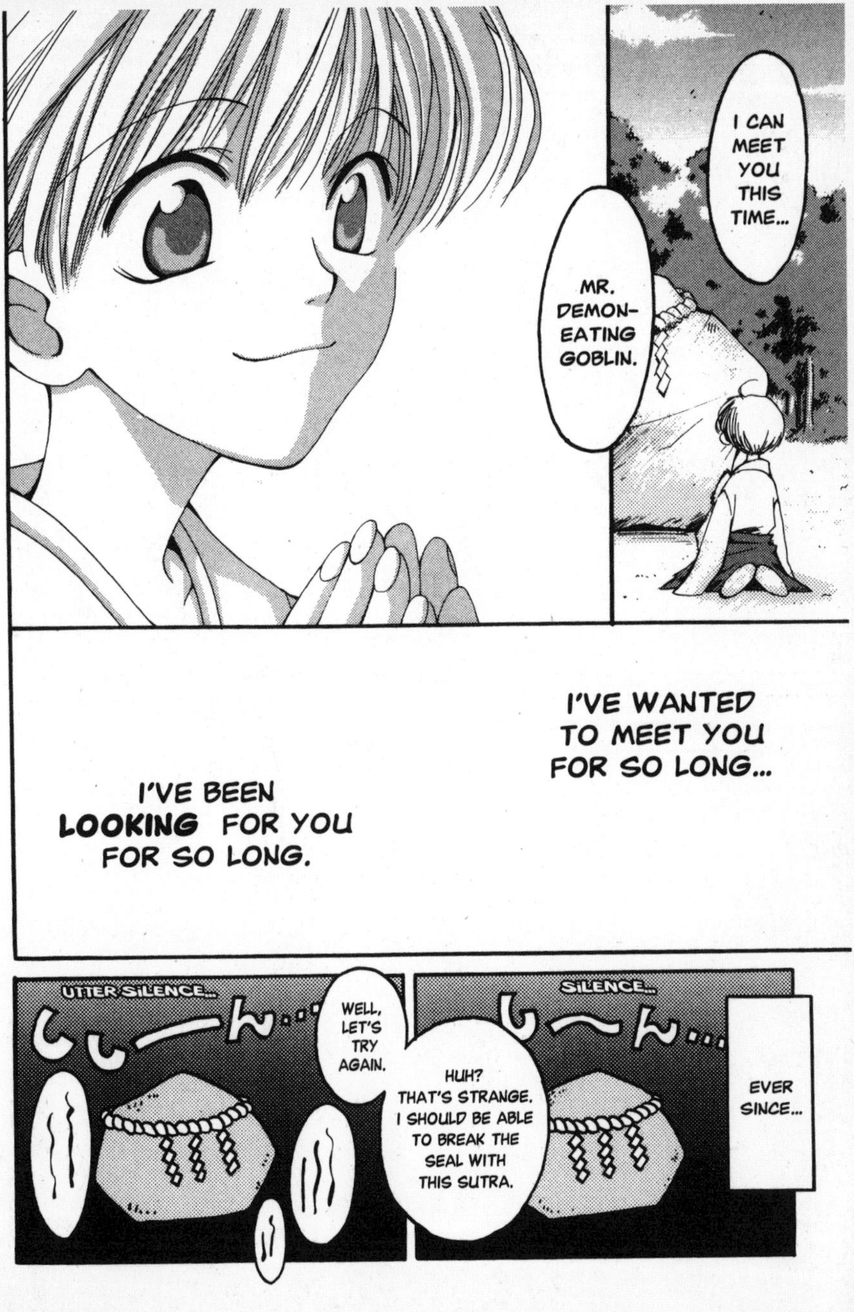
I CAN MEET YOU THIS TIME...
MR. DEMON-EATING GOBLIN.
I'VE WANTED TO MEET YOU FOR SO LONG...
I'VE BEEN **LOOKING** FOR YOU FOR SO LONG.
EVER SINCE...
SILENCE...
し〜ん...
HUH? THAT'S STRANGE. I SHOULD BE ABLE TO BREAK THE SEAL WITH THIS SUTRA.
UTTER SILENCE...
しーん...
WELL, LET'S TRY AGAIN.

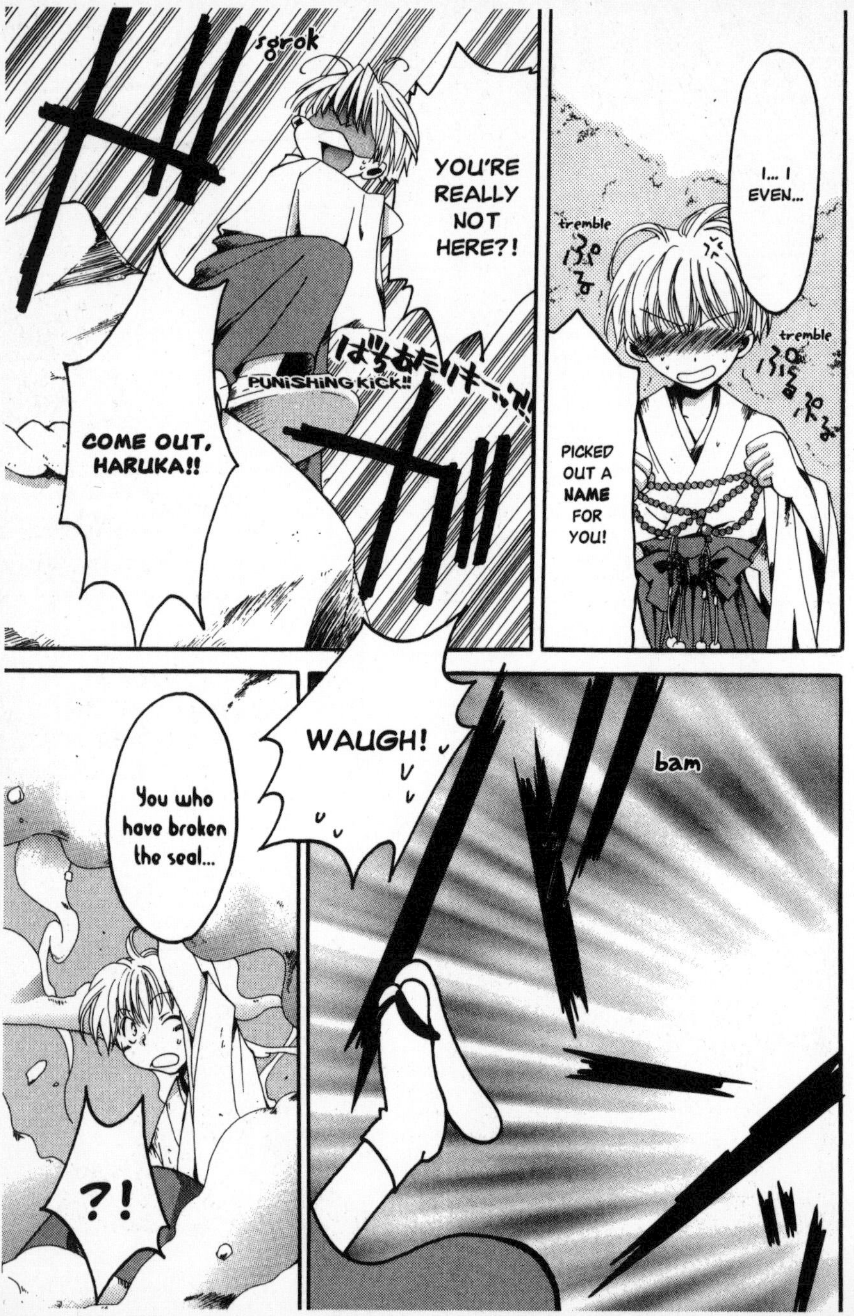
I... I EVEN...
tremble
tremble
PICKED OUT A NAME FOR YOU!
sgrok
YOU'RE REALLY NOT HERE?!
PUNISHING KICK!!
COME OUT, HARUKA!!
WAUGH!
bam
You who have broken the seal...
?!

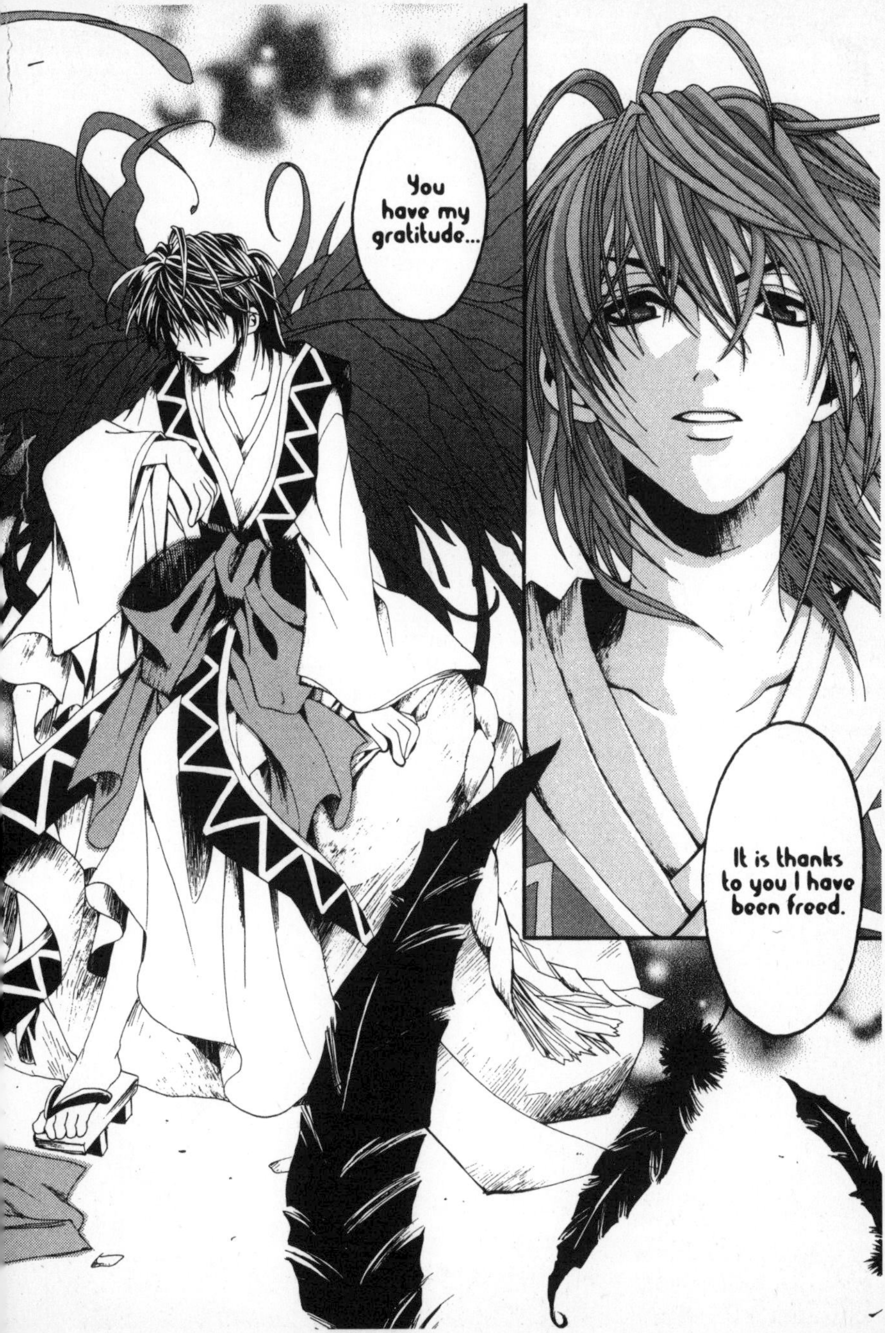
It is thanks to you I have been freed.
You have my gratitude...

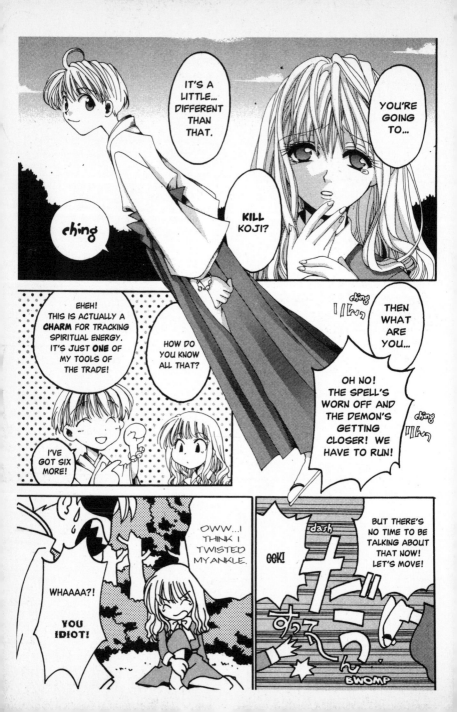

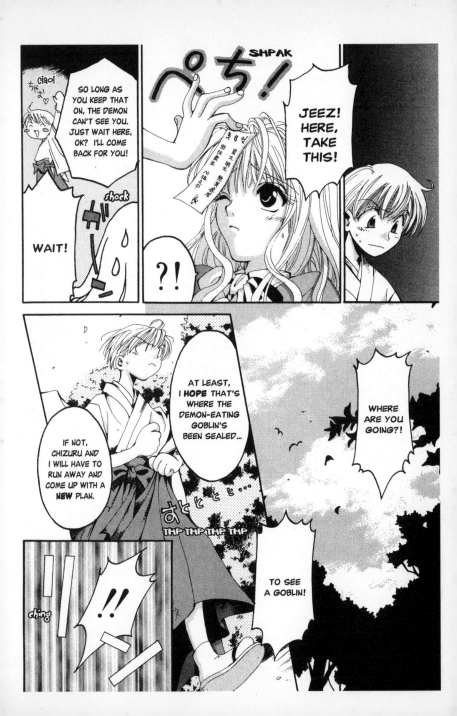

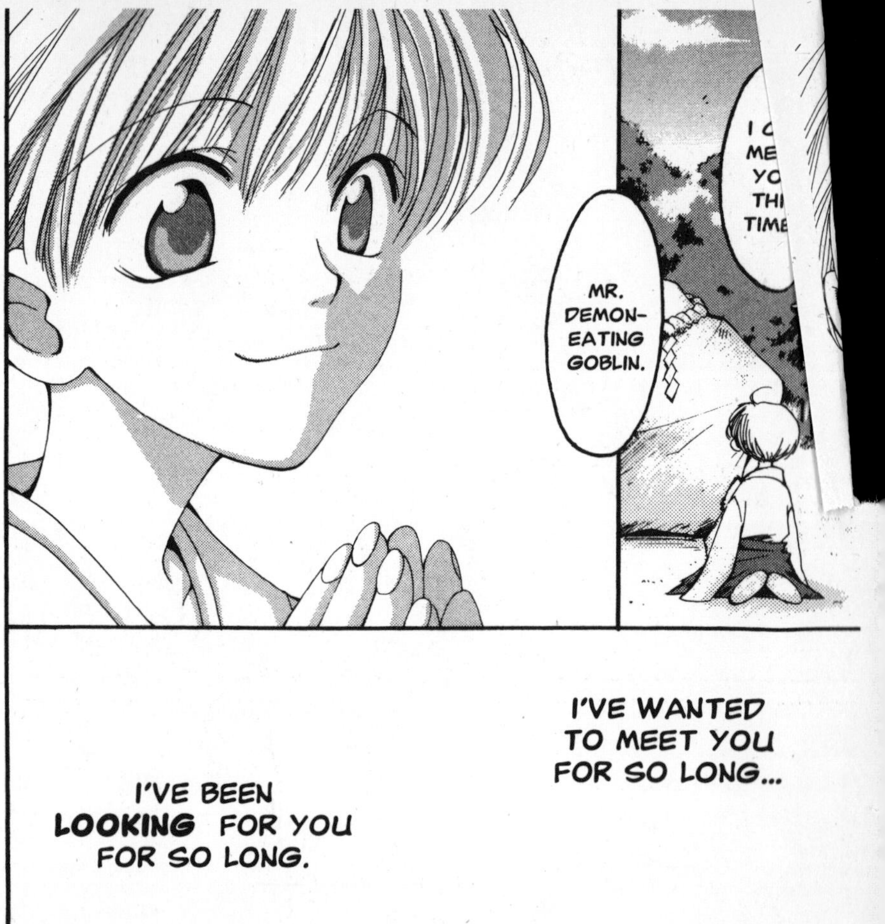
MR. DEMON-EATING GOBLIN.
I'VE WANTED TO MEET YOU FOR SO LONG...
I'VE BEEN LOOKING FOR YOU FOR SO LONG.
EVER SINCE...
SILENCE...
しーん...
HUH? THAT'S STRANGE. I SHOULD BE ABLE TO BREAK THE SEAL WITH THIS SUTRA.
UTTER SILENCE...
しーん...
WELL, LET'S TRY AGAIN.

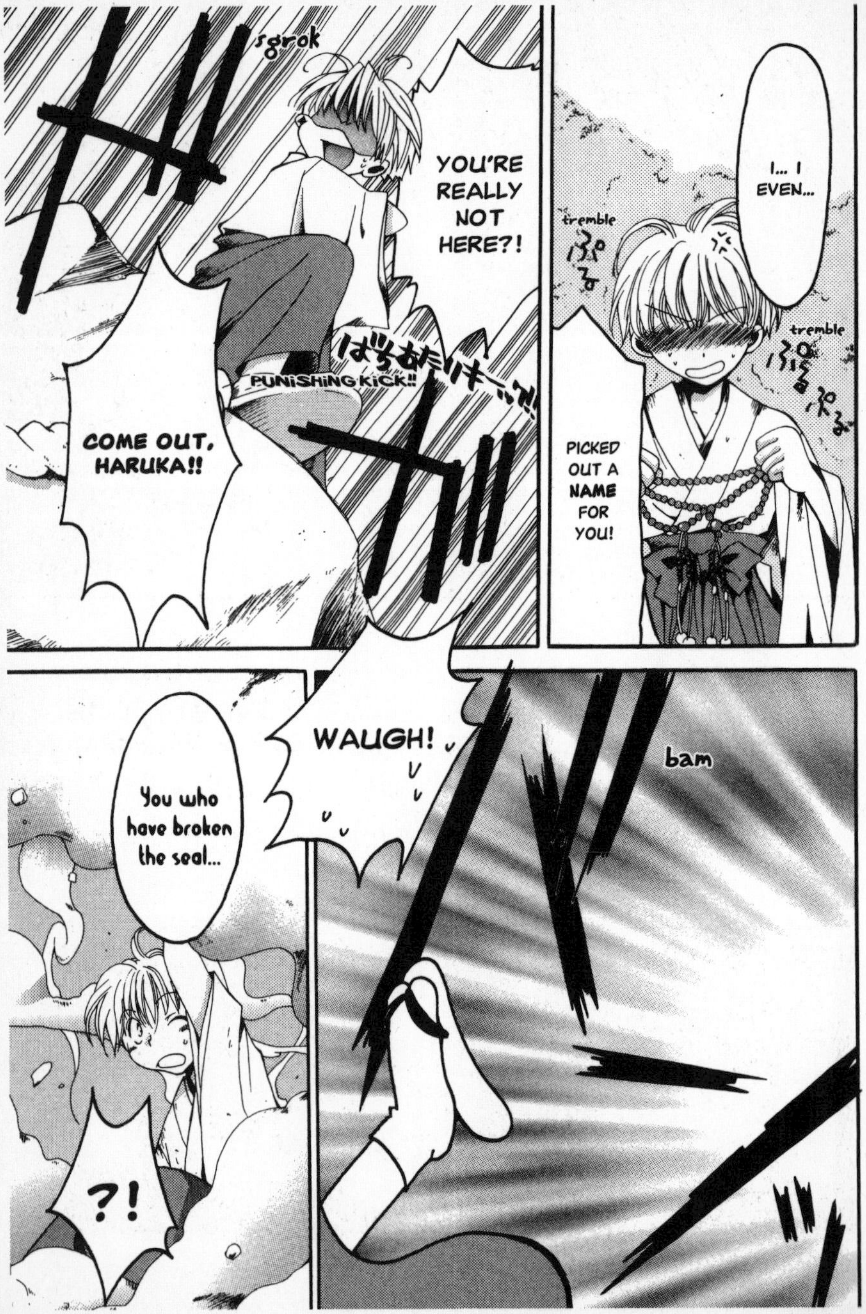
I... I EVEN...
tremble
tremble
PICKED OUT A NAME FOR YOU!
sgrok
YOU'RE REALLY NOT HERE?!
PUNISHING KICK!!
COME OUT, HARUKA!!
WAUGH!
bam
You who have broken the seal...
?!

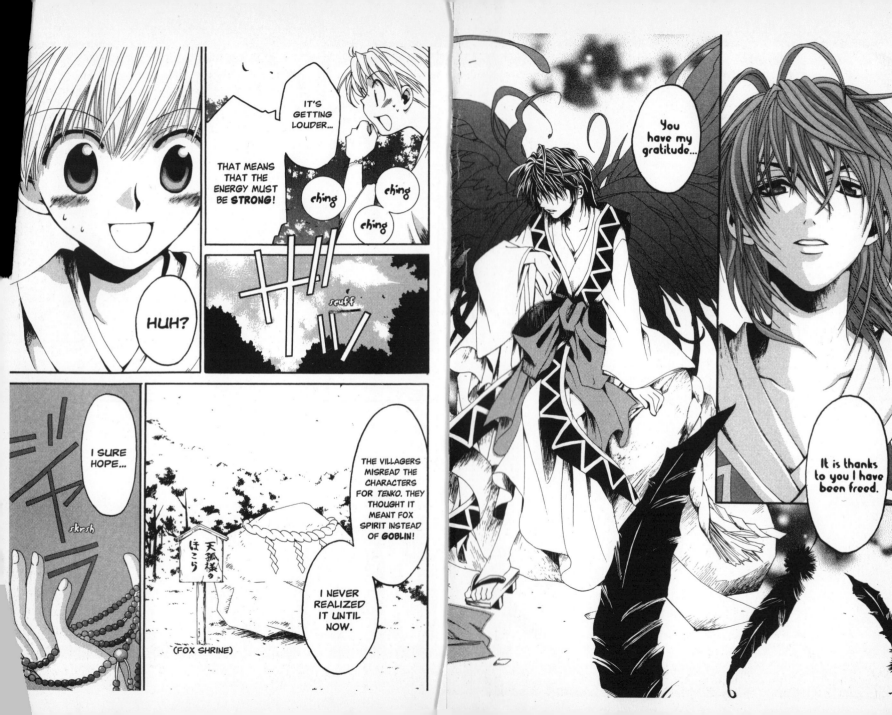

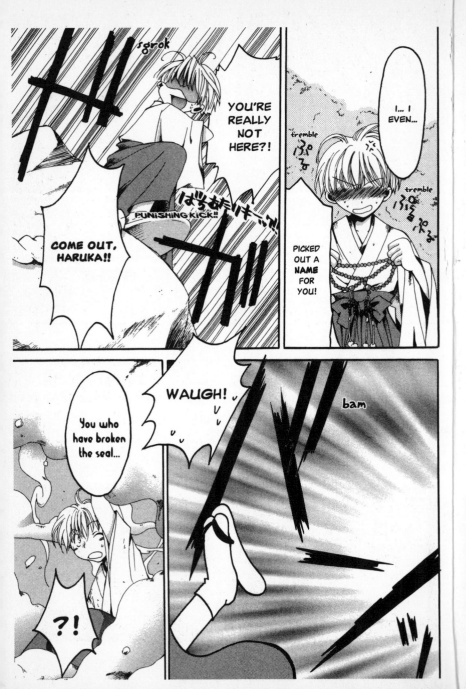

sgrok

YOU'RE REALLY NOT HERE?!

COME OUT, HARUKA!!

PUNISHING KICK!!

tremble

tremble

I... I EVEN...

PICKED OUT A NAME FOR YOU!

You who have broken the seal...

WAUGH!

bam

?!

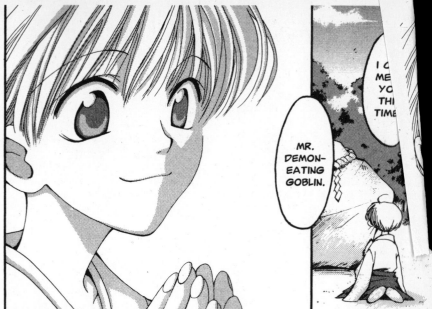

I CAN MEET YOU THIS TIME.

MR. DEMON-EATING GOBLIN.

I'VE WANTED TO MEET YOU FOR SO LONG...

I'VE BEEN **LOOKING** FOR YOU FOR SO LONG.

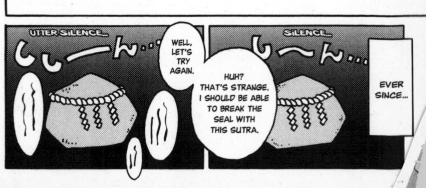

UTTER SILENCE...

WELL, LET'S TRY AGAIN.

HUH? THAT'S STRANGE. I SHOULD BE ABLE TO BREAK THE SEAL WITH THIS SUTRA.

SILENCE...

EVER SINCE...

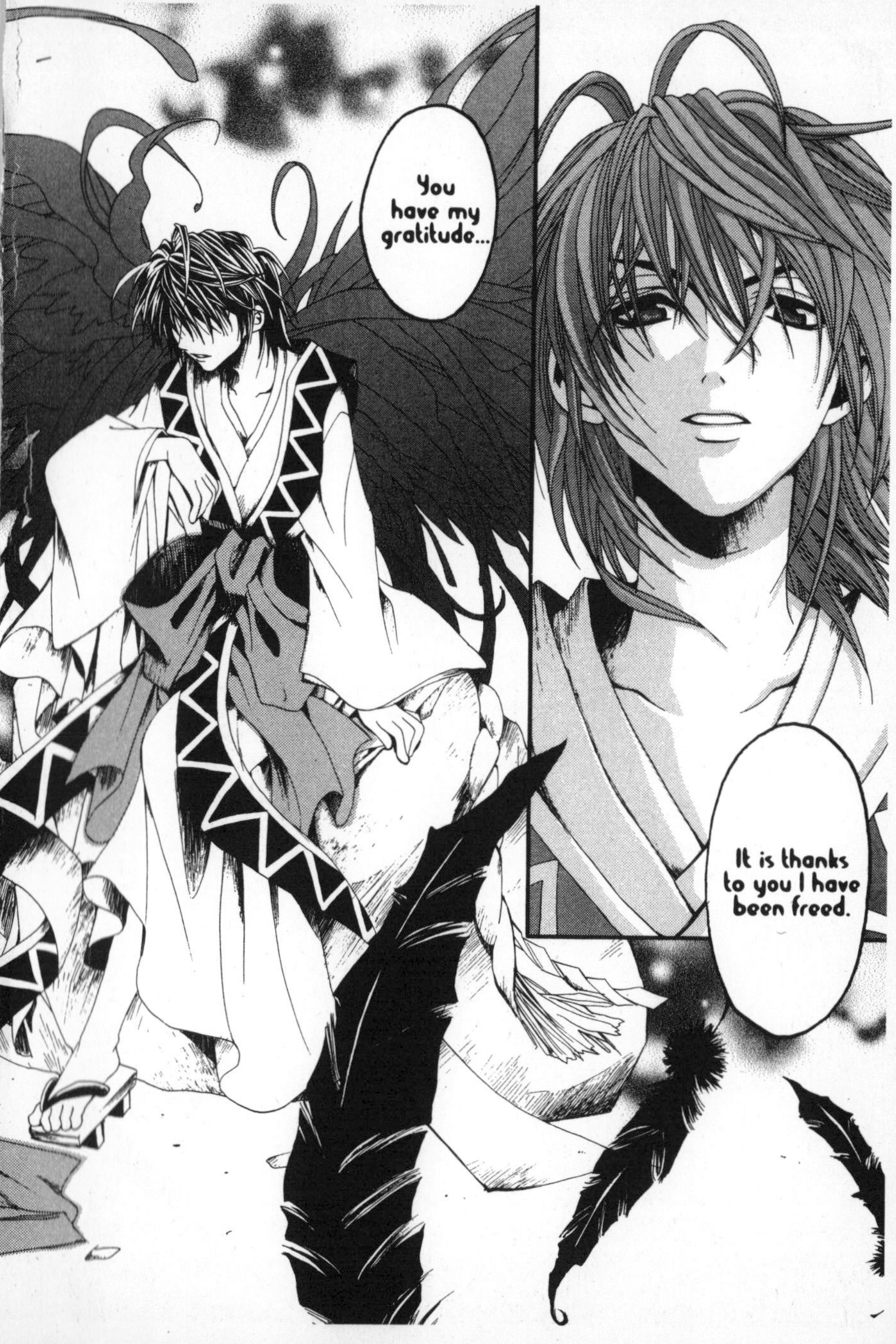
You have my gratitude...
It is thanks to you I have been freed.

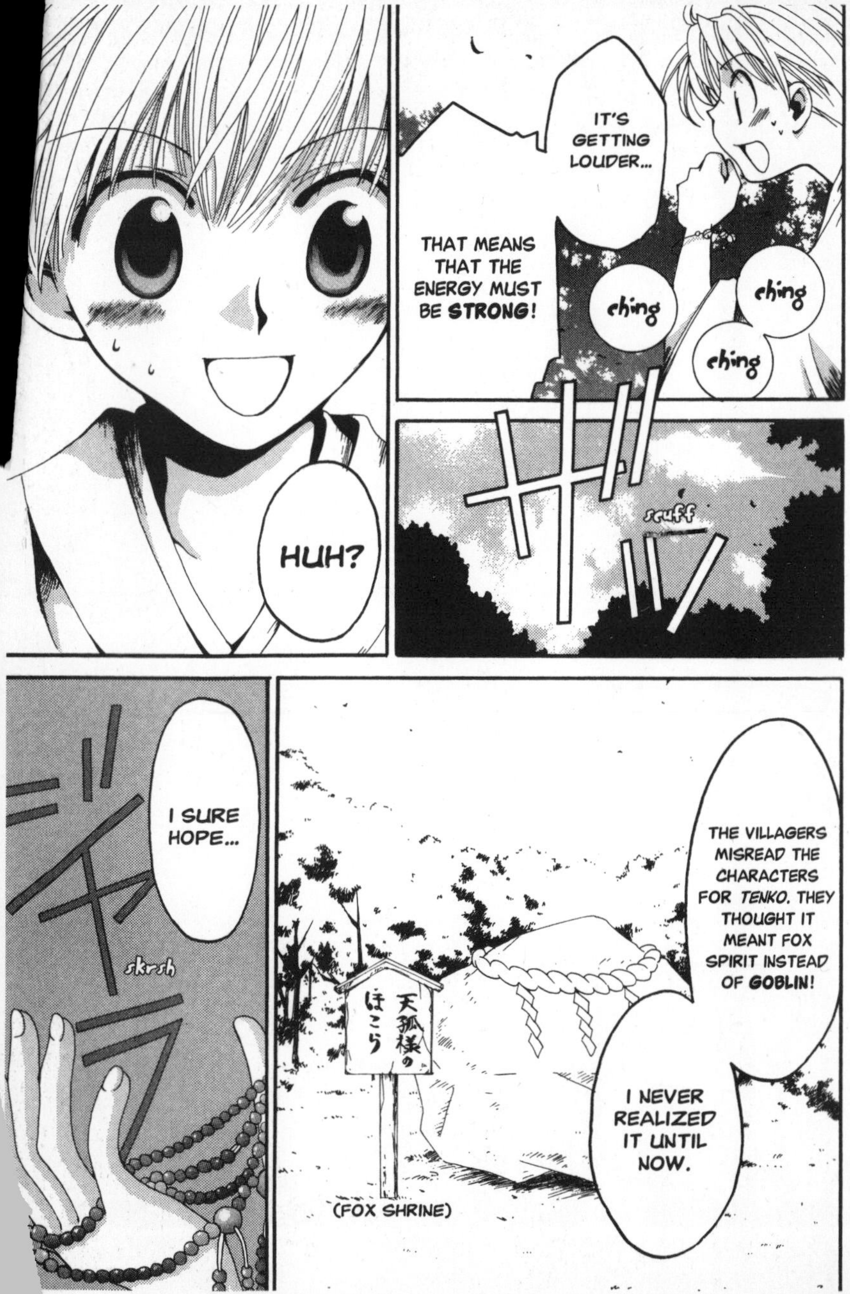
IT'S GETTING LOUDER...
THAT MEANS THAT THE ENERGY MUST BE **STRONG**!
ching
ching
ching
scuff
HUH?
THE VILLAGERS MISREAD THE CHARACTERS FOR *TENKO*. THEY THOUGHT IT MEANT FOX SPIRIT INSTEAD OF **GOBLIN**!
I NEVER REALIZED IT UNTIL NOW.
天狐様のほこら
(FOX SHRINE)
I SURE HOPE...
skrsh

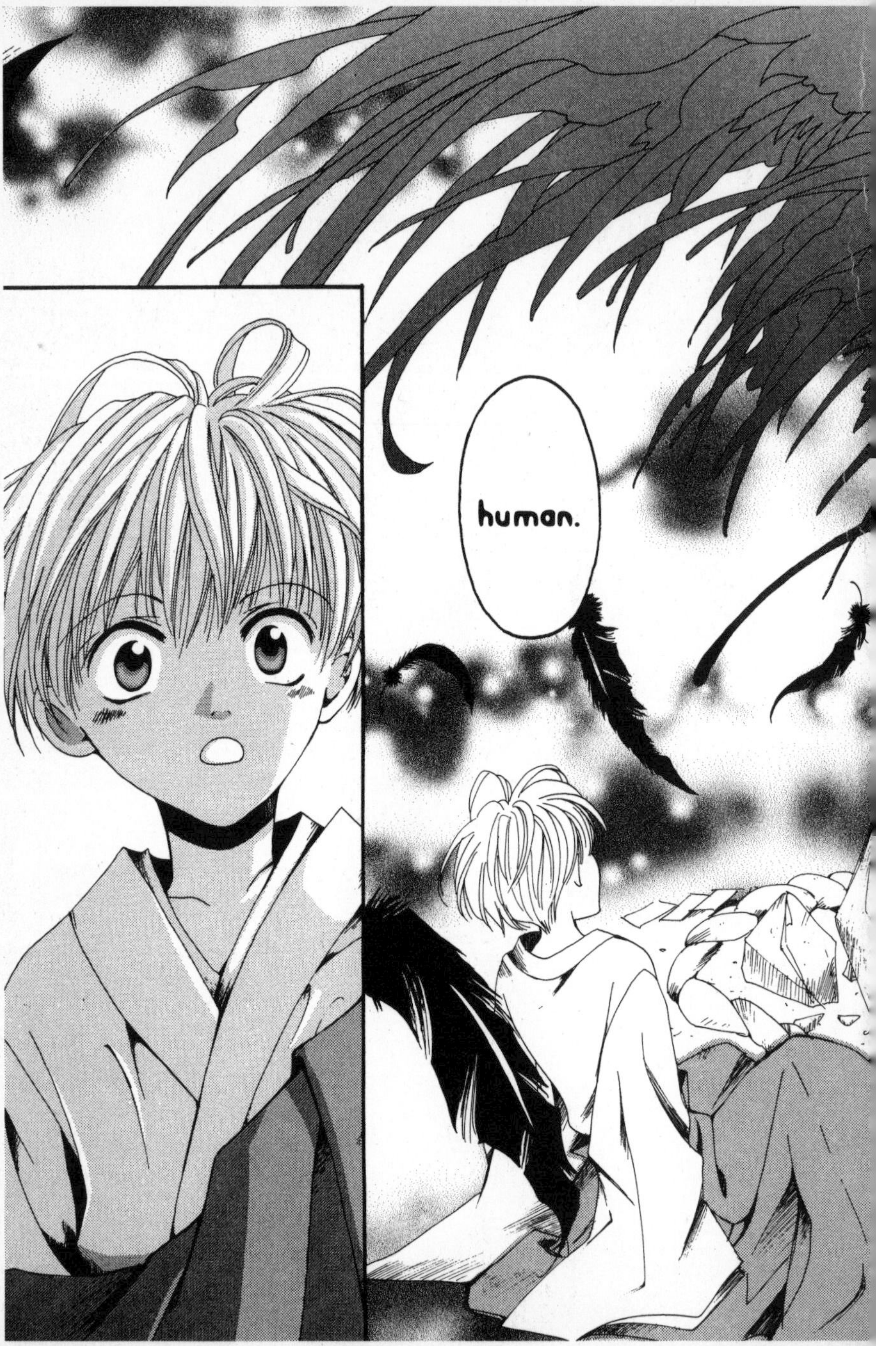
human.

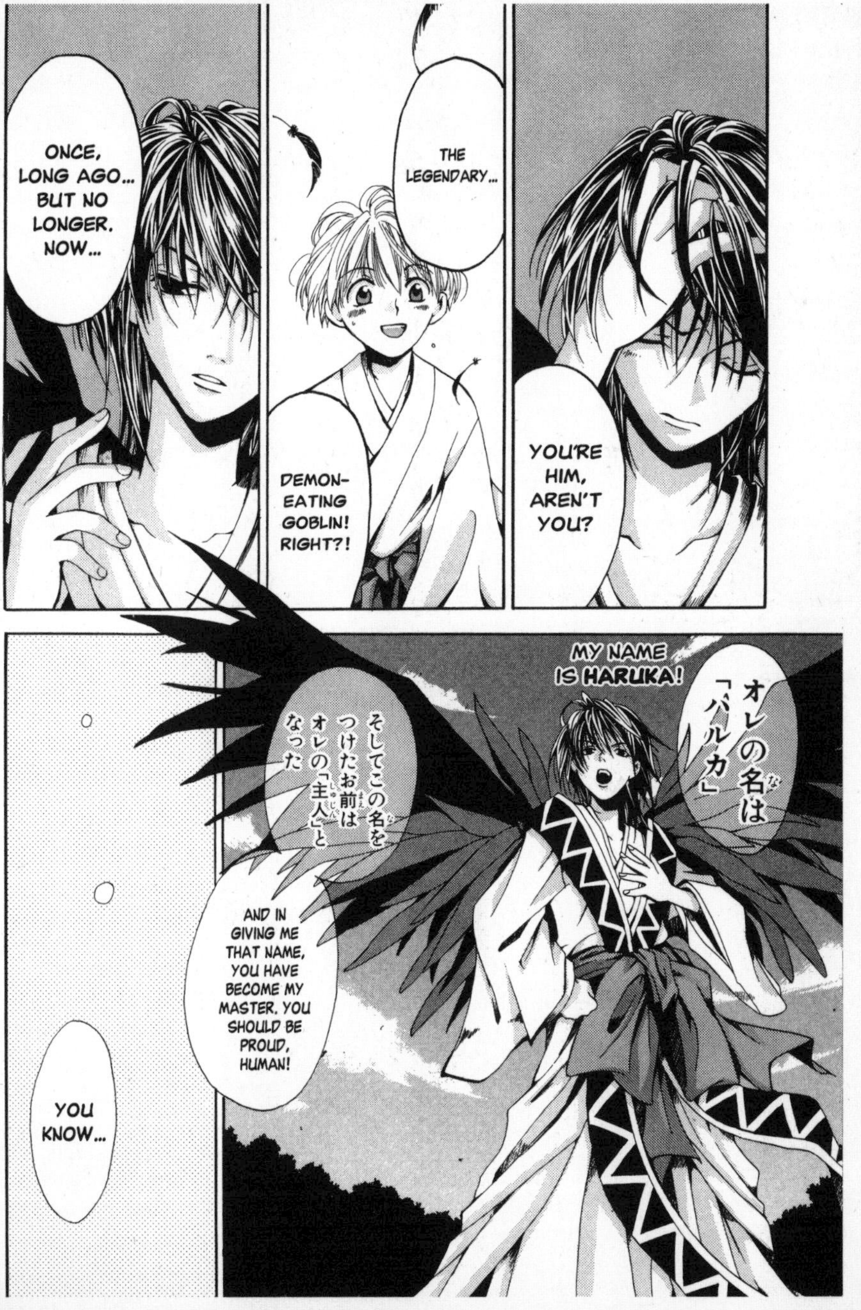
YOU'RE HIM, AREN'T YOU?
THE LEGENDARY...
DEMON-EATING GOBLIN! RIGHT?!
ONCE, LONG AGO... BUT NO LONGER. NOW...
MY NAME IS HARUKA!
オレの名は「ハルカ」
そしてこの名をつけたお前はオレの「主人」となった
AND IN GIVING ME THAT NAME, YOU HAVE BECOME MY MASTER. YOU SHOULD BE PROUD, HUMAN!
YOU KNOW...

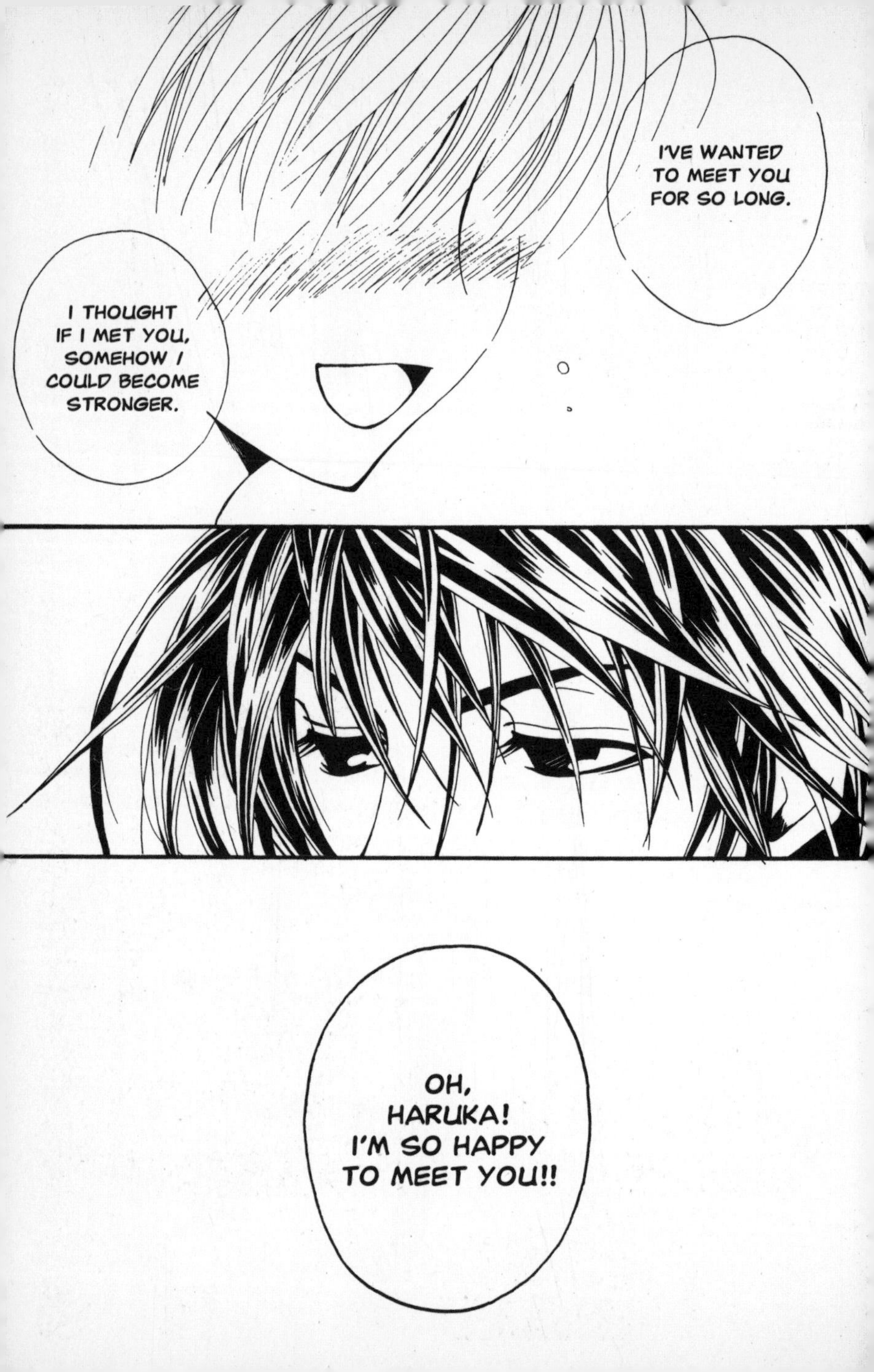
I'VE WANTED TO MEET YOU FOR SO LONG.
I THOUGHT IF I MET YOU, SOMEHOW I COULD BECOME STRONGER.
OH, HARUKA! I'M SO HAPPY TO MEET YOU!!

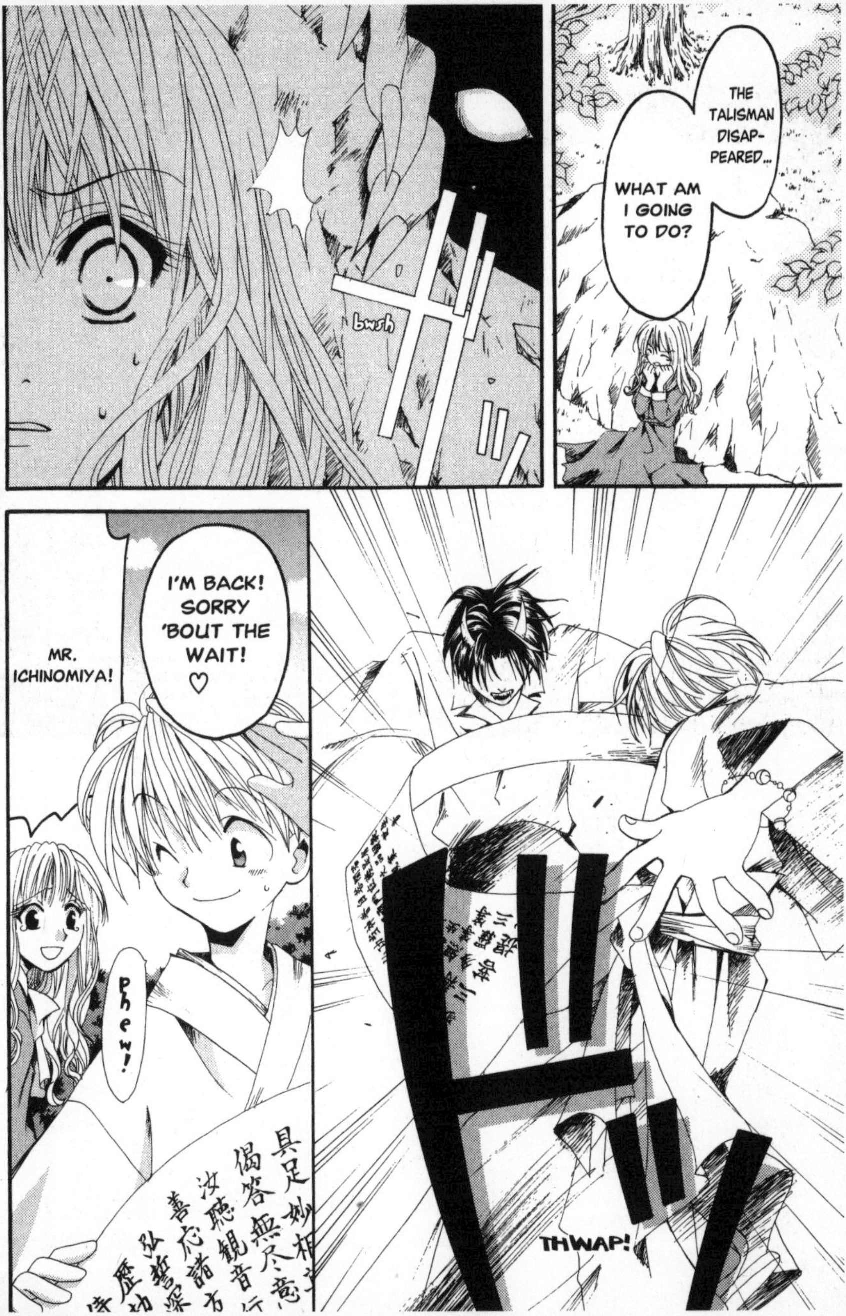
THE TALISMAN DISAP-PEARED...
WHAT AM I GOING TO DO?
bwsh
THWAP!
I'M BACK! SORRY 'BOUT THE WAIT! ♡
MR. ICHINOMIYA!
Phew!

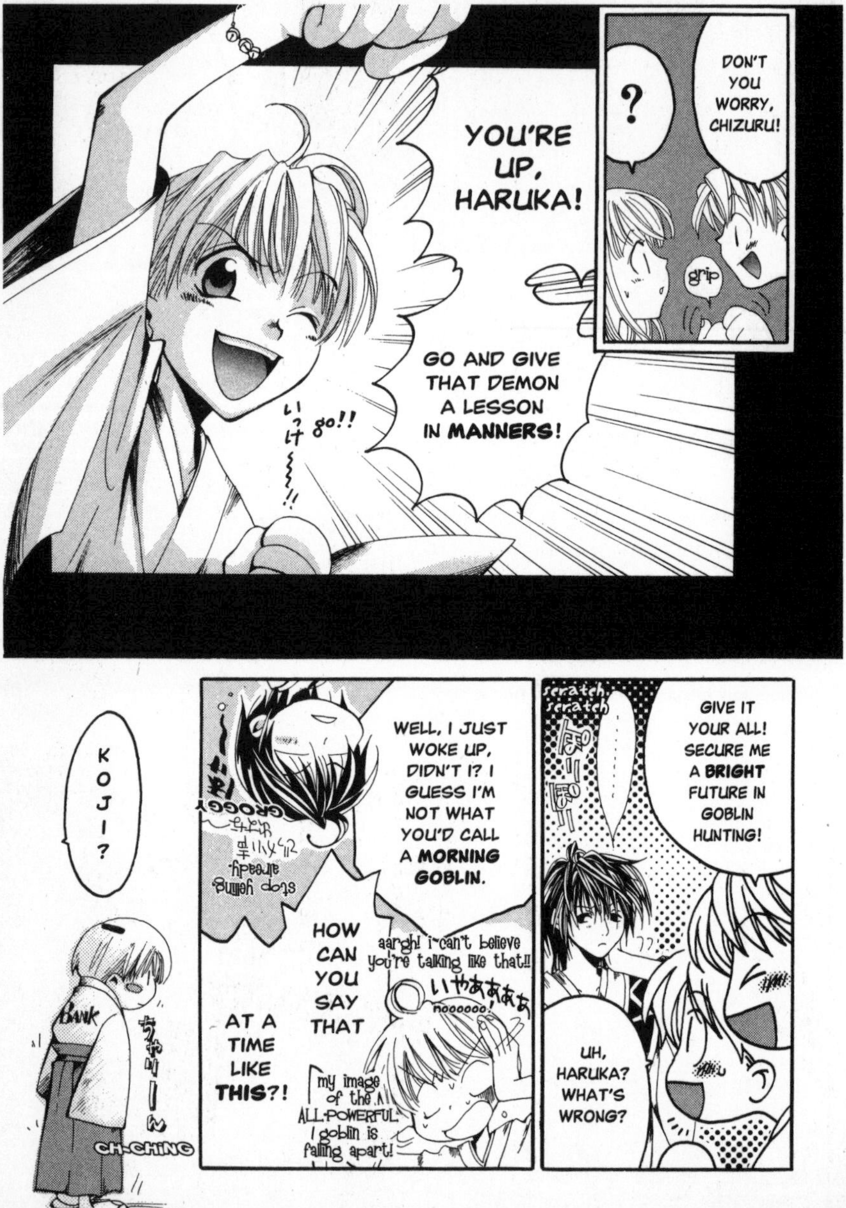
DON'T YOU WORRY, CHIZURU!
?
grip
YOU'RE UP, HARUKA!
GO AND GIVE THAT DEMON A LESSON IN **MANNERS**!
いっけ～～!!
go!!
GIVE IT YOUR ALL! SECURE ME A **BRIGHT** FUTURE IN GOBLIN HUNTING!
scratch scratch
......
UH, HARUKA? WHAT'S WRONG?
WELL, I JUST WOKE UP, DIDN'T I? I GUESS I'M NOT WHAT YOU'D CALL A **MORNING GOBLIN**.
GROGGY
stop yelling already
HOW CAN YOU SAY THAT AT A TIME LIKE **THIS**?!
aargh! i can't believe you're talking like that!!
いやああああ
noooooo!
my image of the ALL-POWERFUL goblin is falling apart!
KOJI?
BANK
CH-CHING

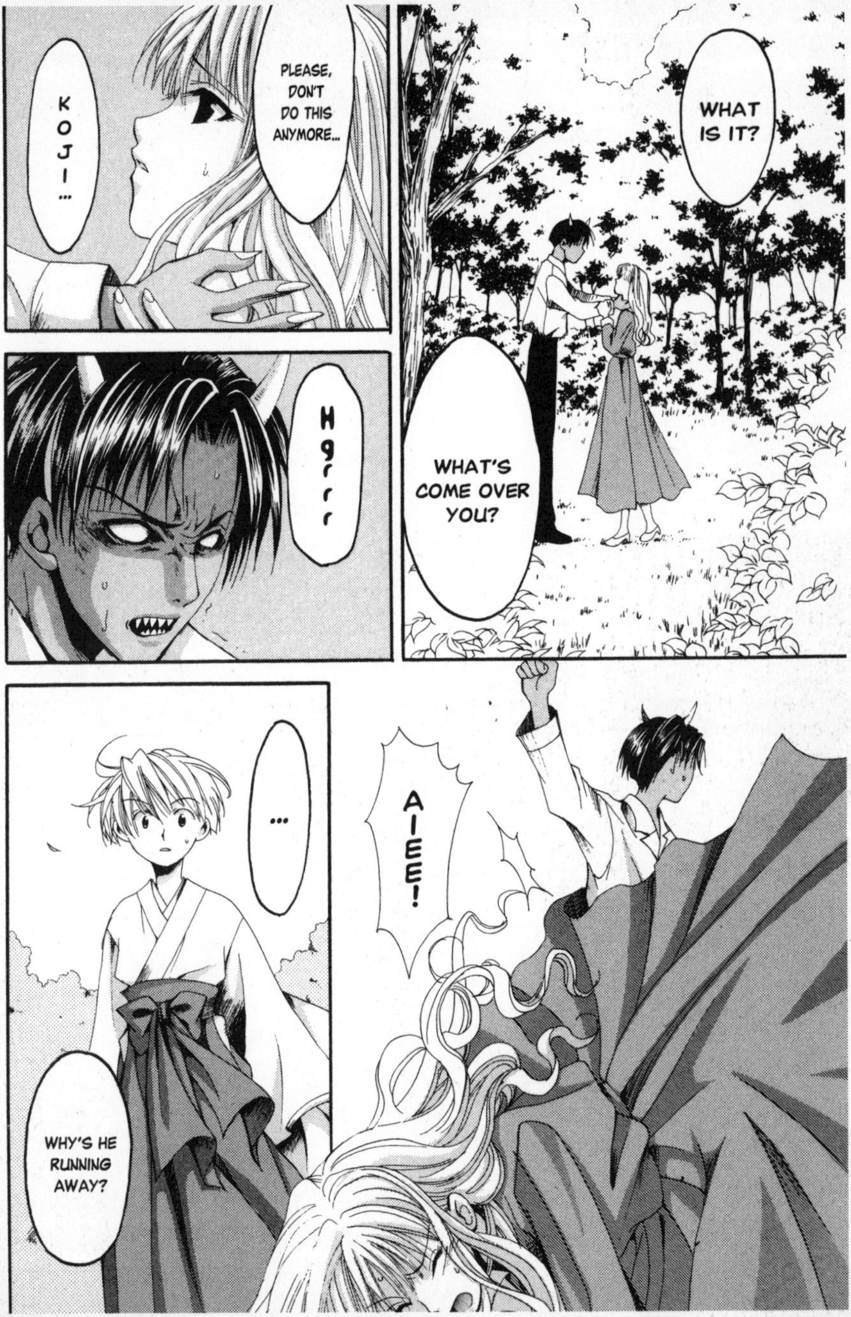
WHAT IS IT?
WHAT'S COME OVER YOU?
PLEASE, DON'T DO THIS ANYMORE...
KOJI...
Hgrrr
AIEE!
...
WHY'S HE RUNNING AWAY?

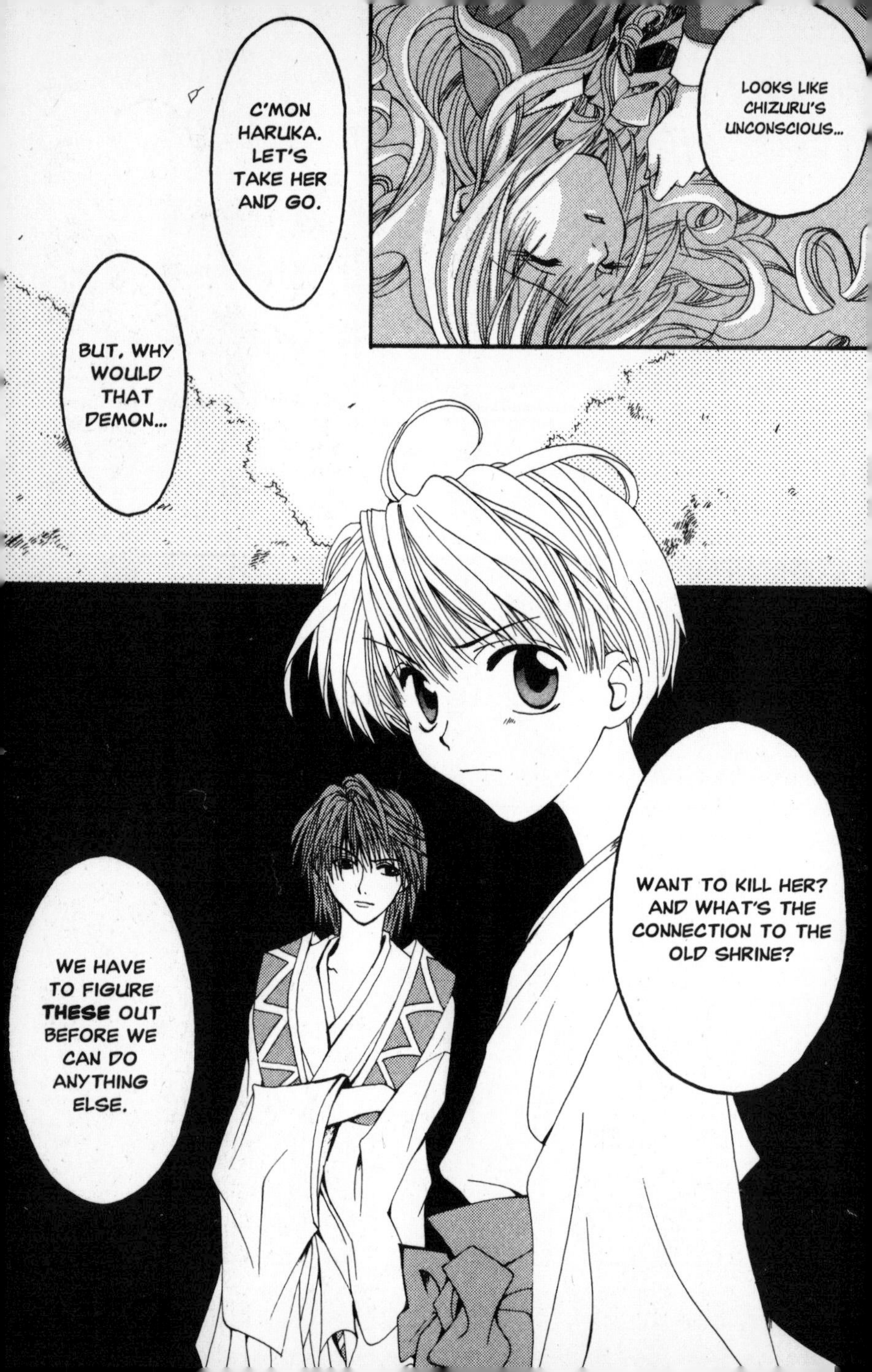
LOOKS LIKE CHIZURU'S UNCONSCIOUS...
C'MON HARUKA. LET'S TAKE HER AND GO.
BUT, WHY WOULD THAT DEMON...
WANT TO KILL HER? AND WHAT'S THE CONNECTION TO THE OLD SHRINE?
WE HAVE TO FIGURE **THESE** OUT BEFORE WE CAN DO ANYTHING ELSE.

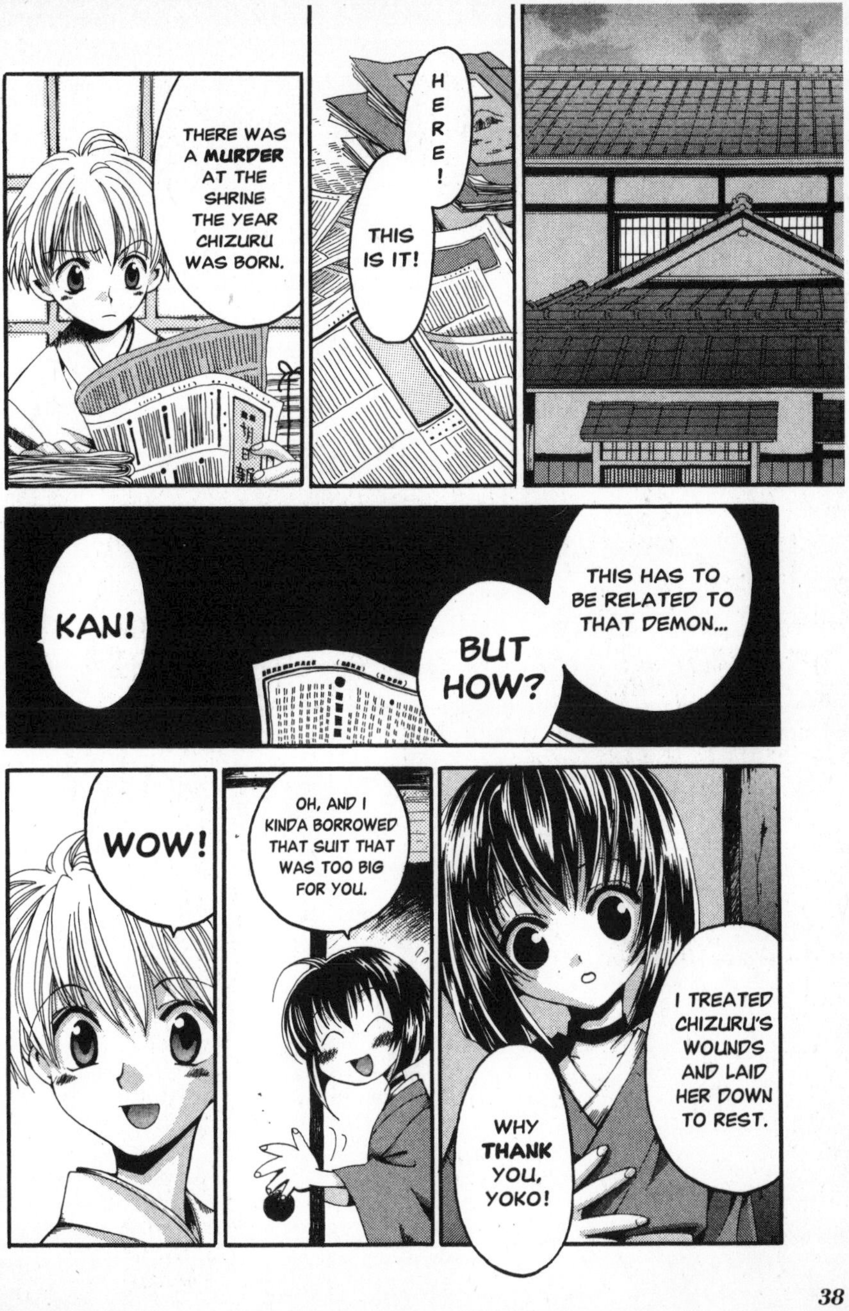
HERE!
THIS IS IT!
THERE WAS A **MURDER** AT THE SHRINE THE YEAR CHIZURU WAS BORN.
THIS HAS TO BE RELATED TO THAT DEMON...
BUT HOW?
KAN!
I TREATED CHIZURU'S WOUNDS AND LAID HER DOWN TO REST.
WHY **THANK** YOU, YOKO!
OH, AND I KINDA BORROWED THAT SUIT THAT WAS TOO BIG FOR YOU.
WOW!

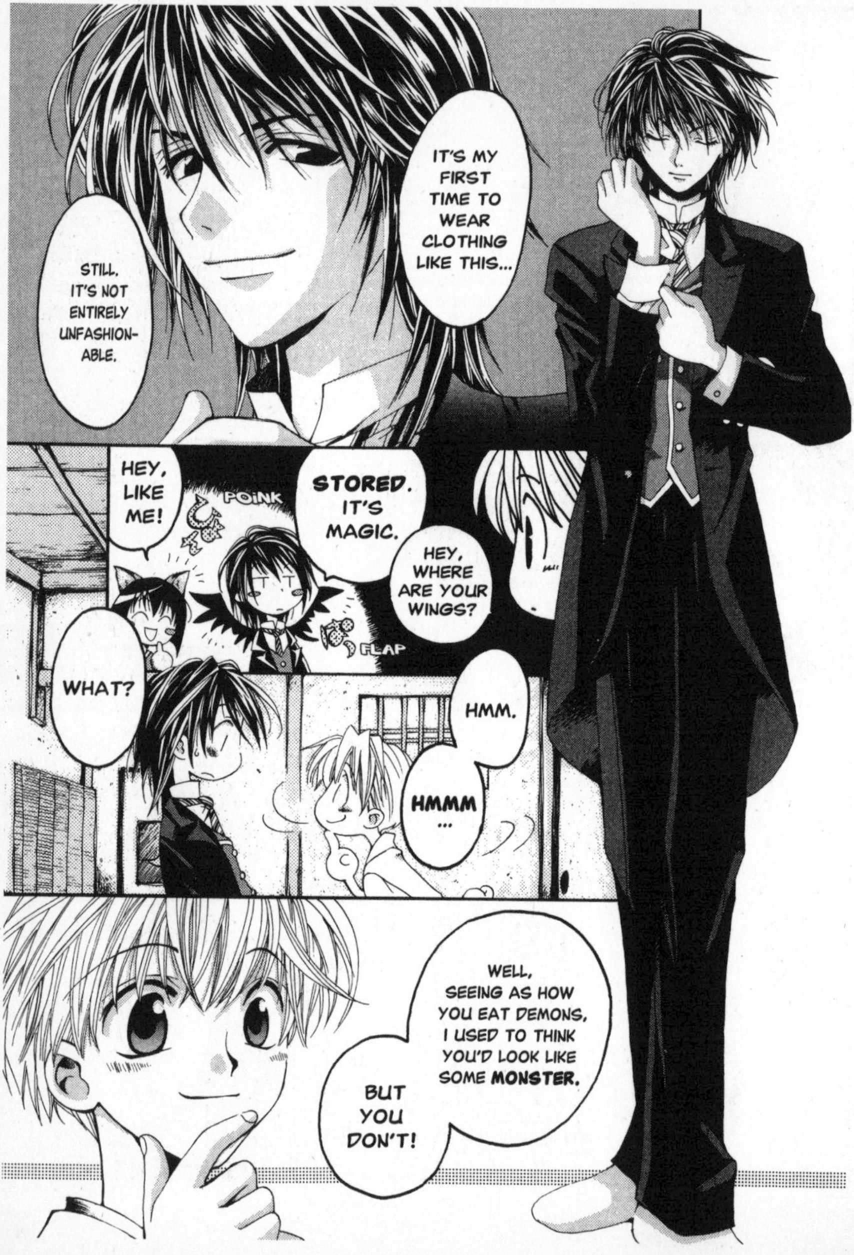
IT'S MY FIRST TIME TO WEAR CLOTHING LIKE THIS...
STILL, IT'S NOT ENTIRELY UNFASHION-ABLE.
HEY, WHERE ARE YOUR WINGS?
STORED. IT'S MAGIC.
POINK
FLAP
HEY, LIKE ME!
HMM.
HMMM ...
WHAT?
WELL, SEEING AS HOW YOU EAT DEMONS, I USED TO THINK YOU'D LOOK LIKE SOME MONSTER.
BUT YOU DON'T!

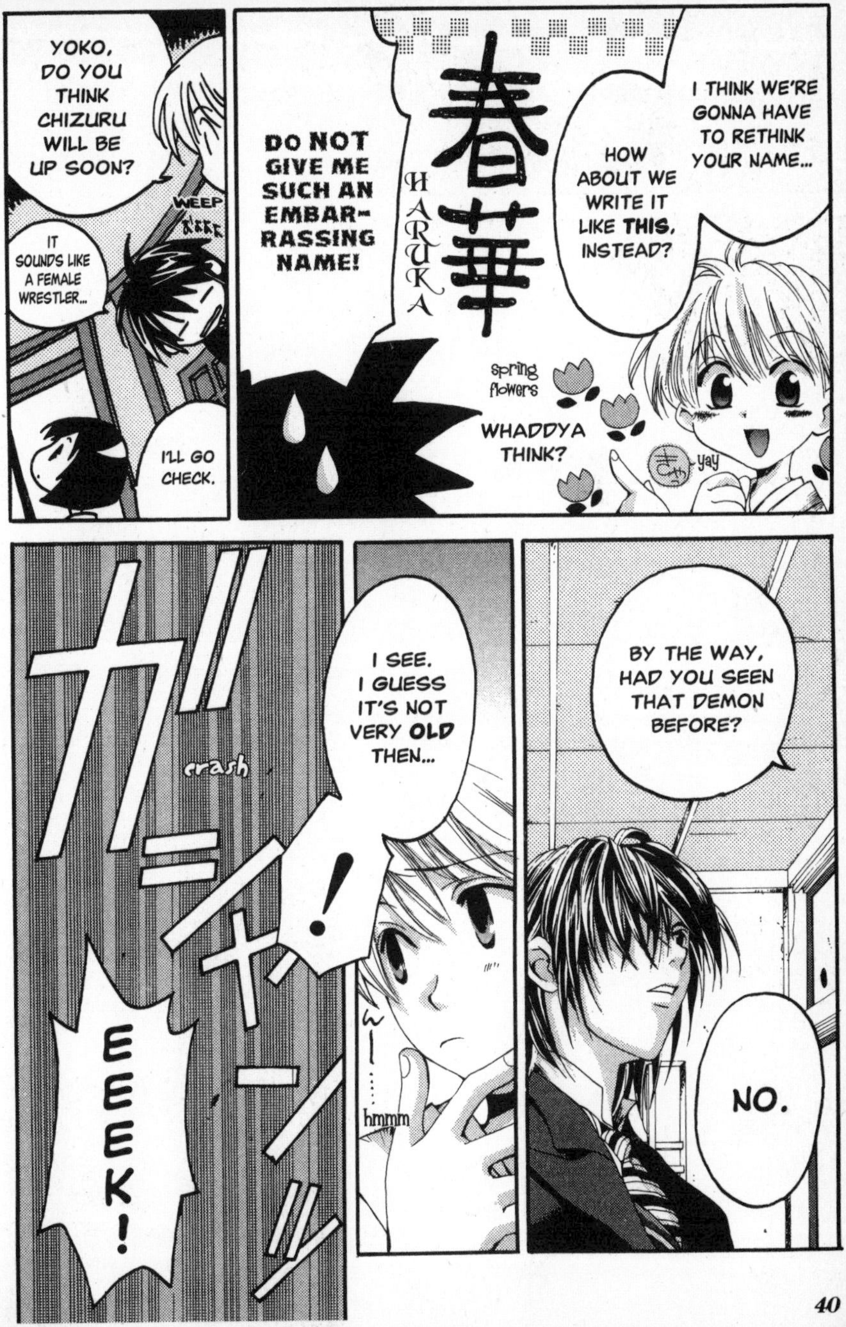
I THINK WE'RE GONNA HAVE TO RETHINK YOUR NAME...
HOW ABOUT WE WRITE IT LIKE THIS, INSTEAD?
春華
HARUKA
DO NOT GIVE ME SUCH AN EMBARRASSING NAME!
spring flowers
WHADDYA THINK?
yay
YOKO, DO YOU THINK CHIZURU WILL BE UP SOON?
WEEP
IT SOUNDS LIKE A FEMALE WRESTLER...
I'LL GO CHECK.
BY THE WAY, HAD YOU SEEN THAT DEMON BEFORE?
NO.
I SEE. I GUESS IT'S NOT VERY OLD THEN...
!
hmmm
crash
EEEEK!

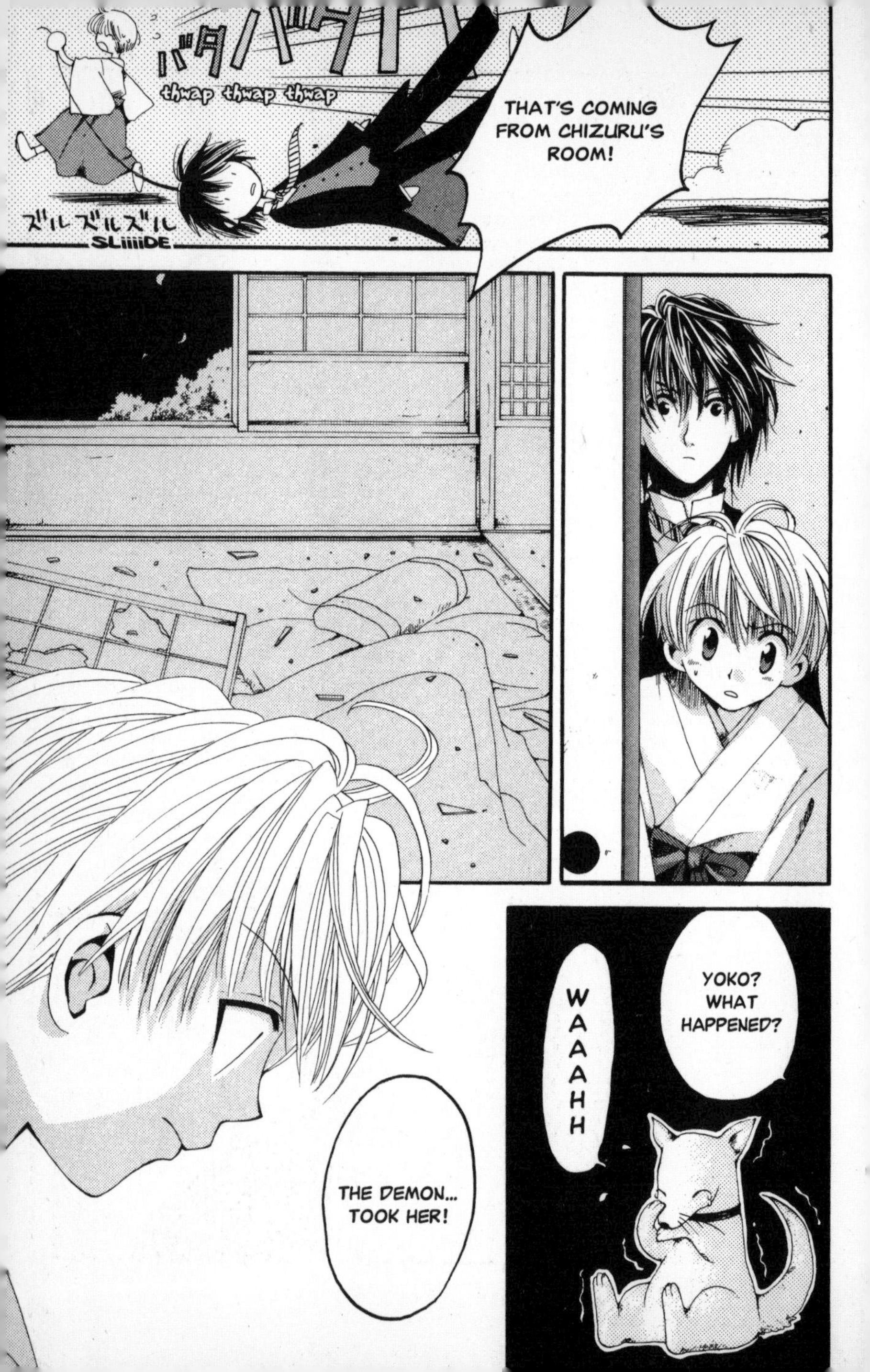
THAT'S COMING FROM CHIZURU'S ROOM!
thwap thwap thwap
ズルズルズル
SLiiiiDE
YOKO? WHAT HAPPENED?
WAAAAHH
THE DEMON... TOOK HER!

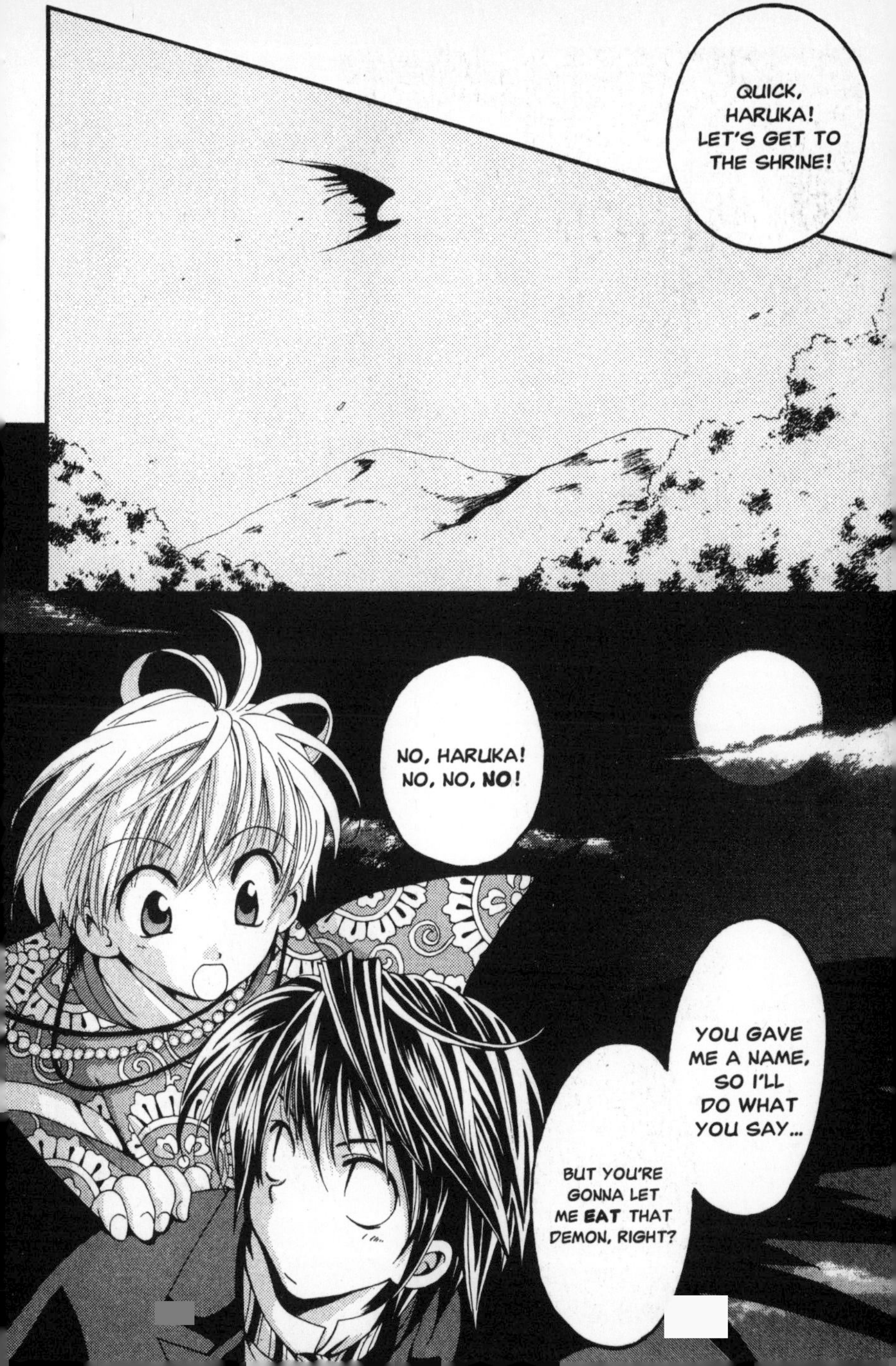
QUICK, HARUKA! LET'S GET TO THE SHRINE!
NO, HARUKA! NO, NO, NO!
YOU GAVE ME A NAME, SO I'LL DO WHAT YOU SAY...
BUT YOU'RE GONNA LET ME EAT THAT DEMON, RIGHT?

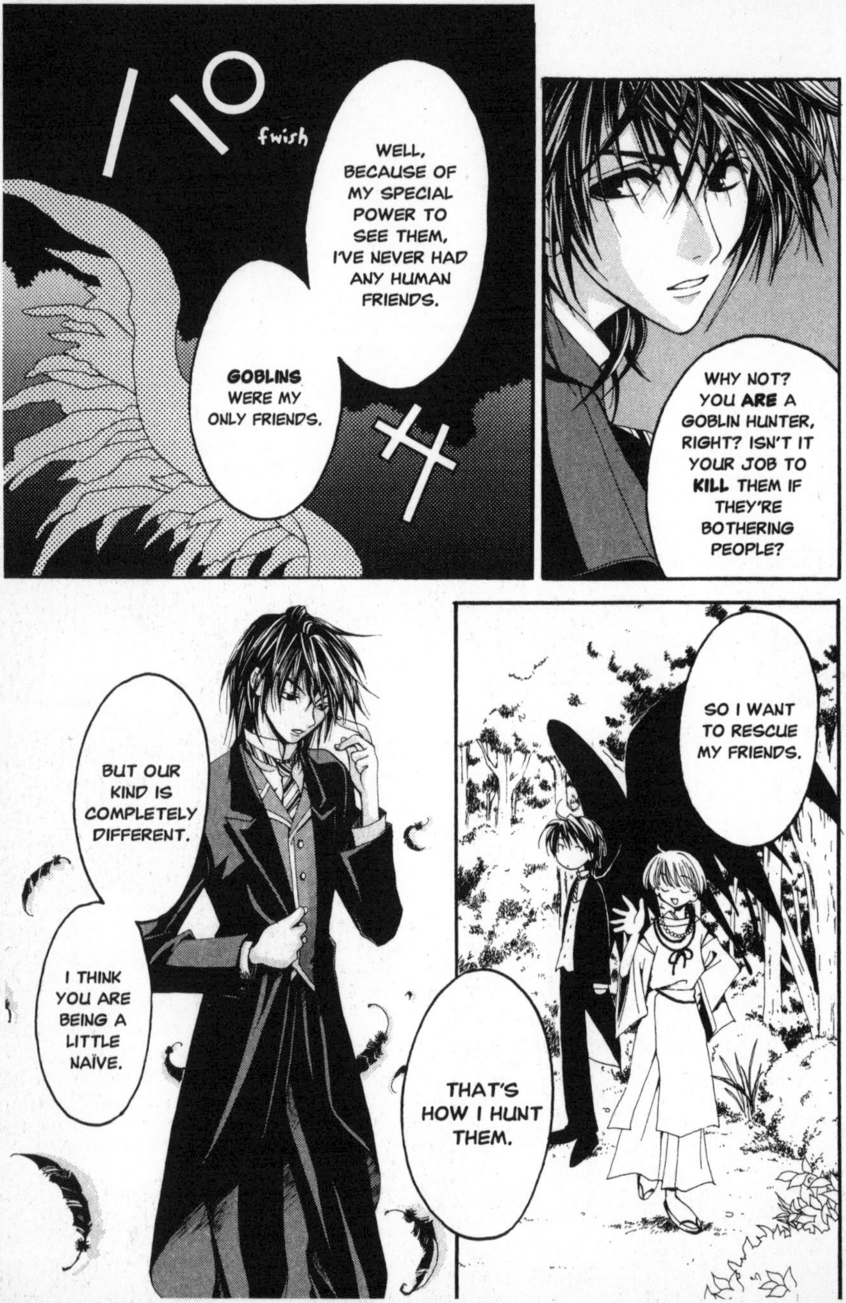
WHY NOT? YOU **ARE** A GOBLIN HUNTER, RIGHT? ISN'T IT YOUR JOB TO **KILL** THEM IF THEY'RE BOTHERING PEOPLE?
fwish
WELL, BECAUSE OF MY SPECIAL POWER TO SEE THEM, I'VE NEVER HAD ANY HUMAN FRIENDS.
GOBLINS WERE MY ONLY FRIENDS.
SO I WANT TO RESCUE MY FRIENDS.
THAT'S HOW I HUNT THEM.
BUT OUR KIND IS COMPLETELY DIFFERENT.
I THINK YOU ARE BEING A LITTLE NAÏVE.

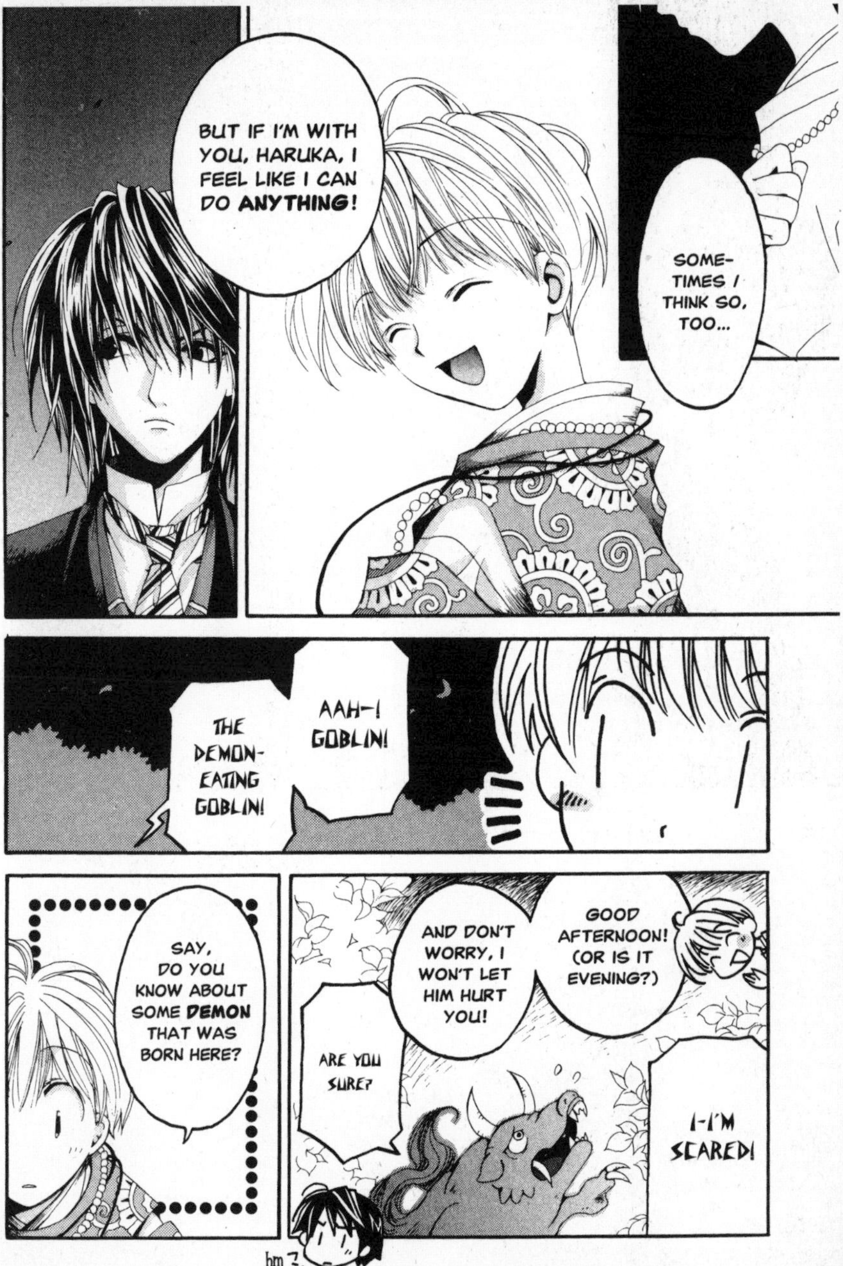
SOME-TIMES I THINK SO, TOO...
BUT IF I'M WITH YOU, HARUKA, I FEEL LIKE I CAN DO **ANYTHING**!
AAH—! GOBLIN!
THE DEMON-EATING GOBLIN!
GOOD AFTERNOON! (OR IS IT EVENING?)
AND DON'T WORRY, I WON'T LET HIM HURT YOU!
I-I'M SCARED!
ARE YOU SURE?
hm
SAY, DO YOU KNOW ABOUT SOME **DEMON** THAT WAS BORN HERE?

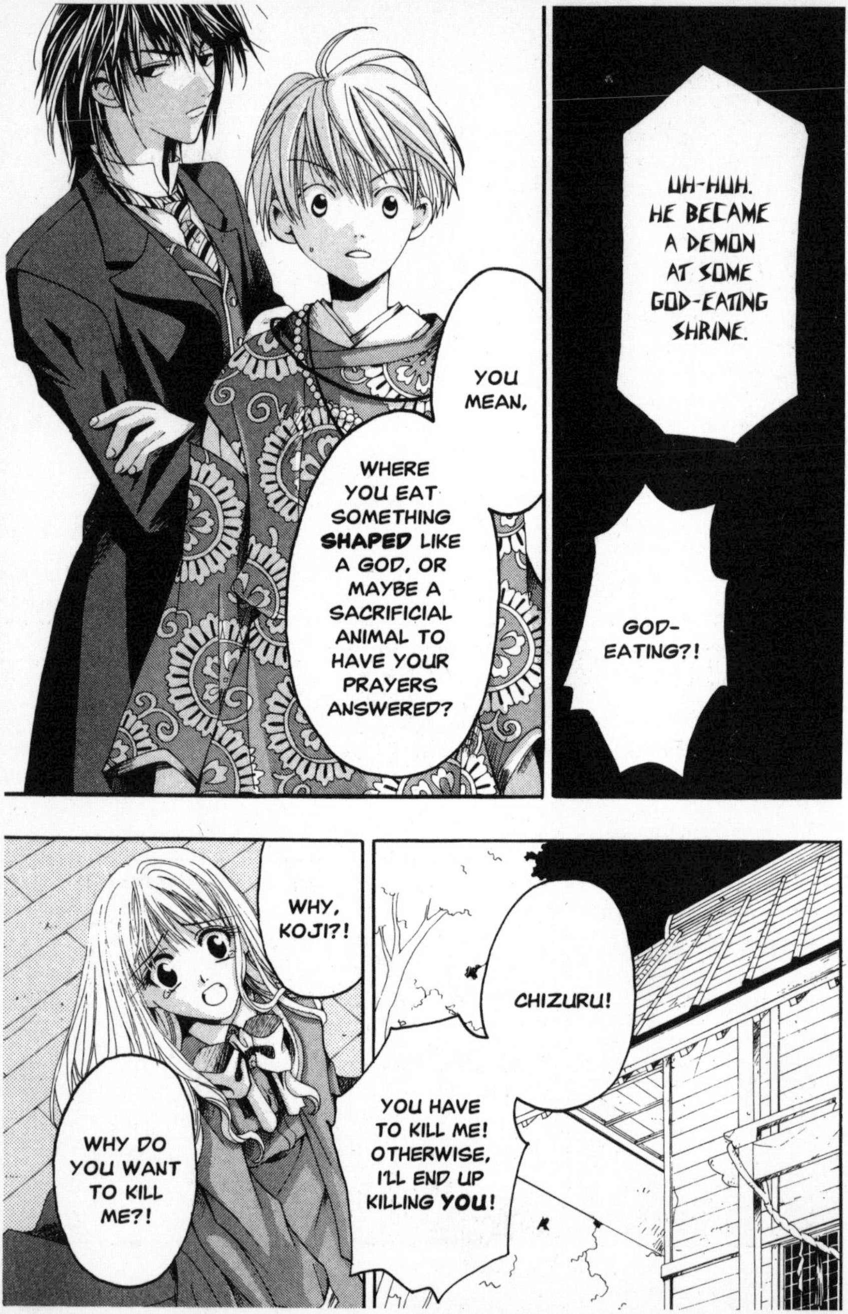
UH-HUH. HE BECAME A DEMON AT SOME GOD-EATING SHRINE.
GOD-EATING?!
YOU MEAN,
WHERE YOU EAT SOMETHING **SHAPED** LIKE A GOD, OR MAYBE A SACRIFICIAL ANIMAL TO HAVE YOUR PRAYERS ANSWERED?
CHIZURU!
YOU HAVE TO KILL ME! OTHERWISE, I'LL END UP KILLING **YOU**!
WHY, KOJI?!
WHY DO YOU WANT TO KILL ME?!

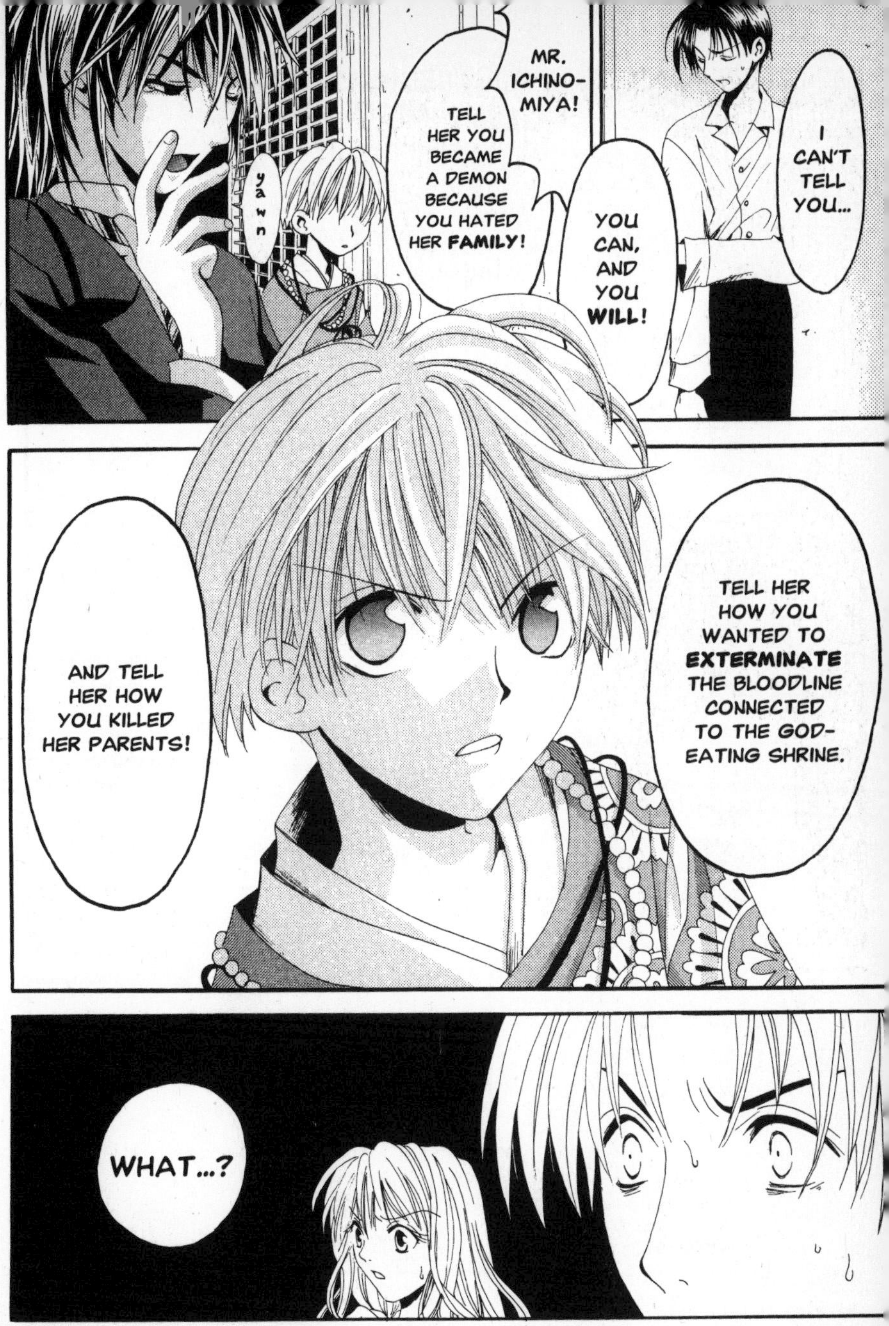
I CAN'T TELL YOU...
YOU CAN, AND YOU **WILL**!
MR. ICHINO-MIYA!
TELL HER YOU BECAME A DEMON BECAUSE YOU HATED HER **FAMILY**!
yawn
TELL HER HOW YOU WANTED TO **EXTERMINATE** THE BLOODLINE CONNECTED TO THE GOD-EATING SHRINE.
AND TELL HER HOW YOU KILLED HER PARENTS!
WHAT...?

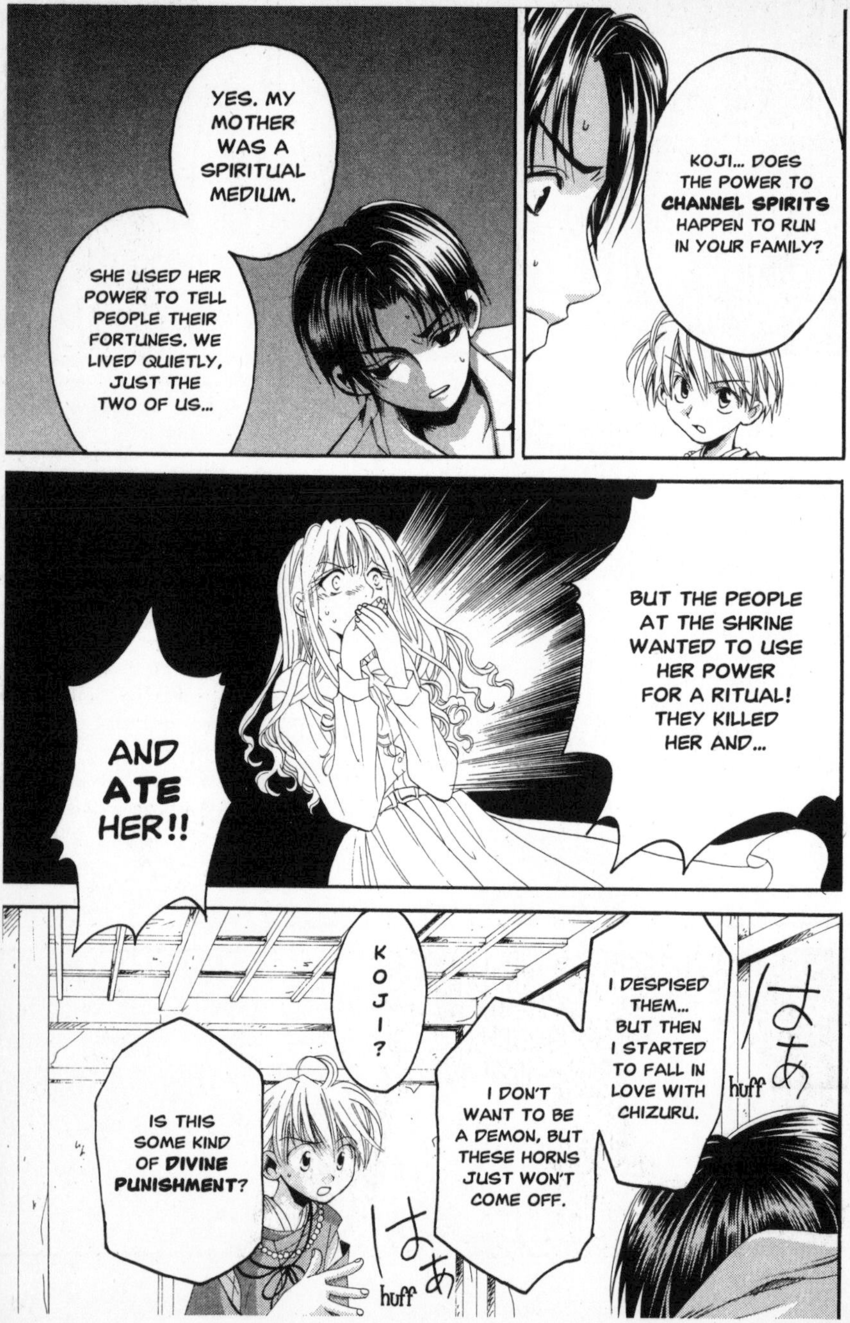
KOJI... DOES THE POWER TO **CHANNEL SPIRITS** HAPPEN TO RUN IN YOUR FAMILY?
YES. MY MOTHER WAS A SPIRITUAL MEDIUM.
SHE USED HER POWER TO TELL PEOPLE THEIR FORTUNES. WE LIVED QUIETLY, JUST THE TWO OF US...
BUT THE PEOPLE AT THE SHRINE WANTED TO USE HER POWER FOR A RITUAL! THEY KILLED HER AND...
AND ATE HER!!
はあ
huff
I DESPISED THEM... BUT THEN I STARTED TO FALL IN LOVE WITH CHIZURU.
I DON'T WANT TO BE A DEMON, BUT THESE HORNS JUST WON'T COME OFF.
KOJI?
IS THIS SOME KIND OF **DIVINE PUNISHMENT**?
はあ
huff

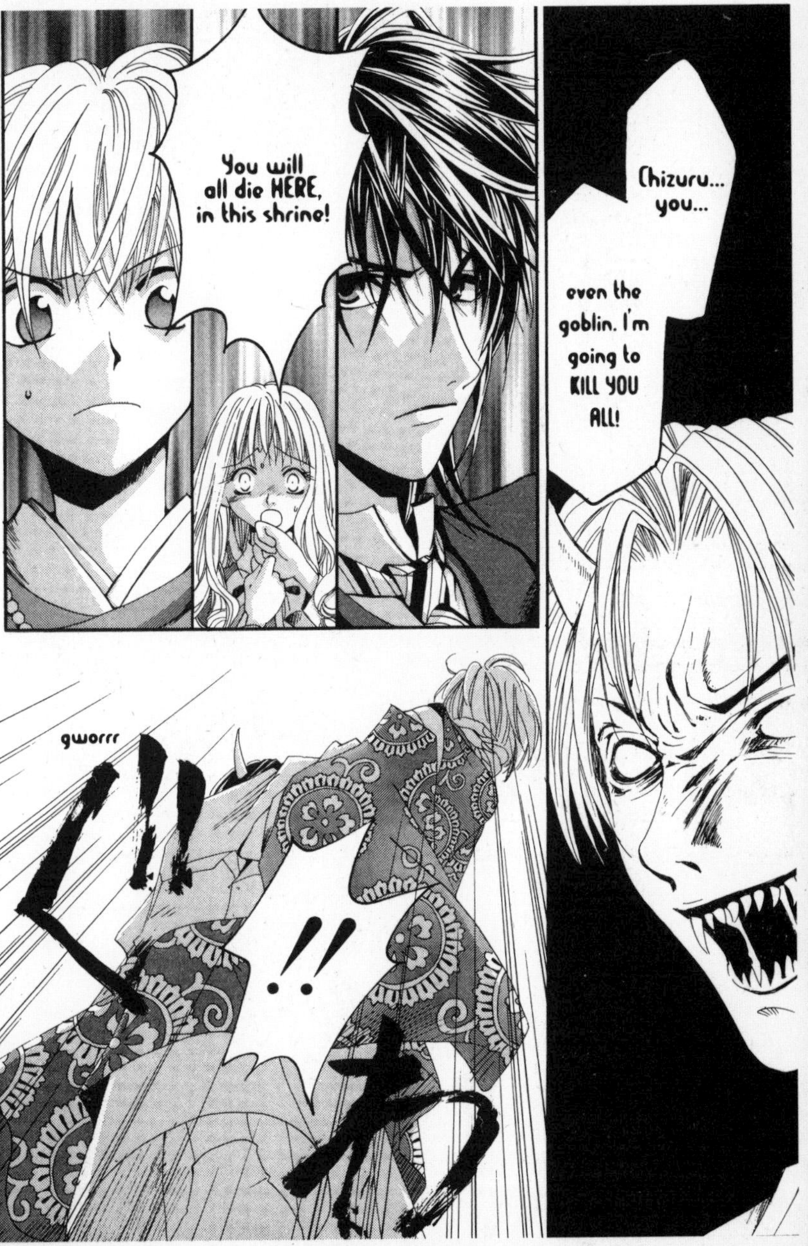
Chizuru... you...
even the goblin. I'm going to KILL YOU ALL!
You will all die HERE, in this shrine!
gworrr
!!

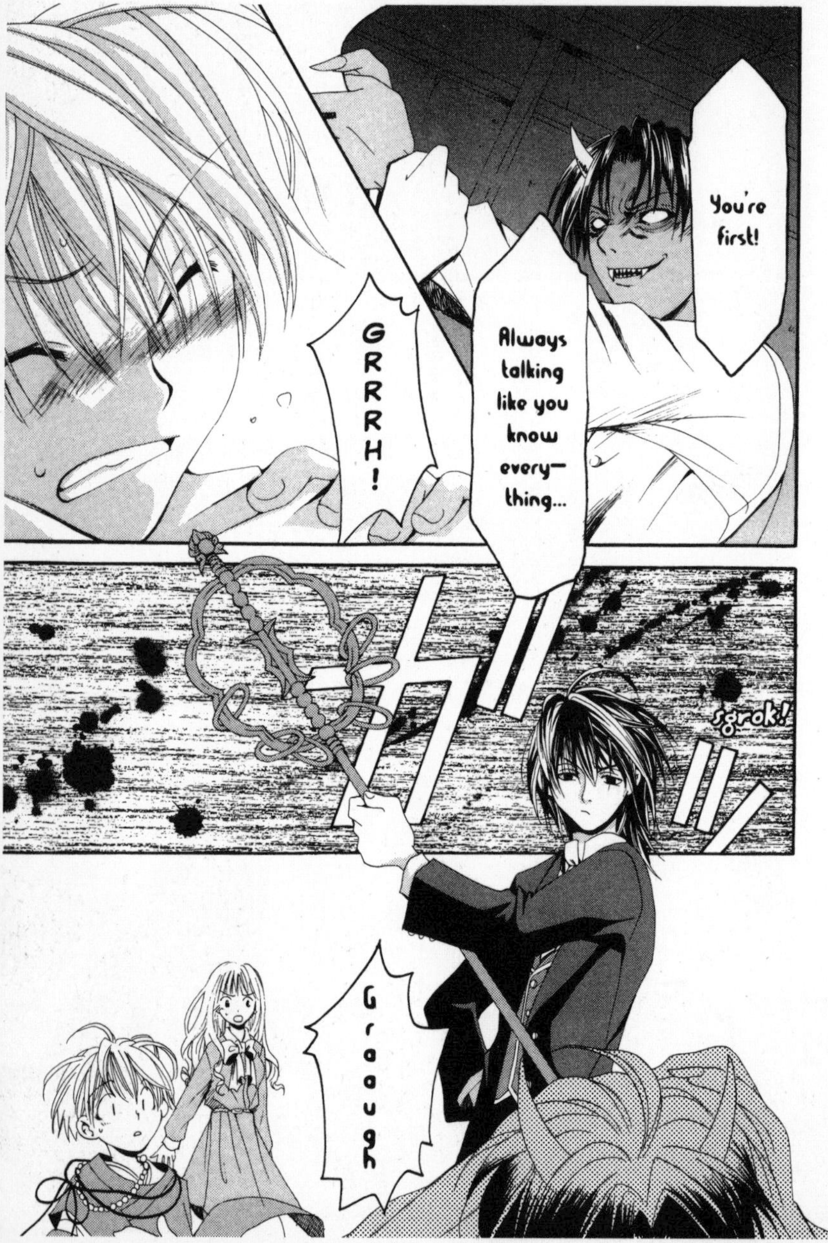
You're first!
Always talking like you know every-thing...
GRRRH!
sgrok!
Graaugh

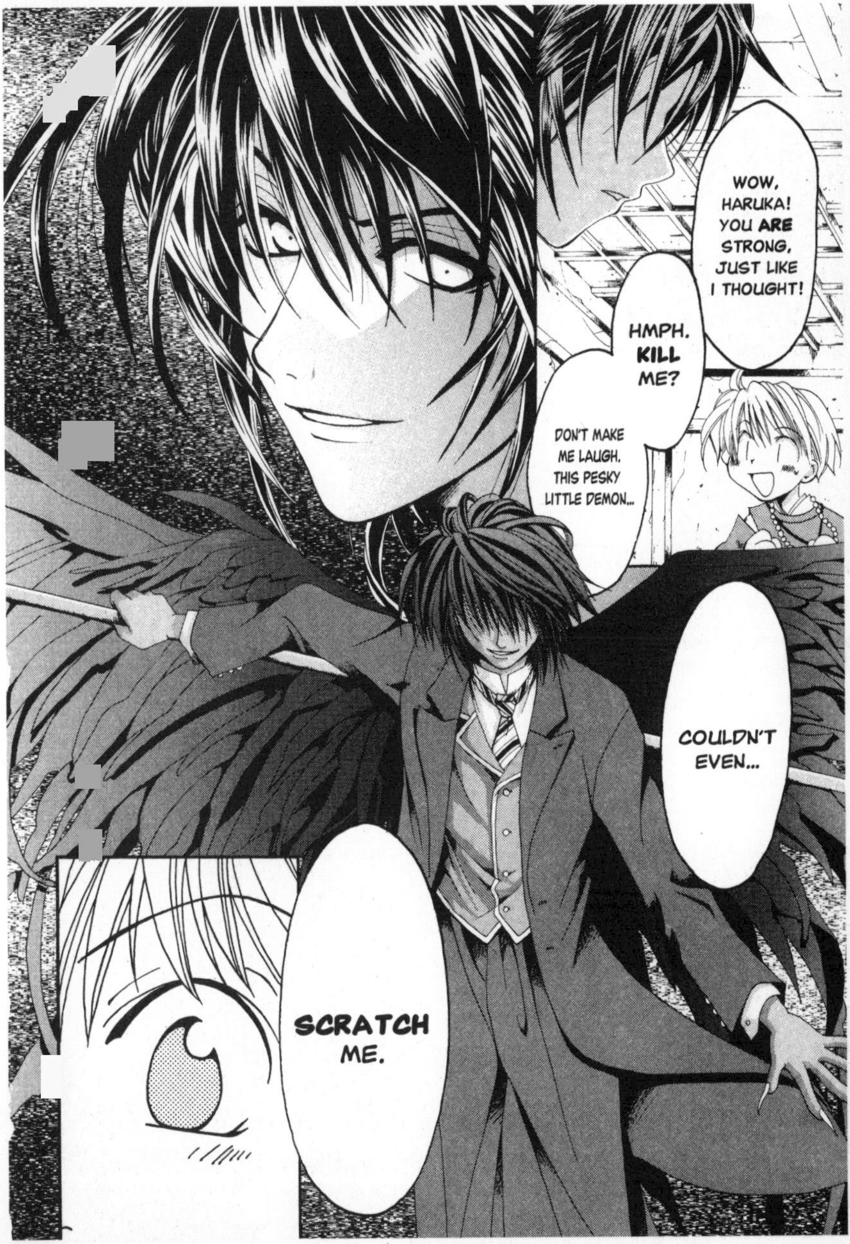
WOW, HARUKA! YOU **ARE** STRONG, JUST LIKE I THOUGHT!
HMPH. **KILL** ME?
DON'T MAKE ME LAUGH. THIS PESKY LITTLE DEMON...
COULDN'T EVEN...
SCRATCH ME.

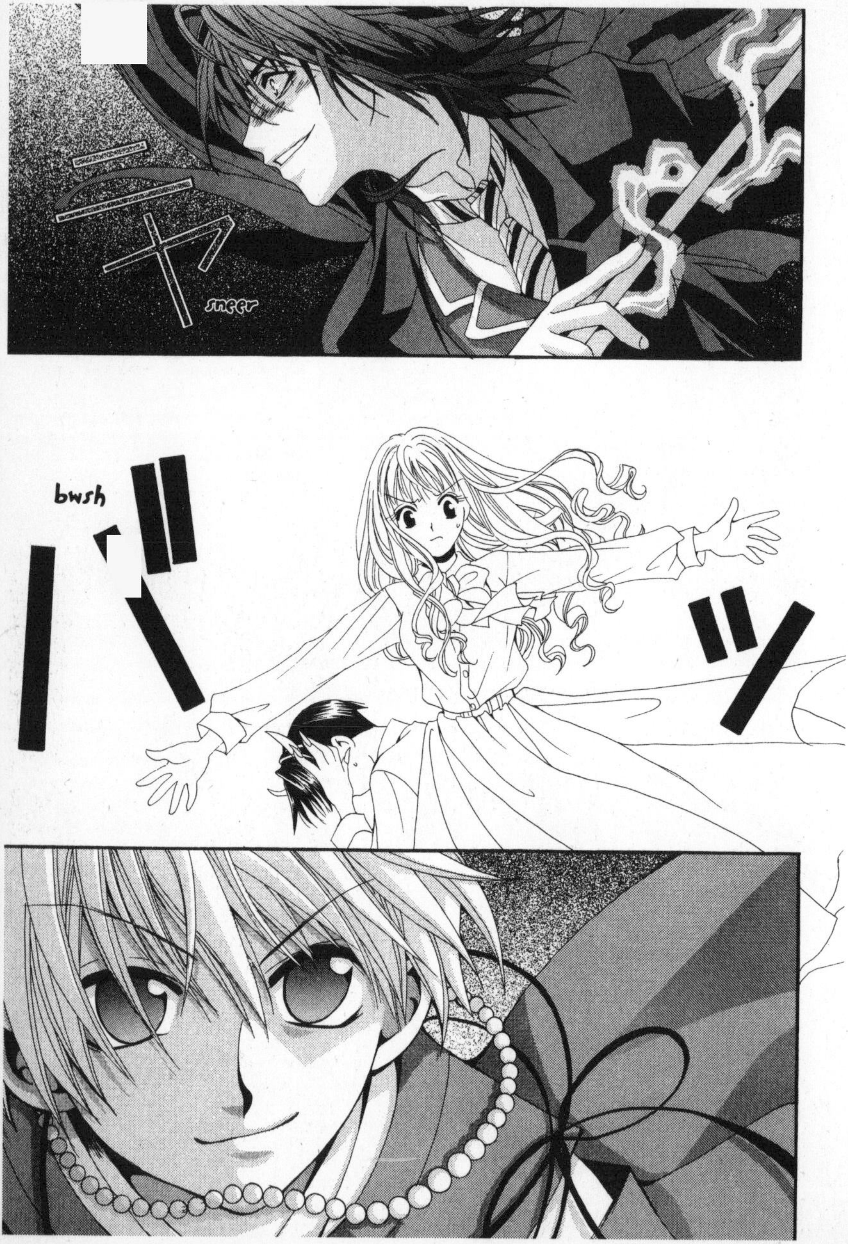
ニヤ
sneer
bwsh

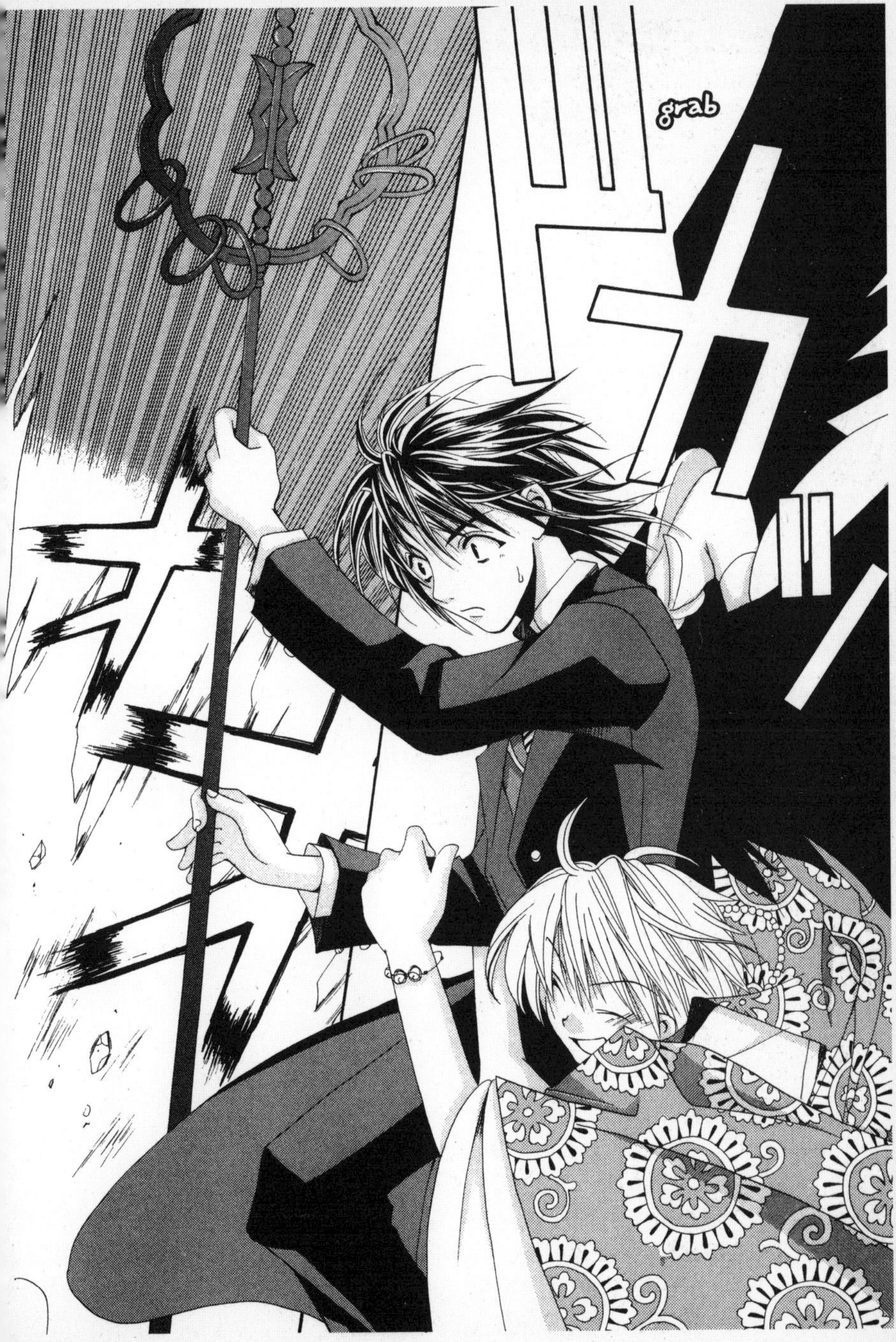
grab

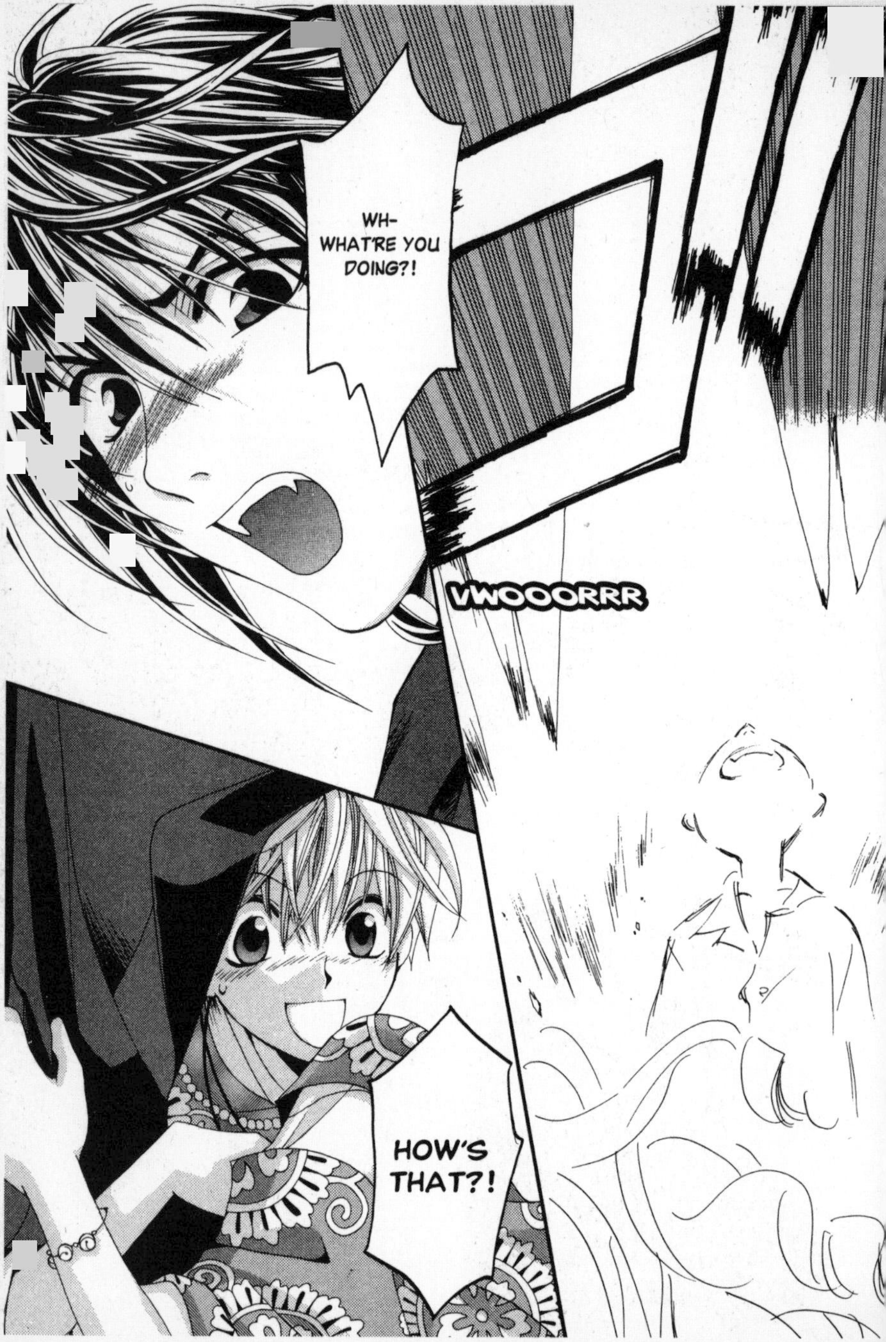
WH-
WHAT'RE YOU
DOING?!
VWOOORRR
HOW'S
THAT?!

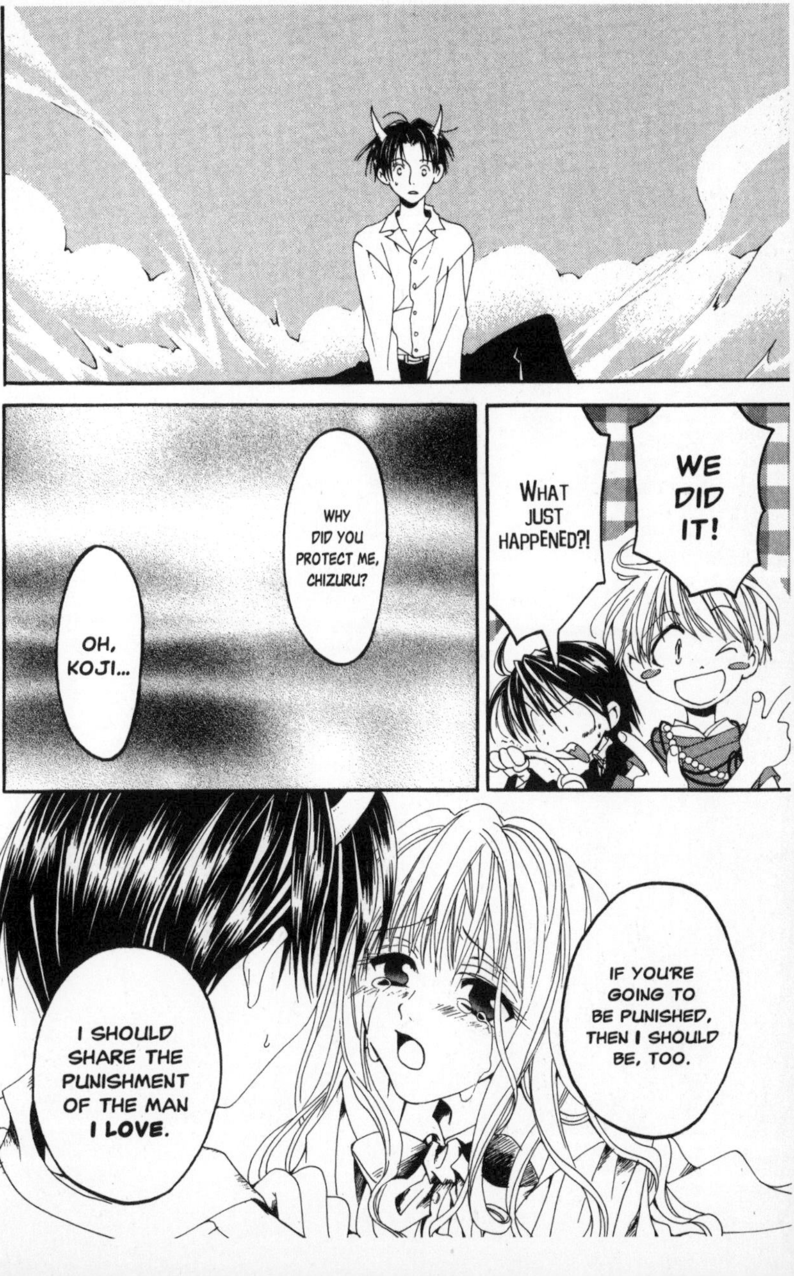
WE DID IT!
WHAT JUST HAPPENED?!
WHY DID YOU PROTECT ME, CHIZURU?
OH, KOJI...
IF YOU'RE GOING TO BE PUNISHED, THEN I SHOULD BE, TOO.
I SHOULD SHARE THE PUNISHMENT OF THE MAN I LOVE.

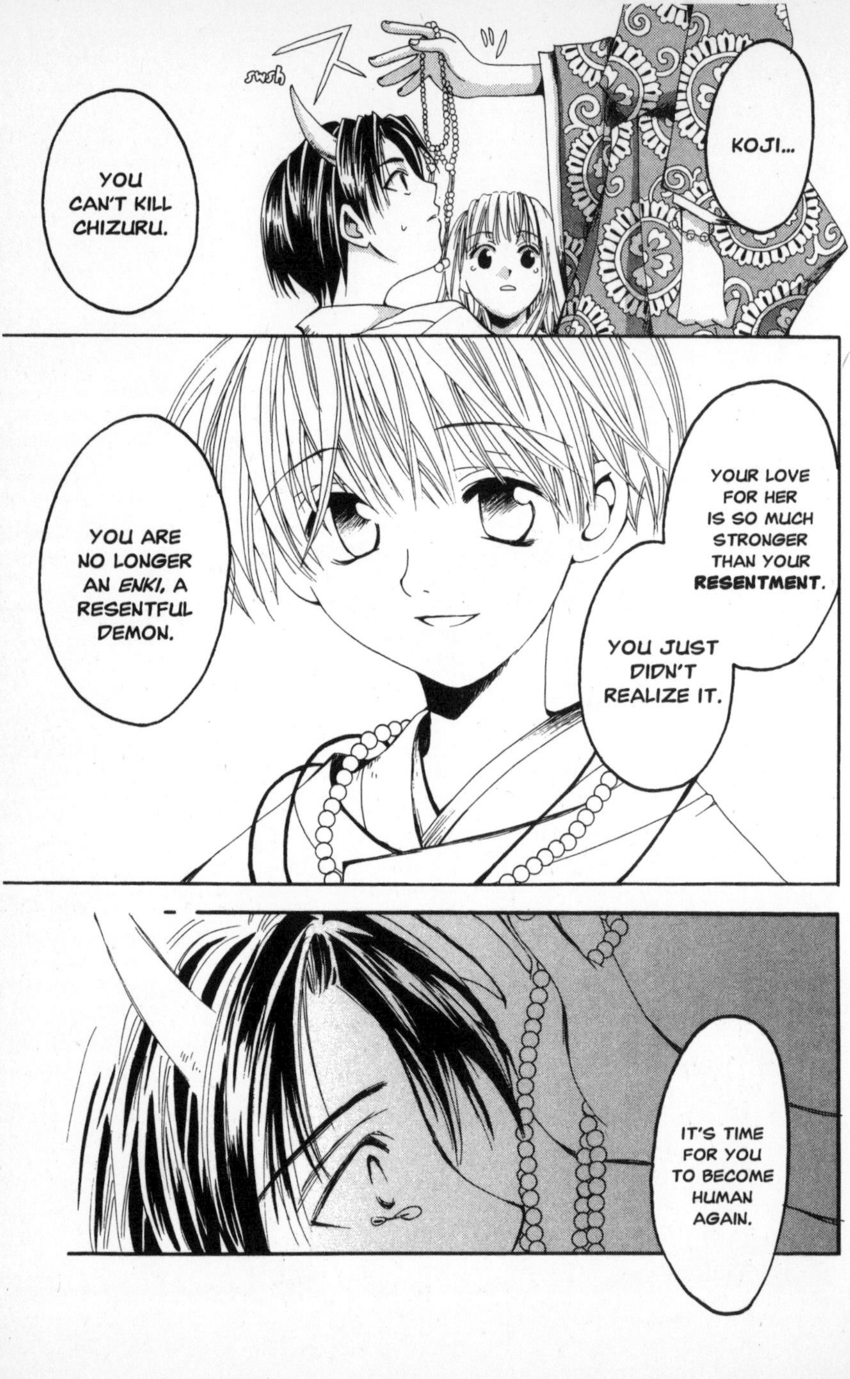
KOJI...
swsh
YOU CAN'T KILL CHIZURU.
YOUR LOVE FOR HER IS SO MUCH STRONGER THAN YOUR **RESENTMENT**.
YOU JUST DIDN'T REALIZE IT.
YOU ARE NO LONGER AN *ENKI*, A RESENTFUL DEMON.
IT'S TIME FOR YOU TO BECOME HUMAN AGAIN.

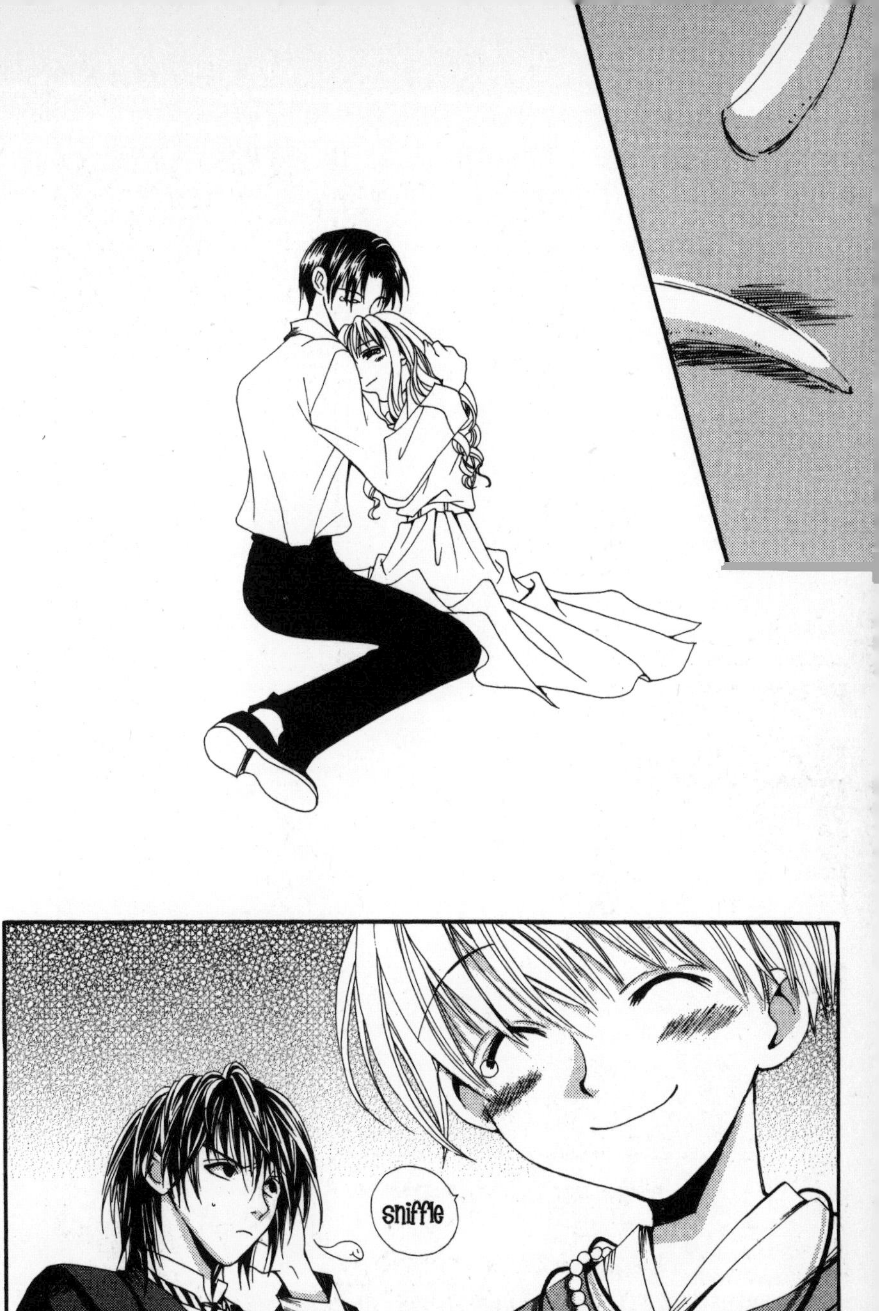
sniffle

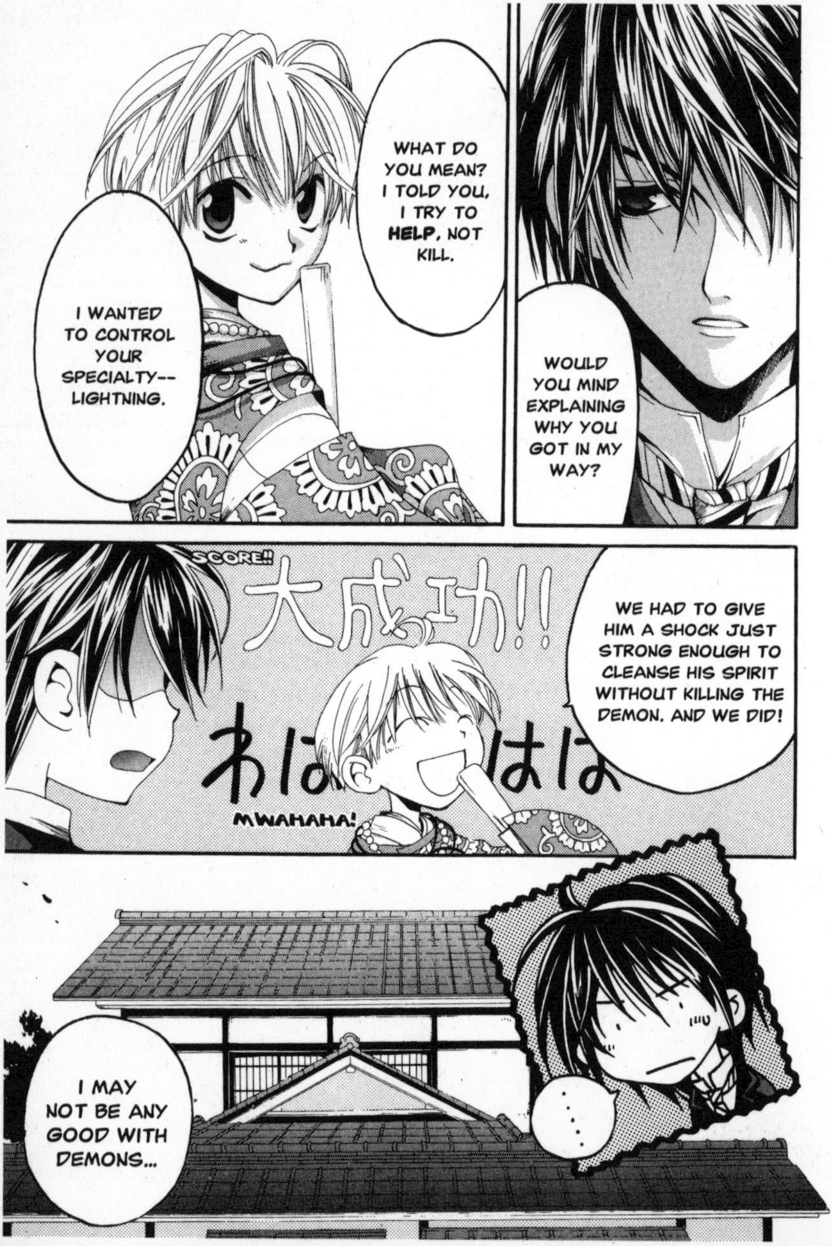
WOULD YOU MIND EXPLAINING WHY YOU GOT IN MY WAY?
WHAT DO YOU MEAN? I TOLD YOU, I TRY TO **HELP**, NOT KILL.
I WANTED TO CONTROL YOUR SPECIALTY-- LIGHTNING.
WE HAD TO GIVE HIM A SHOCK JUST STRONG ENOUGH TO CLEANSE HIS SPIRIT WITHOUT KILLING THE DEMON. AND WE DID!
SCORE!!
大成功!!
わは はは
MWAHAHA!
...
I MAY NOT BE ANY GOOD WITH DEMONS...

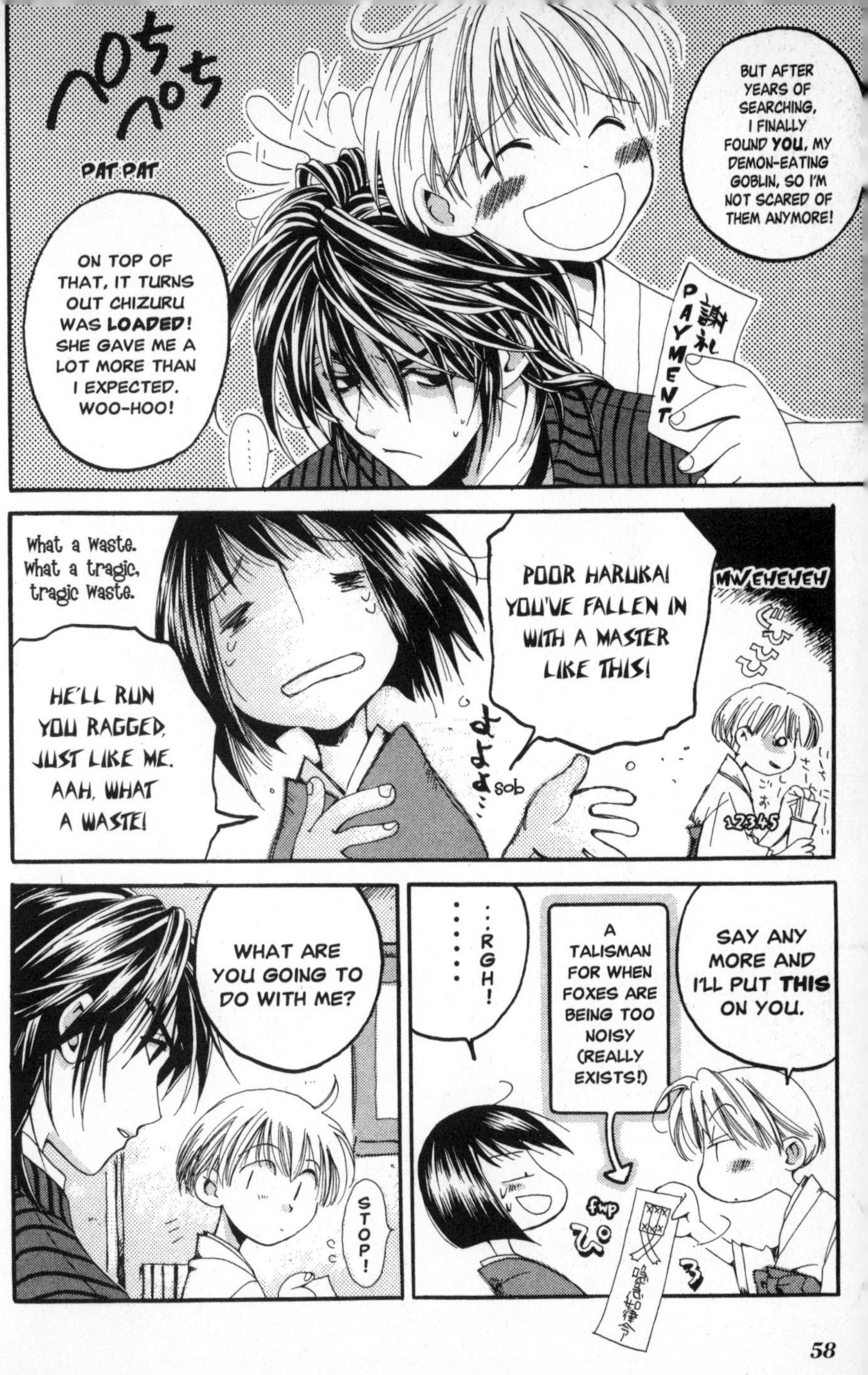
BUT AFTER YEARS OF SEARCHING, I FINALLY FOUND YOU, MY DEMON-EATING GOBLIN, SO I'M NOT SCARED OF THEM ANYMORE!
ぺちぺち
PAT PAT
謝礼
PAYMENT
ON TOP OF THAT, IT TURNS OUT CHIZURU WAS LOADED! SHE GAVE ME A LOT MORE THAN I EXPECTED. WOO-HOO!
......
MWEHEHEH
POOR HARUKA! YOU'VE FALLEN IN WITH A MASTER LIKE THIS!
What a waste. What a tragic, tragic waste.
HE'LL RUN YOU RAGGED, JUST LIKE ME. AAH, WHAT A WASTE!
sob
12345
SAY ANY MORE AND I'LL PUT THIS ON YOU.
A TALISMAN FOR WHEN FOXES ARE BEING TOO NOISY (REALLY EXISTS!)
...RGH!
......
fwp
WHAT ARE YOU GOING TO DO WITH ME?
STOP!

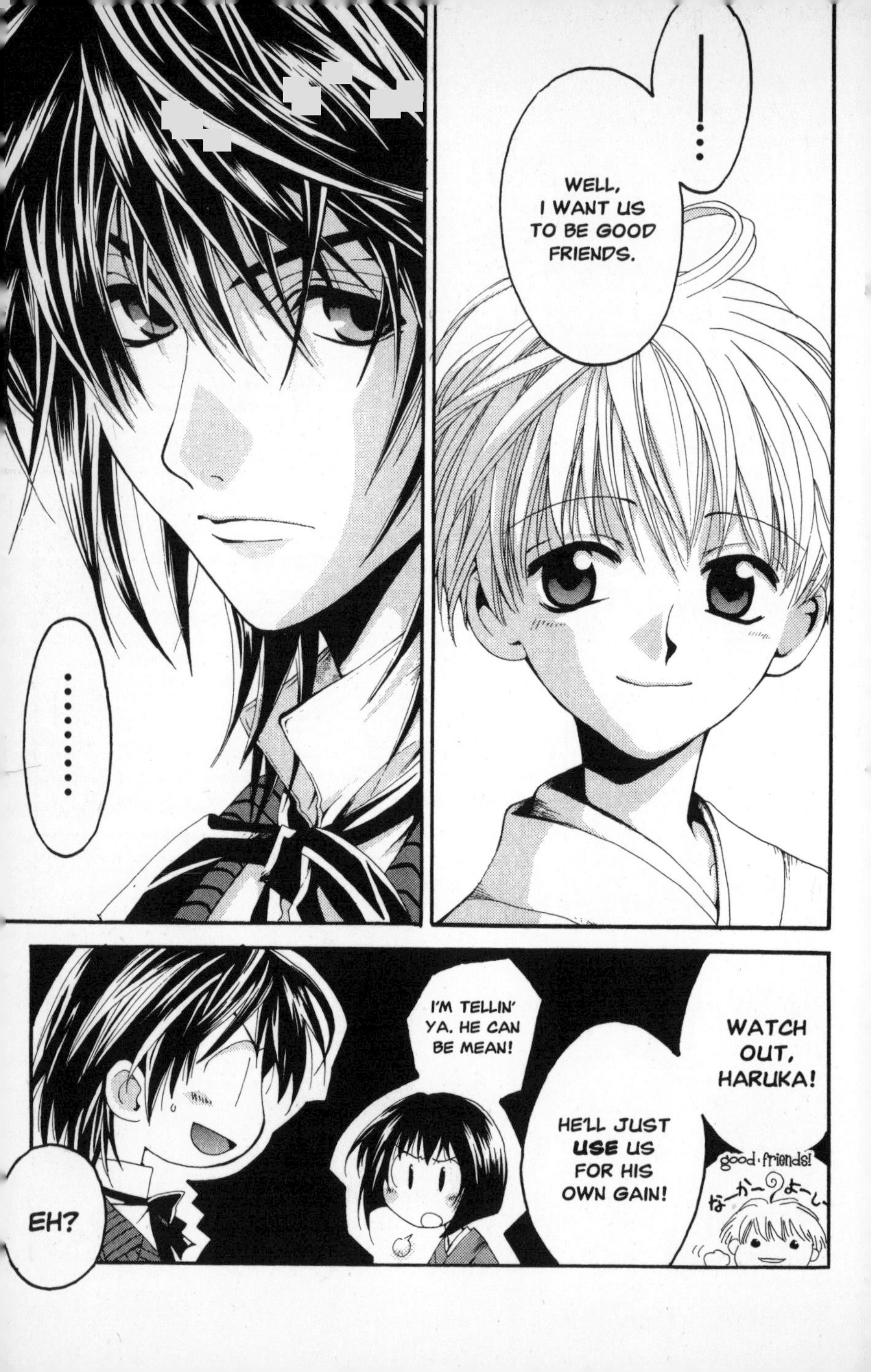
...!
WELL, I WANT US TO BE GOOD FRIENDS.
....
WATCH OUT, HARUKA!
good friends!
なーかーよーしー
HE'LL JUST **USE** US FOR HIS OWN GAIN!
I'M TELLIN' YA. HE CAN BE MEAN!
EH?

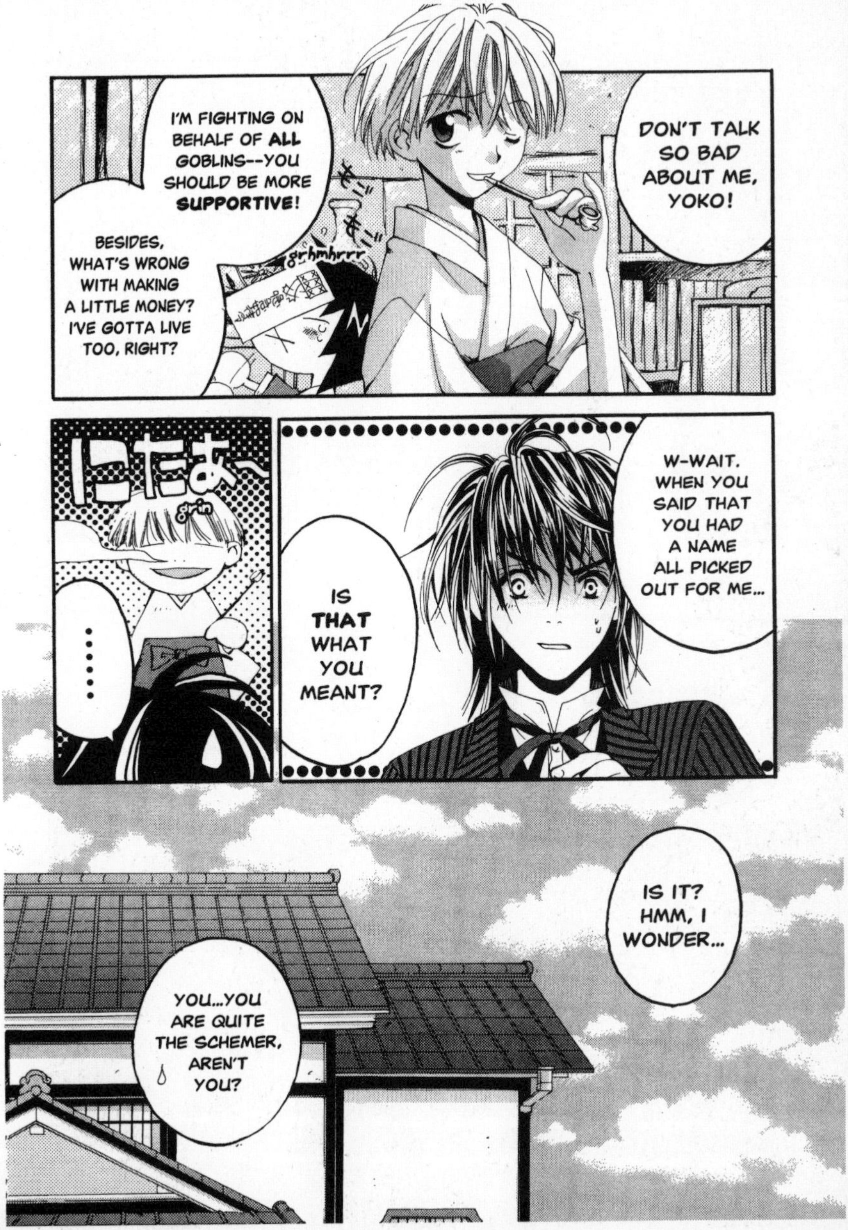
DON'T TALK SO BAD ABOUT ME, YOKO!
I'M FIGHTING ON BEHALF OF ALL GOBLINS--YOU SHOULD BE MORE SUPPORTIVE!
もご もご
grhmhrrr
BESIDES, WHAT'S WRONG WITH MAKING A LITTLE MONEY? I'VE GOTTA LIVE TOO, RIGHT?
W-WAIT. WHEN YOU SAID THAT YOU HAD A NAME ALL PICKED OUT FOR ME...
IS THAT WHAT YOU MEANT?
にたぁ〜
grin
......
IS IT? HMM, I WONDER...
YOU...YOU ARE QUITE THE SCHEMER, AREN'T YOU?

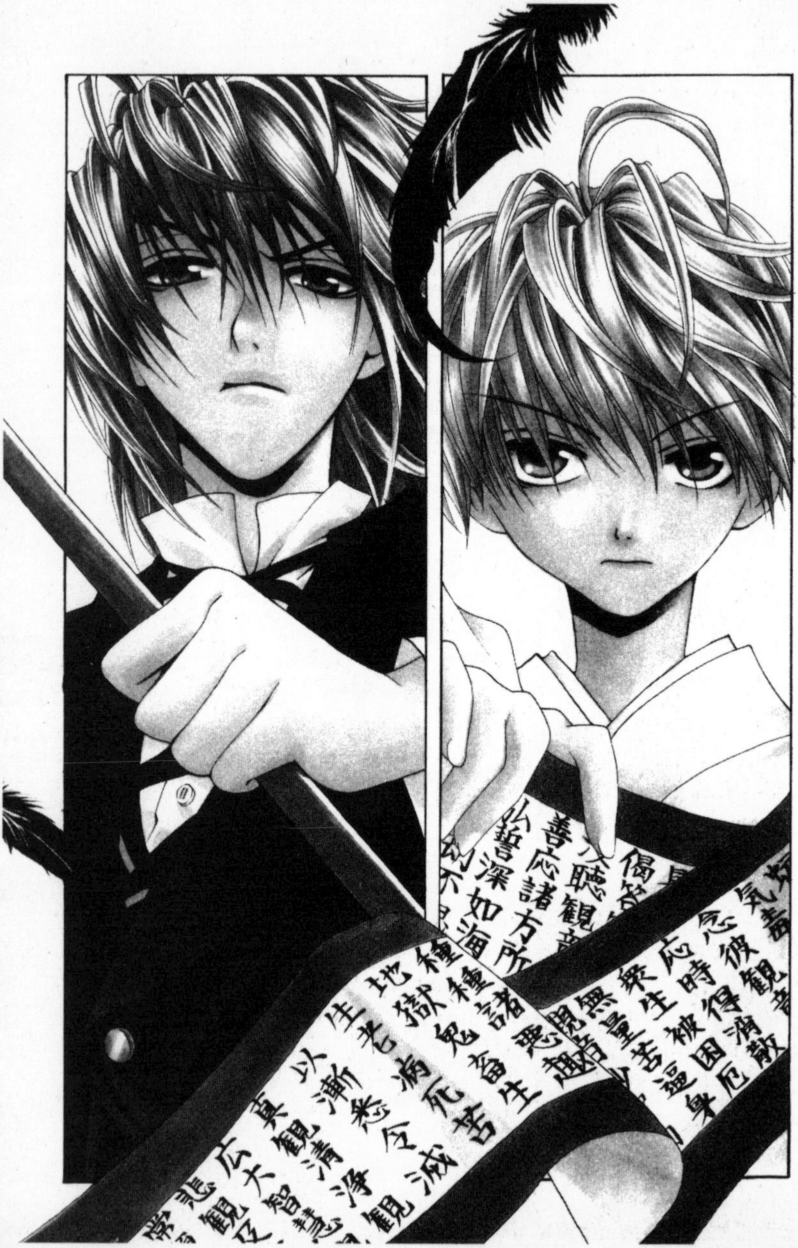

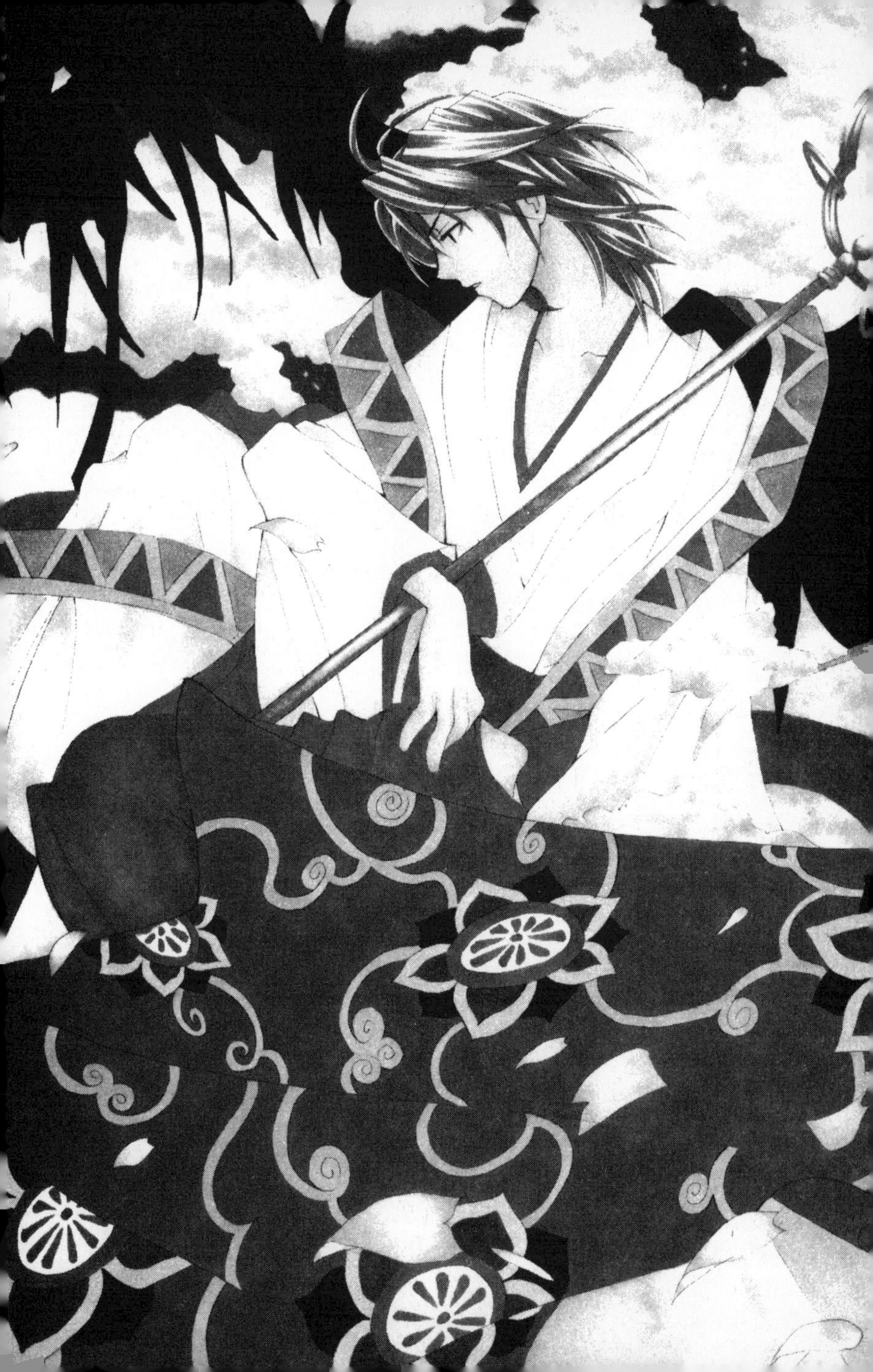

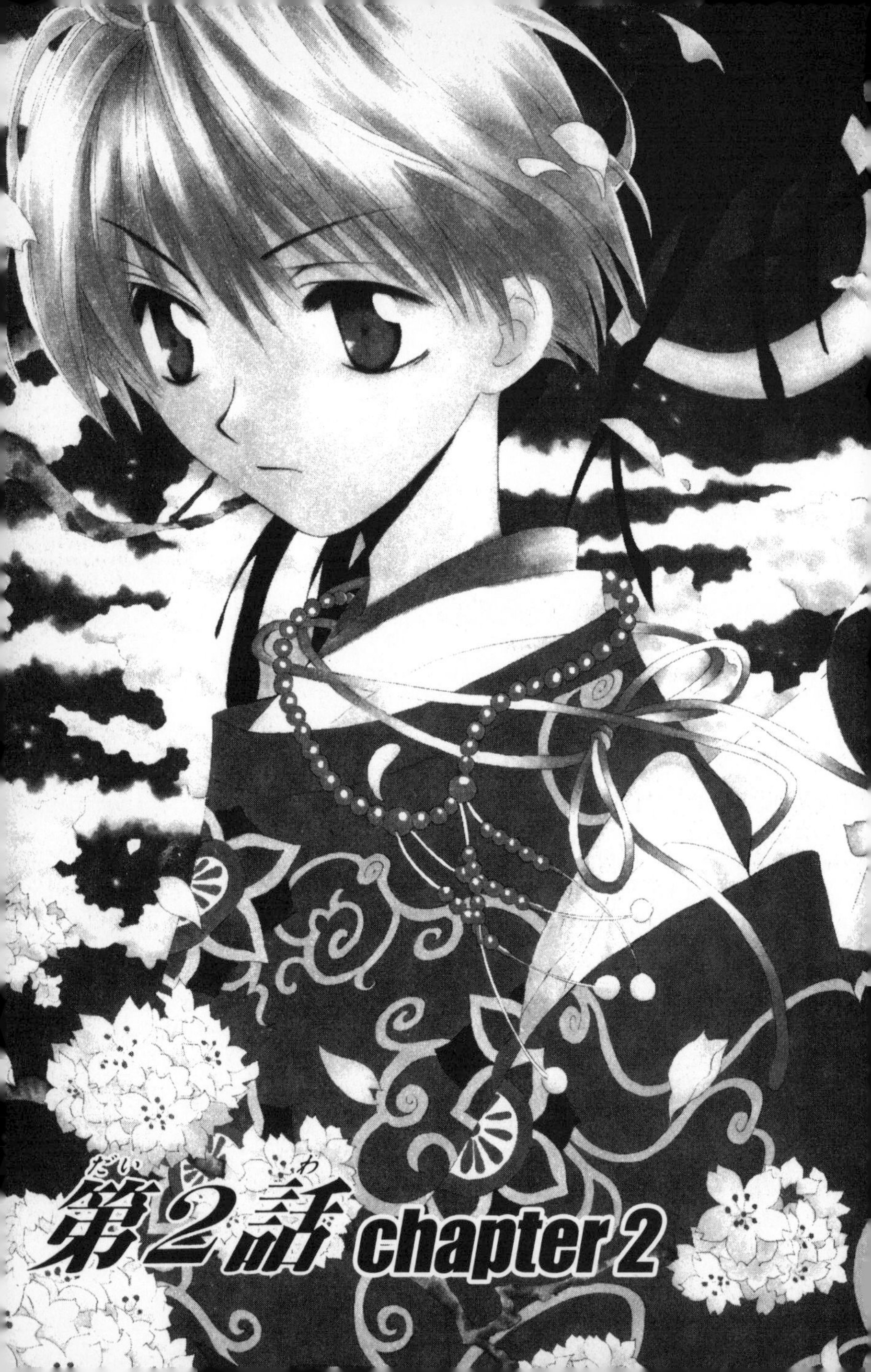
第2話
chapter 2

Tactics

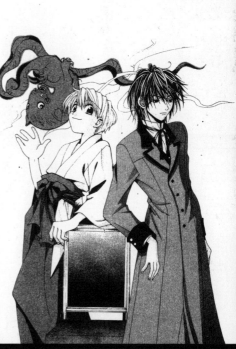

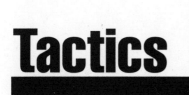

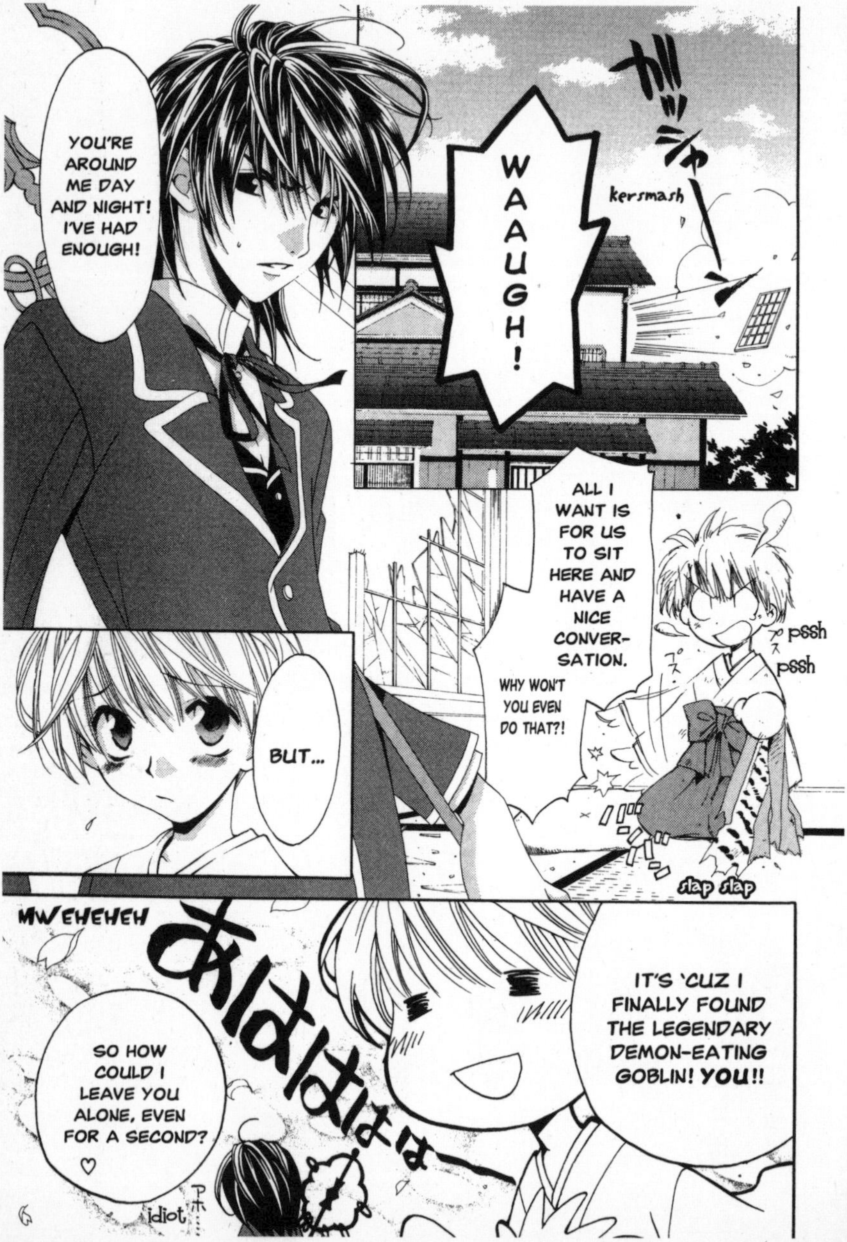

kersmash
WAAUGH!
YOU'RE AROUND ME DAY AND NIGHT! I'VE HAD ENOUGH!
ALL I WANT IS FOR US TO SIT HERE AND HAVE A NICE CONVERSATION.
pssh pssh
WHY WON'T YOU EVEN DO THAT?!
slap slap
BUT...
IT'S 'CUZ I FINALLY FOUND THE LEGENDARY DEMON-EATING GOBLIN! **YOU**!!
あははははー
MWEHEHEH
SO HOW COULD I LEAVE YOU ALONE, EVEN FOR A SECOND? ♡
アホ…
idiot

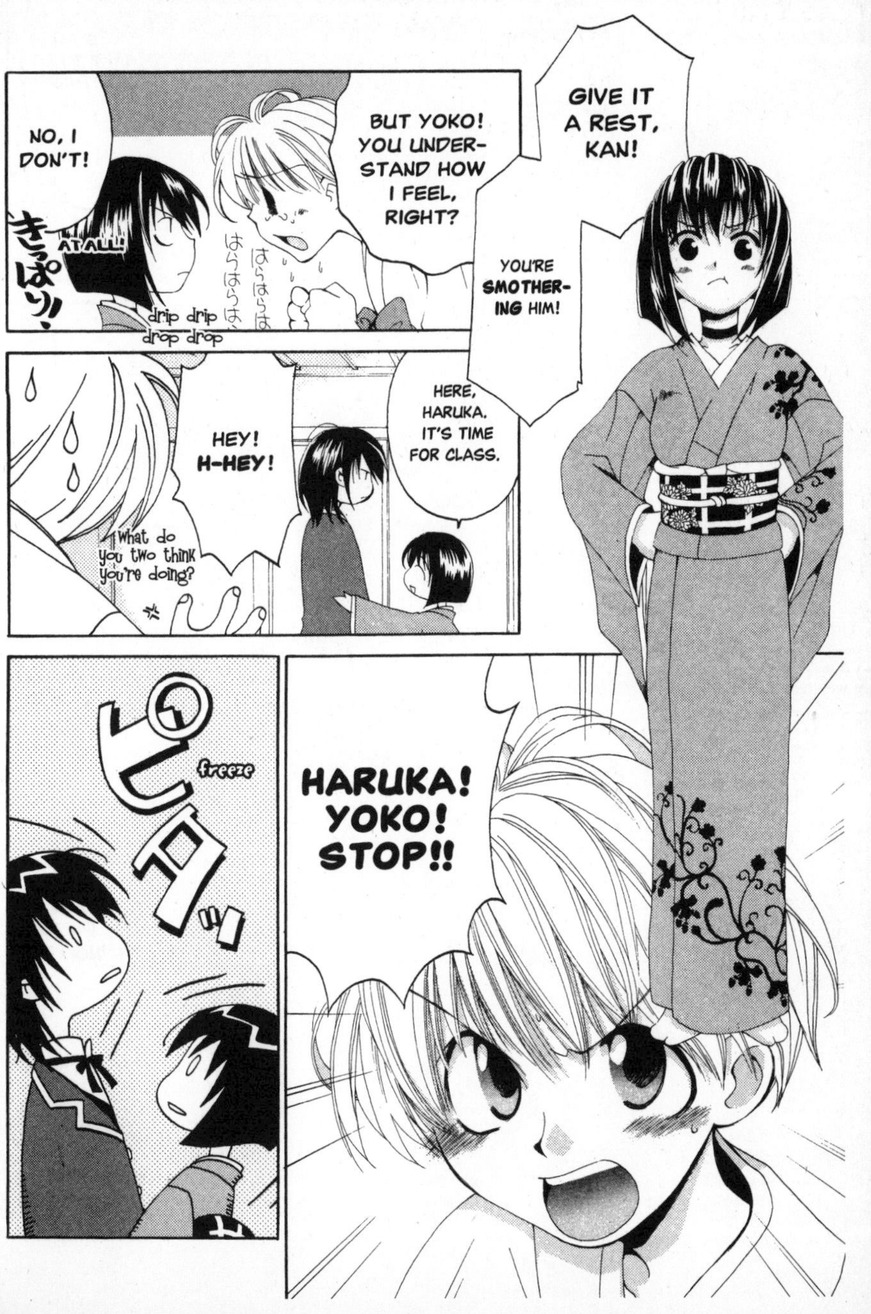

GIVE IT A REST, KAN!
YOU'RE SMOTHERING HIM!
BUT YOKO! YOU UNDER-STAND HOW I FEEL, RIGHT?
はらはらは
drip drip drop drop
NO, I DON'T!
きっぱり!
AT ALL.
HERE, HARUKA. IT'S TIME FOR CLASS.
HEY! H-HEY!
What do you two think you're doing?
HARUKA! YOKO! STOP!!
ピタッ
freeze

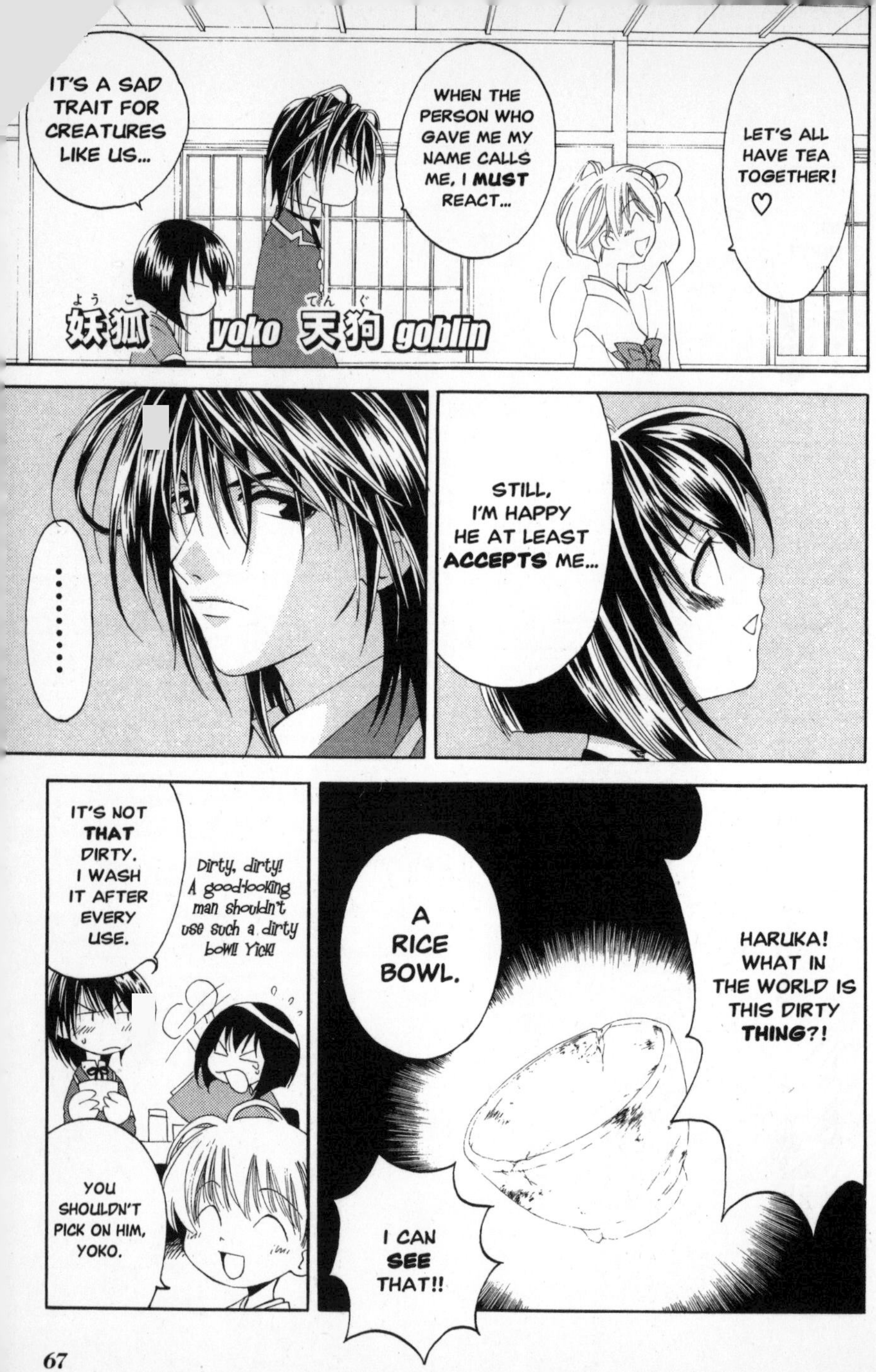
LET'S ALL HAVE TEA TOGETHER! ♡
WHEN THE PERSON WHO GAVE ME MY NAME CALLS ME, I MUST REACT...
IT'S A SAD TRAIT FOR CREATURES LIKE US...
妖狐 yoko 天狗 goblin
STILL, I'M HAPPY HE AT LEAST ACCEPTS ME...
....
HARUKA! WHAT IN THE WORLD IS THIS DIRTY THING?!
A RICE BOWL.
I CAN SEE THAT!!
Dirty, dirty! A good-looking man shouldn't use such a dirty bowl! Yick!
IT'S NOT THAT DIRTY. I WASH IT AFTER EVERY USE.
YOU SHOULDN'T PICK ON HIM, YOKO.

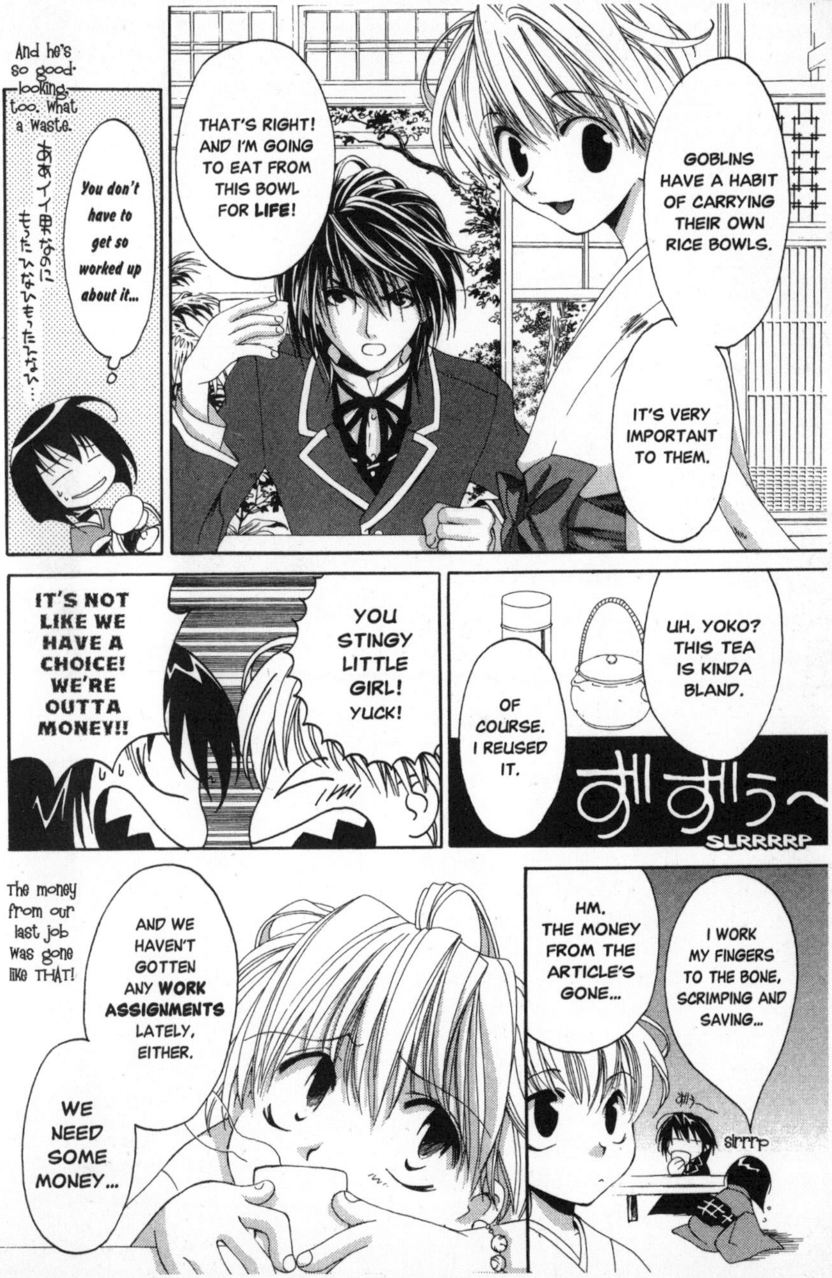
GOBLINS HAVE A HABIT OF CARRYING THEIR OWN RICE BOWLS.
IT'S VERY IMPORTANT TO THEM.
THAT'S RIGHT! AND I'M GOING TO EAT FROM THIS BOWL FOR LIFE!
And he's so good-looking, too. What a waste.
ああイイ男なのに もったいなぃもったいなぃ…
You don't have to get so worked up about it...
UH, YOKO? THIS TEA IS KINDA BLAND.
OF COURSE. I REUSED IT.
ずずう～
SLRRRRP
YOU STINGY LITTLE GIRL! YUCK!
IT'S NOT LIKE WE HAVE A CHOICE! WE'RE OUTTA MONEY!!
I WORK MY FINGERS TO THE BONE, SCRIMPING AND SAVING...
HM. THE MONEY FROM THE ARTICLE'S GONE...
sirrrp
The money from our last job was gone like THAT!
AND WE HAVEN'T GOTTEN ANY WORK ASSIGNMENTS LATELY, EITHER.
WE NEED SOME MONEY...

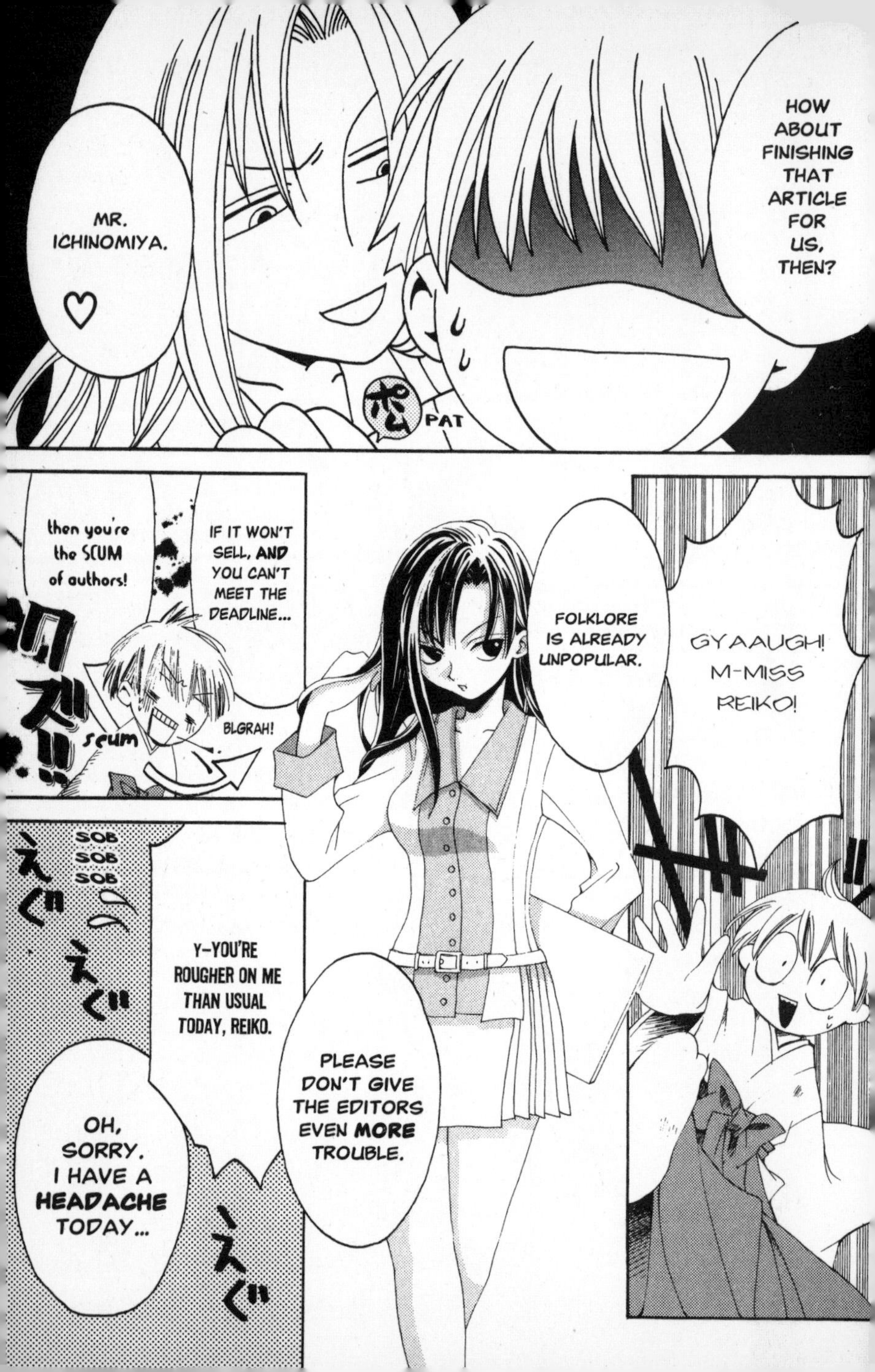
HOW ABOUT FINISHING THAT ARTICLE FOR US, THEN?
MR. ICHINOMIYA. ♡
ポン
PAT
GYAAUGH! M-MISS REIKO!
FOLKLORE IS ALREADY UNPOPULAR.
IF IT WON'T SELL, AND YOU CAN'T MEET THE DEADLINE...
then you're the SCUM of authors!
SCUM
BLGRAH!
PLEASE DON'T GIVE THE EDITORS EVEN MORE TROUBLE.
Y-YOU'RE ROUGHER ON ME THAN USUAL TODAY, REIKO.
SOB SOB SOB
えぐ えぐ えぐ
OH, SORRY. I HAVE A HEADACHE TODAY...

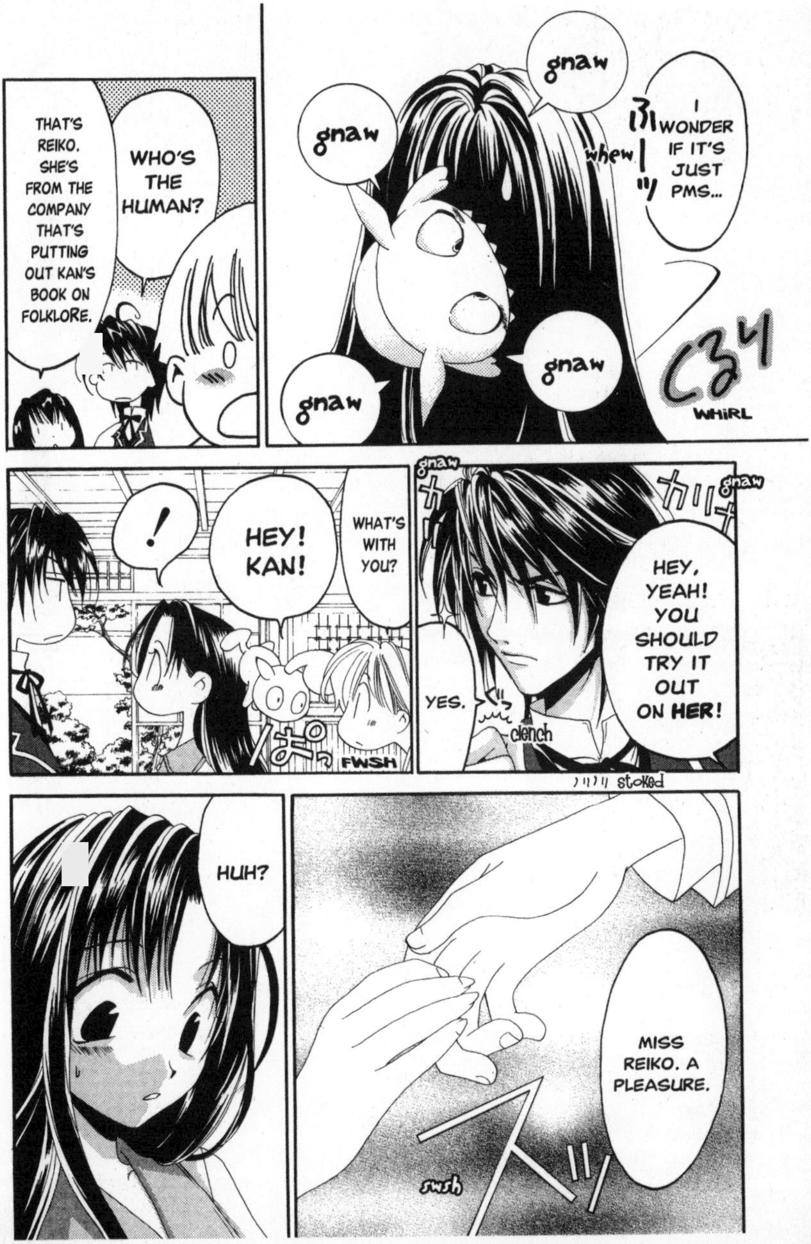
gnaw
gnaw
I WONDER IF IT'S JUST PMS...
whew
gnaw
gnaw
WHIRL
WHO'S THE HUMAN?
THAT'S REIKO. SHE'S FROM THE COMPANY THAT'S PUTTING OUT KAN'S BOOK ON FOLKLORE.
gnaw
gnaw
HEY, YEAH! YOU SHOULD TRY IT OUT ON HER!
YES.
clench
stoked
WHAT'S WITH YOU?
HEY! KAN!
!
FWSH
MISS REIKO. A PLEASURE.
swsh
HUH?

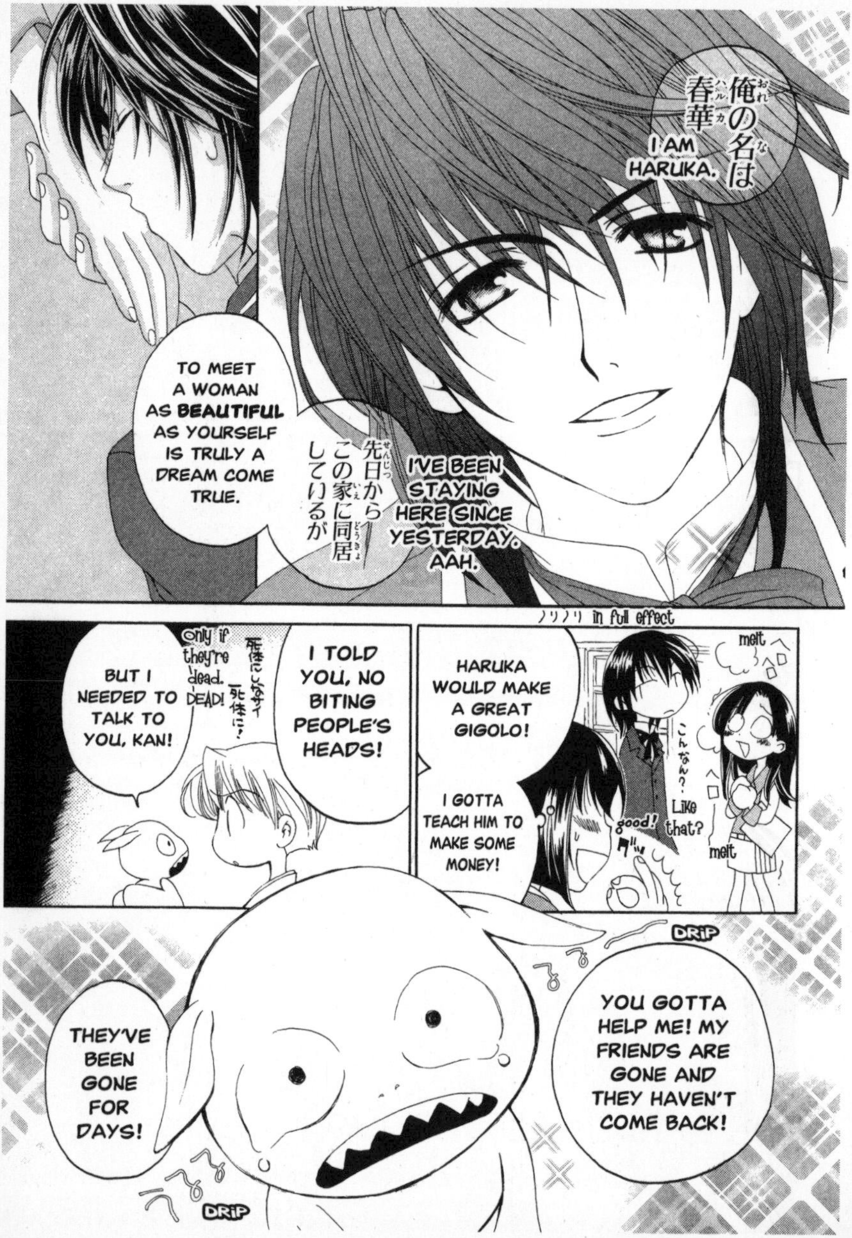

俺の名は春華
I AM HARUKA.
先日からこの家に同居しているが
I'VE BEEN STAYING HERE SINCE YESTERDAY. AAH.
TO MEET A WOMAN AS **BEAUTIFUL** AS YOURSELF IS TRULY A DREAM COME TRUE.
ノリノリ in full effect
HARUKA WOULD MAKE A GREAT GIGOLO!
melt
こんなん？
Like that?
melt
good!
I GOTTA TEACH HIM TO MAKE SOME MONEY!
I TOLD YOU, NO BITING PEOPLE'S HEADS!
死体にしなさい 死体に！
only if they're dead. DEAD!
BUT I NEEDED TO TALK TO YOU, KAN!
DRIP
YOU GOTTA HELP ME! MY FRIENDS ARE GONE AND THEY HAVEN'T COME BACK!
THEY'VE BEEN GONE FOR DAYS!
DRIP

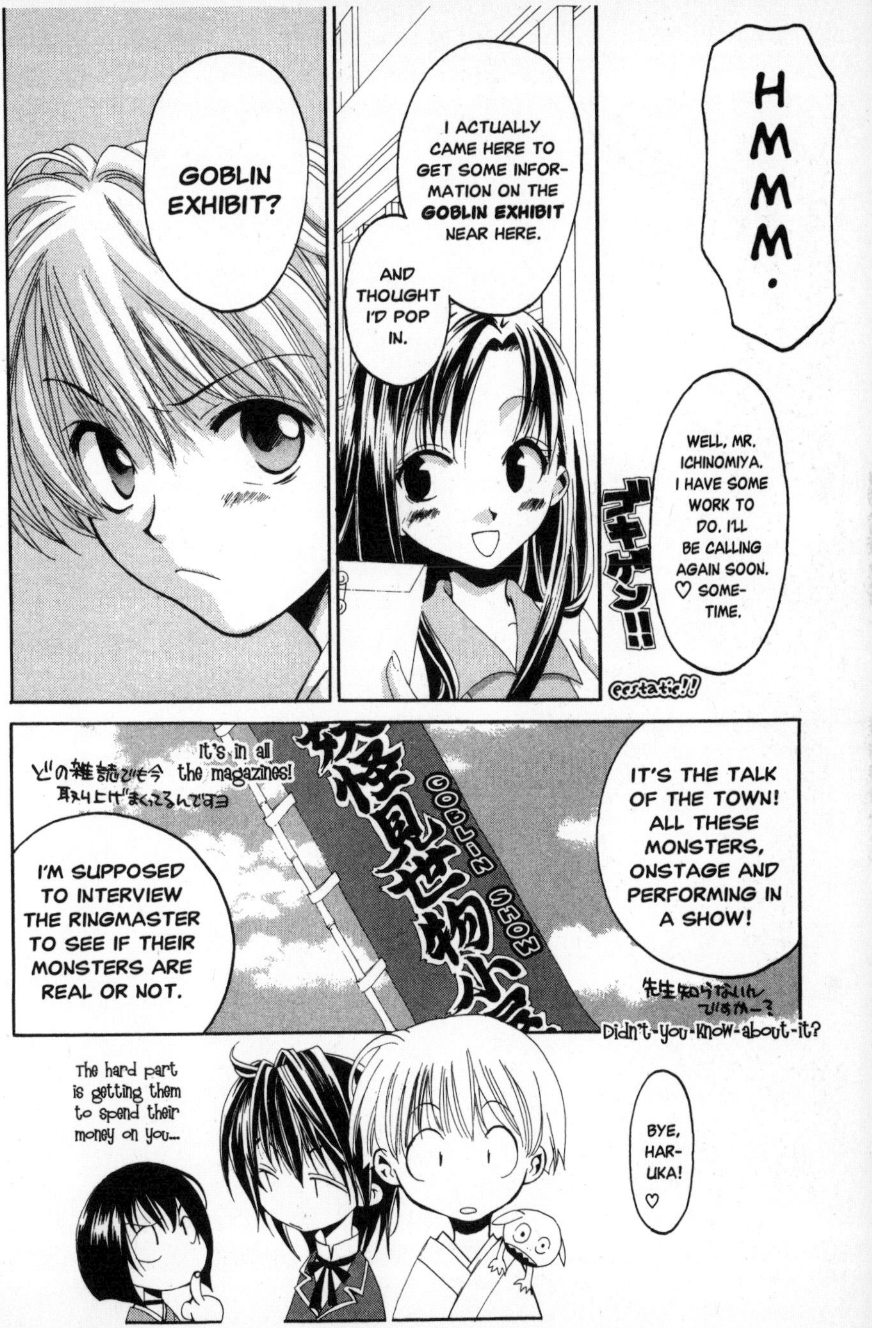
HMMM.
I ACTUALLY CAME HERE TO GET SOME INFORMATION ON THE GOBLIN EXHIBIT NEAR HERE.
AND THOUGHT I'D POP IN.
GOBLIN EXHIBIT?
WELL, MR. ICHINOMIYA. I HAVE SOME WORK TO DO. I'LL BE CALLING AGAIN SOON. ♡ SOMETIME.
ecstatic!!
IT'S THE TALK OF THE TOWN! ALL THESE MONSTERS, ONSTAGE AND PERFORMING IN A SHOW!
先生知らないんですか～？
Didn't-you-know-about-it?
GOBLIN SHOW
どの雑誌でも今取り上げまくってるんですヨ
It's in all the magazines!
I'M SUPPOSED TO INTERVIEW THE RINGMASTER TO SEE IF THEIR MONSTERS ARE REAL OR NOT.
BYE, HARUKA! ♡
The hard part is getting them to spend their money on you...

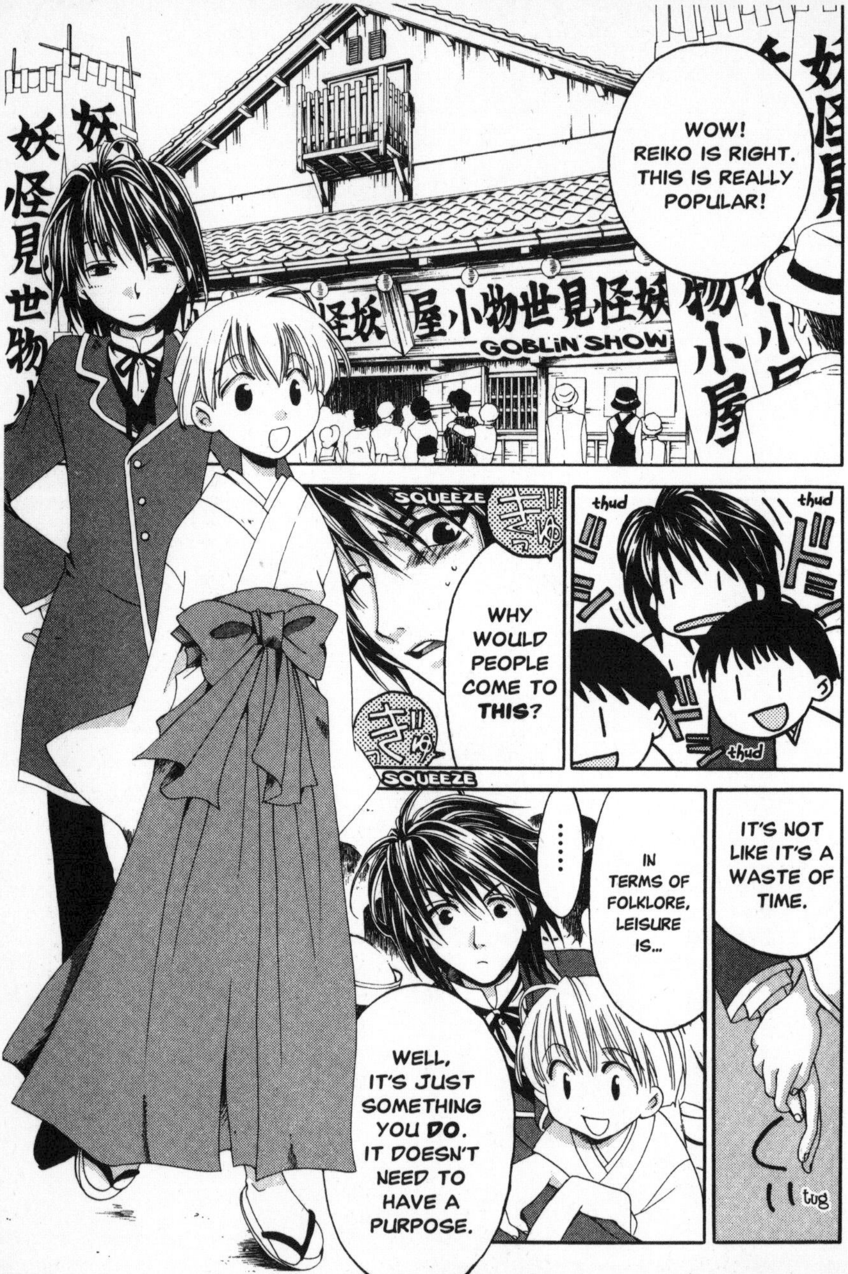
妖怪見世物小屋
GOBLIN SHOW
WOW! REIKO IS RIGHT. THIS IS REALLY POPULAR!
thud
thud
thud
SQUEEZE
WHY WOULD PEOPLE COME TO THIS?
SQUEEZE
IT'S NOT LIKE IT'S A WASTE OF TIME.
tug
......
IN TERMS OF FOLKLORE, LEISURE IS...
WELL, IT'S JUST SOMETHING YOU DO. IT DOESN'T NEED TO HAVE A PURPOSE.

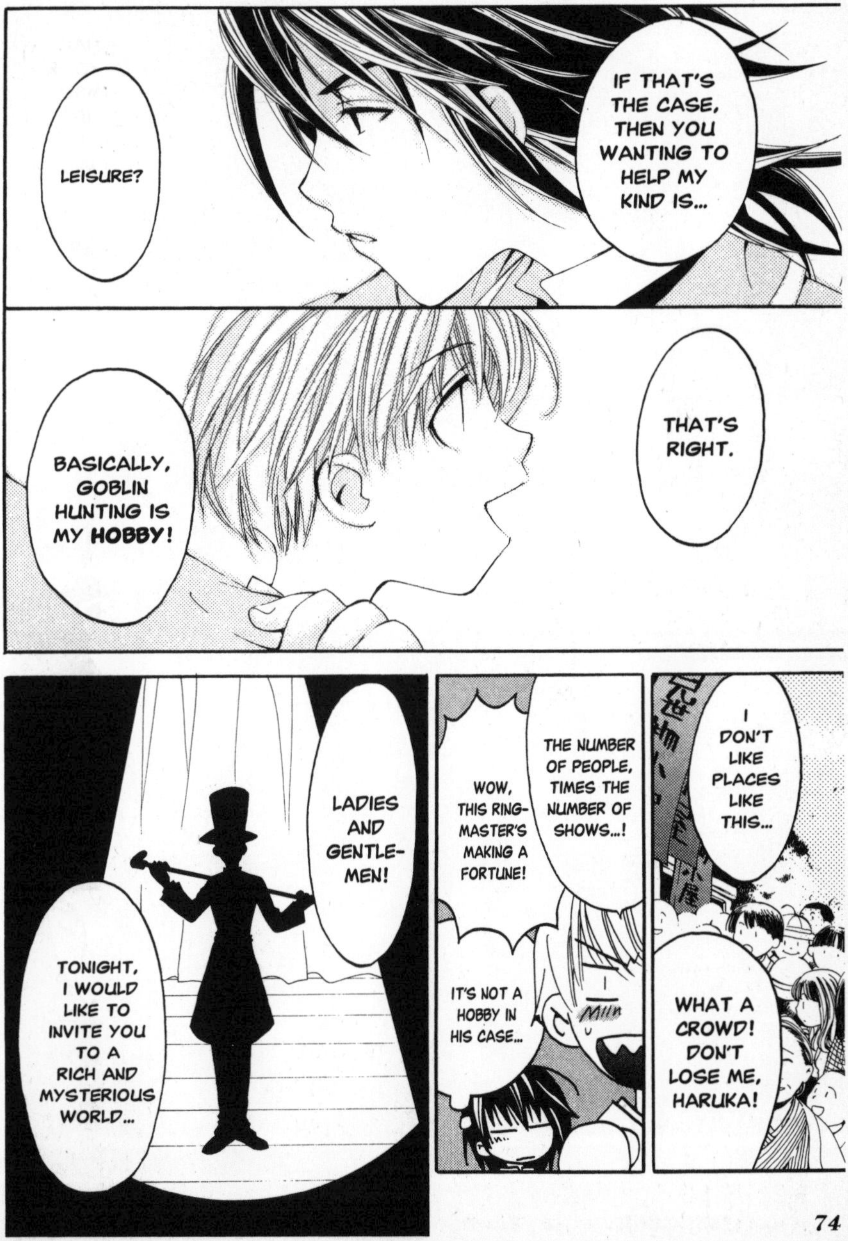
IF THAT'S THE CASE, THEN YOU WANTING TO HELP MY KIND IS...
LEISURE?
THAT'S RIGHT.
BASICALLY, GOBLIN HUNTING IS MY **HOBBY**!
I DON'T LIKE PLACES LIKE THIS...
WHAT A CROWD! DON'T LOSE ME, HARUKA!
THE NUMBER OF PEOPLE, TIMES THE NUMBER OF SHOWS...!
WOW, THIS RING-MASTER'S MAKING A FORTUNE!
IT'S NOT A HOBBY IN HIS CASE...
LADIES AND GENTLE-MEN!
TONIGHT, I WOULD LIKE TO INVITE YOU TO A RICH AND MYSTERIOUS WORLD...

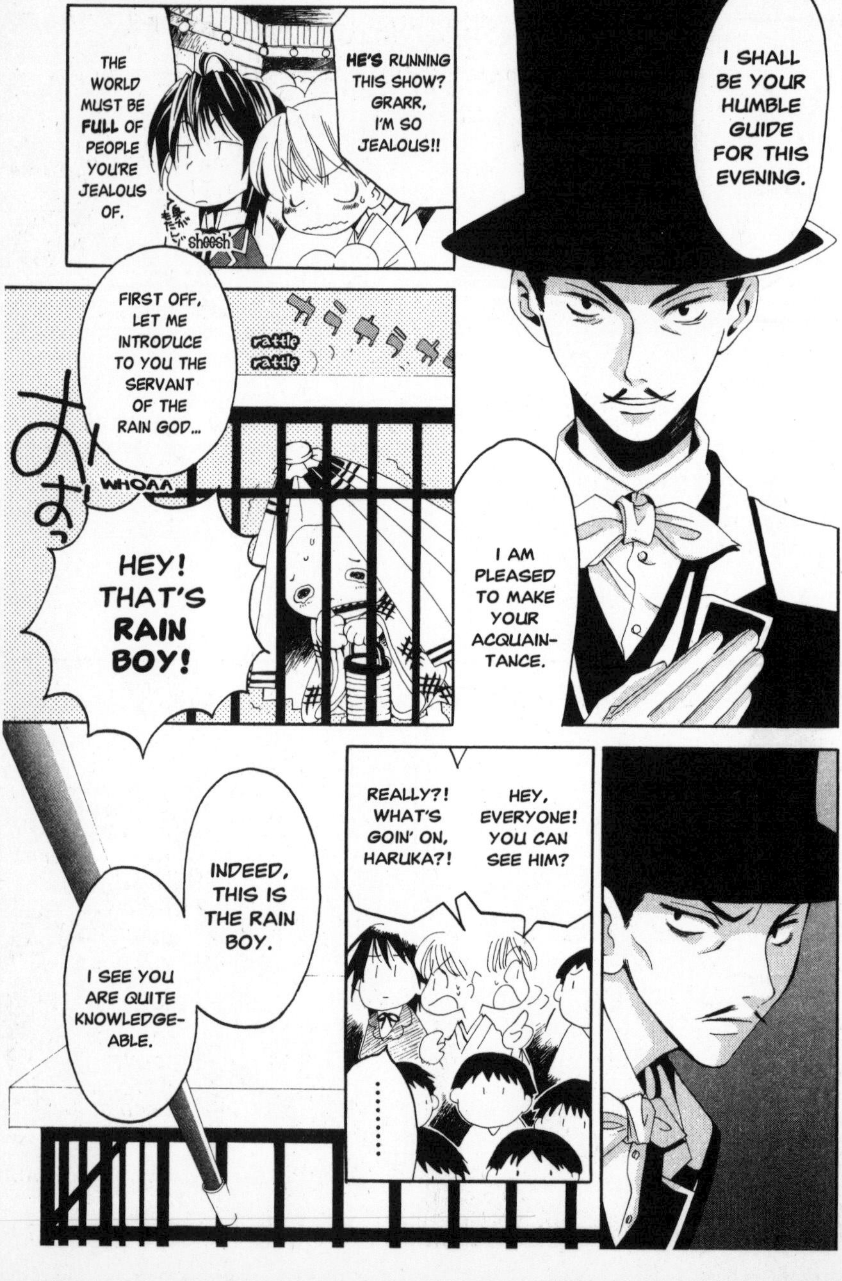
I SHALL BE YOUR HUMBLE GUIDE FOR THIS EVENING.
I AM PLEASED TO MAKE YOUR ACQUAINTANCE.
HE'S RUNNING THIS SHOW? GRARR, I'M SO JEALOUS!!
THE WORLD MUST BE FULL OF PEOPLE YOU'RE JEALOUS OF.
sheesh
FIRST OFF, LET ME INTRODUCE TO YOU THE SERVANT OF THE RAIN GOD...
rattle rattle
WHOAA
HEY! THAT'S RAIN BOY!
HEY, EVERYONE! YOU CAN SEE HIM?
REALLY?! WHAT'S GOIN' ON, HARUKA?!
......
INDEED, THIS IS THE RAIN BOY.
I SEE YOU ARE QUITE KNOWLEDGE-ABLE.

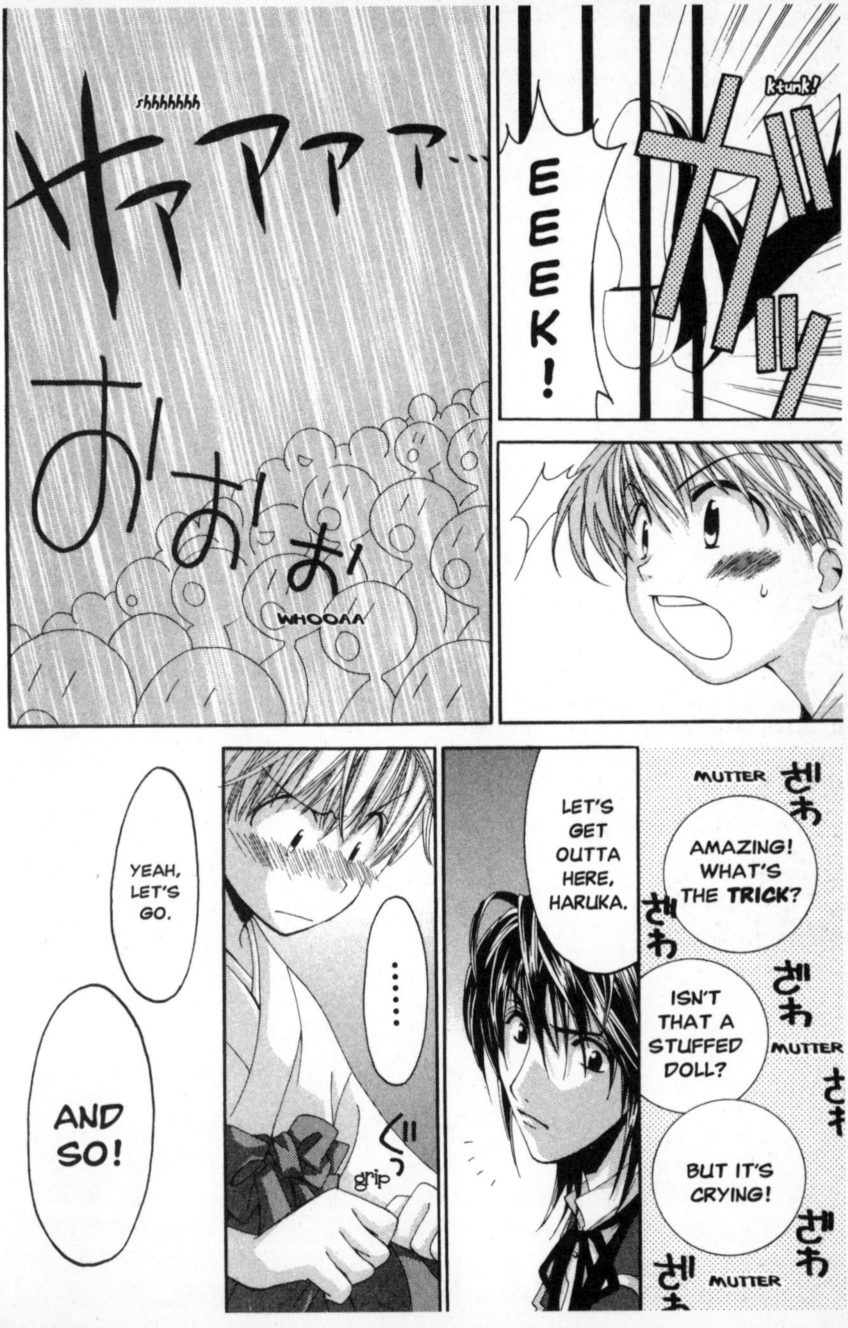
ktunk!
ガッ
EEEEK!
shhhhhhhh
サァァァ…
おおおお
WHOOAA
MUTTER
ざわ
ざわ
AMAZING! WHAT'S THE TRICK?
ISN'T THAT A STUFFED DOLL?
ざわ
MUTTER
BUT IT'S CRYING!
ざわ
ざわ
MUTTER
LET'S GET OUTTA HERE, HARUKA.
……
ぐっ
grip
YEAH, LET'S GO.
AND SO!

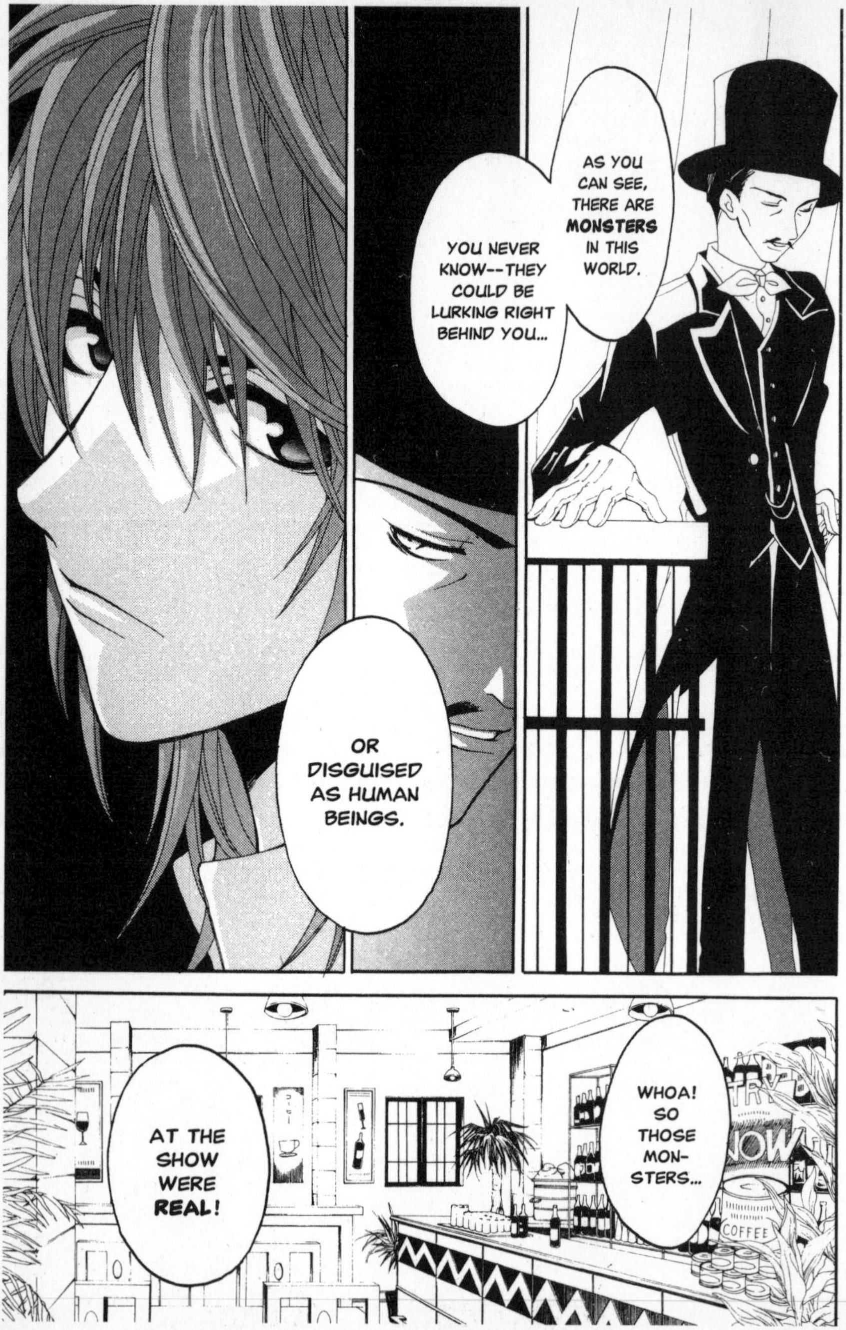
AS YOU CAN SEE, THERE ARE **MONSTERS** IN THIS WORLD.
YOU NEVER KNOW--THEY COULD BE LURKING RIGHT BEHIND YOU...
OR DISGUISED AS HUMAN BEINGS.
WHOA! SO THOSE MON-STERS...
AT THE SHOW WERE **REAL**!
COFFEE

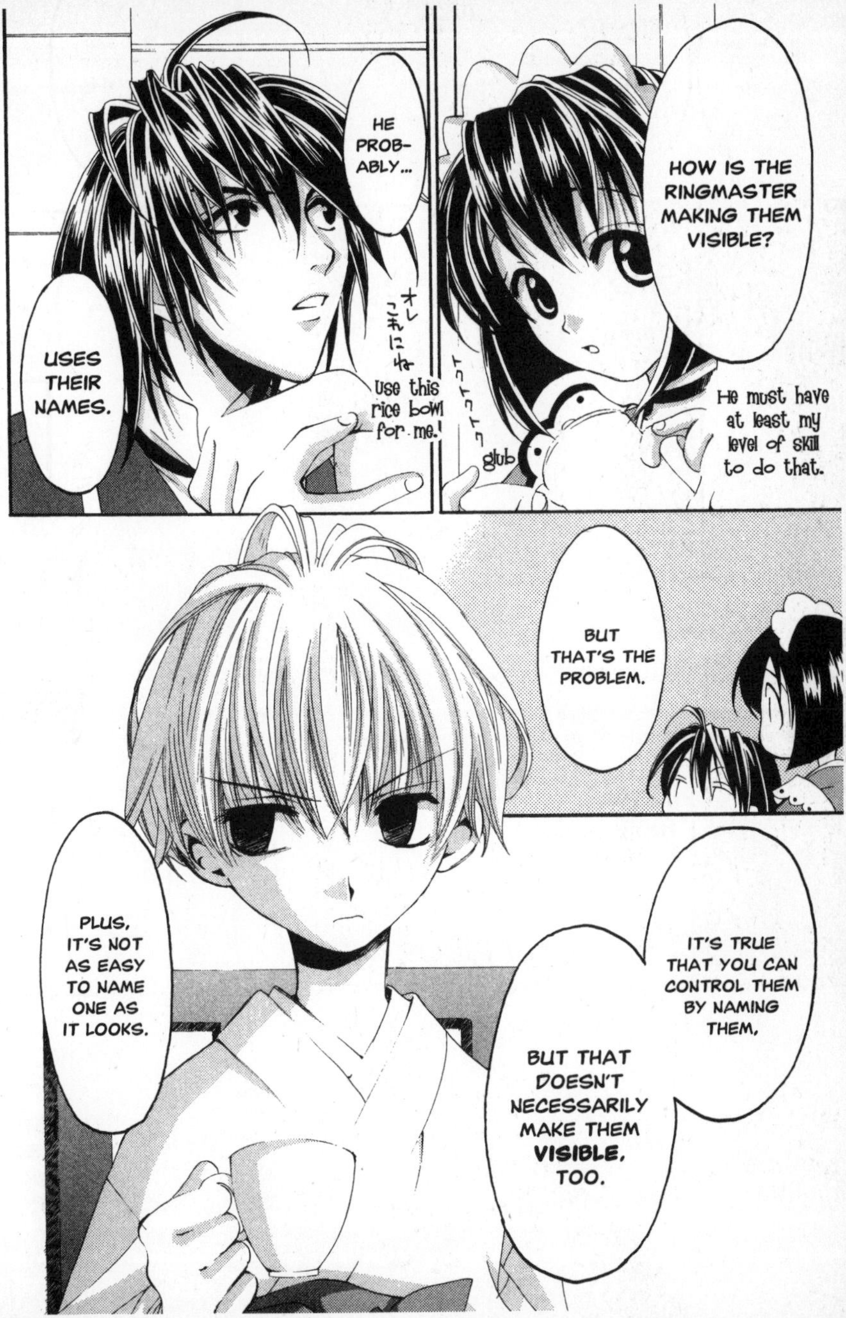
HOW IS THE RINGMASTER MAKING THEM VISIBLE?
He must have at least my level of skill to do that.
glub
HE PROBABLY...
USES THEIR NAMES.
オレこれにね
Use this rice bowl for me.
BUT THAT'S THE PROBLEM.
IT'S TRUE THAT YOU CAN CONTROL THEM BY NAMING THEM,
BUT THAT DOESN'T NECESSARILY MAKE THEM **VISIBLE**, TOO.
PLUS, IT'S NOT AS EASY TO NAME ONE AS IT LOOKS.

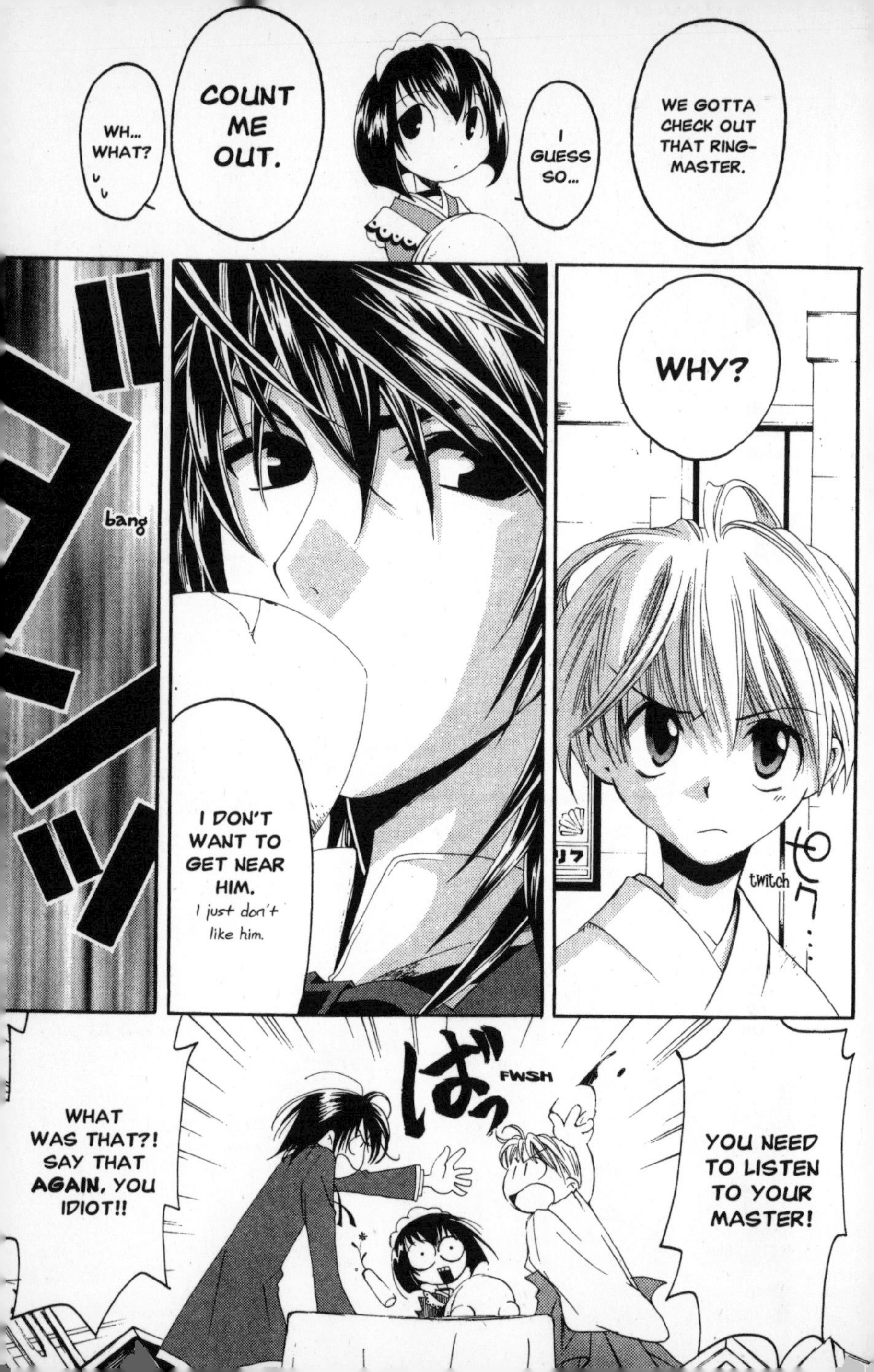
WE GOTTA CHECK OUT THAT RING-MASTER.
I GUESS SO...
COUNT ME OUT.
WH... WHAT?
WHY?
twitch
I DON'T WANT TO GET NEAR HIM.
I just don't like him.
bang
YOU NEED TO LISTEN TO YOUR MASTER!
FWSH
WHAT WAS THAT?! SAY THAT AGAIN, YOU IDIOT!!

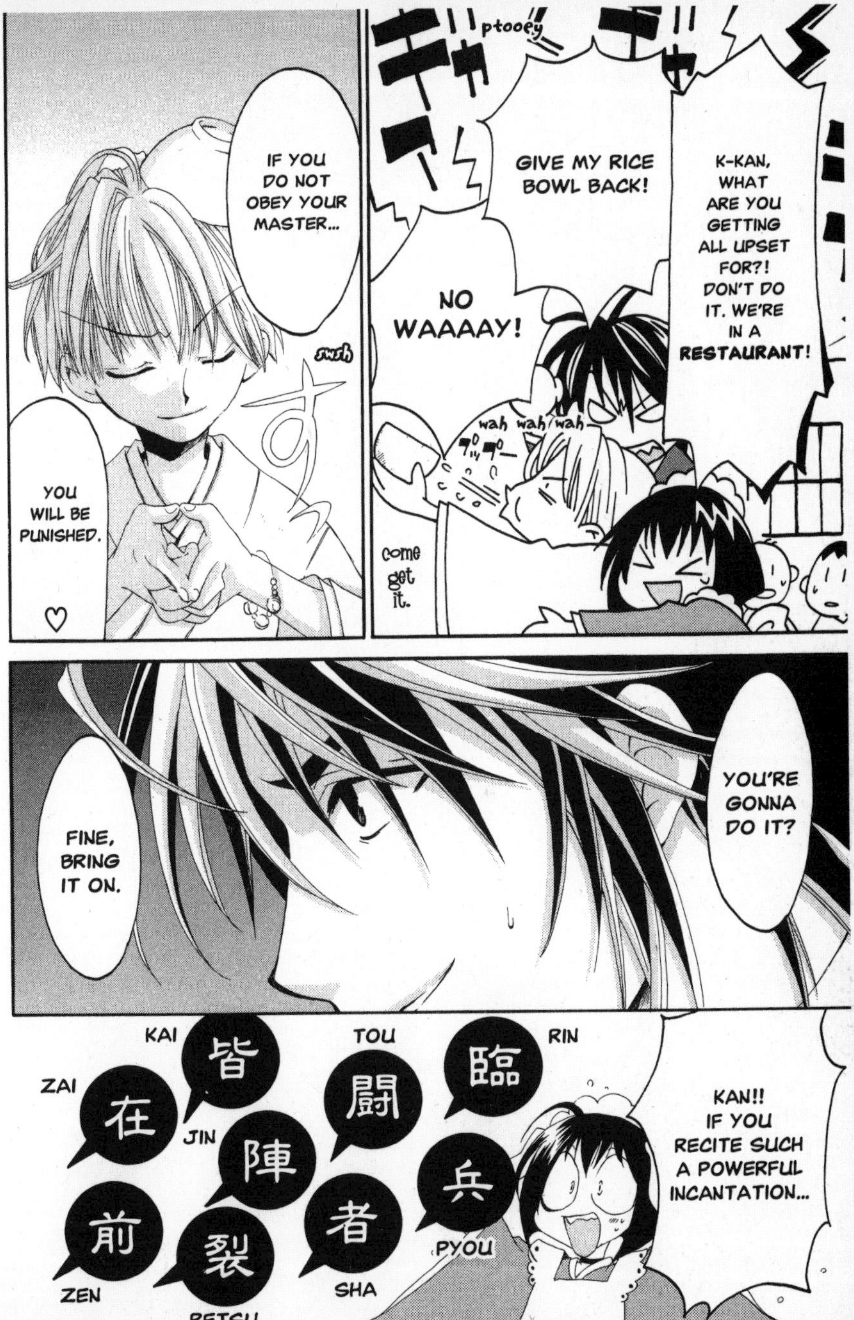
ptooey
K-KAN, WHAT ARE YOU GETTING ALL UPSET FOR?! DON'T DO IT. WE'RE IN A RESTAURANT!
GIVE MY RICE BOWL BACK!
NO WAAAAY!
wah wah wah
come get it.
IF YOU DO NOT OBEY YOUR MASTER...
swsh
YOU WILL BE PUNISHED.
♡
YOU'RE GONNA DO IT?
FINE, BRING IT ON.
KAN!! IF YOU RECITE SUCH A POWERFUL INCANTATION...
臨 RIN
兵 PYOU
闘 TOU
者 SHA
皆 KAI
陣 JIN
裂 RETSU
在 ZAI
前 ZEN

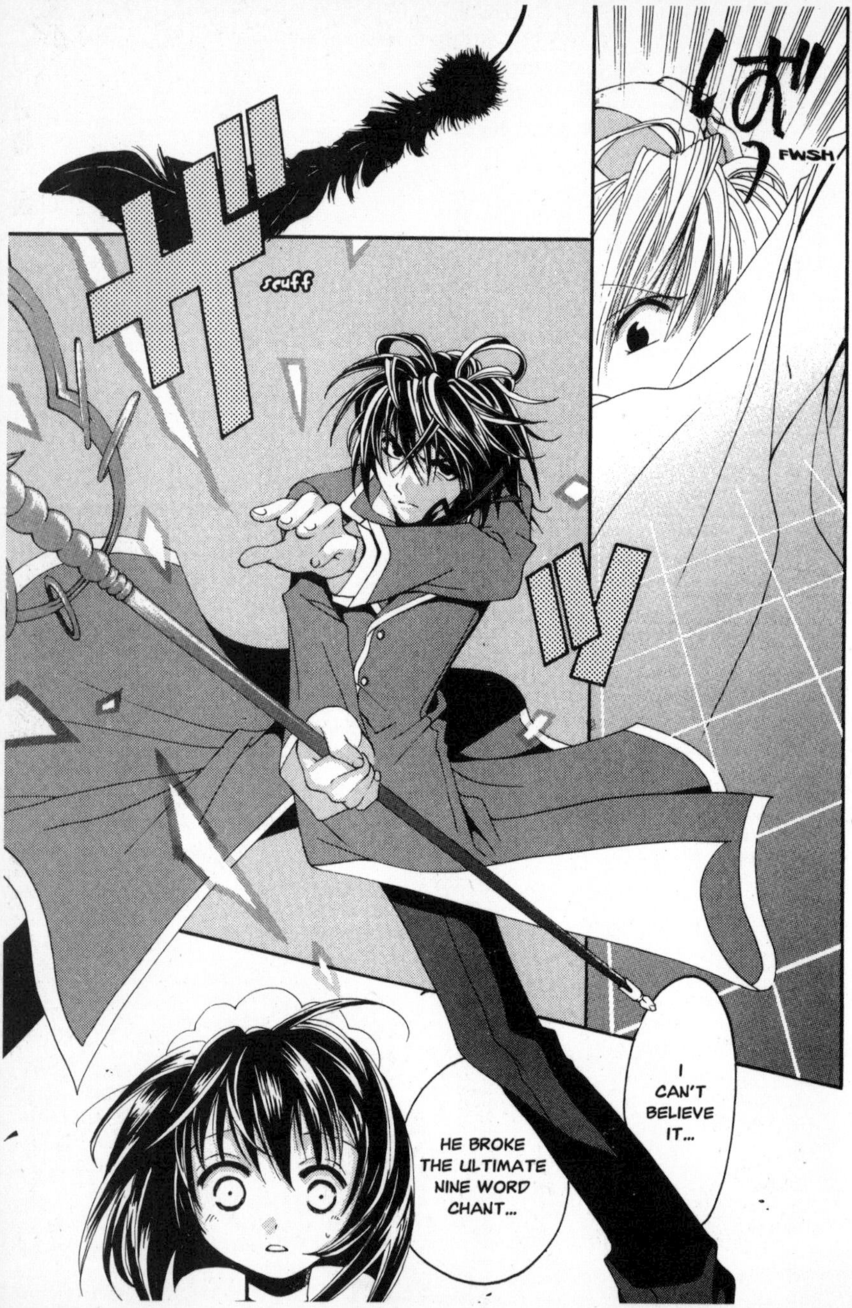
FWSH
scuff
I CAN'T BELIEVE IT...
HE BROKE THE ULTIMATE NINE WORD CHANT...

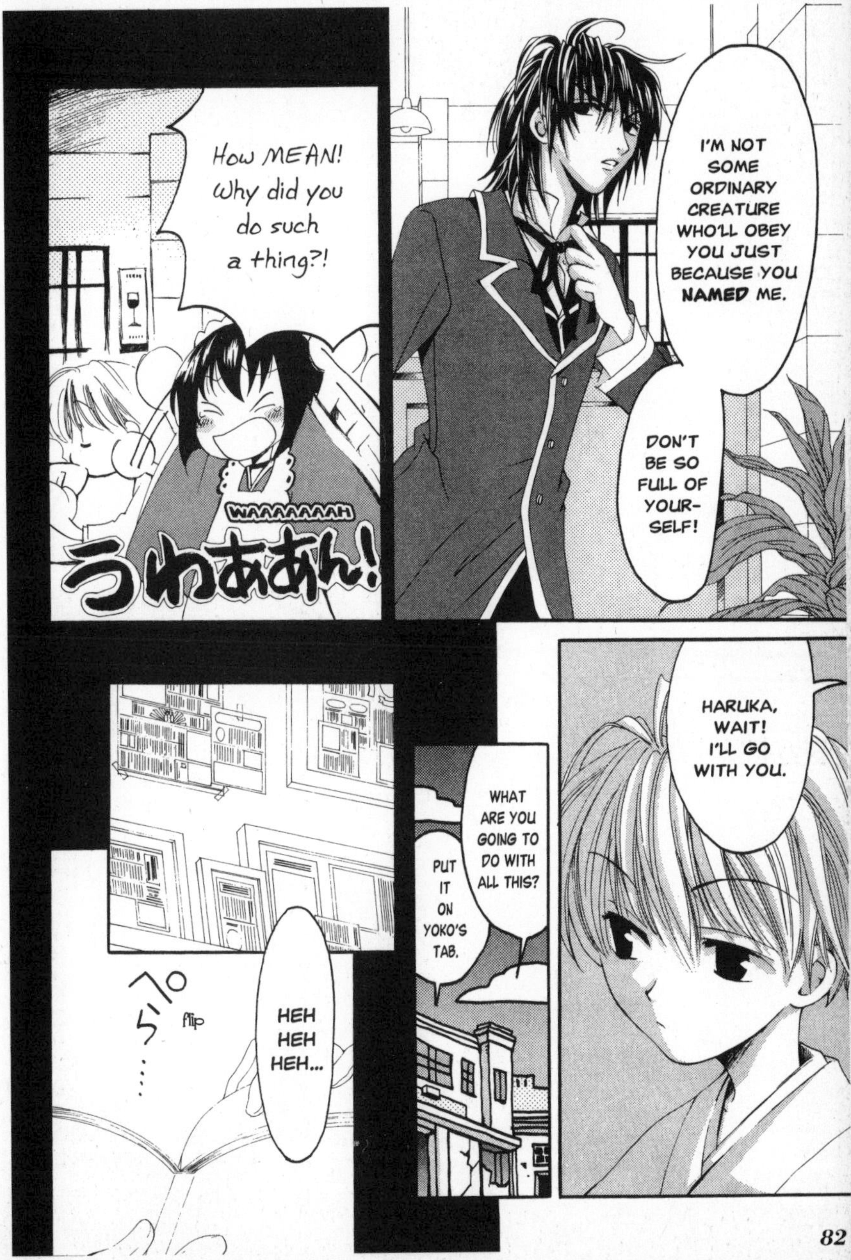
I'M NOT SOME ORDINARY CREATURE WHO'LL OBEY YOU JUST BECAUSE YOU **NAMED** ME.
DON'T BE SO FULL OF YOUR-SELF!
How MEAN! Why did you do such a thing?!
WAAAAAAAH
うわああん!
HARUKA, WAIT! I'LL GO WITH YOU.
WHAT ARE YOU GOING TO DO WITH ALL THIS?
PUT IT ON YOKO'S TAB.
HEH HEH HEH...
ぺら…
flip

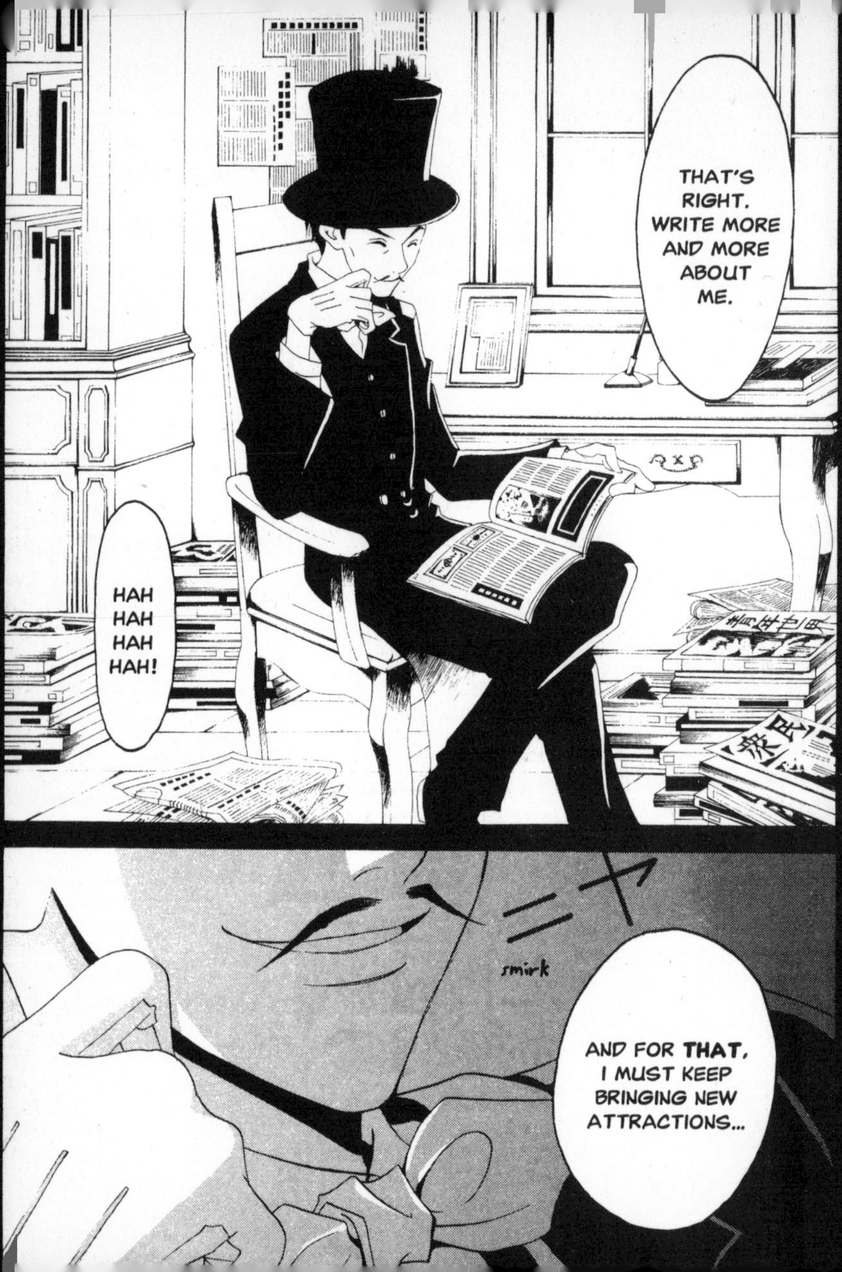
THAT'S RIGHT. WRITE MORE AND MORE ABOUT ME.
HAH HAH HAH HAH!
ニヤ
smirk
AND FOR **THAT**, I MUST KEEP BRINGING NEW ATTRACTIONS...

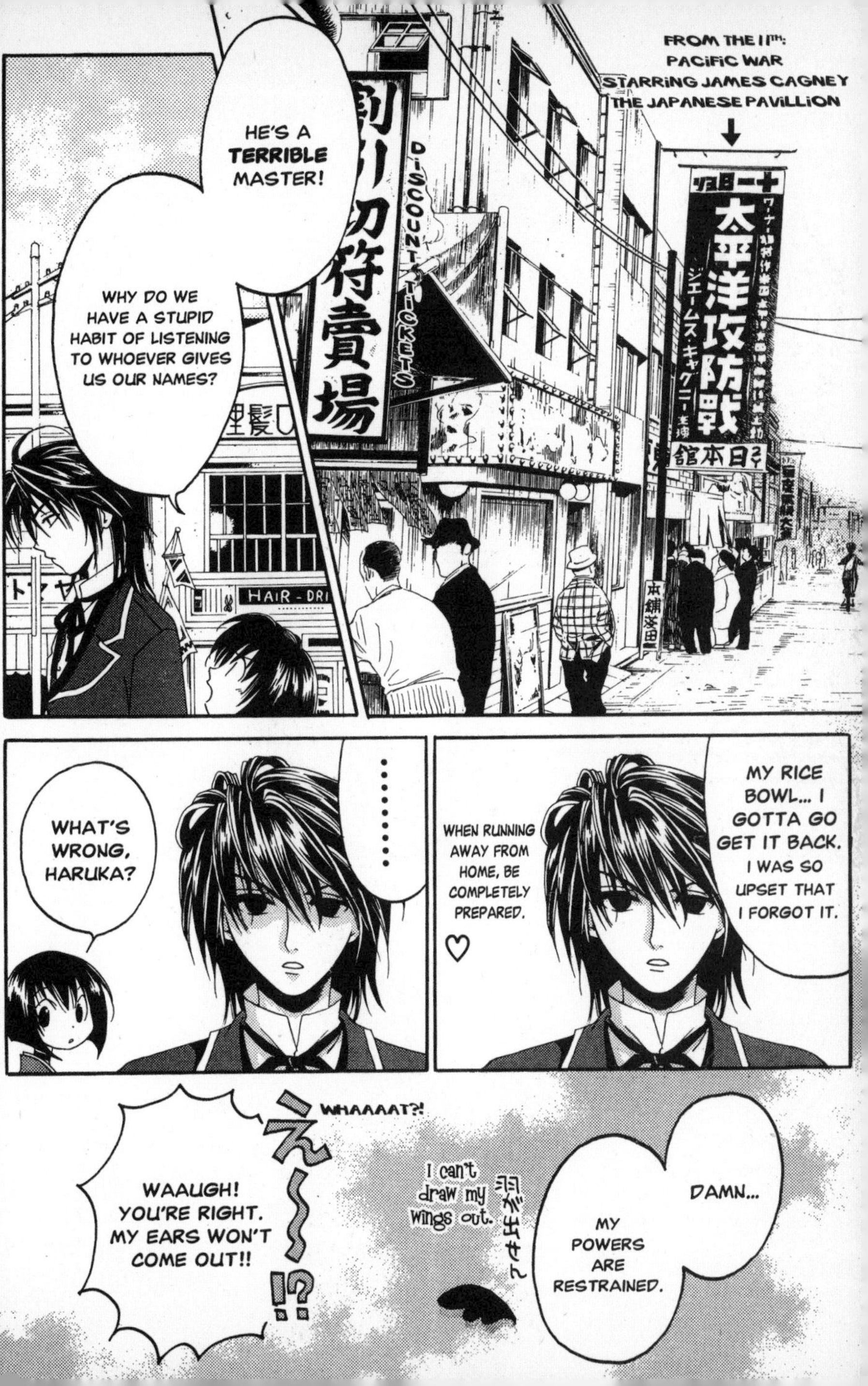
FROM THE 11TH: PACIFIC WAR STARRING JAMES CAGNEY THE JAPANESE PAVILLION
太平洋攻防戦
ジェームス・キャグニー
日本館
DISCOUNT TICKETS
HE'S A TERRIBLE MASTER!
WHY DO WE HAVE A STUPID HABIT OF LISTENING TO WHOEVER GIVES US OUR NAMES?
MY RICE BOWL... I GOTTA GO GET IT BACK. I WAS SO UPSET THAT I FORGOT IT.
WHEN RUNNING AWAY FROM HOME, BE COMPLETELY PREPARED. ♡
......
WHAT'S WRONG, HARUKA?
DAMN... MY POWERS ARE RESTRAINED.
羽が出せん
I can't draw my wings out.
えーー!?
WHAAAAT?!
WAAUGH! YOU'RE RIGHT. MY EARS WON'T COME OUT!!

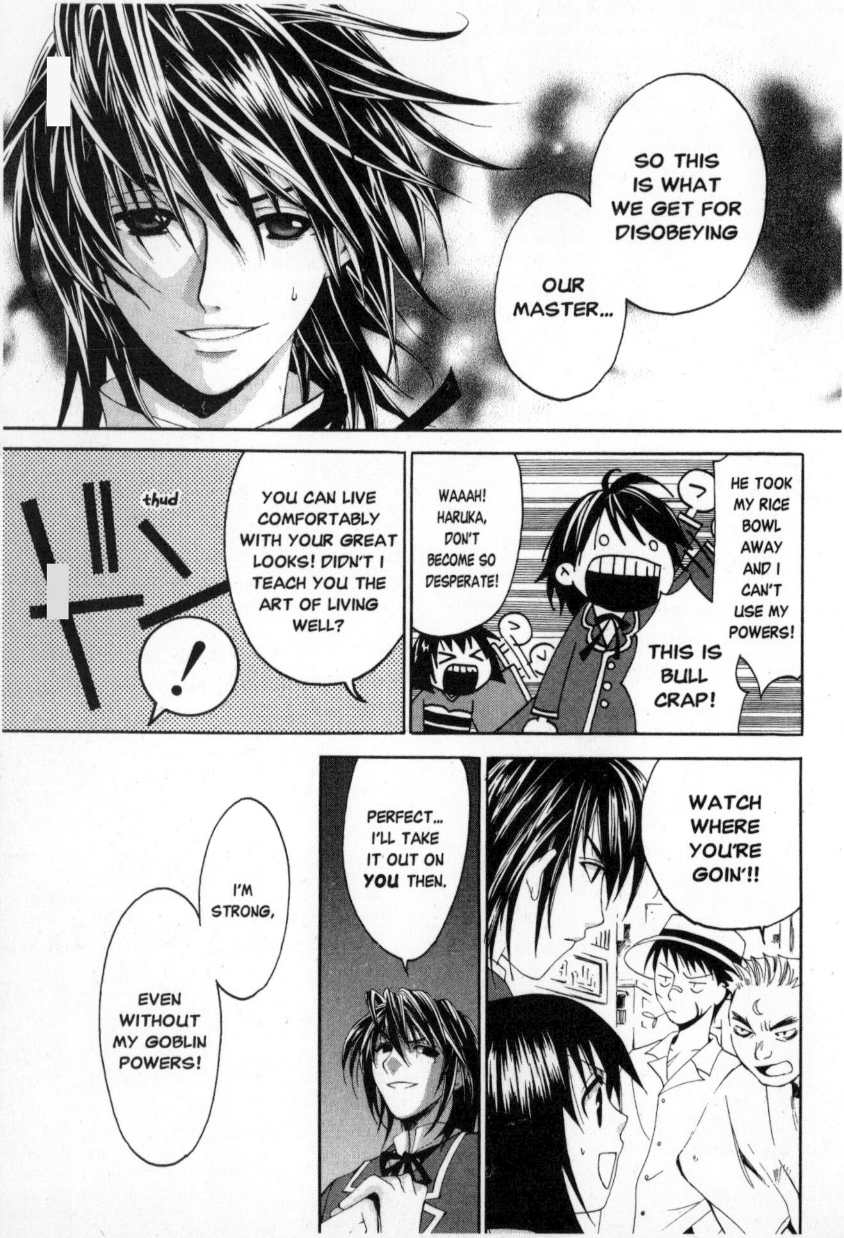
SO THIS IS WHAT WE GET FOR DISOBEYING
OUR MASTER...
HE TOOK MY RICE BOWL AWAY AND I CAN'T USE MY POWERS!
THIS IS BULL CRAP!
WAAAH! HARUKA, DON'T BECOME SO DESPERATE!
YOU CAN LIVE COMFORTABLY WITH YOUR GREAT LOOKS! DIDN'T I TEACH YOU THE ART OF LIVING WELL?
thud
!
WATCH WHERE YOU'RE GOIN'!!
PERFECT... I'LL TAKE IT OUT ON **YOU** THEN.
I'M STRONG,
EVEN WITHOUT MY GOBLIN POWERS!

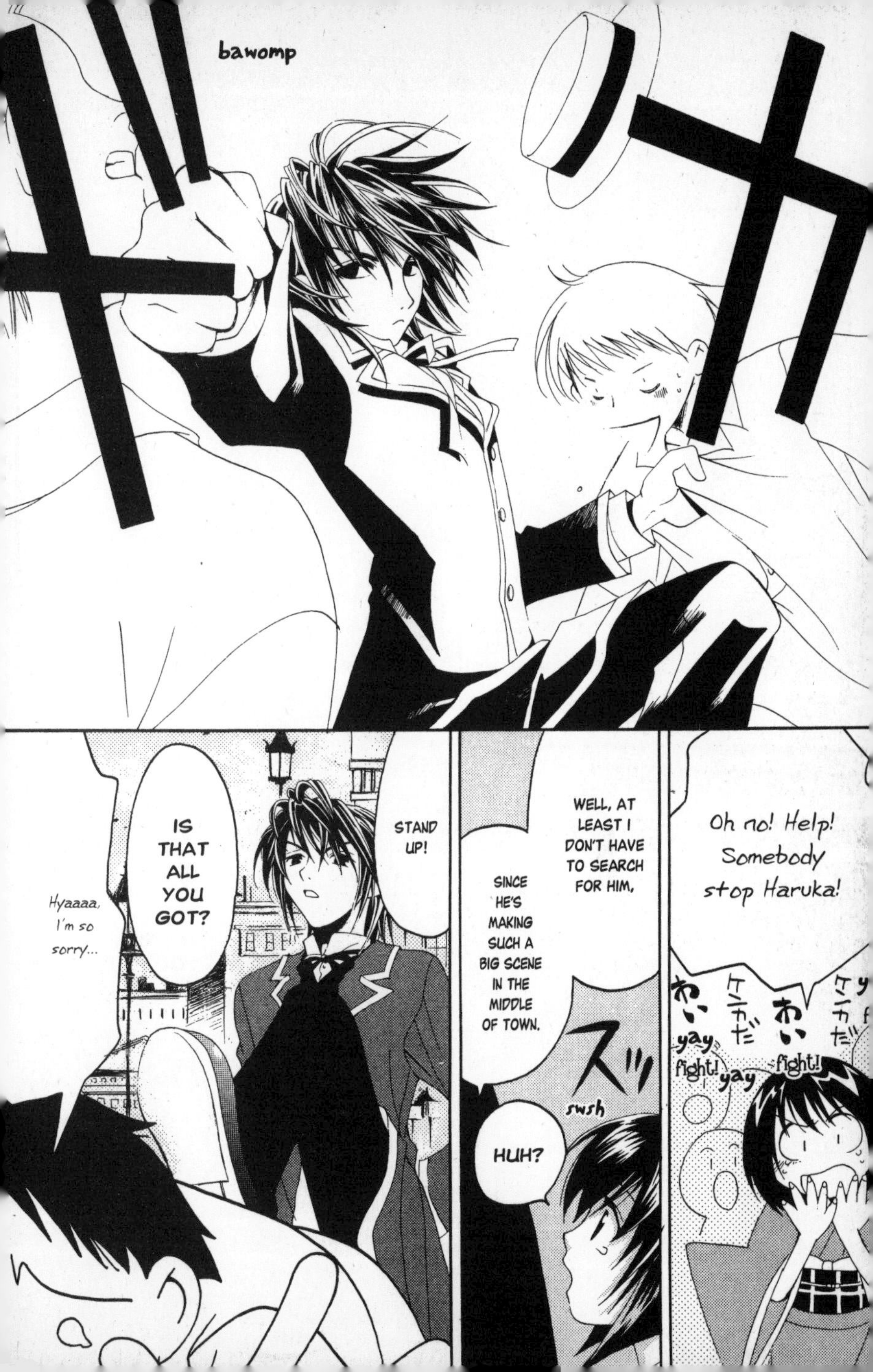

bawomp
Oh no! Help! Somebody stop Haruka!
わい
ケンカだ
yay
fight!
わい
ケンカだ
yay
fight!
WELL, AT LEAST I DON'T HAVE TO SEARCH FOR HIM,
SINCE HE'S MAKING SUCH A BIG SCENE IN THE MIDDLE OF TOWN.
swsh
HUH?
STAND UP!
IS THAT ALL YOU GOT?
Hyaaaa, I'm so sorry...

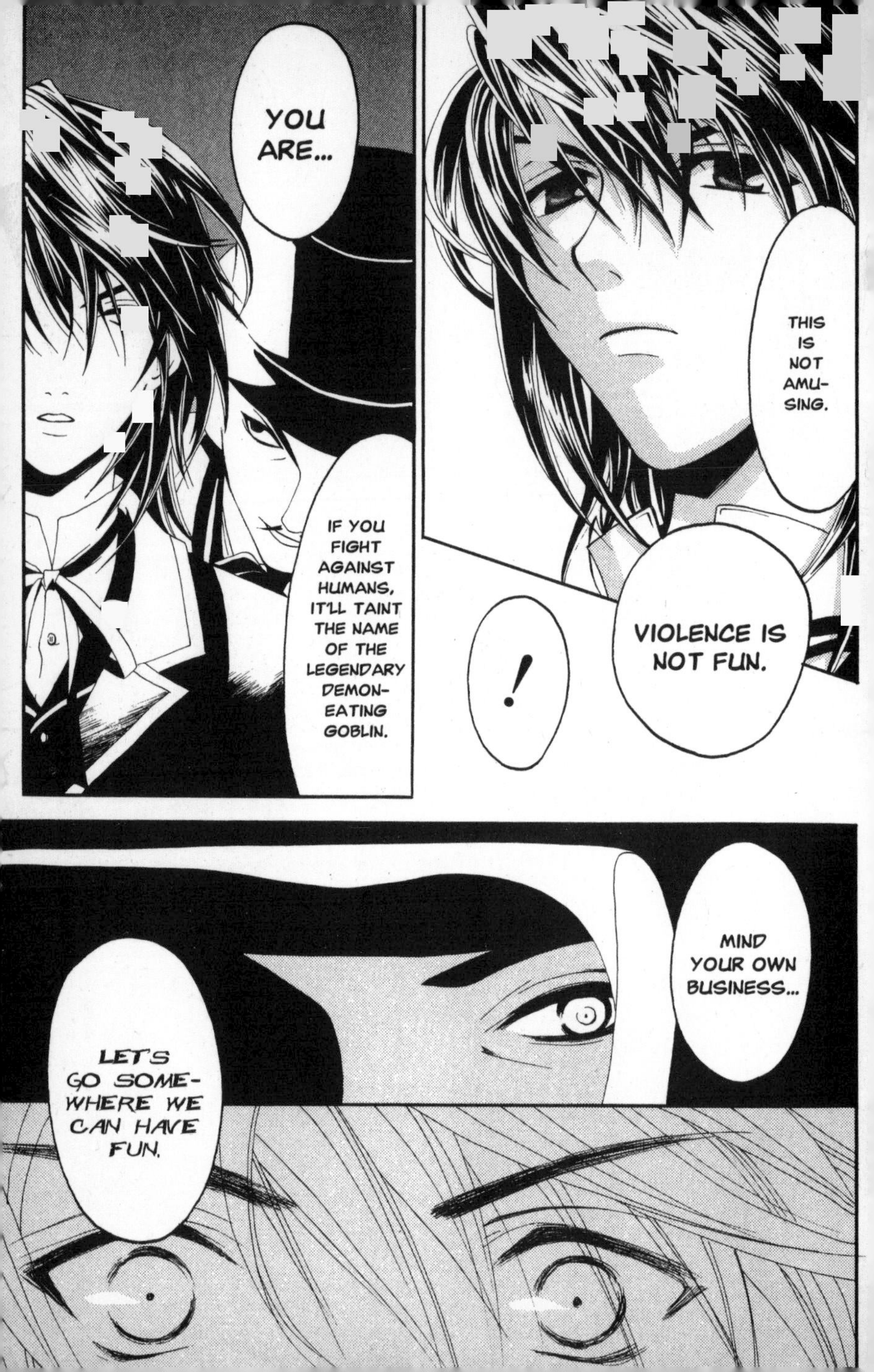
THIS IS NOT AMUSING.
VIOLENCE IS NOT FUN.
!
YOU ARE...
IF YOU FIGHT AGAINST HUMANS, IT'LL TAINT THE NAME OF THE LEGENDARY DEMON-EATING GOBLIN.
MIND YOUR OWN BUSINESS...
LET'S GO SOMEWHERE WE CAN HAVE FUN.

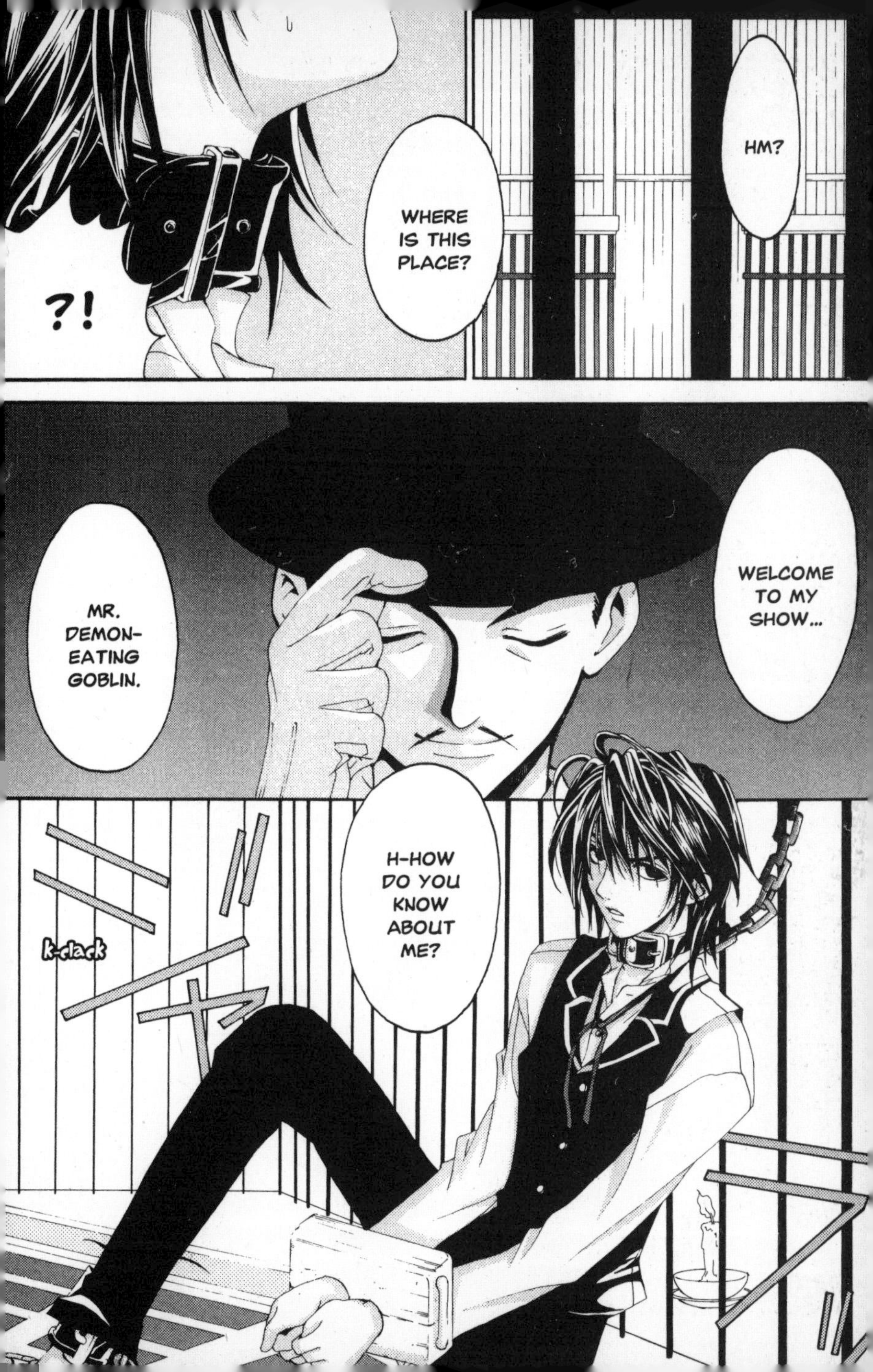
HM?
WHERE IS THIS PLACE?
?!
WELCOME TO MY SHOW...
MR. DEMON-EATING GOBLIN.
H-HOW DO YOU KNOW ABOUT ME?
k-clack

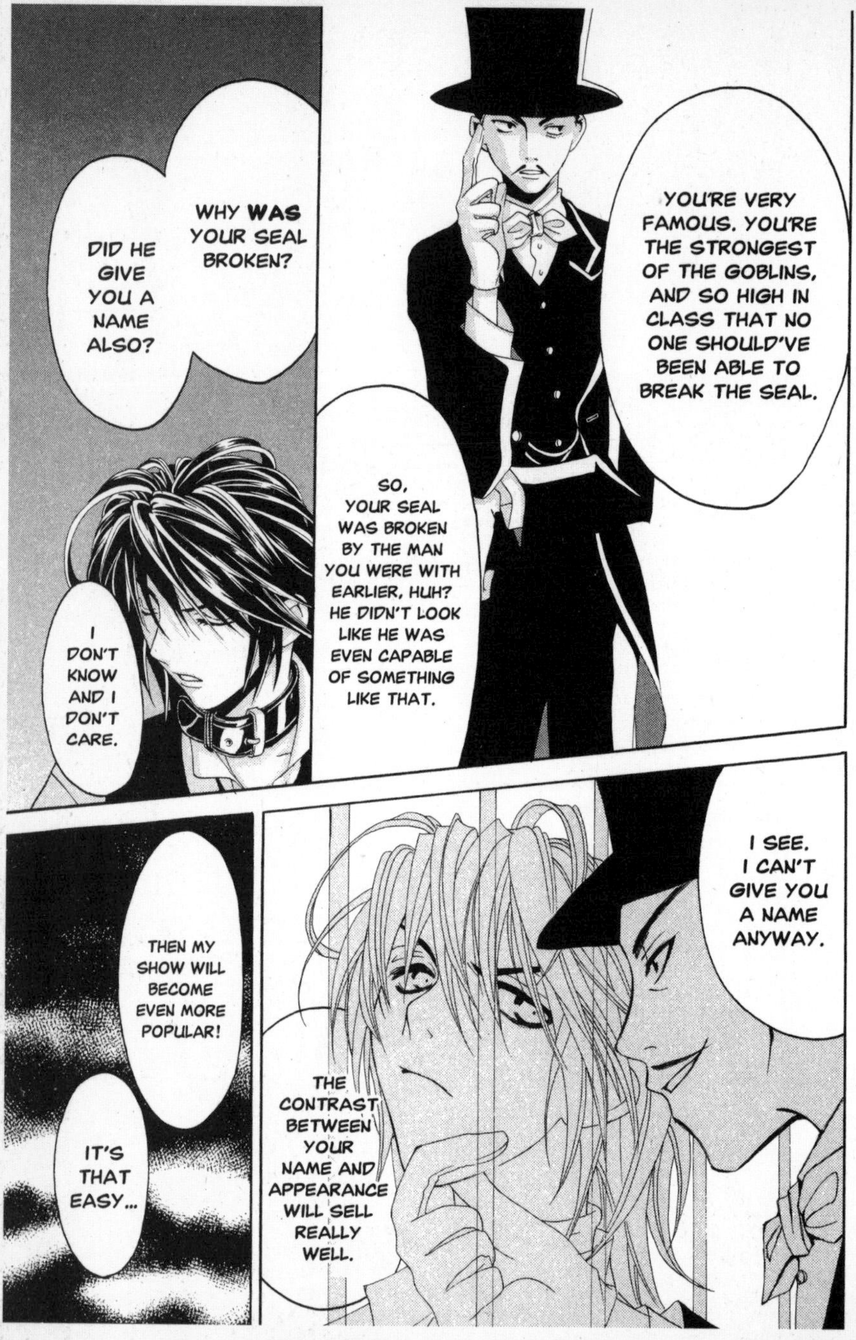
YOU'RE VERY FAMOUS. YOU'RE THE STRONGEST OF THE GOBLINS, AND SO HIGH IN CLASS THAT NO ONE SHOULD'VE BEEN ABLE TO BREAK THE SEAL.
SO, YOUR SEAL WAS BROKEN BY THE MAN YOU WERE WITH EARLIER, HUH? HE DIDN'T LOOK LIKE HE WAS EVEN CAPABLE OF SOMETHING LIKE THAT.
WHY **WAS** YOUR SEAL BROKEN?
DID HE GIVE YOU A NAME ALSO?
I DON'T KNOW AND I DON'T CARE.
I SEE. I CAN'T GIVE YOU A NAME ANYWAY.
THE CONTRAST BETWEEN YOUR NAME AND APPEARANCE WILL SELL REALLY WELL.
THEN MY SHOW WILL BECOME EVEN MORE POPULAR!
IT'S THAT EASY...

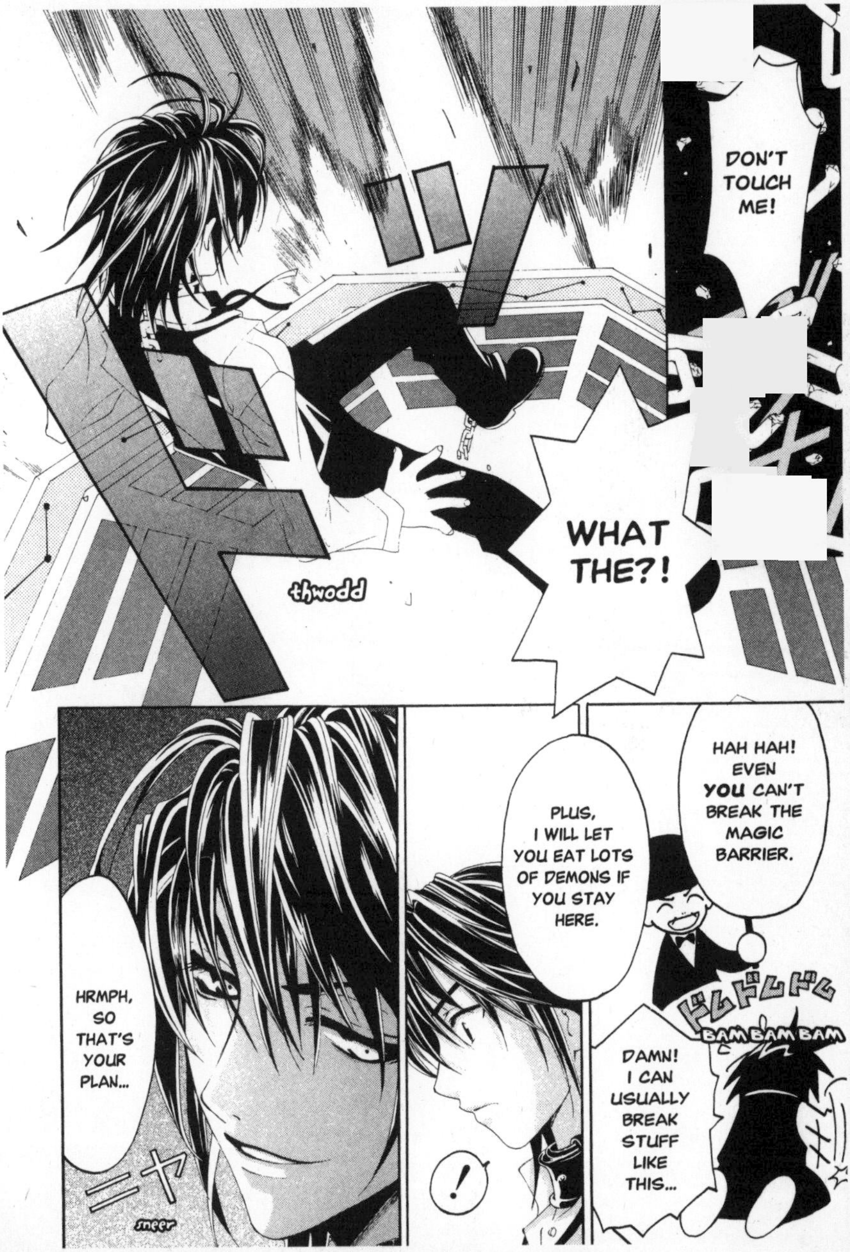
DON'T TOUCH ME!
WHAT THE?!
thwodd
HAH HAH! EVEN **YOU** CAN'T BREAK THE MAGIC BARRIER.
BAM BAM BAM
DAMN! I CAN USUALLY BREAK STUFF LIKE THIS...
PLUS, I WILL LET YOU EAT LOTS OF DEMONS IF YOU STAY HERE.
!
HRMPH, SO THAT'S YOUR PLAN...
ニヤ
sneer

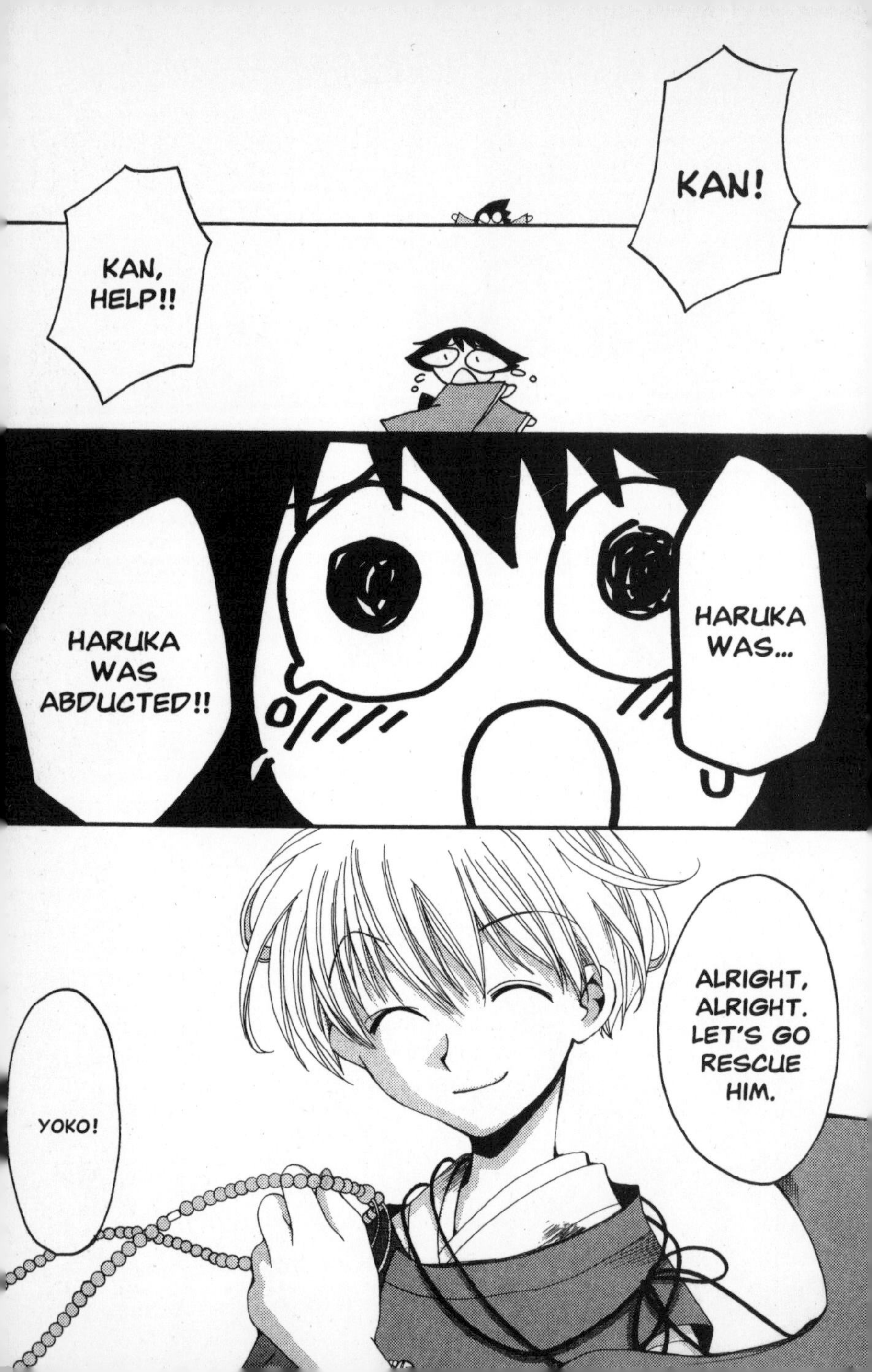
KAN!
KAN, HELP!!
HARUKA WAS...
HARUKA WAS ABDUCTED!!
ALRIGHT, ALRIGHT. LET'S GO RESCUE HIM.
YOKO!

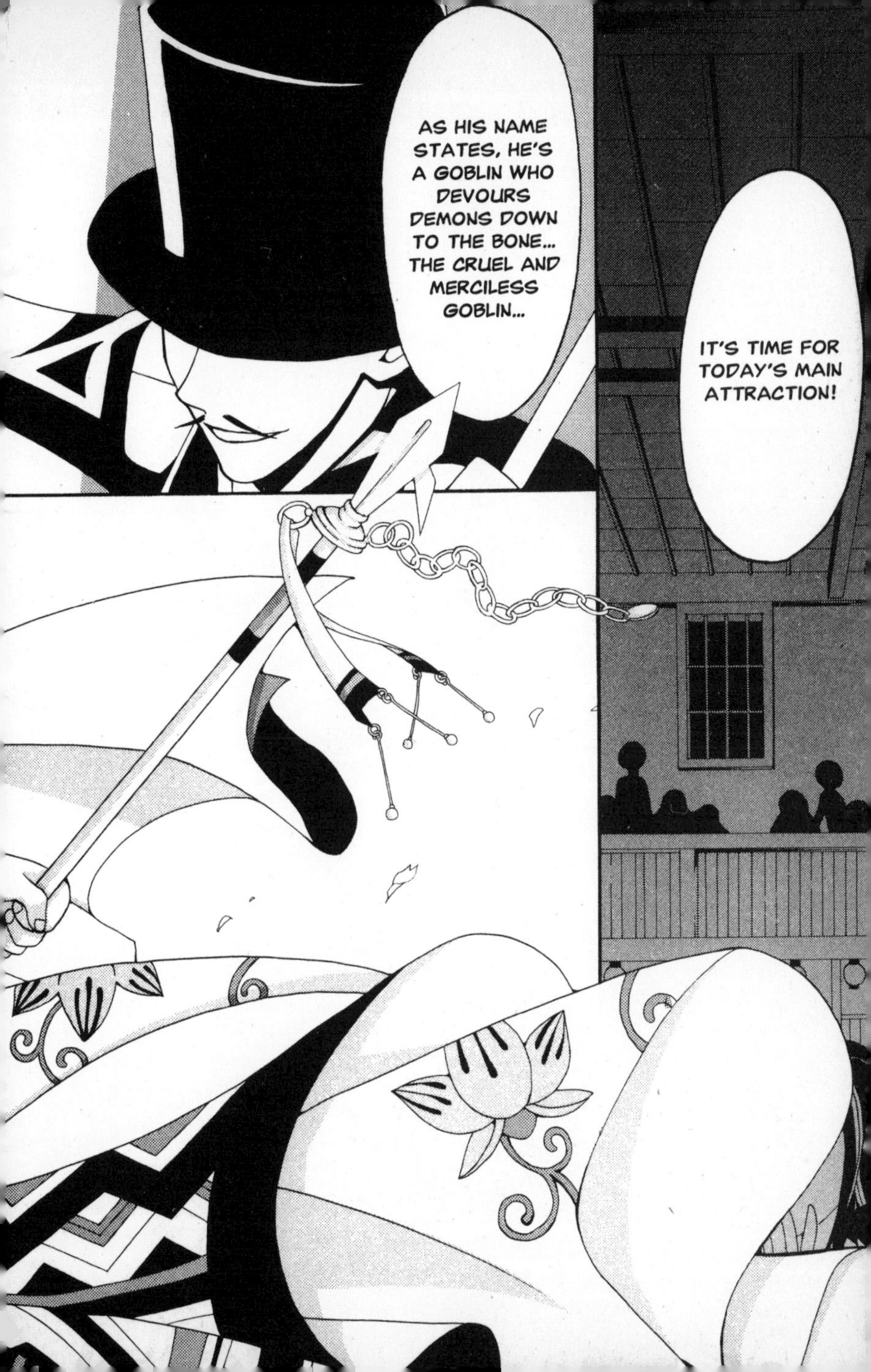
IT'S TIME FOR TODAY'S MAIN ATTRACTION!
AS HIS NAME STATES, HE'S A GOBLIN WHO DEVOURS DEMONS DOWN TO THE BONE... THE CRUEL AND MERCILESS GOBLIN...

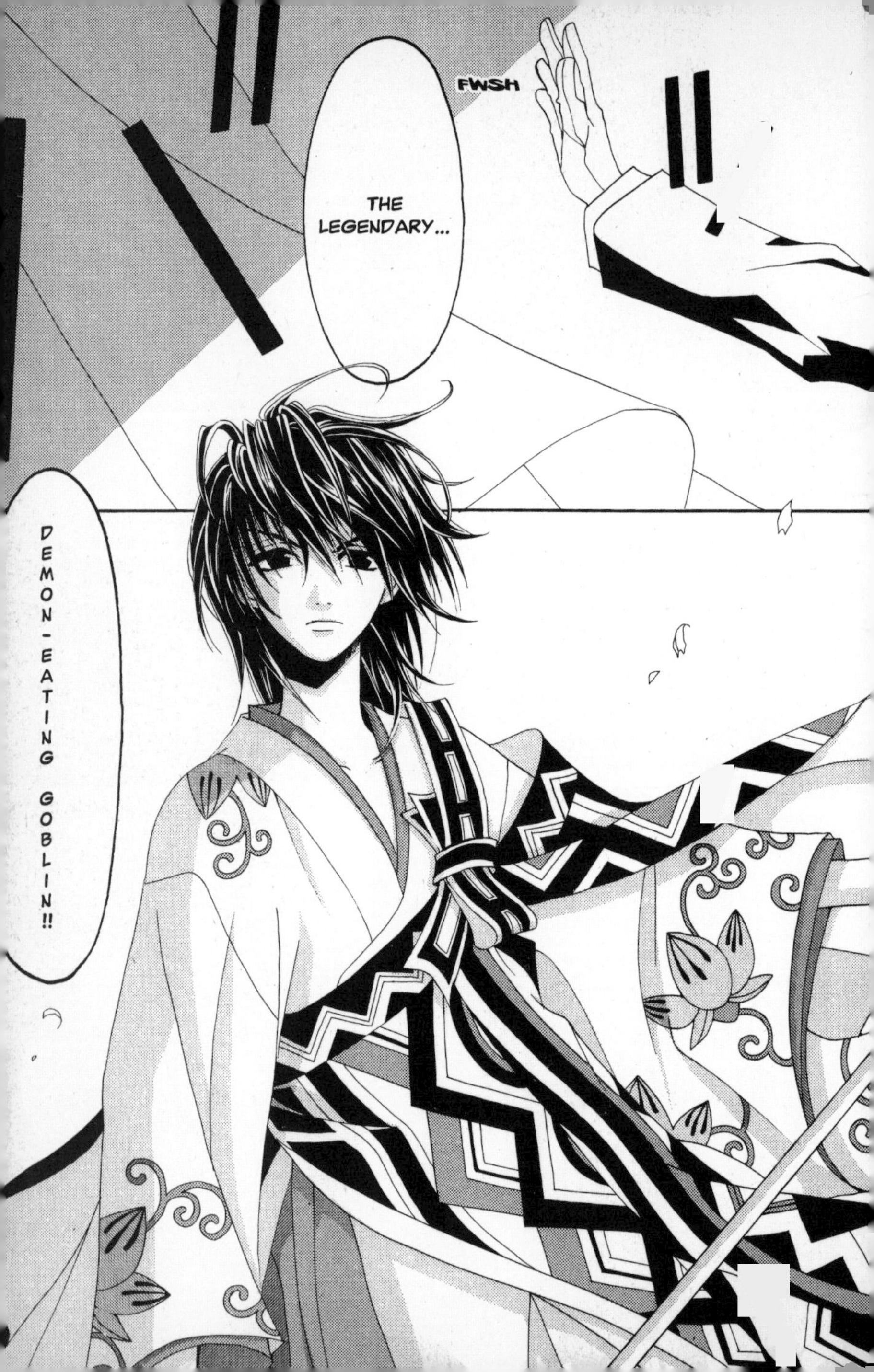
FWSH
THE LEGENDARY...
DEMON-EATING GOBLIN!!

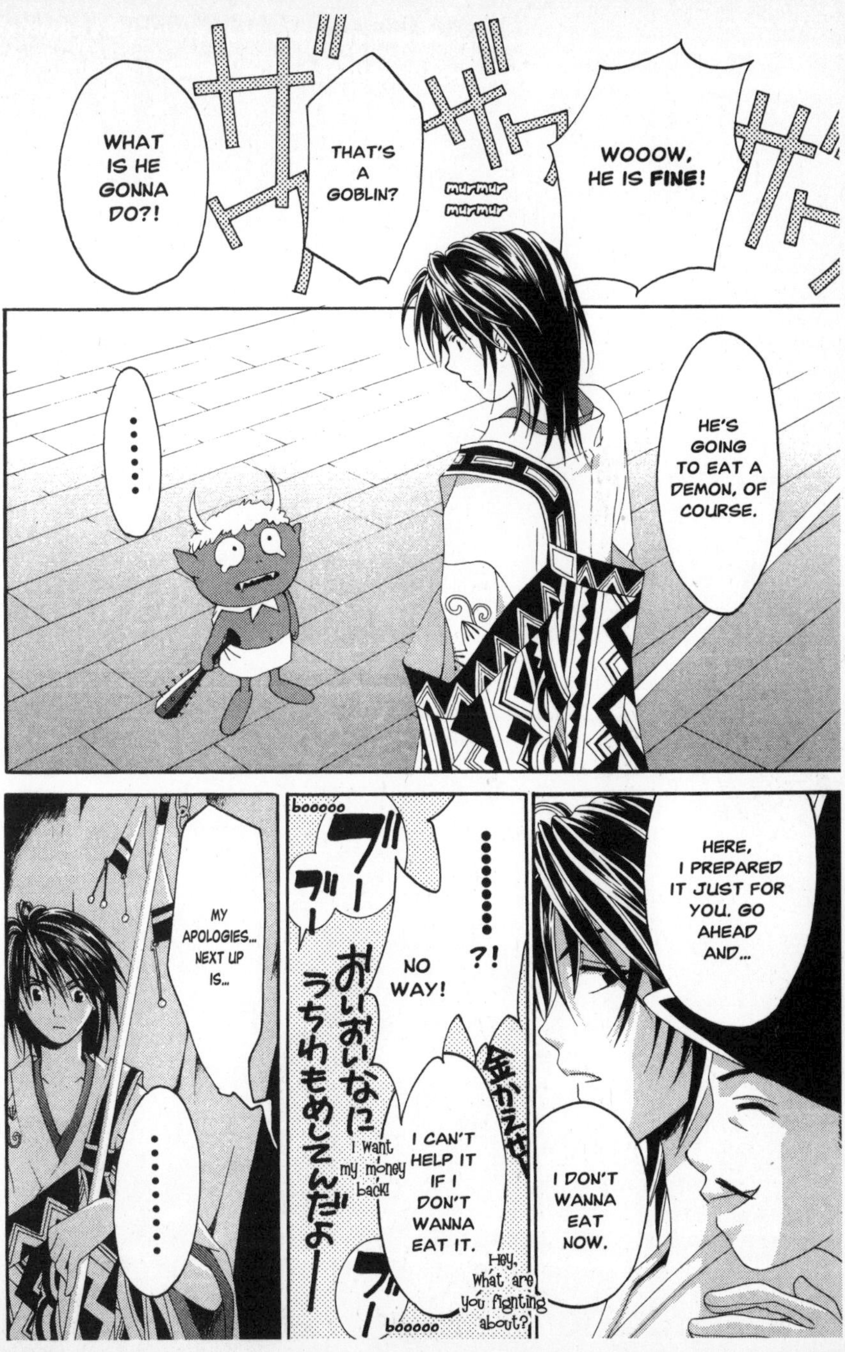
ザワ ザワ ザワ
WOOOW, HE IS **FINE**!
murmur murmur
THAT'S A GOBLIN?
WHAT IS HE GONNA DO?!
HE'S GOING TO EAT A DEMON, OF COURSE.
......
HERE, I PREPARED IT JUST FOR YOU. GO AHEAD AND...
I DON'T WANNA EAT NOW.
........?!
NO WAY!
ブーブー
boooo
金かえせ
I want my money back!
おいおいなにうちわもめしてんだよー
Hey, what are you fighting about?
I CAN'T HELP IT IF I DON'T WANNA EAT IT.
ブー
boooo
MY APOLOGIES... NEXT UP IS...
......

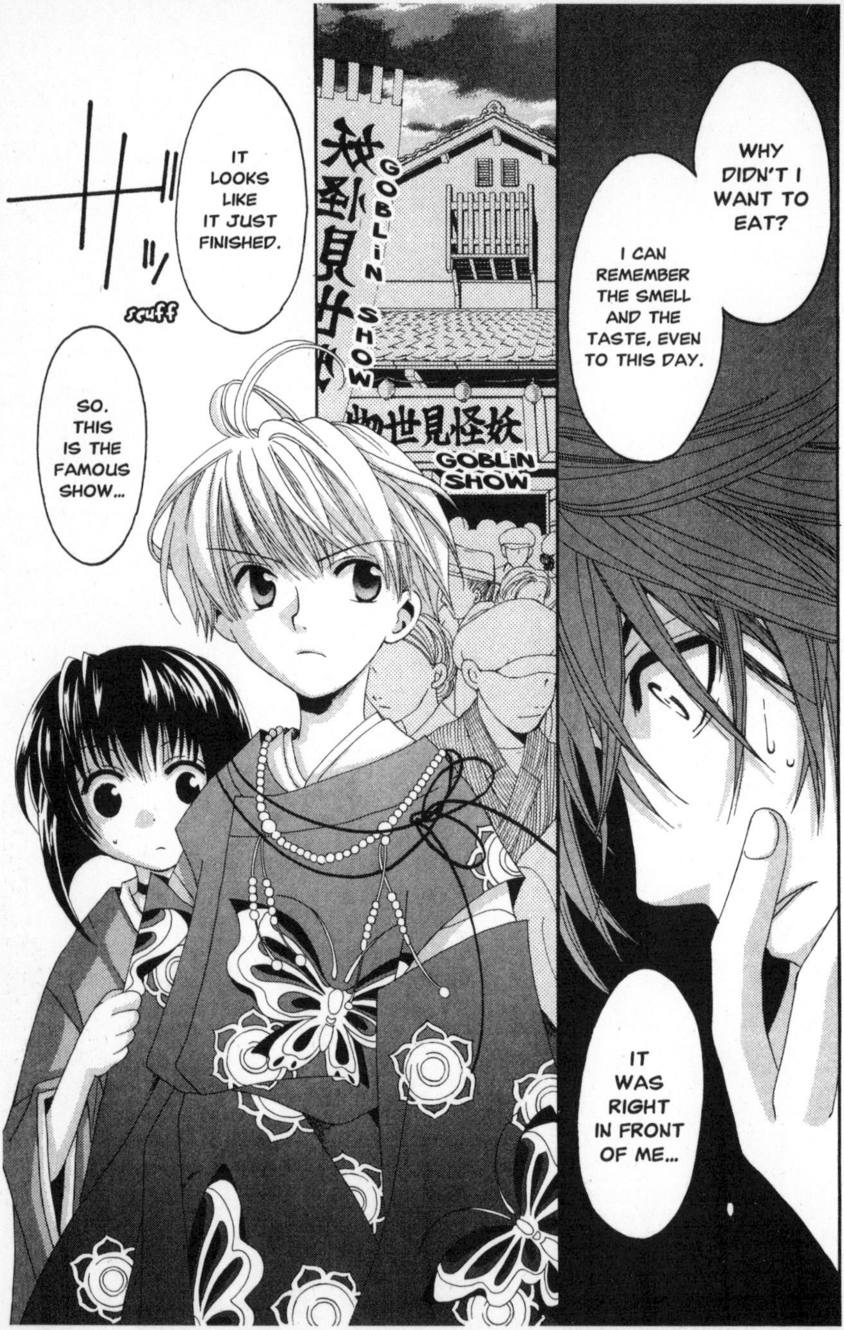
WHY DIDN'T I WANT TO EAT?
I CAN REMEMBER THE SMELL AND THE TASTE, EVEN TO THIS DAY.
IT WAS RIGHT IN FRONT OF ME...
IT LOOKS LIKE IT JUST FINISHED.
GOBLIN SHOW
物世見怪妖
GOBLIN SHOW
scuff
SO. THIS IS THE FAMOUS SHOW...

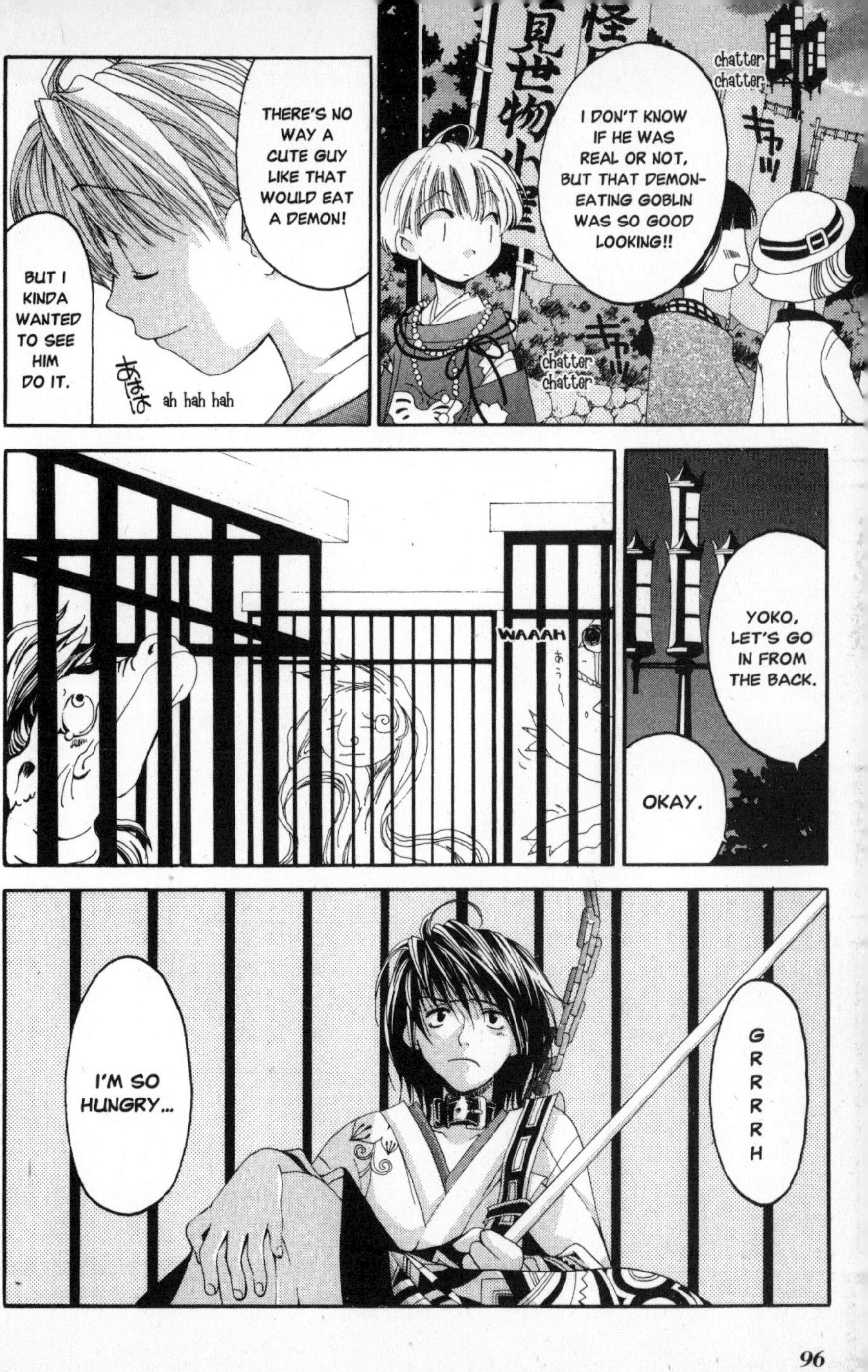
chatter chatter
怪
見世物小
I DON'T KNOW IF HE WAS REAL OR NOT, BUT THAT DEMON-EATING GOBLIN WAS SO GOOD LOOKING!!
キャッ
キャッ
chatter chatter
THERE'S NO WAY A CUTE GUY LIKE THAT WOULD EAT A DEMON!
BUT I KINDA WANTED TO SEE HIM DO IT.
あはは
ah hah hah
YOKO, LET'S GO IN FROM THE BACK.
OKAY.
WAAAH
あう～
GRRRRH
I'M SO HUNGRY...

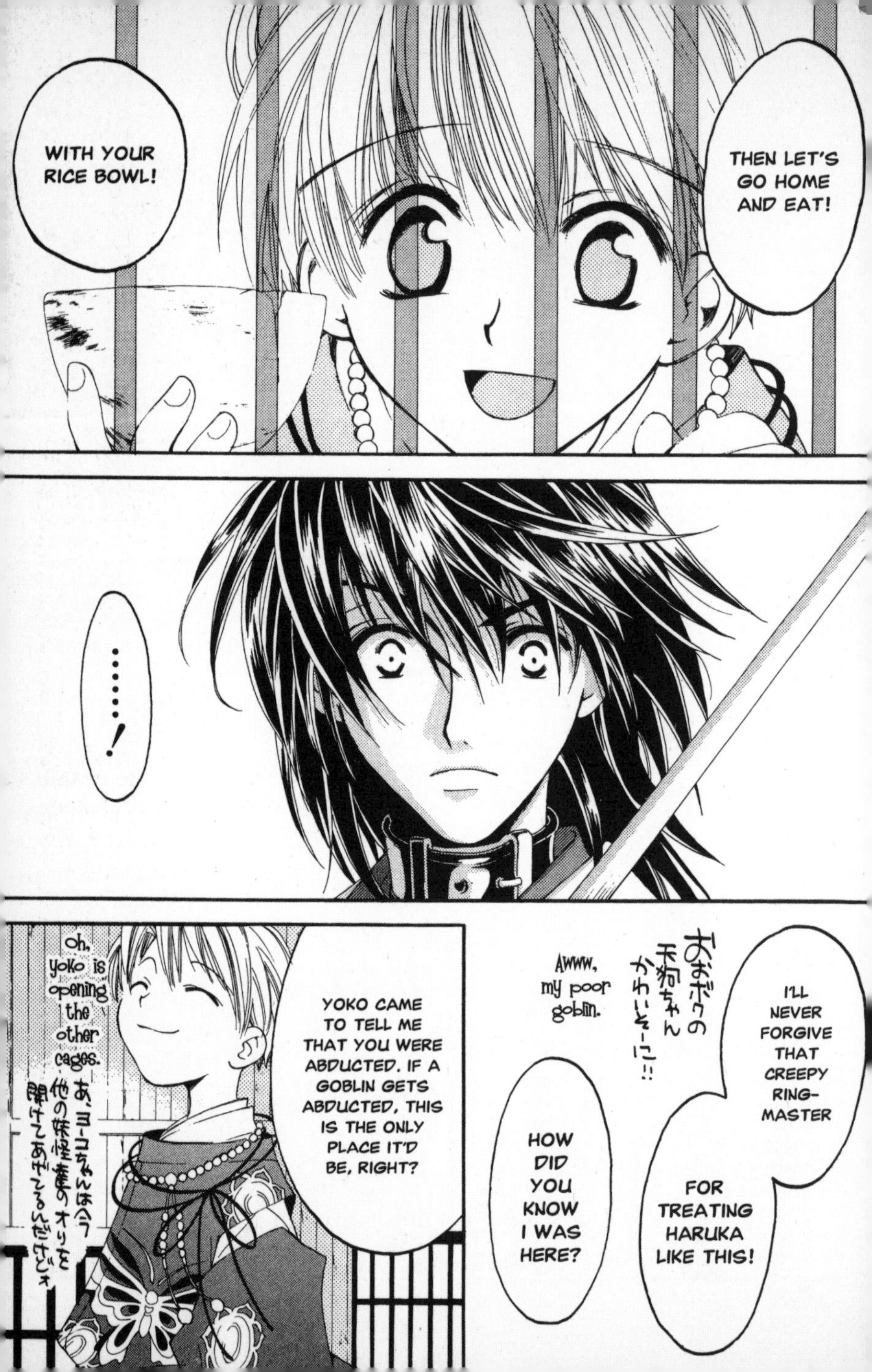
THEN LET'S GO HOME AND EAT!
WITH YOUR RICE BOWL!
......!
I'LL NEVER FORGIVE THAT CREEPY RING-MASTER
FOR TREATING HARUKA LIKE THIS!
おおボクの天狗ちゃんかわいそーに!!
Awww, my poor goblin.
HOW DID YOU KNOW I WAS HERE?
YOKO CAME TO TELL ME THAT YOU WERE ABDUCTED. IF A GOBLIN GETS ABDUCTED, THIS IS THE ONLY PLACE IT'D BE, RIGHT?
Oh, Yoko is opening the other cages.
あ、ヨーコちゃんは今他の妖怪達のオリを開けてあげてるんだけどォ

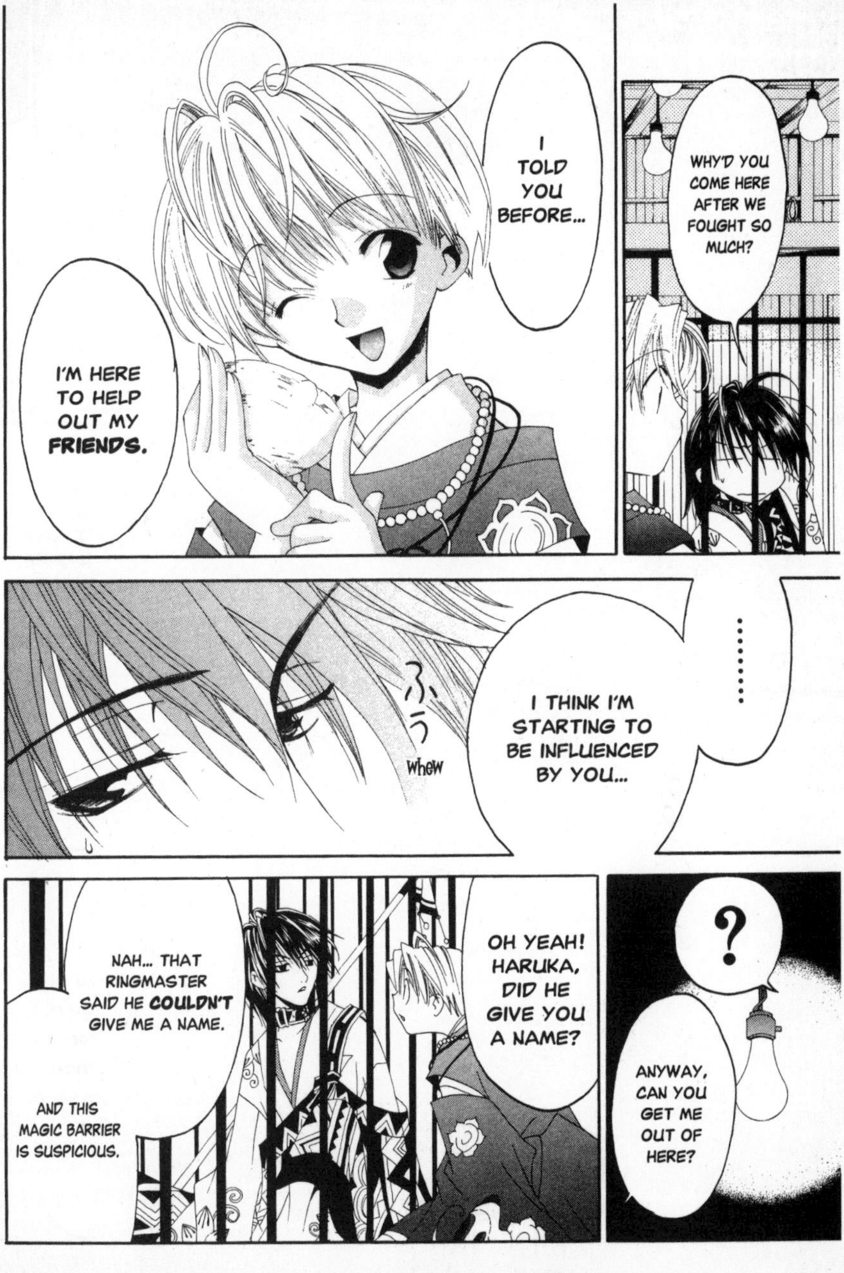
WHY'D YOU COME HERE AFTER WE FOUGHT SO MUCH?
I TOLD YOU BEFORE...
I'M HERE TO HELP OUT MY **FRIENDS.**
......
I THINK I'M STARTING TO BE INFLUENCED BY YOU...
ふう
whew
?
ANYWAY, CAN YOU GET ME OUT OF HERE?
OH YEAH! HARUKA, DID HE GIVE YOU A NAME?
NAH... THAT RINGMASTER SAID HE **COULDN'T** GIVE ME A NAME.
AND THIS MAGIC BARRIER IS SUSPICIOUS.

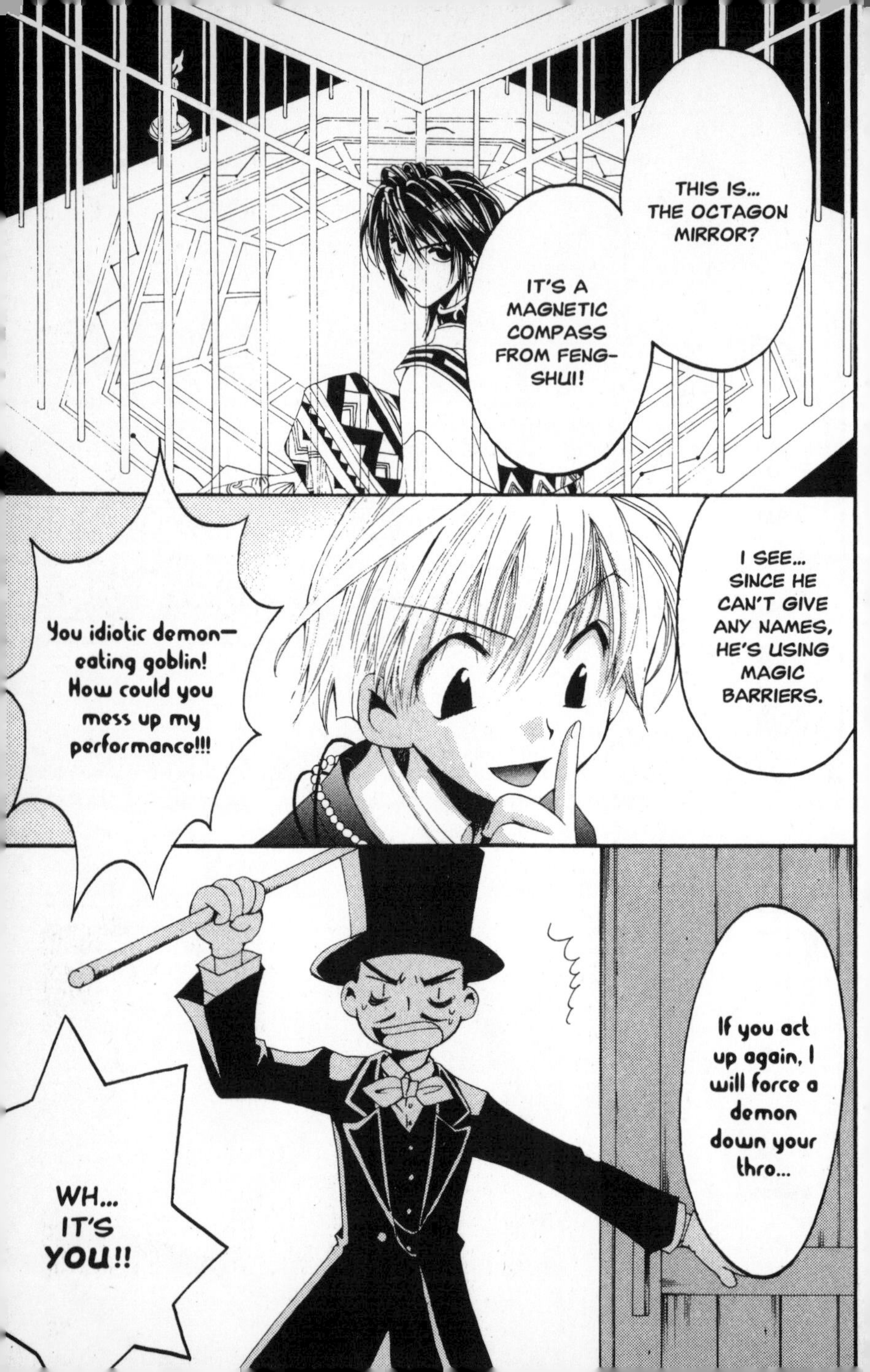
THIS IS... THE OCTAGON MIRROR?
IT'S A MAGNETIC COMPASS FROM FENG-SHUI!
I SEE... SINCE HE CAN'T GIVE ANY NAMES, HE'S USING MAGIC BARRIERS.
You idiotic demon-eating goblin! How could you mess up my performance!!!
If you act up again, I will force a demon down your thro...
WH... IT'S YOU!!

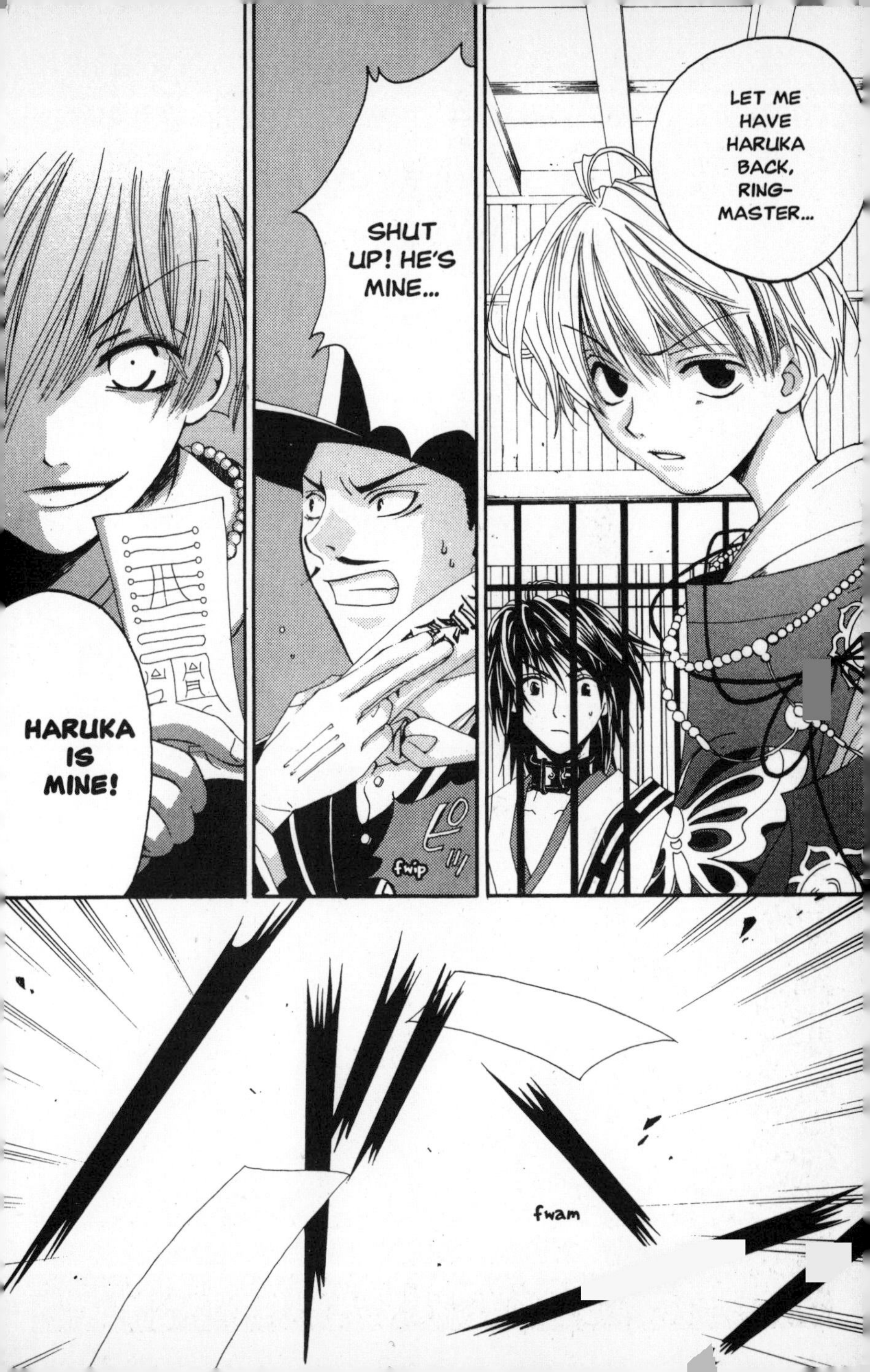
LET ME HAVE HARUKA BACK, RING-MASTER...
SHUT UP! HE'S MINE...
fwip
HARUKA IS MINE!
fwam

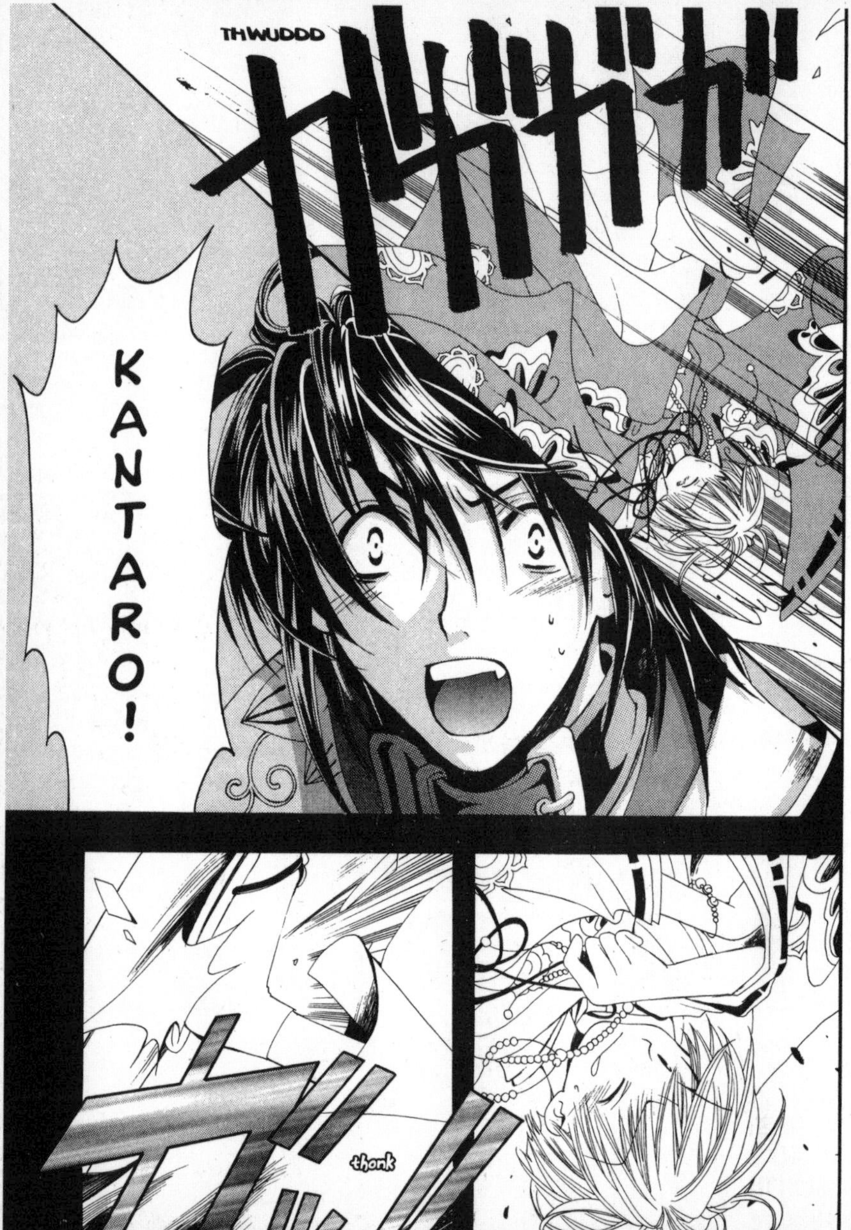
THWUDDD
KANTARO!
thonk

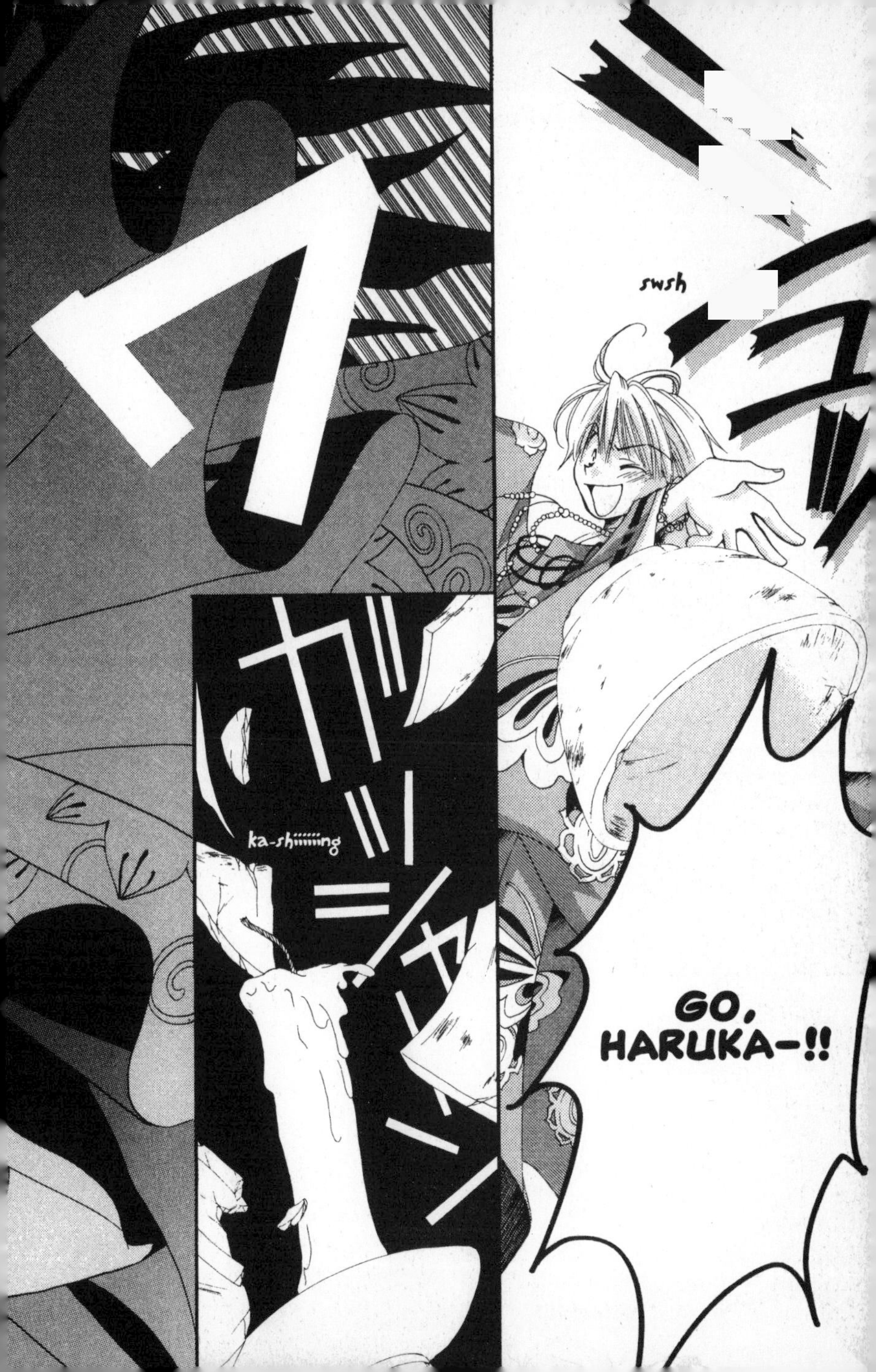
swsh
GO, HARUKA–!!
ka-shiiiiiiiing

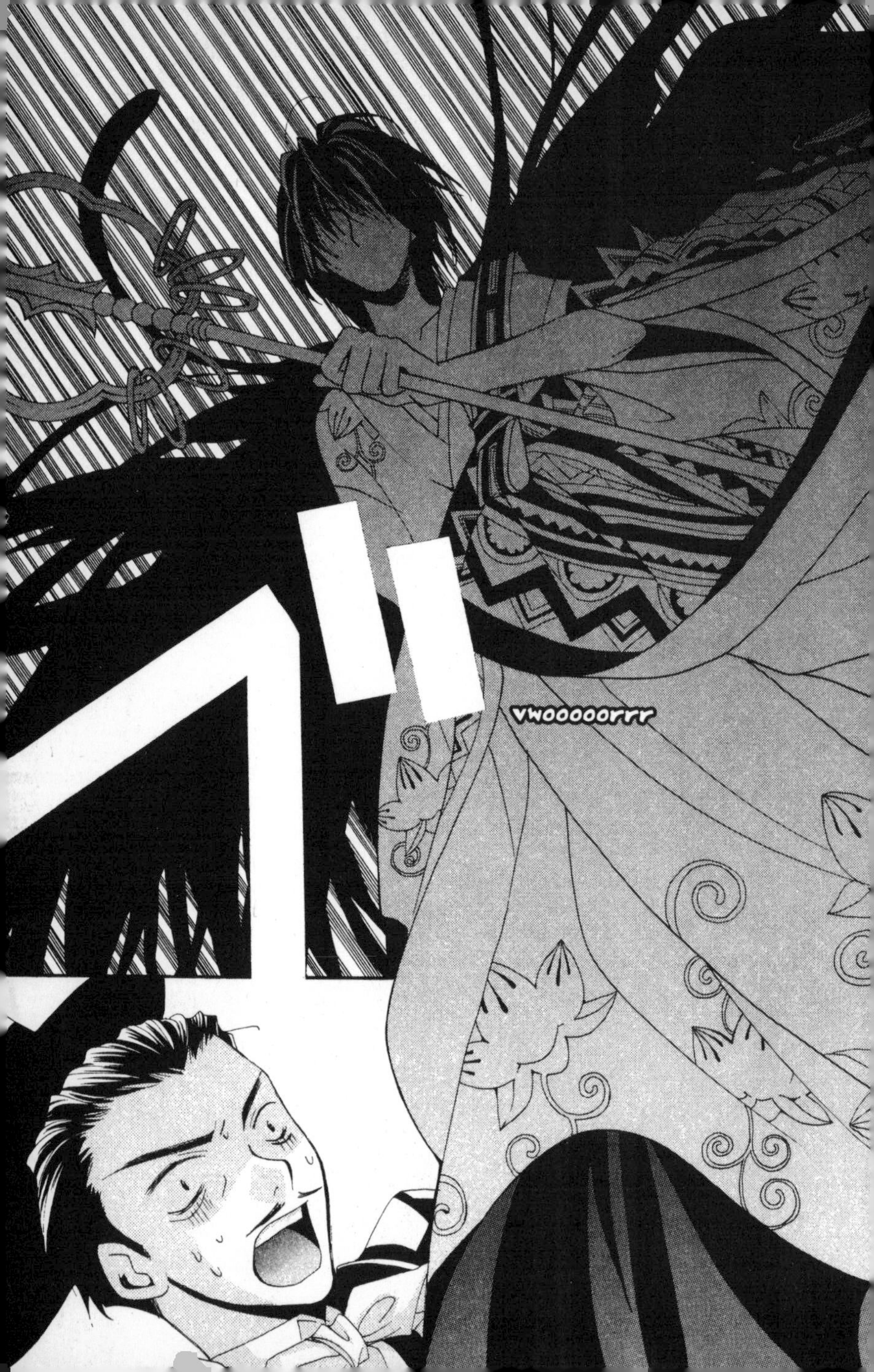
vwoooorrr

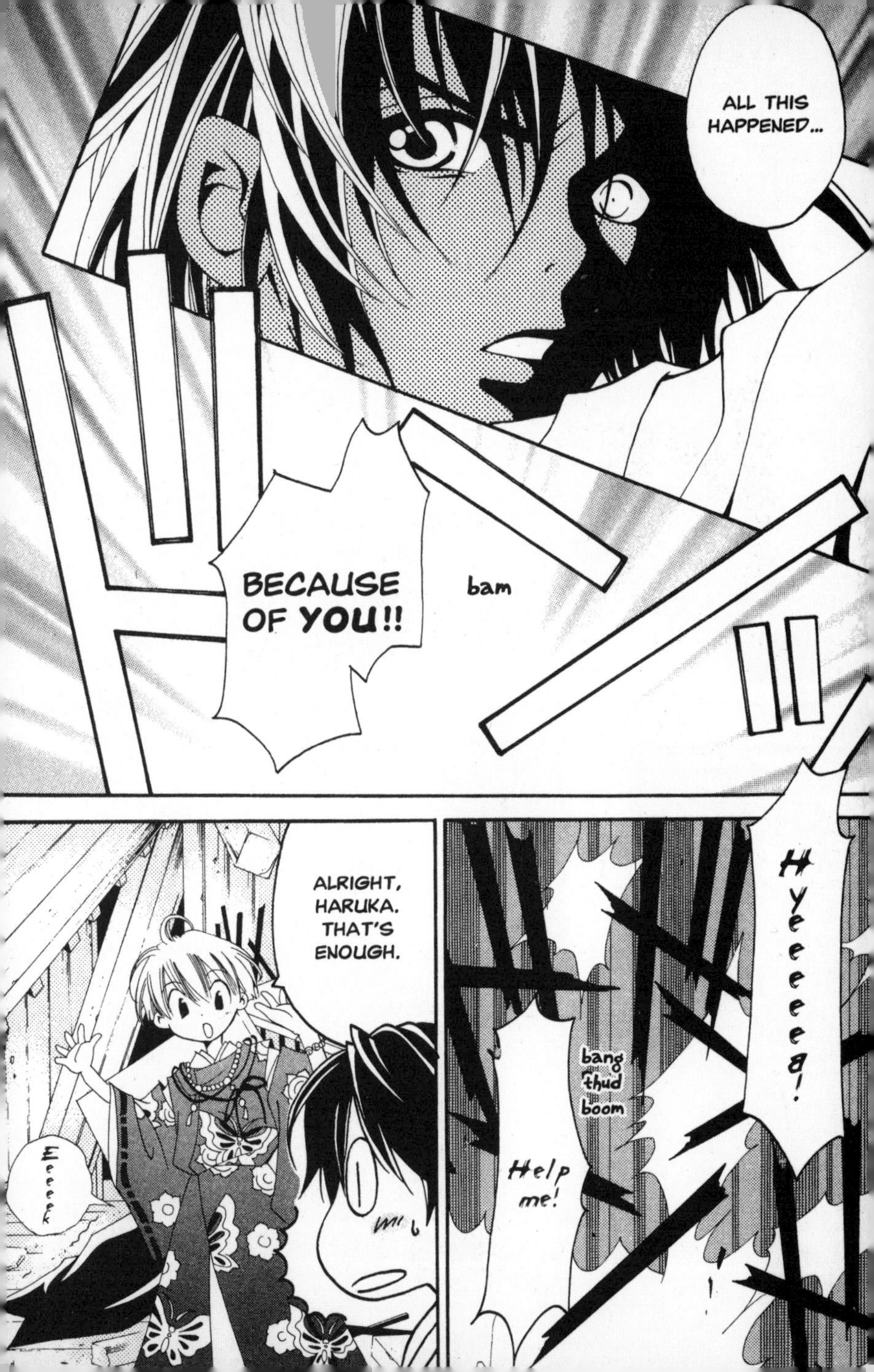
ALL THIS HAPPENED...
BECAUSE OF YOU!!
bam
Hyeeeeea!
bang thud boom
Help me!
ALRIGHT, HARUKA. THAT'S ENOUGH.
Eeeeek

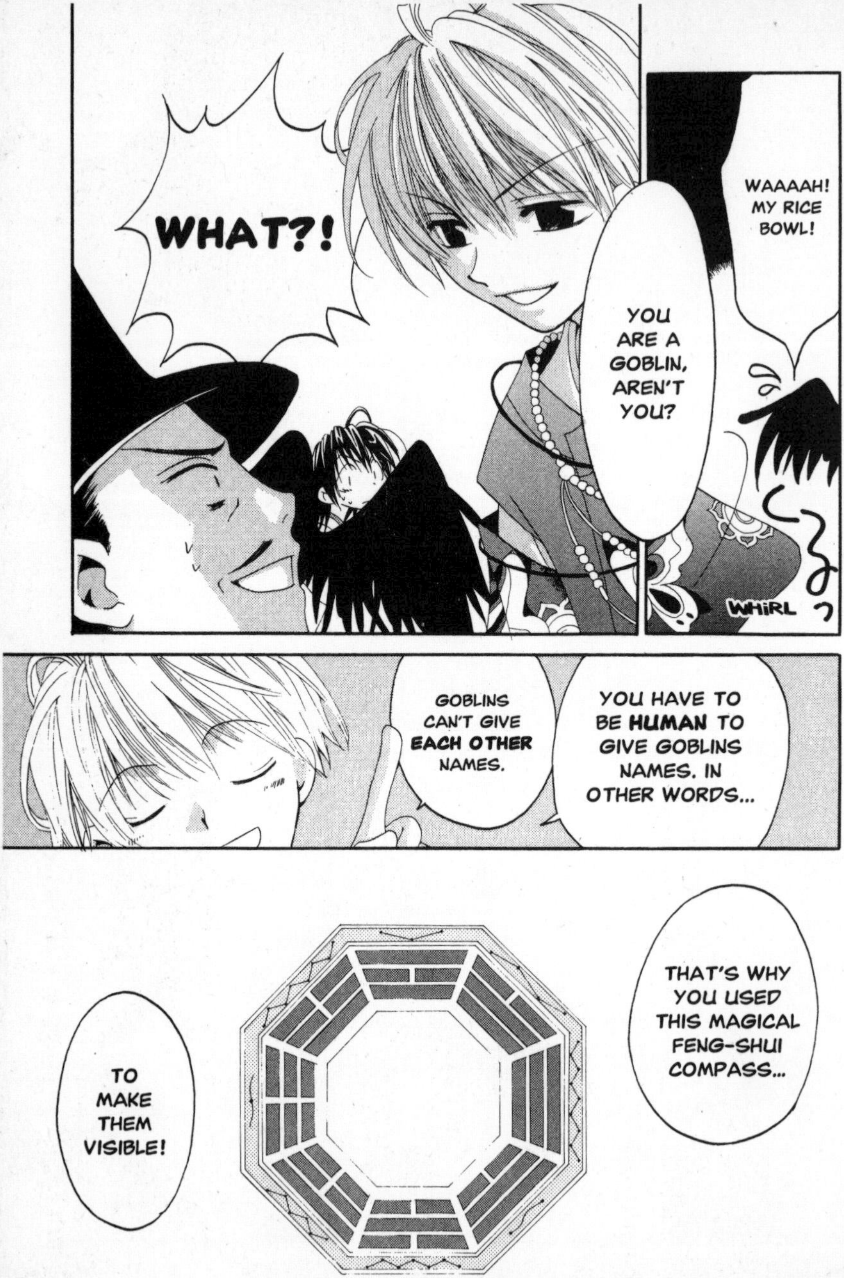
WAAAAH! MY RICE BOWL!
WHIRL
YOU ARE A GOBLIN, AREN'T YOU?
WHAT?!
YOU HAVE TO BE **HUMAN** TO GIVE GOBLINS NAMES. IN OTHER WORDS...
GOBLINS CAN'T GIVE **EACH OTHER** NAMES.
THAT'S WHY YOU USED THIS MAGICAL FENG-SHUI COMPASS...
TO MAKE THEM VISIBLE!

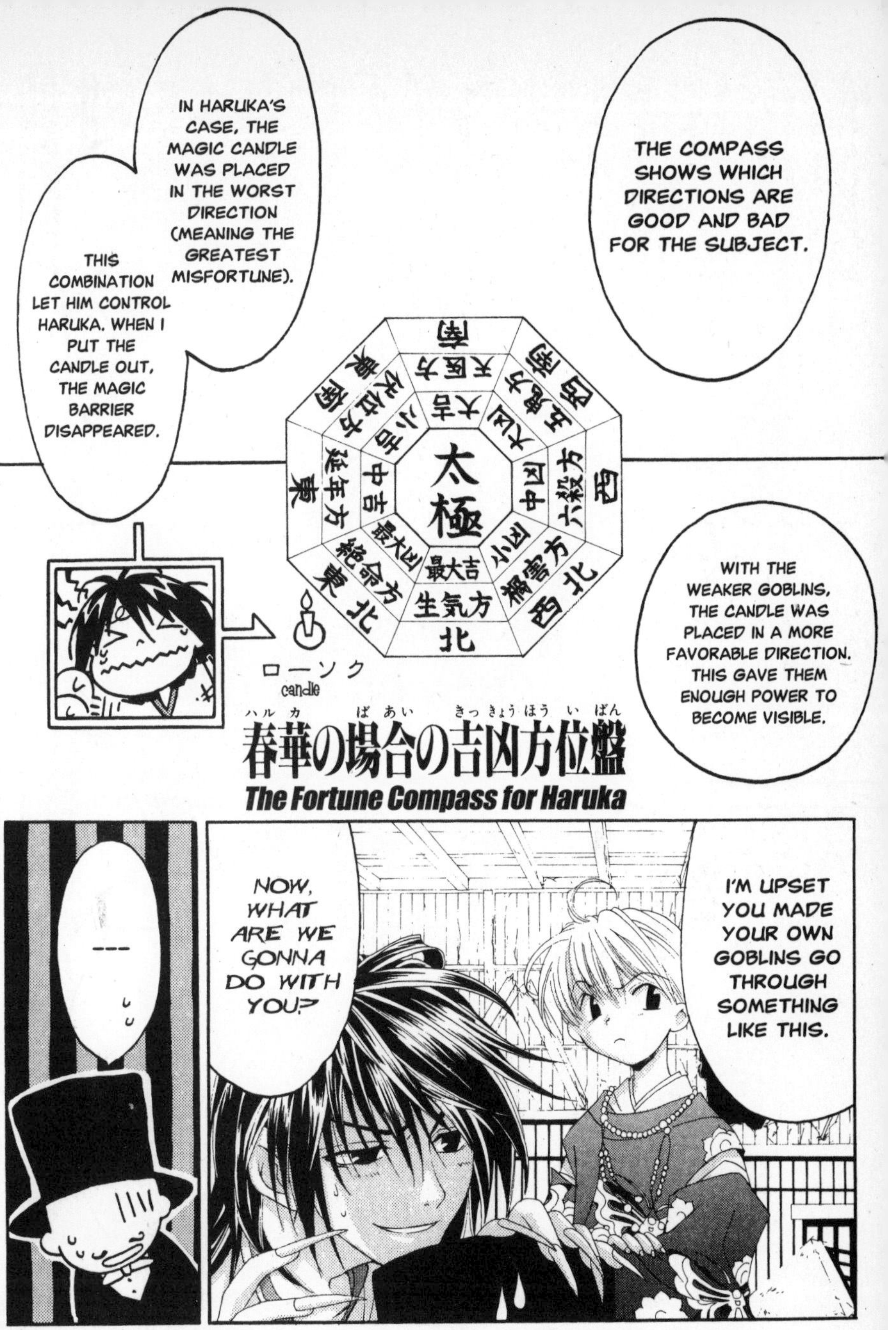
THE COMPASS SHOWS WHICH DIRECTIONS ARE GOOD AND BAD FOR THE SUBJECT.
IN HARUKA'S CASE, THE MAGIC CANDLE WAS PLACED IN THE WORST DIRECTION (MEANING THE GREATEST MISFORTUNE).
THIS COMBINATION LET HIM CONTROL HARUKA. WHEN I PUT THE CANDLE OUT, THE MAGIC BARRIER DISAPPEARED.
太極
南
天医方
大吉
五鬼方
大凶
西
六殺方
中凶
禍害方
小凶
北
生気方
最大吉
絶命方
最大凶
東
延年方
中吉
伏位方
小吉
ローソク
candle
WITH THE WEAKER GOBLINS, THE CANDLE WAS PLACED IN A MORE FAVORABLE DIRECTION. THIS GAVE THEM ENOUGH POWER TO BECOME VISIBLE.
春華の場合の吉凶方位盤
The Fortune Compass for Haruka
I'M UPSET YOU MADE YOUR OWN GOBLINS GO THROUGH SOMETHING LIKE THIS.
NOW, WHAT ARE WE GONNA DO WITH YOU?

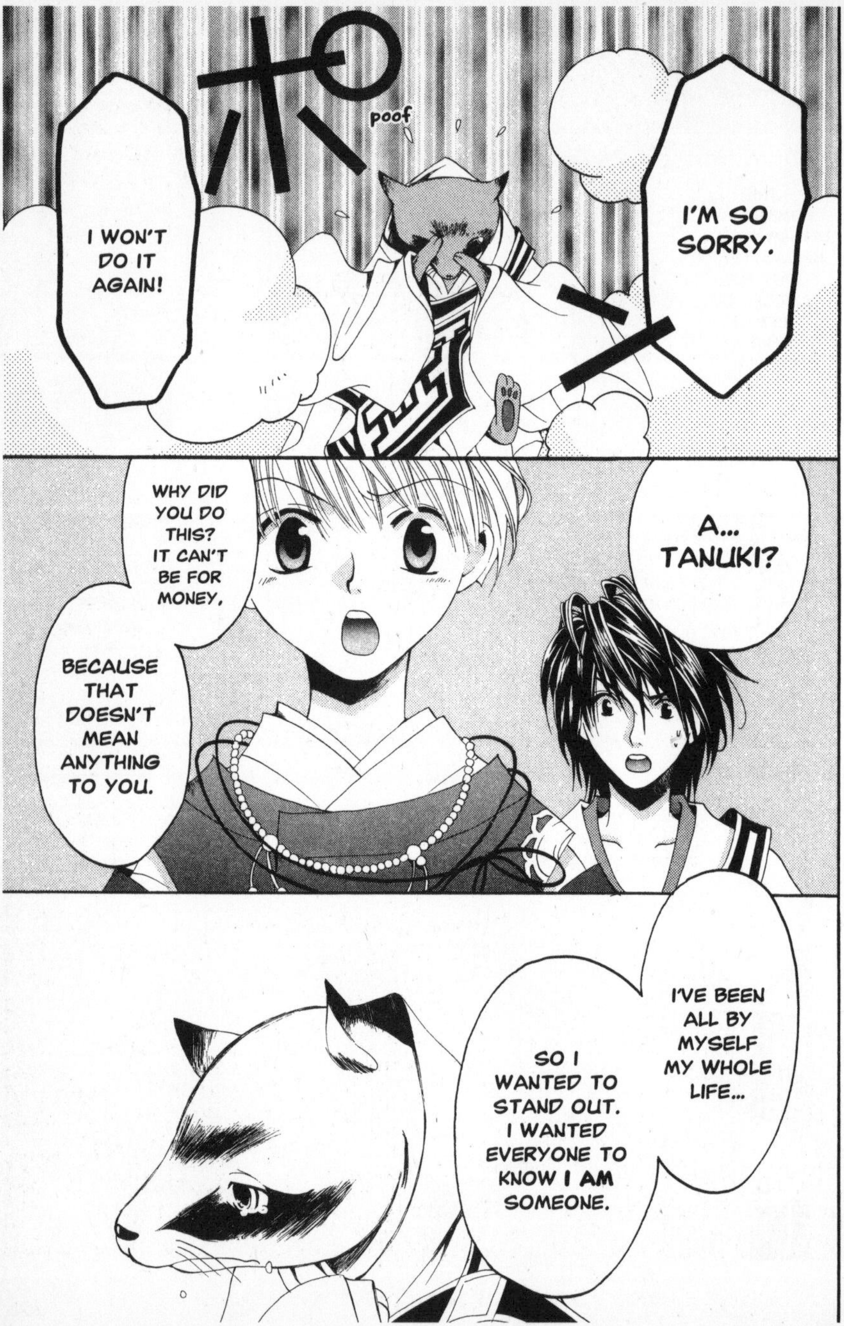
I'M SO SORRY.
poof
I WON'T DO IT AGAIN!
A... TANUKI?
WHY DID YOU DO THIS? IT CAN'T BE FOR MONEY,
BECAUSE THAT DOESN'T MEAN ANYTHING TO YOU.
I'VE BEEN ALL BY MYSELF MY WHOLE LIFE...
SO I WANTED TO STAND OUT. I WANTED EVERYONE TO KNOW I AM SOMEONE.

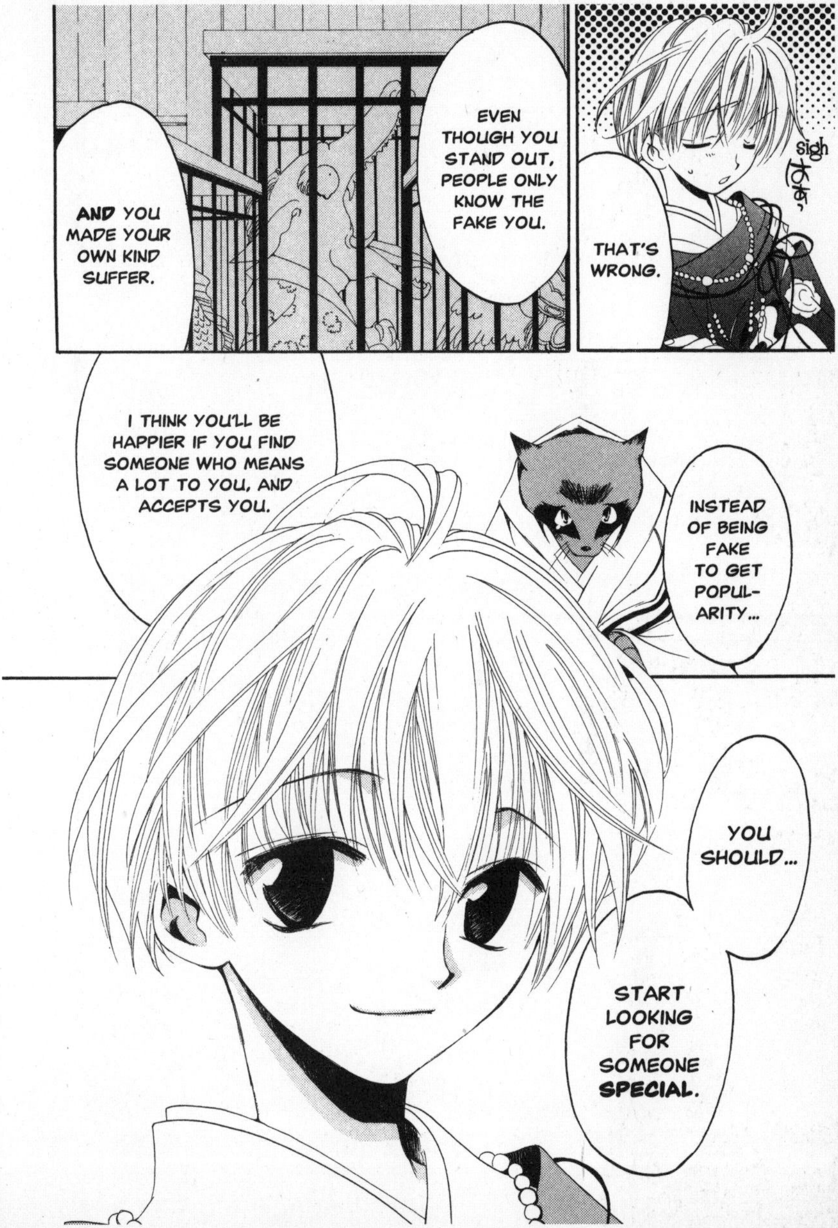
sigh
THAT'S WRONG.
EVEN THOUGH YOU STAND OUT, PEOPLE ONLY KNOW THE FAKE YOU.
AND YOU MADE YOUR OWN KIND SUFFER.
INSTEAD OF BEING FAKE TO GET POPUL- ARITY...
I THINK YOU'LL BE HAPPIER IF YOU FIND SOMEONE WHO MEANS A LOT TO YOU, AND ACCEPTS YOU.
YOU SHOULD...
START LOOKING FOR SOMEONE SPECIAL.

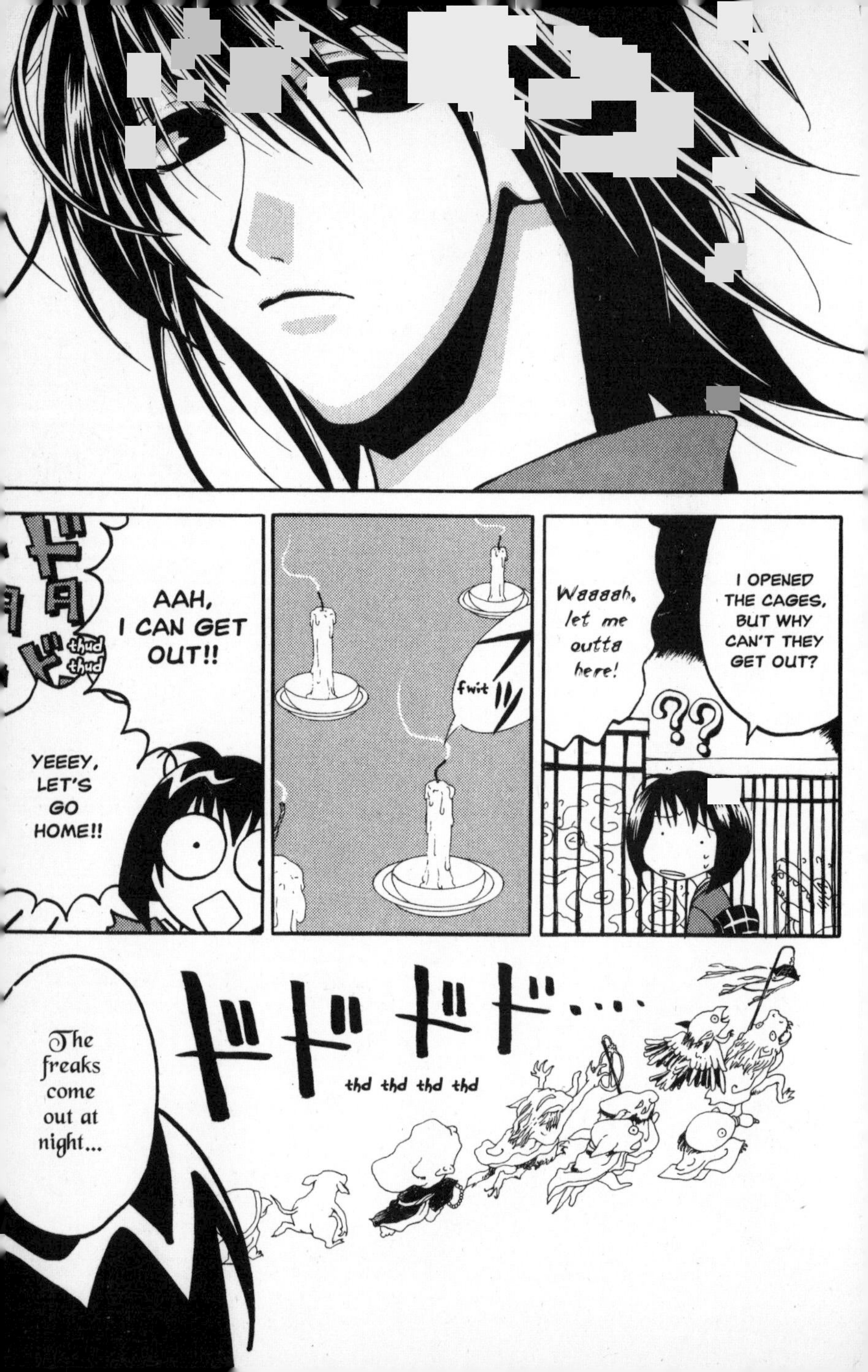
I OPENED THE CAGES, BUT WHY CAN'T THEY GET OUT?
Waaaah, let me outta here!
fwit
AAH, I CAN GET OUT!!
thud thud
YEEEY, LET'S GO HOME!!
ドドドド…
thd thd thd thd
The freaks come out at night...

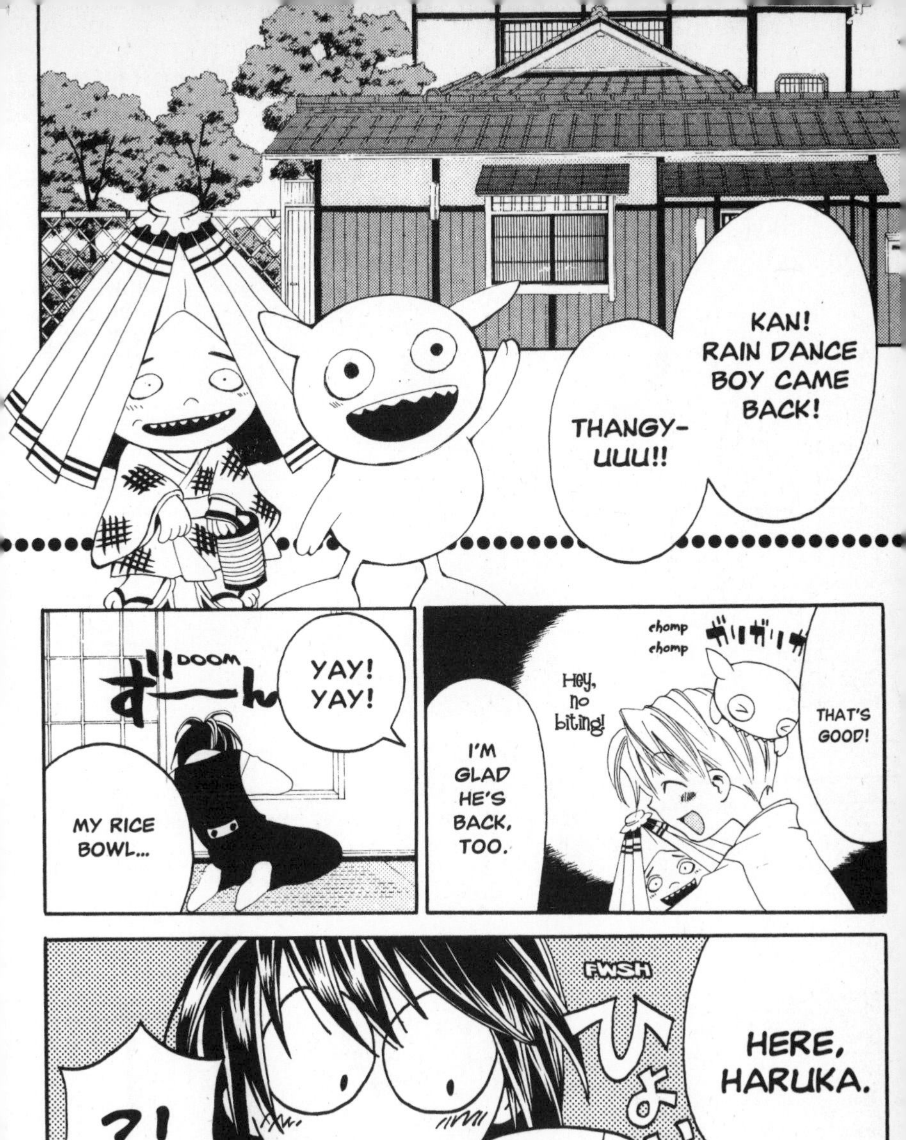
KAN! RAIN DANCE BOY CAME BACK!
THANGY-UUU!!
chomp chomp
ガジガジ
THAT'S GOOD!
Hey, no biting!
I'M GLAD HE'S BACK, TOO.
YAY! YAY!
ずーん
DOOM
MY RICE BOWL...
FWSH
ひょい
HERE, HARUKA.
?!

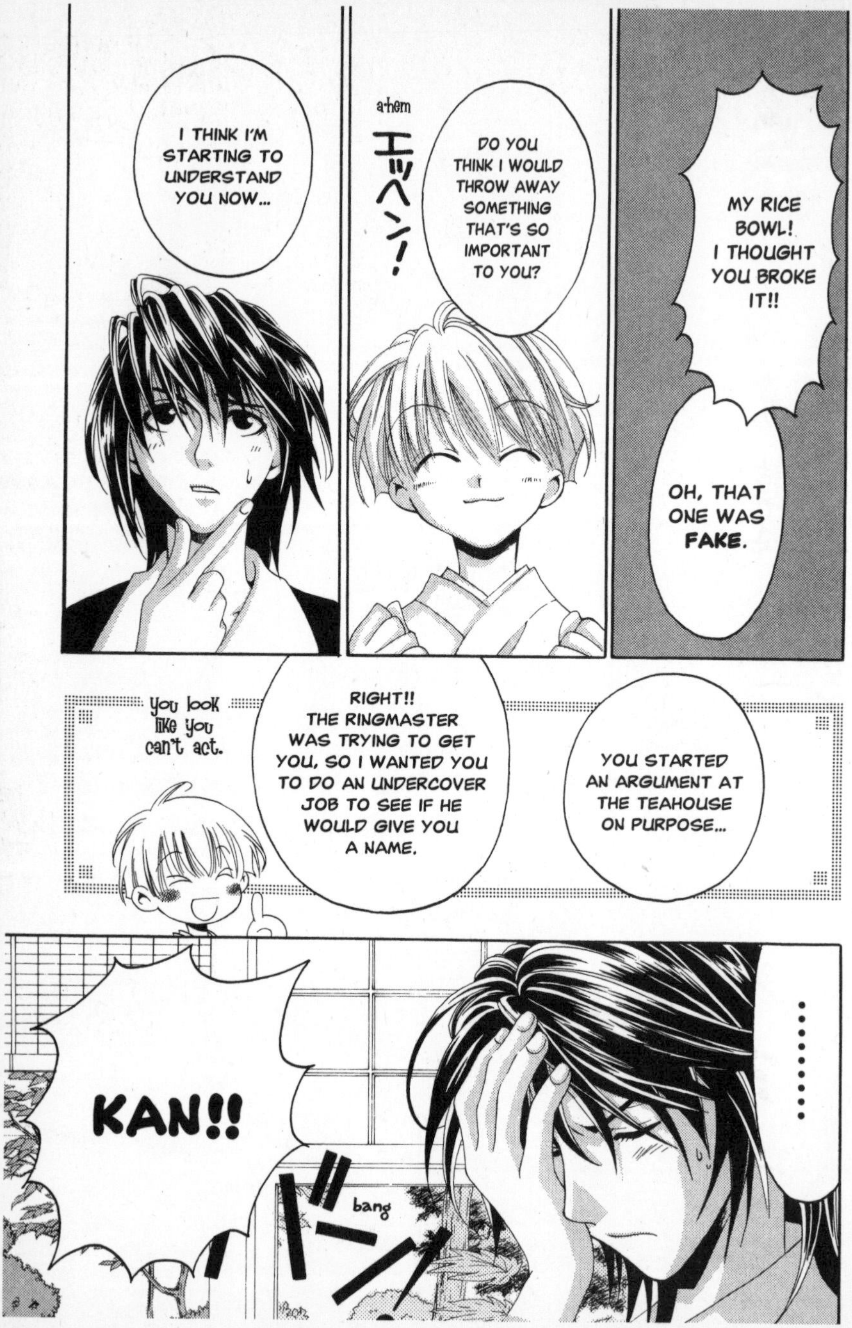
MY RICE BOWL! I THOUGHT YOU BROKE IT!!
OH, THAT ONE WAS **FAKE.**
a-hem
エッヘン!
DO YOU THINK I WOULD THROW AWAY SOMETHING THAT'S SO IMPORTANT TO YOU?
I THINK I'M STARTING TO UNDERSTAND YOU NOW...
YOU STARTED AN ARGUMENT AT THE TEAHOUSE ON PURPOSE...
RIGHT!! THE RINGMASTER WAS TRYING TO GET YOU, SO I WANTED YOU TO DO AN UNDERCOVER JOB TO SEE IF HE WOULD GIVE YOU A NAME.
You look like you can't act.
......
KAN!!
bang

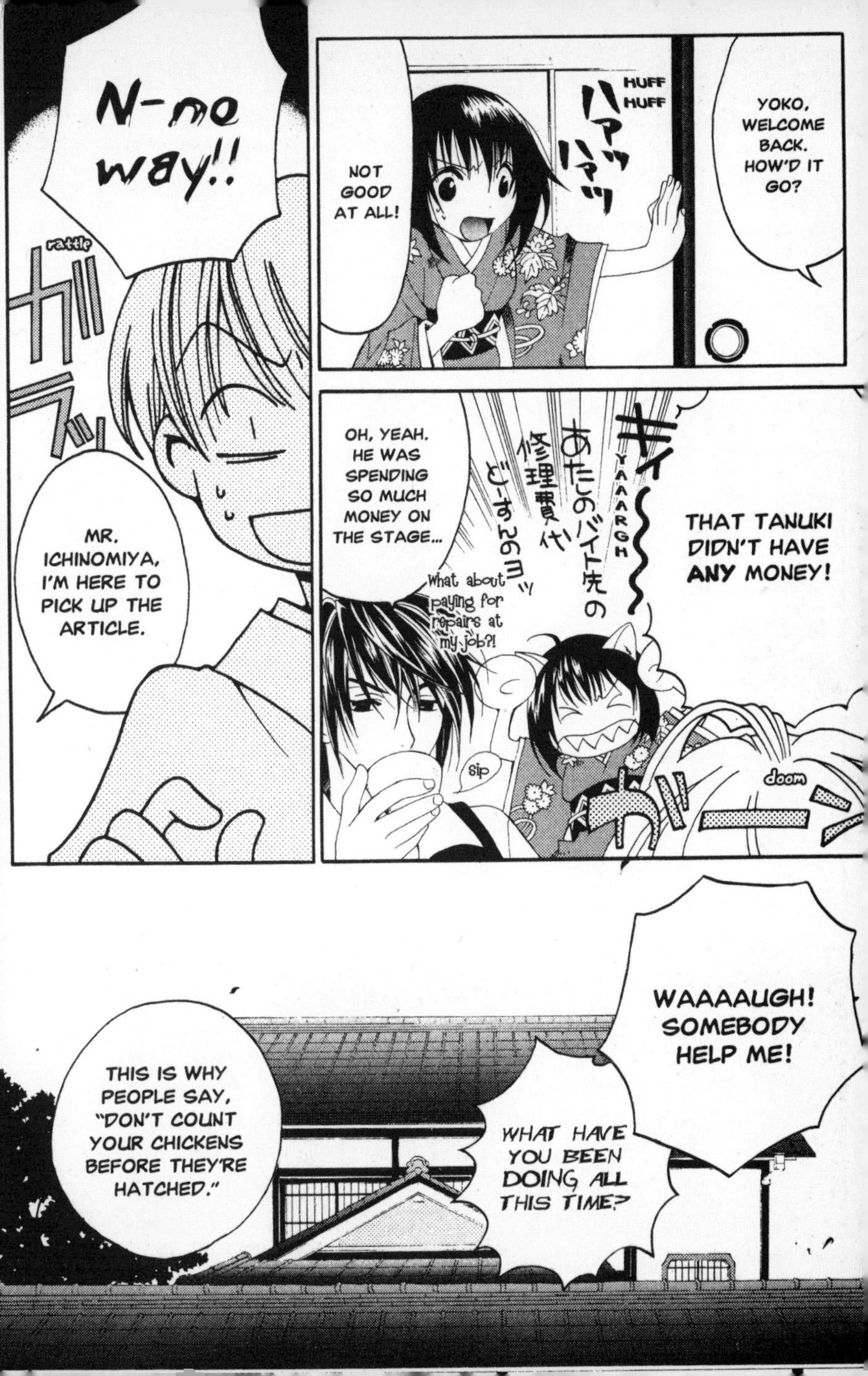
YOKO, WELCOME BACK. HOW'D IT GO?
ハァッ ハァッ
HUFF HUFF
NOT GOOD AT ALL!
THAT TANUKI DIDN'T HAVE ANY MONEY!
キィ〜
YAAAARGH
あたしのバイト先の修理費代どーすんのヨッ
What about paying for repairs at my job?!
OH, YEAH. HE WAS SPENDING SO MUCH MONEY ON THE STAGE...
sip
doom
N-no way!!
rattle
MR. ICHINOMIYA, I'M HERE TO PICK UP THE ARTICLE.
WAAAAUGH! SOMEBODY HELP ME!
WHAT HAVE YOU BEEN DOING ALL THIS TIME?
THIS IS WHY PEOPLE SAY, "DON'T COUNT YOUR CHICKENS BEFORE THEY'RE HATCHED."

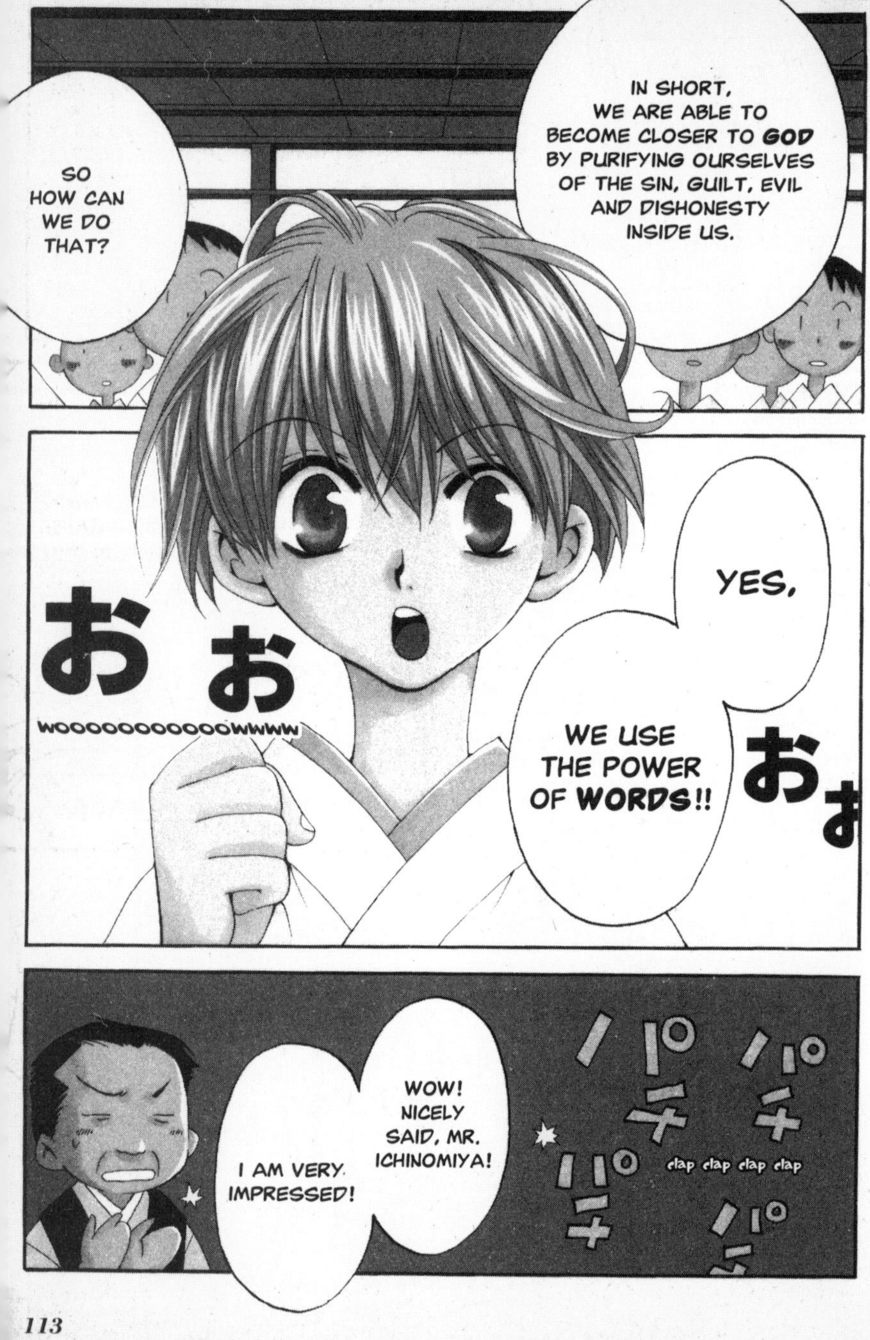
IN SHORT, WE ARE ABLE TO BECOME CLOSER TO GOD BY PURIFYING OURSELVES OF THE SIN, GUILT, EVIL AND DISHONESTY INSIDE US.
SO HOW CAN WE DO THAT?
YES,
WE USE THE POWER OF WORDS!!
おぉ
おぉ
WOOOOOOOOOOOWWWW
パチパチパチパチ
clap clap clap clap
WOW! NICELY SAID, MR. ICHINOMIYA!
I AM VERY IMPRESSED!

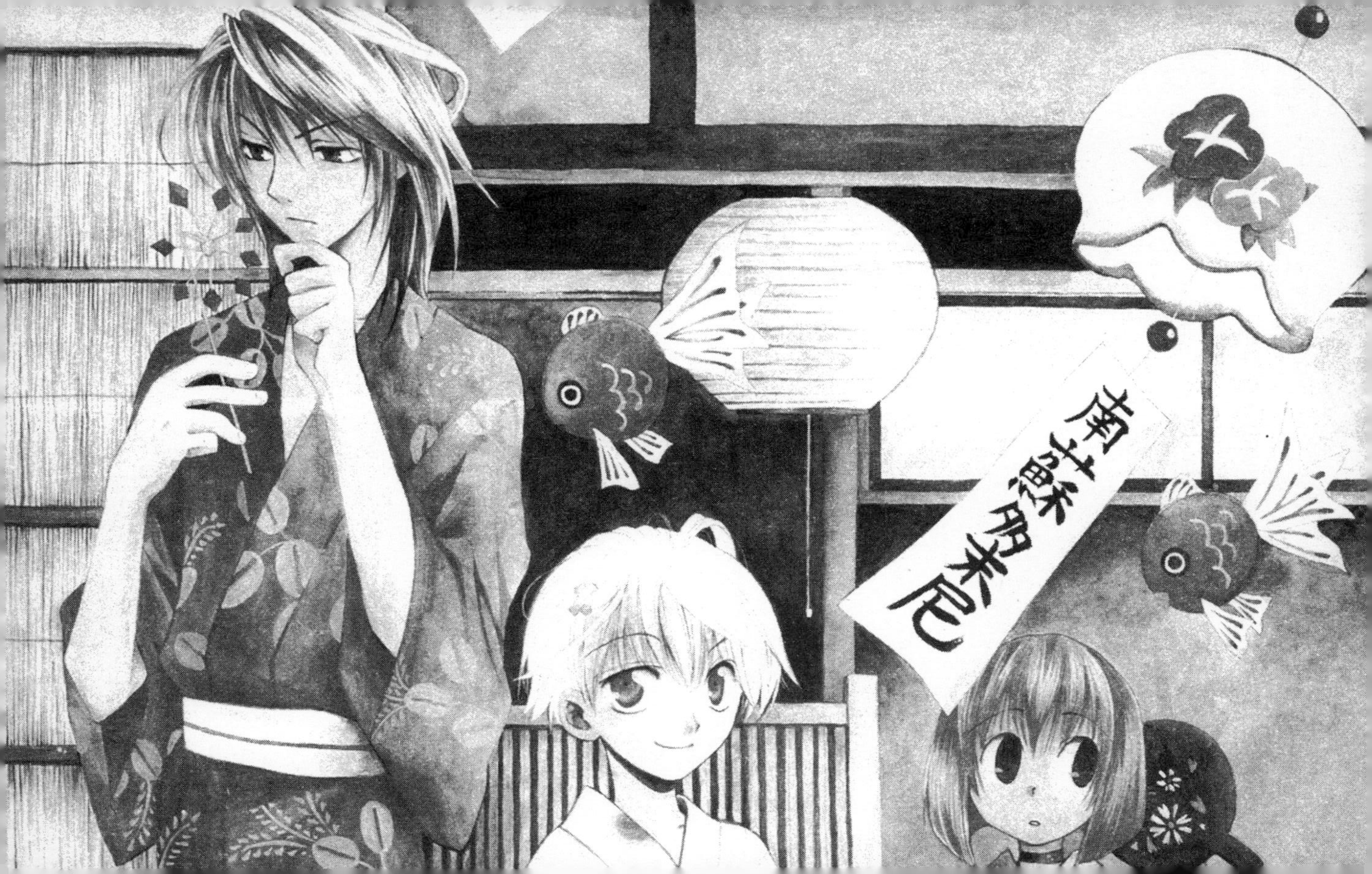

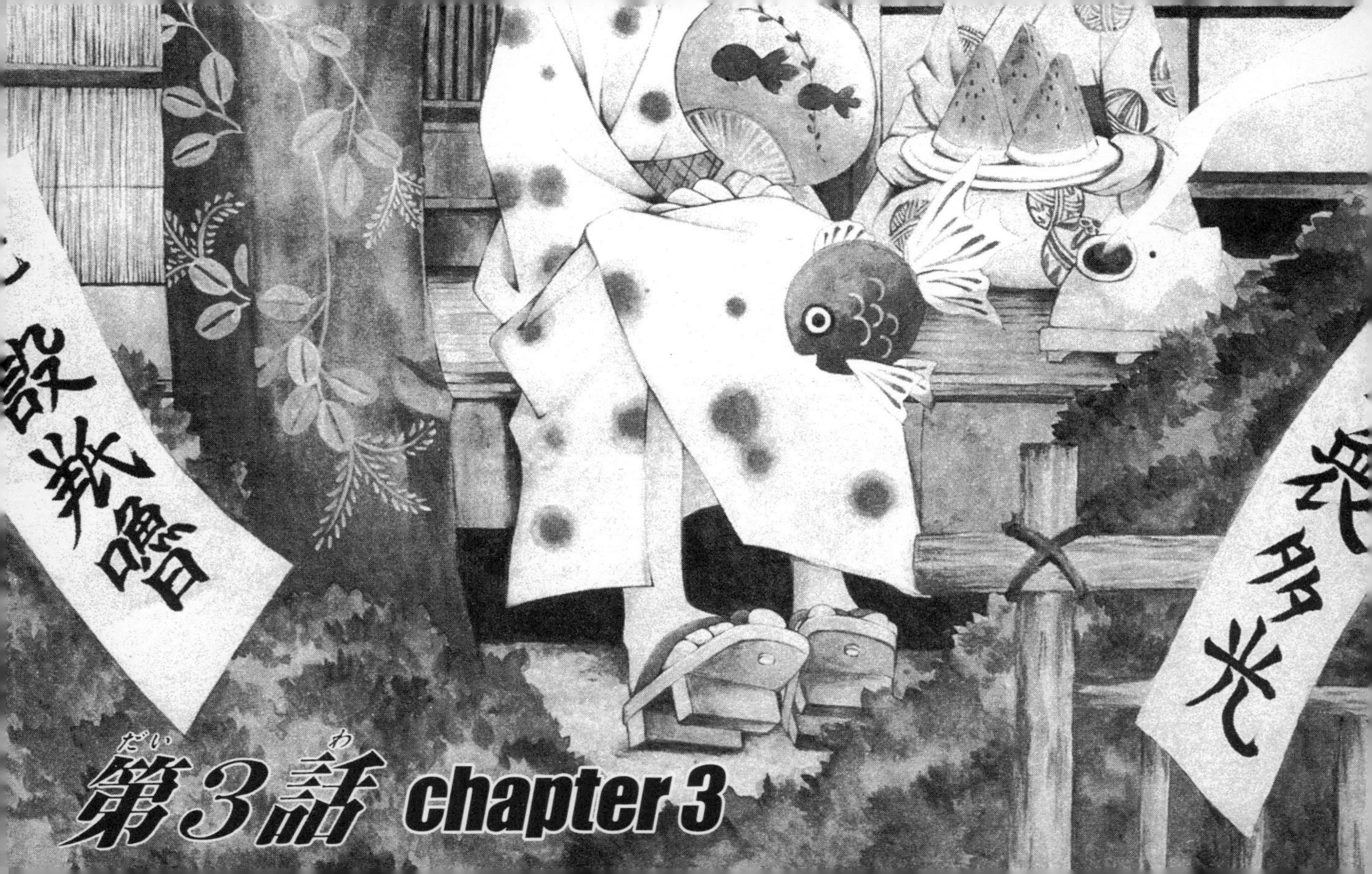
第3話（だいわ） chapter 3

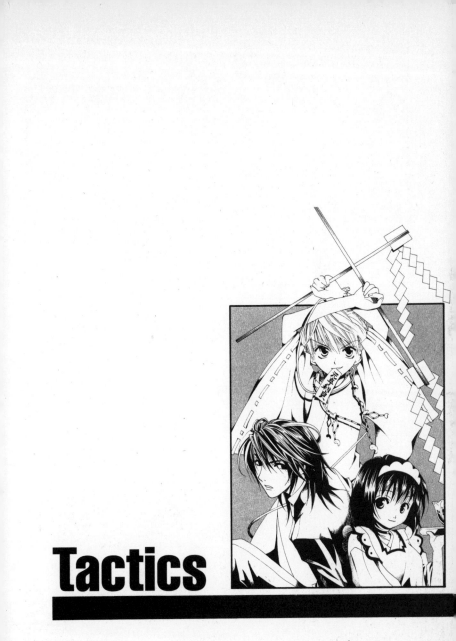

Tactics

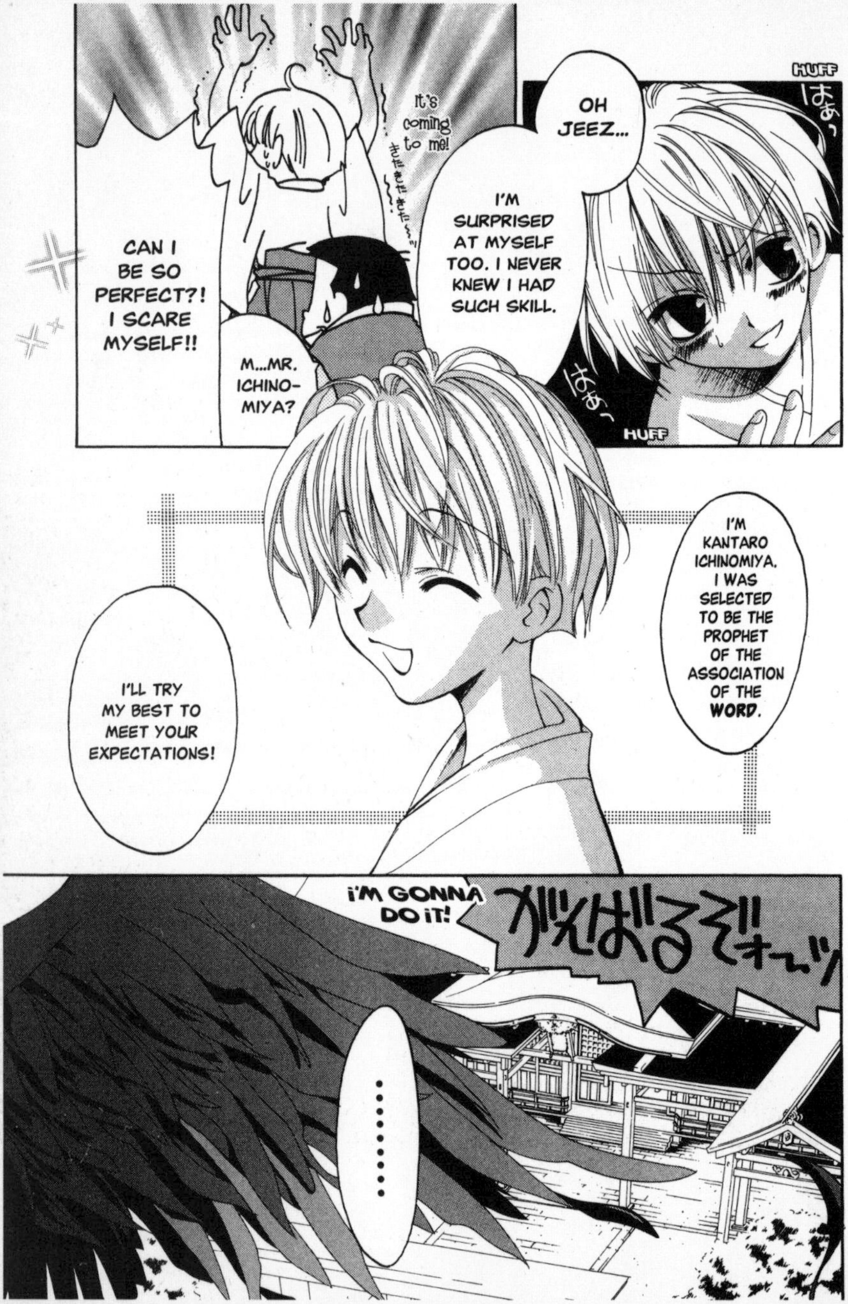
HUFF
はぁっ
OH JEEZ...
I'M SURPRISED AT MYSELF TOO. I NEVER KNEW I HAD SUCH SKILL.
はぁっ
HUFF
It's coming to me!
CAN I BE SO PERFECT?! I SCARE MYSELF!!
M...MR. ICHINOMIYA?
I'M KANTARO ICHINOMIYA. I WAS SELECTED TO BE THE PROPHET OF THE ASSOCIATION OF THE WORD.
I'LL TRY MY BEST TO MEET YOUR EXPECTATIONS!
I'M GONNA DO IT!
がんばるぞォーッ
....

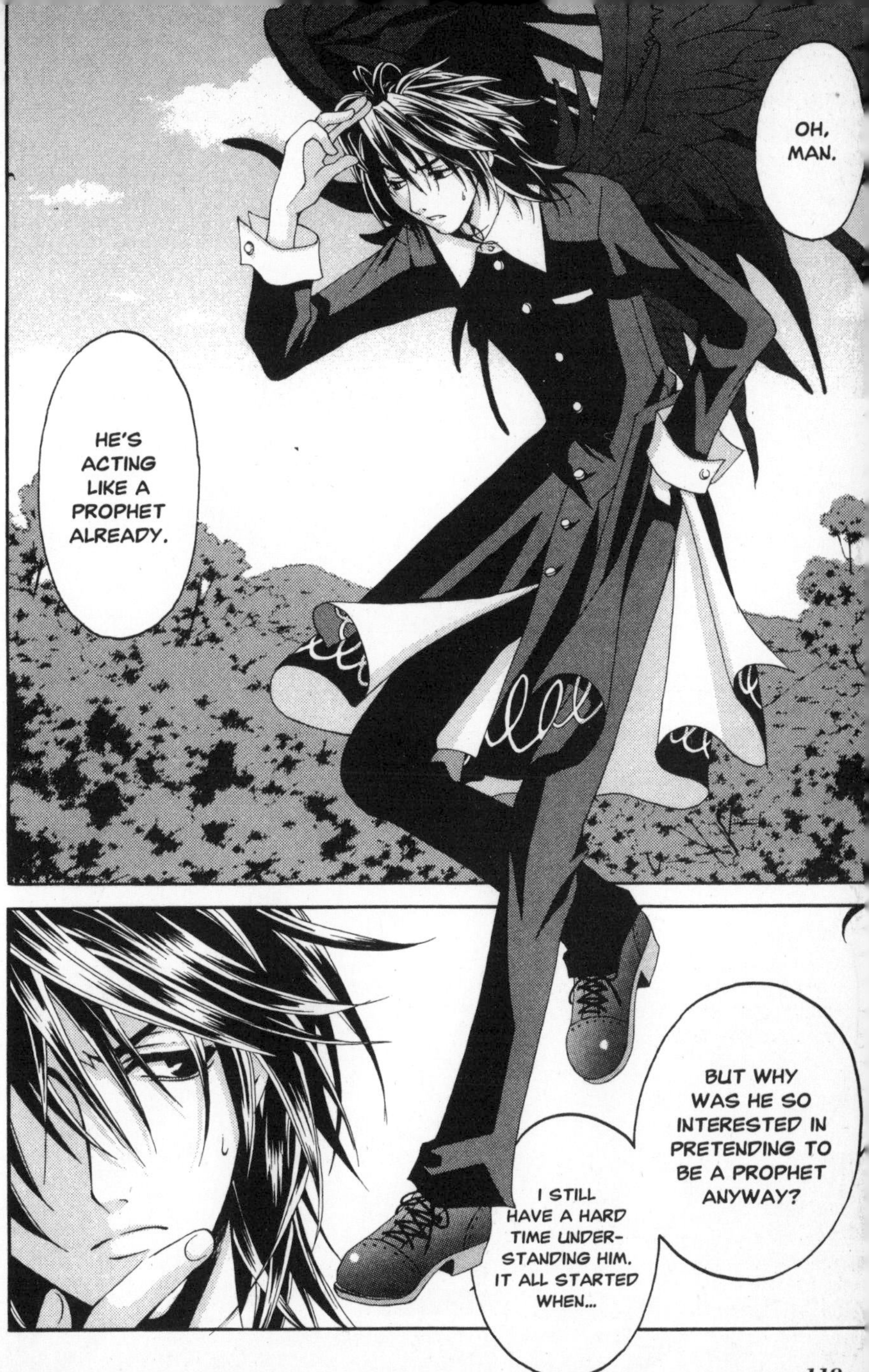
OH, MAN.
HE'S ACTING LIKE A PROPHET ALREADY.
BUT WHY WAS HE SO INTERESTED IN PRETENDING TO BE A PROPHET ANYWAY?
I STILL HAVE A HARD TIME UNDER-STANDING HIM. IT ALL STARTED WHEN...

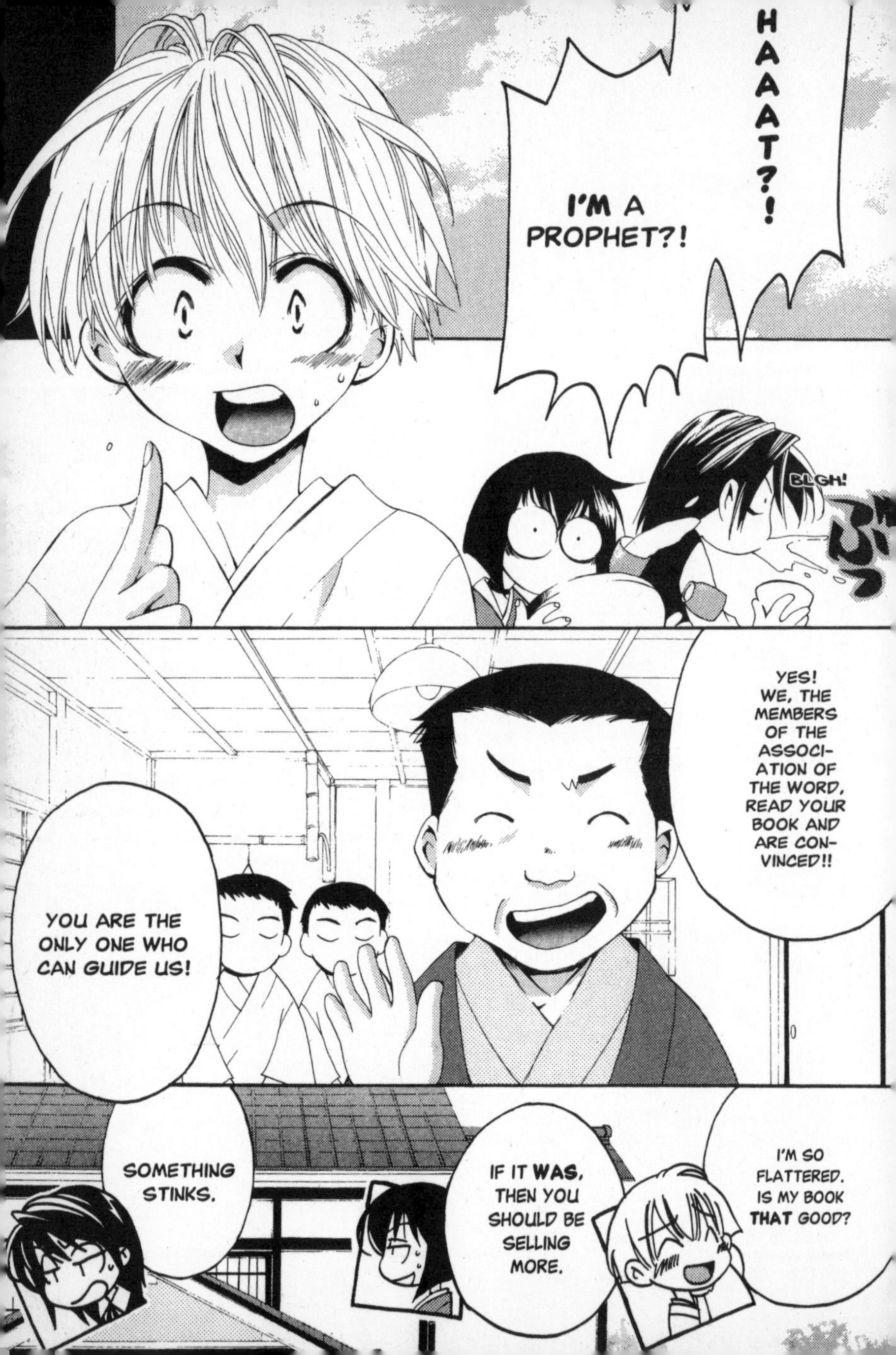
HAAAT?!
I'M A PROPHET?!
BLGH!
YES! WE, THE MEMBERS OF THE ASSOCI-ATION OF THE WORD, READ YOUR BOOK AND ARE CON-VINCED!!
YOU ARE THE ONLY ONE WHO CAN GUIDE US!
I'M SO FLATTERED. IS MY BOOK THAT GOOD?
IF IT WAS, THEN YOU SHOULD BE SELLING MORE.
SOMETHING STINKS.

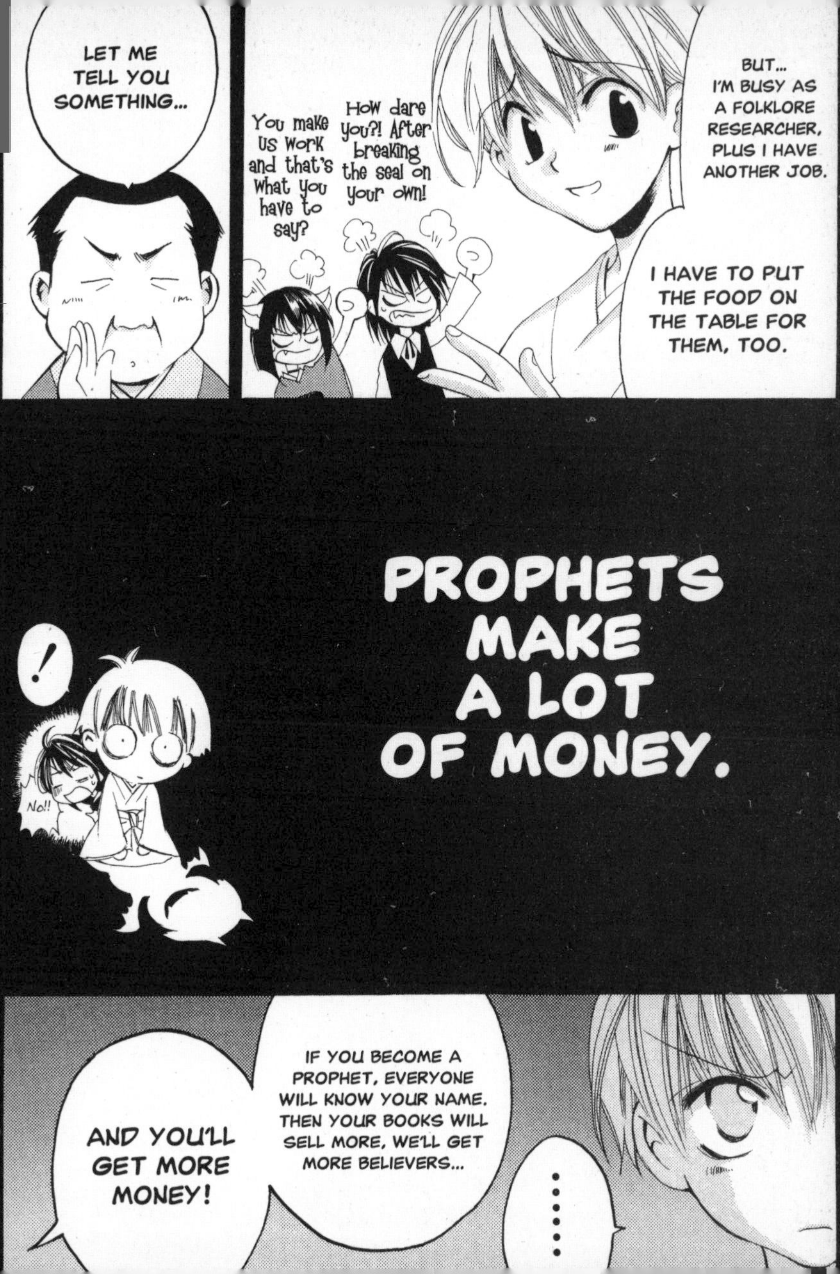
BUT... I'M BUSY AS A FOLKLORE RESEARCHER, PLUS I HAVE ANOTHER JOB.
I HAVE TO PUT THE FOOD ON THE TABLE FOR THEM, TOO.
How dare you?! After breaking the seal on your own!
You make us work and that's what you have to say?
LET ME TELL YOU SOMETHING...
PROPHETS MAKE A LOT OF MONEY.
!
No!!
......
IF YOU BECOME A PROPHET, EVERYONE WILL KNOW YOUR NAME. THEN YOUR BOOKS WILL SELL MORE, WE'LL GET MORE BELIEVERS...
AND YOU'LL GET MORE MONEY!

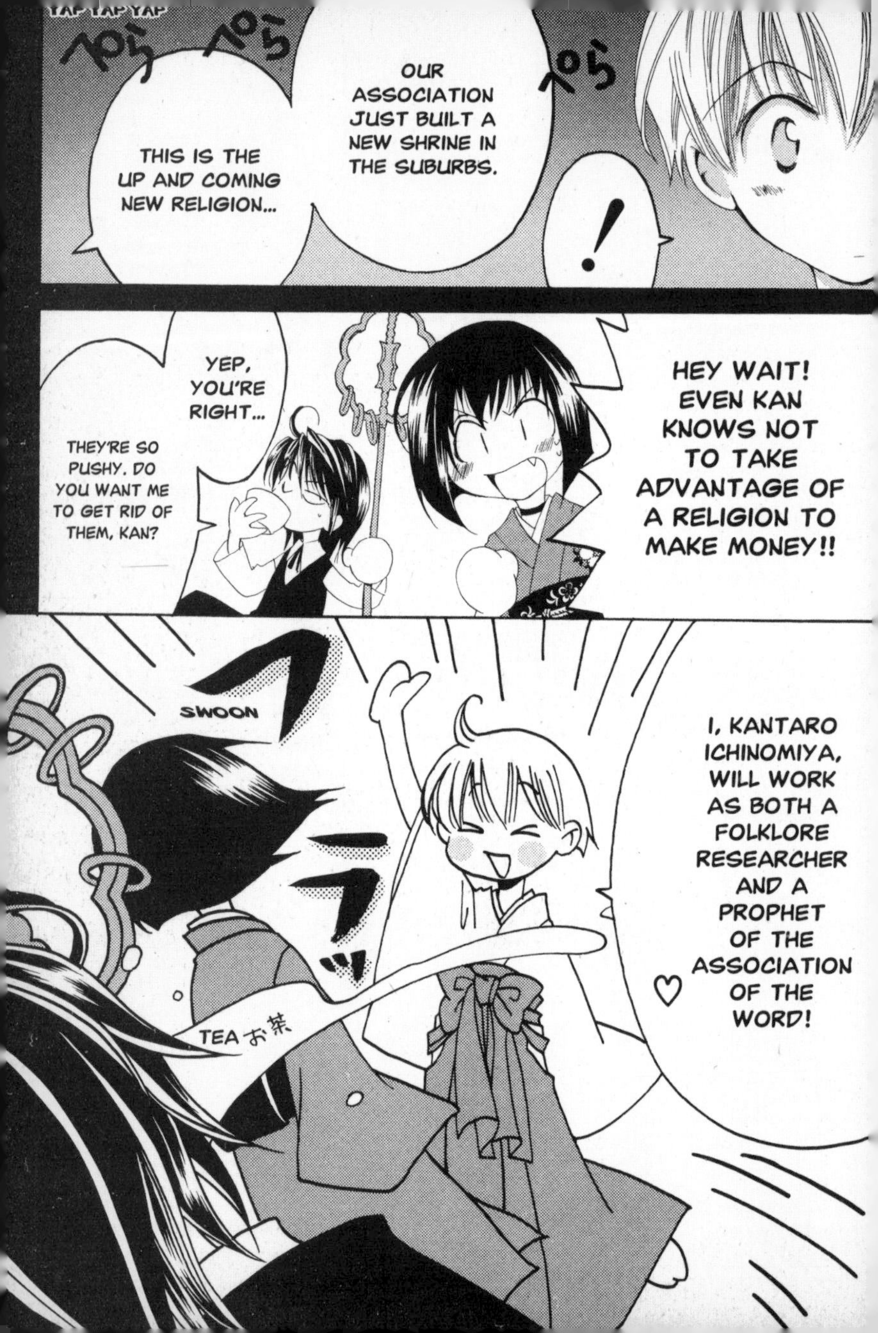
!
ぺら
OUR ASSOCIATION JUST BUILT A NEW SHRINE IN THE SUBURBS.
THIS IS THE UP AND COMING NEW RELIGION...
ぺら ぺら
YAP YAP YAP
HEY WAIT! EVEN KAN KNOWS NOT TO TAKE ADVANTAGE OF A RELIGION TO MAKE MONEY!!
YEP, YOU'RE RIGHT...
THEY'RE SO PUSHY. DO YOU WANT ME TO GET RID OF THEM, KAN?
I, KANTARO ICHINOMIYA, WILL WORK AS BOTH A FOLKLORE RESEARCHER AND A PROPHET OF THE ASSOCIATION OF THE WORD!
♡
SWOON
TEA お茶

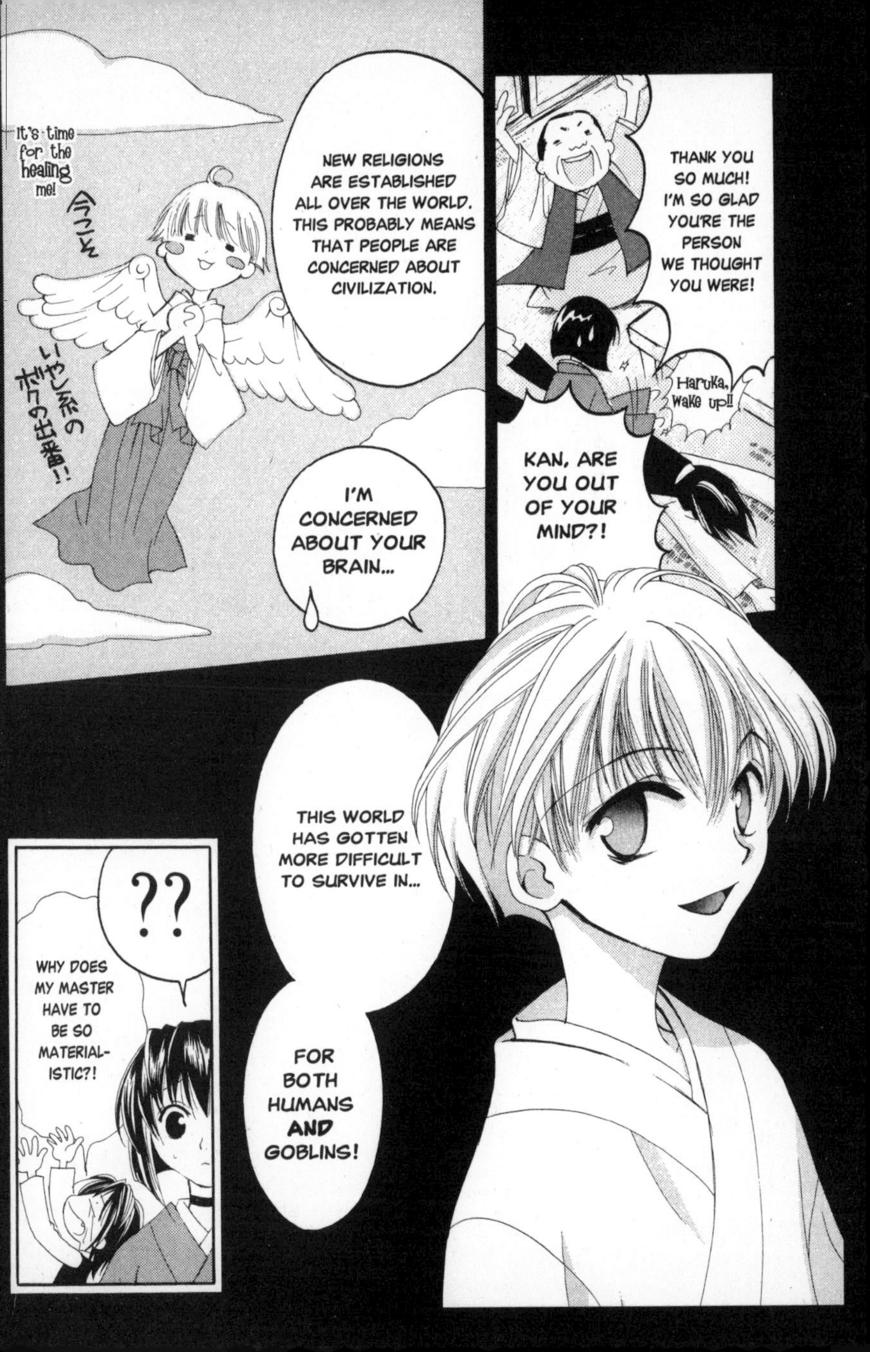
THANK YOU SO MUCH! I'M SO GLAD YOU'RE THE PERSON WE THOUGHT YOU WERE!
Haruka, Wake up!!
KAN, ARE YOU OUT OF YOUR MIND?!
NEW RELIGIONS ARE ESTABLISHED ALL OVER THE WORLD. THIS PROBABLY MEANS THAT PEOPLE ARE CONCERNED ABOUT CIVILIZATION.
It's time for the healing me!
今こそいやし系のボクの出番!!
I'M CONCERNED ABOUT YOUR BRAIN...
THIS WORLD HAS GOTTEN MORE DIFFICULT TO SURVIVE IN...
FOR BOTH HUMANS AND GOBLINS!
??
WHY DOES MY MASTER HAVE TO BE SO MATERIAL-ISTIC?!

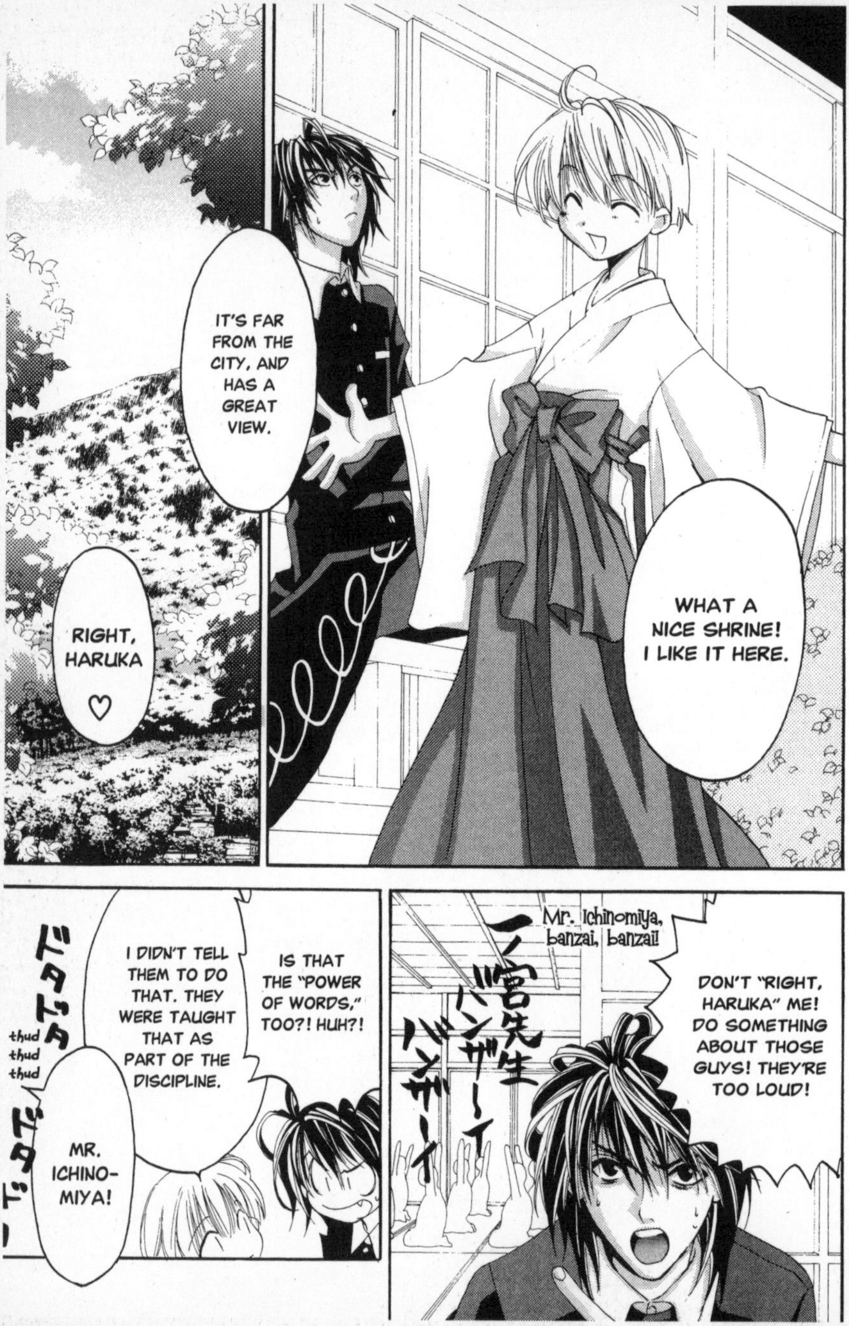
WHAT A NICE SHRINE! I LIKE IT HERE.
IT'S FAR FROM THE CITY, AND HAS A GREAT VIEW.
RIGHT, HARUKA ♡
Mr. Ichinomiya, banzai, banzai!
一ノ宮先生バンザーイバンザーイ
DON'T "RIGHT, HARUKA" ME! DO SOMETHING ABOUT THOSE GUYS! THEY'RE TOO LOUD!
IS THAT THE "POWER OF WORDS," TOO?! HUH?!
I DIDN'T TELL THEM TO DO THAT. THEY WERE TAUGHT THAT AS PART OF THE DISCIPLINE.
thud thud thud
MR. ICHINOMIYA!

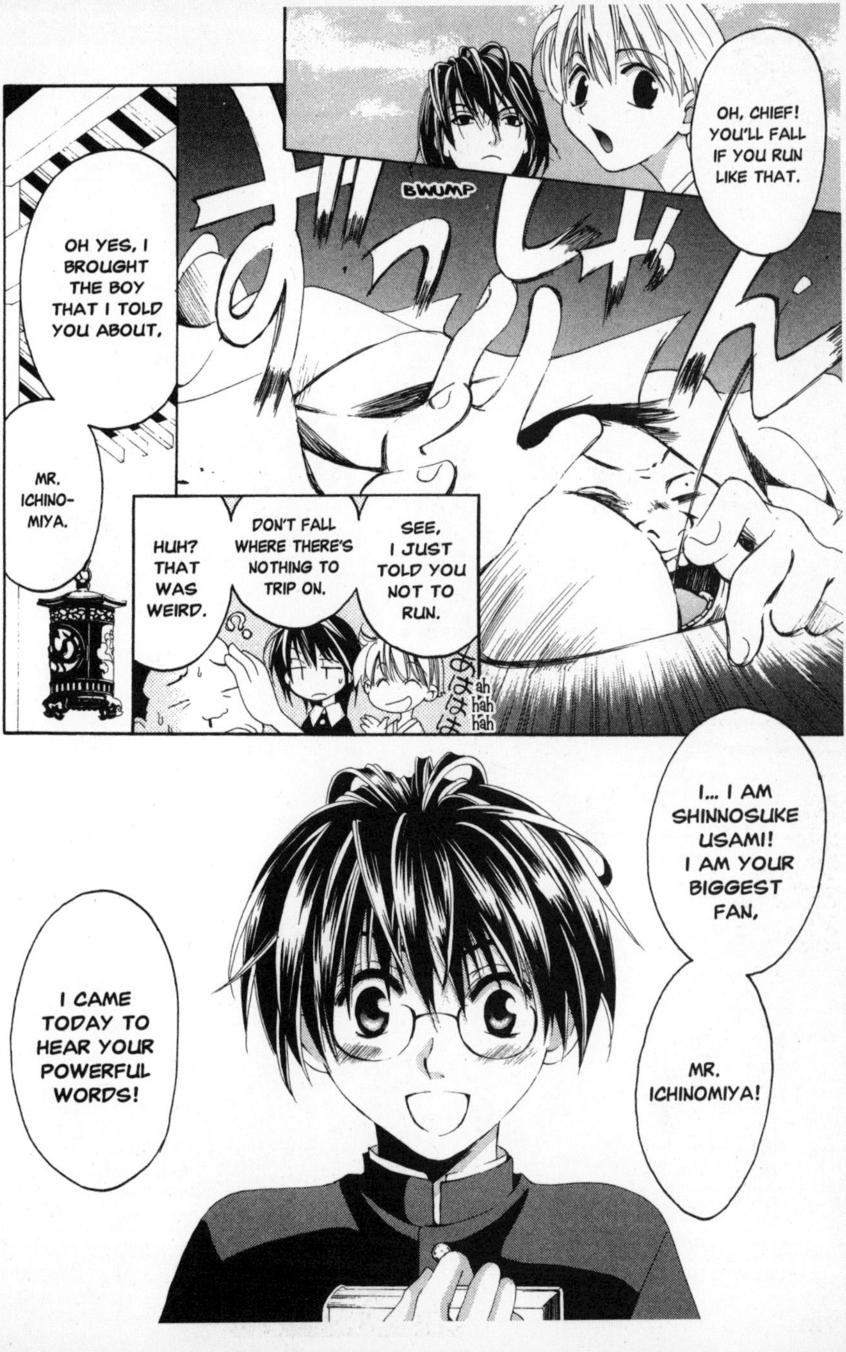
OH, CHIEF! YOU'LL FALL IF YOU RUN LIKE THAT.
BWUMP
SEE, I JUST TOLD YOU NOT TO RUN.
DON'T FALL WHERE THERE'S NOTHING TO TRIP ON.
HUH? THAT WAS WEIRD.
ah hah hah
OH YES, I BROUGHT THE BOY THAT I TOLD YOU ABOUT,
MR. ICHINO-MIYA.
I... I AM SHINNOSUKE USAMI! I AM YOUR BIGGEST FAN,
MR. ICHINOMIYA!
I CAME TODAY TO HEAR YOUR POWERFUL WORDS!

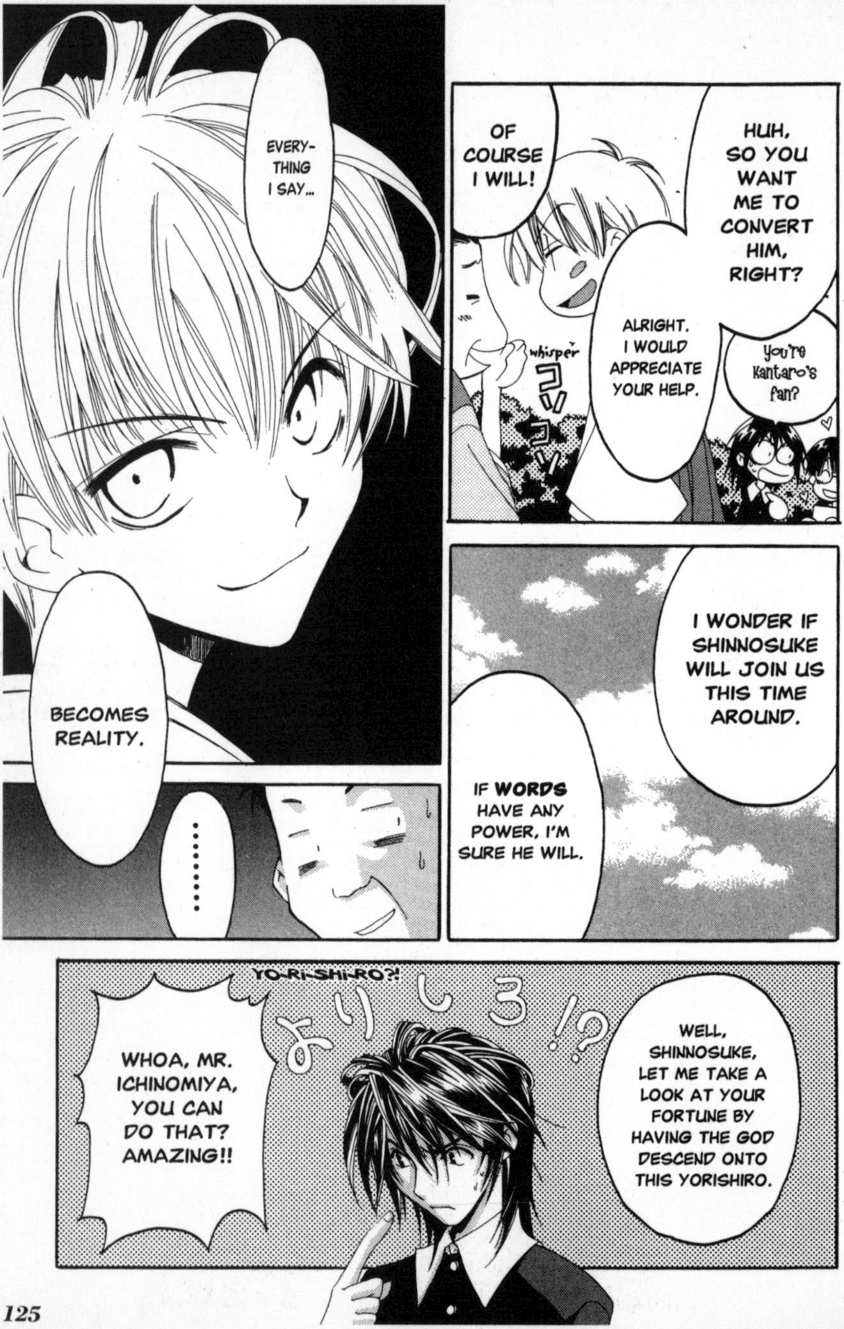
HUH, SO YOU WANT ME TO CONVERT HIM, RIGHT?
OF COURSE I WILL!
You're Kantaro's fan?
ALRIGHT. I WOULD APPRECIATE YOUR HELP.
whisper
コソコソ
I WONDER IF SHINNOSUKE WILL JOIN US THIS TIME AROUND.
IF **WORDS** HAVE ANY POWER, I'M SURE HE WILL.
EVERY-THING I SAY...
BECOMES REALITY.
....
WELL, SHINNOSUKE, LET ME TAKE A LOOK AT YOUR FORTUNE BY HAVING THE GOD DESCEND ONTO THIS YORISHIRO.
YO-RI-SHI-RO?!
よりしろ!?
WHOA, MR. ICHINOMIYA, YOU CAN DO THAT? AMAZING!!

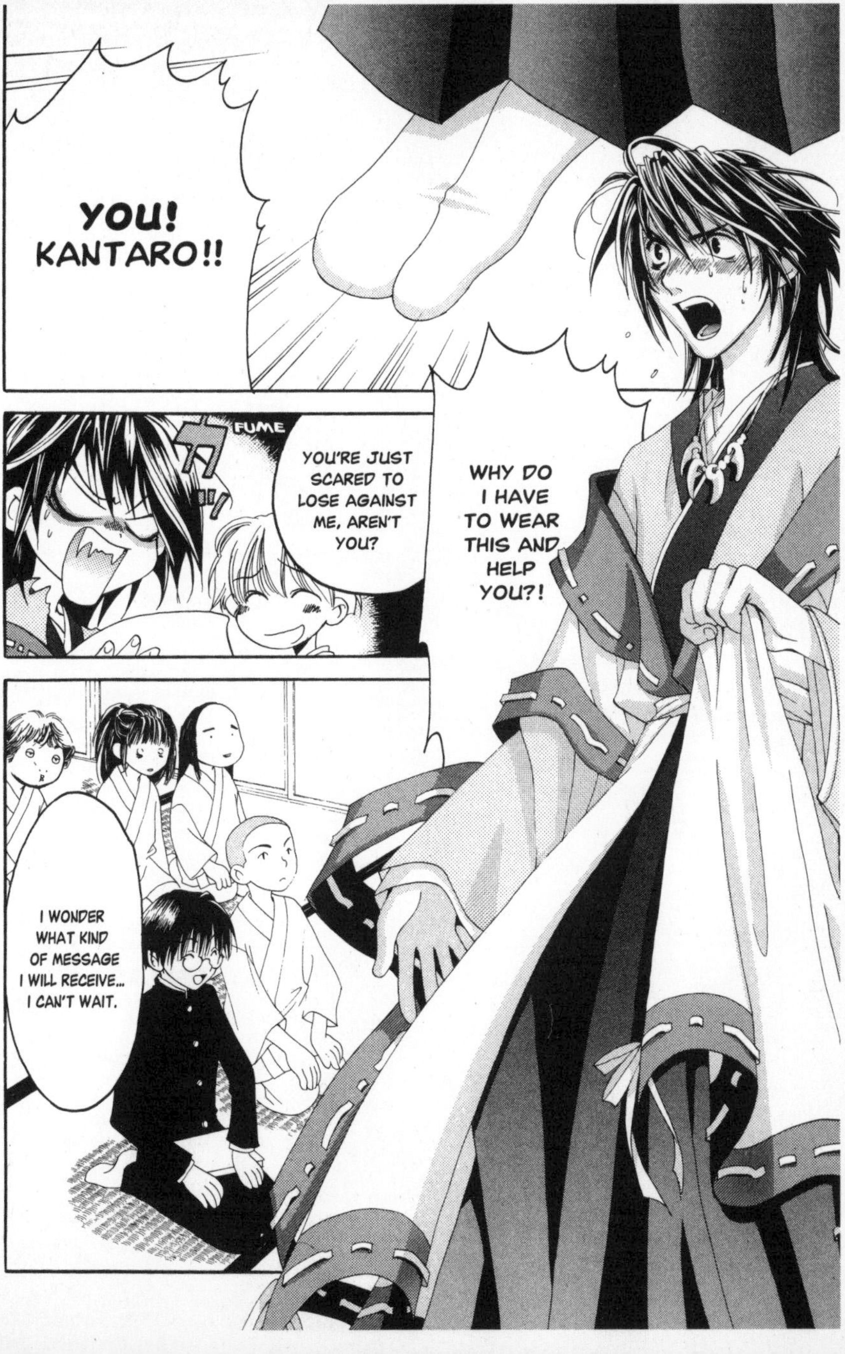
YOU! KANTARO!!
WHY DO I HAVE TO WEAR THIS AND HELP YOU?!
FUME
YOU'RE JUST SCARED TO LOSE AGAINST ME, AREN'T YOU?
I WONDER WHAT KIND OF MESSAGE I WILL RECEIVE... I CAN'T WAIT.

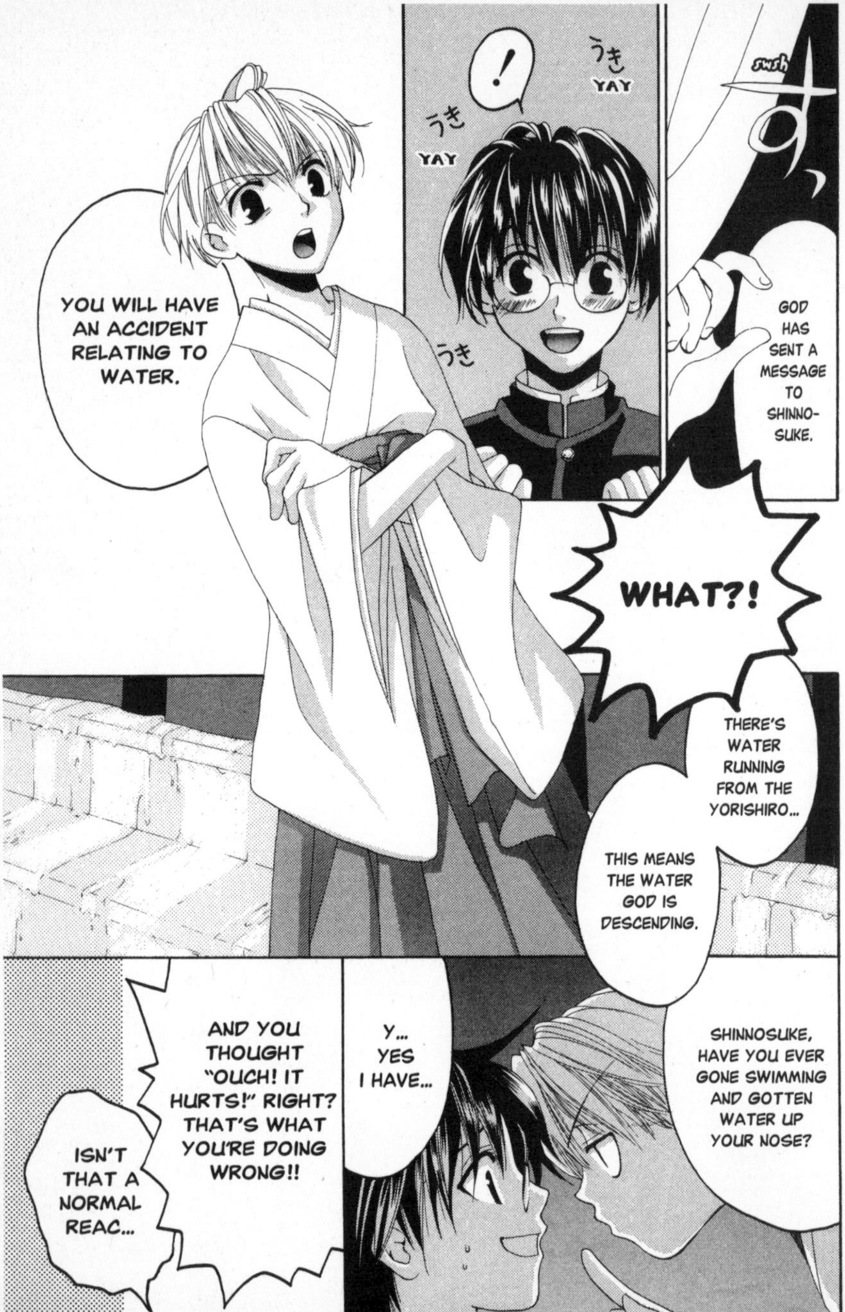
swsh
す
GOD HAS SENT A MESSAGE TO SHINNO-SUKE.
うき
YAY
!
うき
YAY
うき
YOU WILL HAVE AN ACCIDENT RELATING TO WATER.
WHAT?!
THERE'S WATER RUNNING FROM THE YORISHIRO...
THIS MEANS THE WATER GOD IS DESCENDING.
SHINNOSUKE, HAVE YOU EVER GONE SWIMMING AND GOTTEN WATER UP YOUR NOSE?
Y... YES I HAVE...
AND YOU THOUGHT "OUCH! IT HURTS!" RIGHT? THAT'S WHAT YOU'RE DOING WRONG!!
ISN'T THAT A NORMAL REAC...

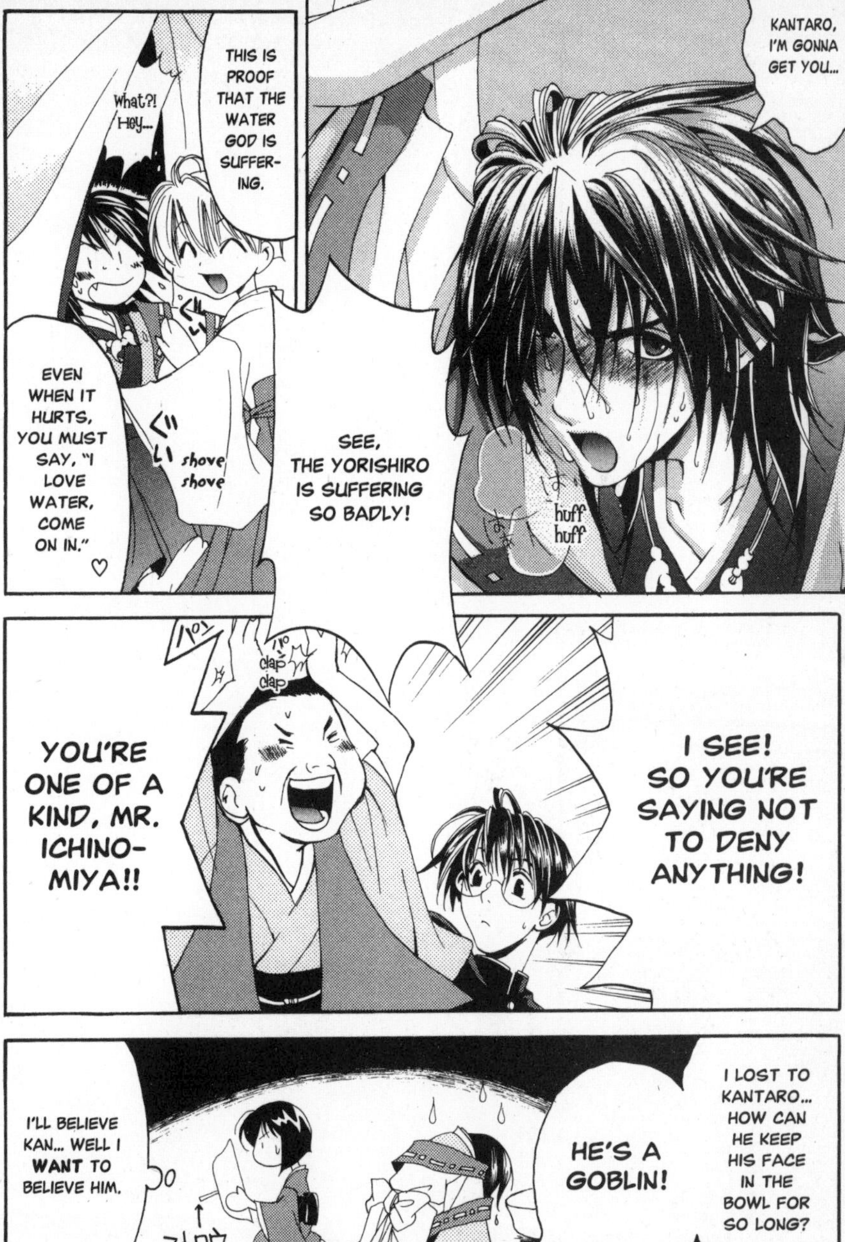
KANTARO, I'M GONNA GET YOU...
huff huff
THIS IS PROOF THAT THE WATER GOD IS SUFFER-ING.
What?! Hey...
EVEN WHEN IT HURTS, YOU MUST SAY, "I LOVE WATER, COME ON IN." ♡
shove shove
SEE, THE YORISHIRO IS SUFFERING SO BADLY!
I SEE! SO YOU'RE SAYING NOT TO DENY ANYTHING!
clap clap
YOU'RE ONE OF A KIND, MR. ICHINO-MIYA!!
I LOST TO KANTARO... HOW CAN HE KEEP HIS FACE IN THE BOWL FOR SO LONG?
HE'S A GOBLIN!
I'LL BELIEVE KAN... WELL I **WANT** TO BELIEVE HIM.
ストロウ
straw

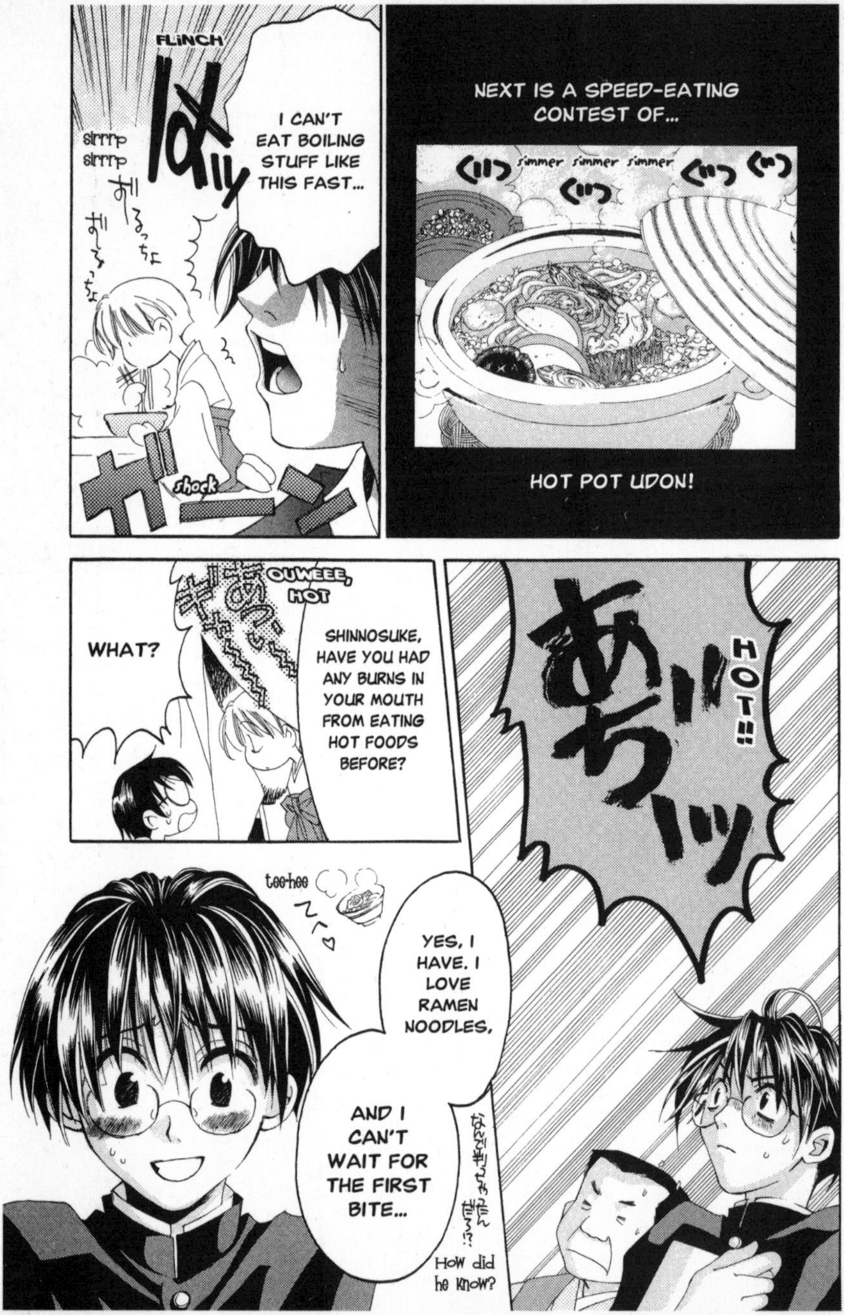
NEXT IS A SPEED-EATING CONTEST OF...
simmer simmer simmer
HOT POT UDON!
FLINCH
I CAN'T EAT BOILING STUFF LIKE THIS FAST...
sirrrp sirrrp
shock
HOT!!
OUWEEE, HOT
SHINNOSUKE, HAVE YOU HAD ANY BURNS IN YOUR MOUTH FROM EATING HOT FOODS BEFORE?
WHAT?
tee-hee
YES, I HAVE. I LOVE RAMEN NOODLES.
AND I CAN'T WAIT FOR THE FIRST BITE...
How did he know?

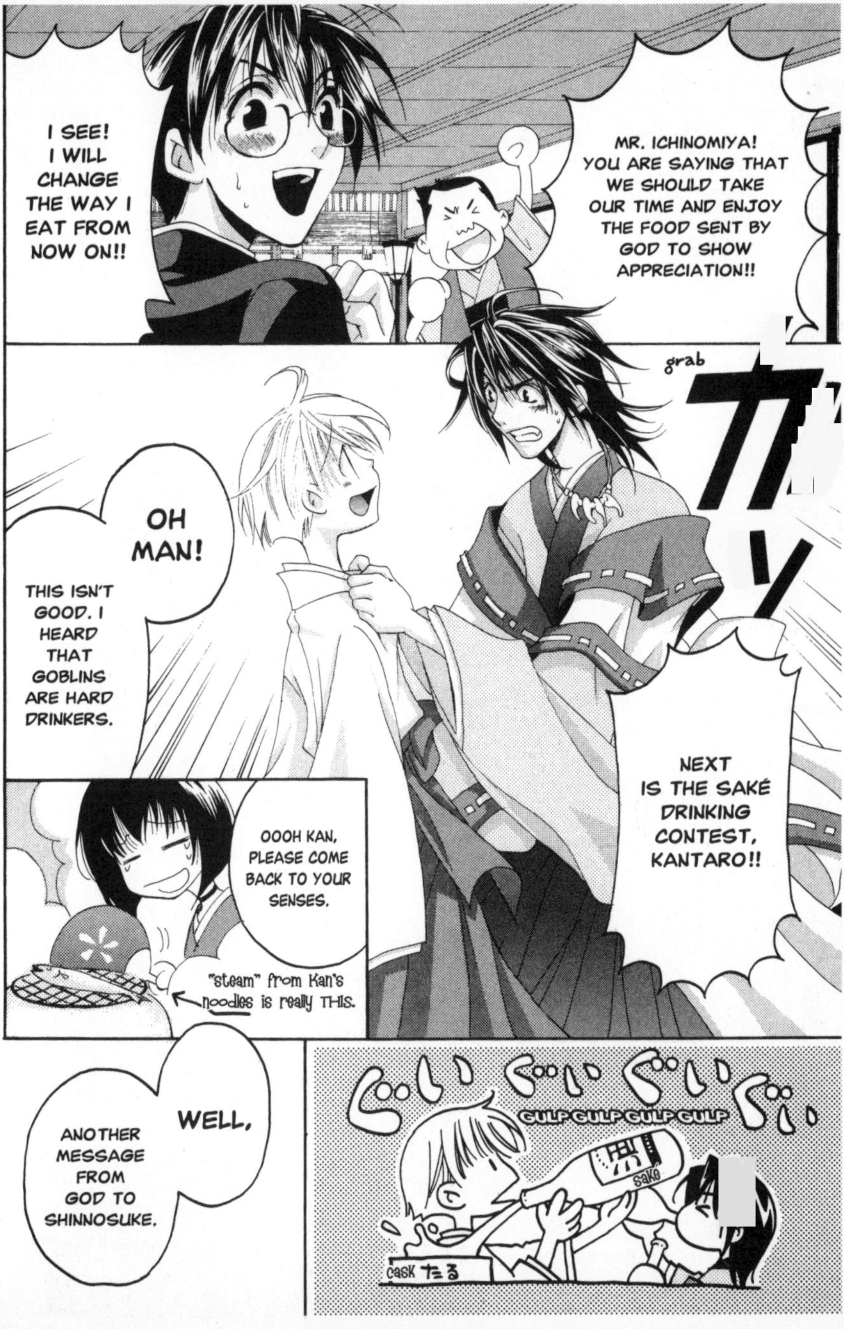
MR. ICHINOMIYA! YOU ARE SAYING THAT WE SHOULD TAKE OUR TIME AND ENJOY THE FOOD SENT BY GOD TO SHOW APPRECIATION!!
I SEE! I WILL CHANGE THE WAY I EAT FROM NOW ON!!
grab
NEXT IS THE SAKÉ DRINKING CONTEST, KANTARO!!
OH MAN!
THIS ISN'T GOOD. I HEARD THAT GOBLINS ARE HARD DRINKERS.
OOOH KAN, PLEASE COME BACK TO YOUR SENSES.
"steam" from Kan's noodles is really THIS.
GULP GULP GULP GULP
sake
cask たる
WELL,
ANOTHER MESSAGE FROM GOD TO SHINNOSUKE.

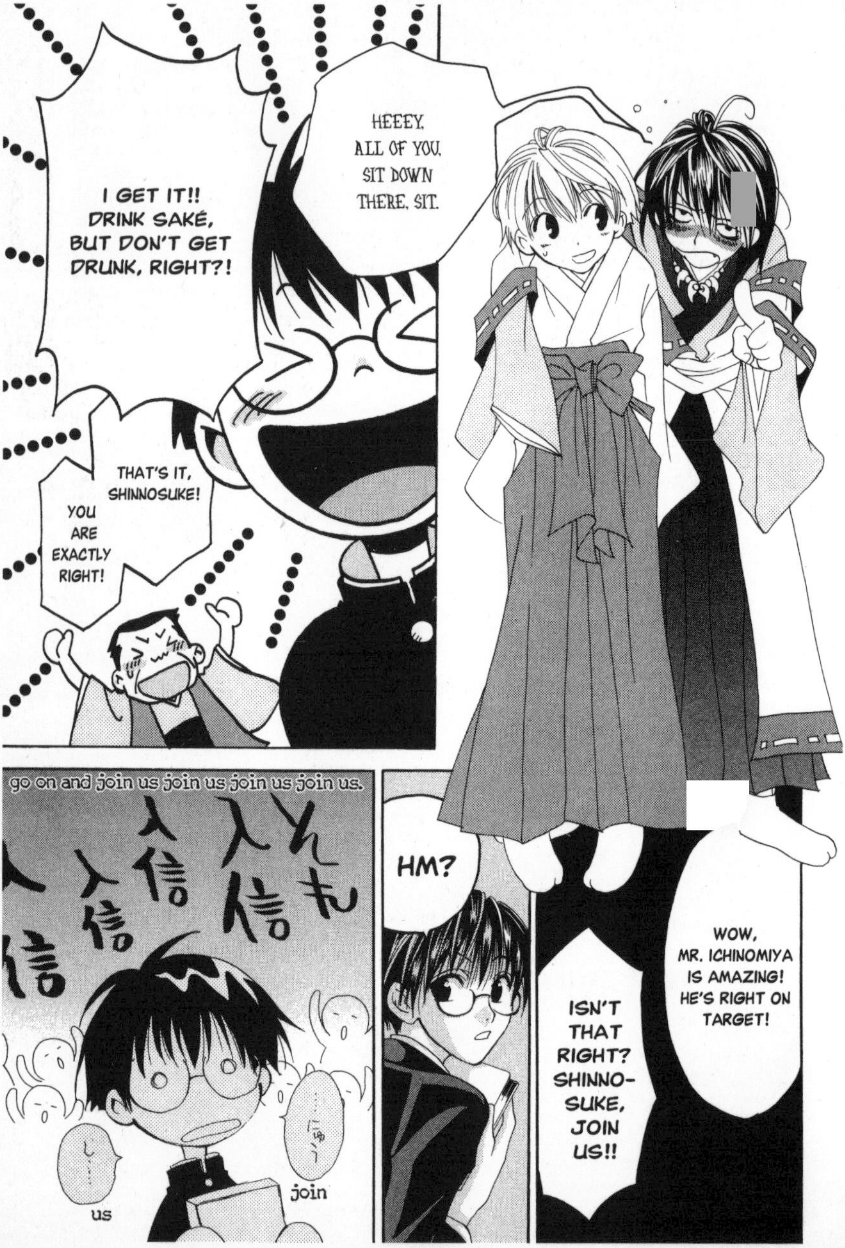
HEEEY, ALL OF YOU, SIT DOWN THERE, SIT.
I GET IT!! DRINK SAKÉ, BUT DON'T GET DRUNK, RIGHT?!
THAT'S IT, SHINNOSUKE!
YOU ARE EXACTLY RIGHT!
WOW, MR. ICHINOMIYA IS AMAZING! HE'S RIGHT ON TARGET!
ISN'T THAT RIGHT? SHINNO-SUKE, JOIN US!!
HM?
go on and join us join us join us join us.
join
us

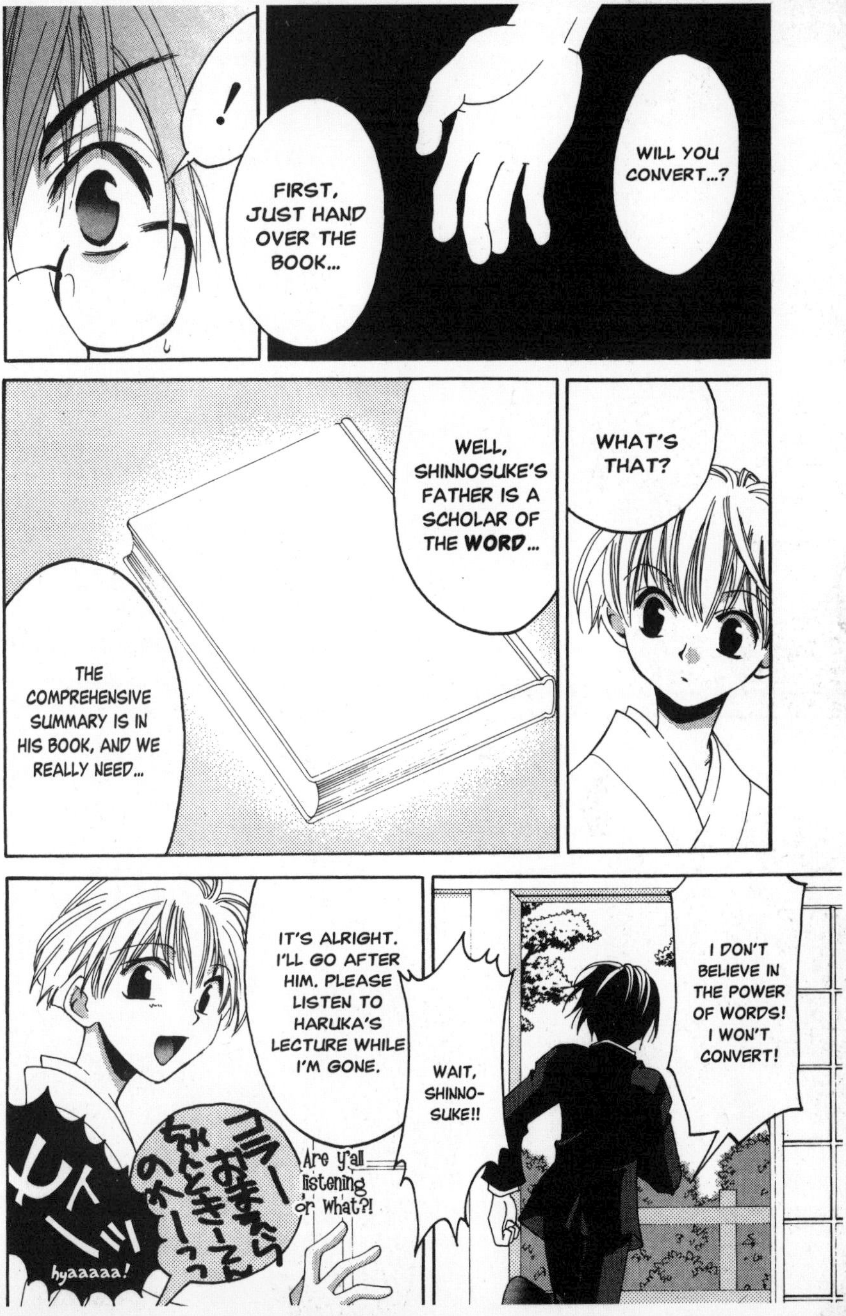
WILL YOU CONVERT...?
FIRST, JUST HAND OVER THE BOOK...
!
WHAT'S THAT?
WELL, SHINNOSUKE'S FATHER IS A SCHOLAR OF THE **WORD**...
THE COMPREHENSIVE SUMMARY IS IN HIS BOOK, AND WE REALLY NEED...
I DON'T BELIEVE IN THE POWER OF WORDS! I WON'T CONVERT!
WAIT, SHINNO-SUKE!!
IT'S ALRIGHT. I'LL GO AFTER HIM. PLEASE LISTEN TO HARUKA'S LECTURE WHILE I'M GONE.
コラー おまえら ちゃんときーてんのかーっ
Are y'all listening or What?!
hyaaaaa!

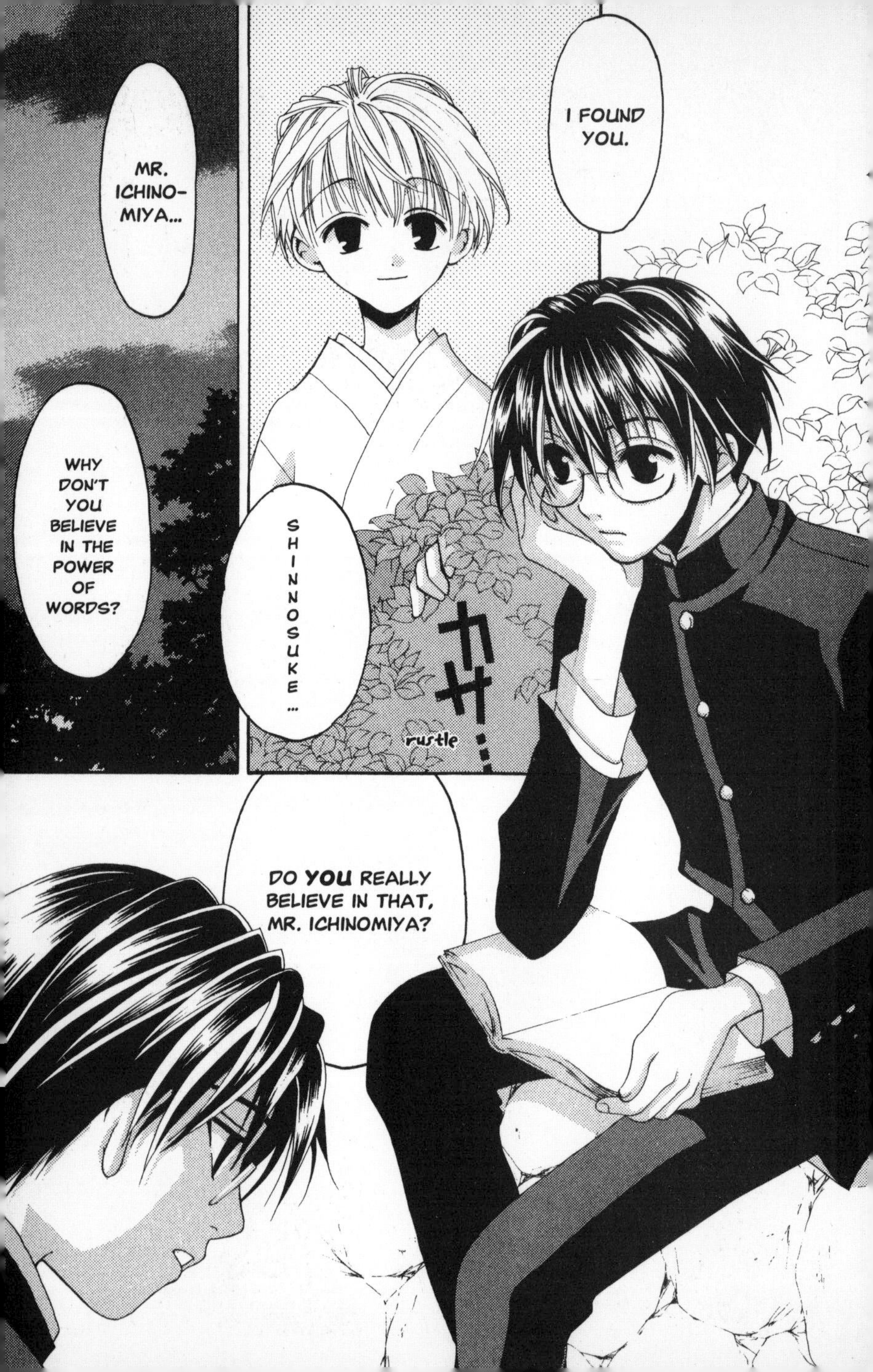

I FOUND YOU.
SHINNOSUKE...
カサ…
rustle
MR. ICHINOMIYA...
WHY DON'T YOU BELIEVE IN THE POWER OF WORDS?
DO **YOU** REALLY BELIEVE IN THAT, MR. ICHINOMIYA?

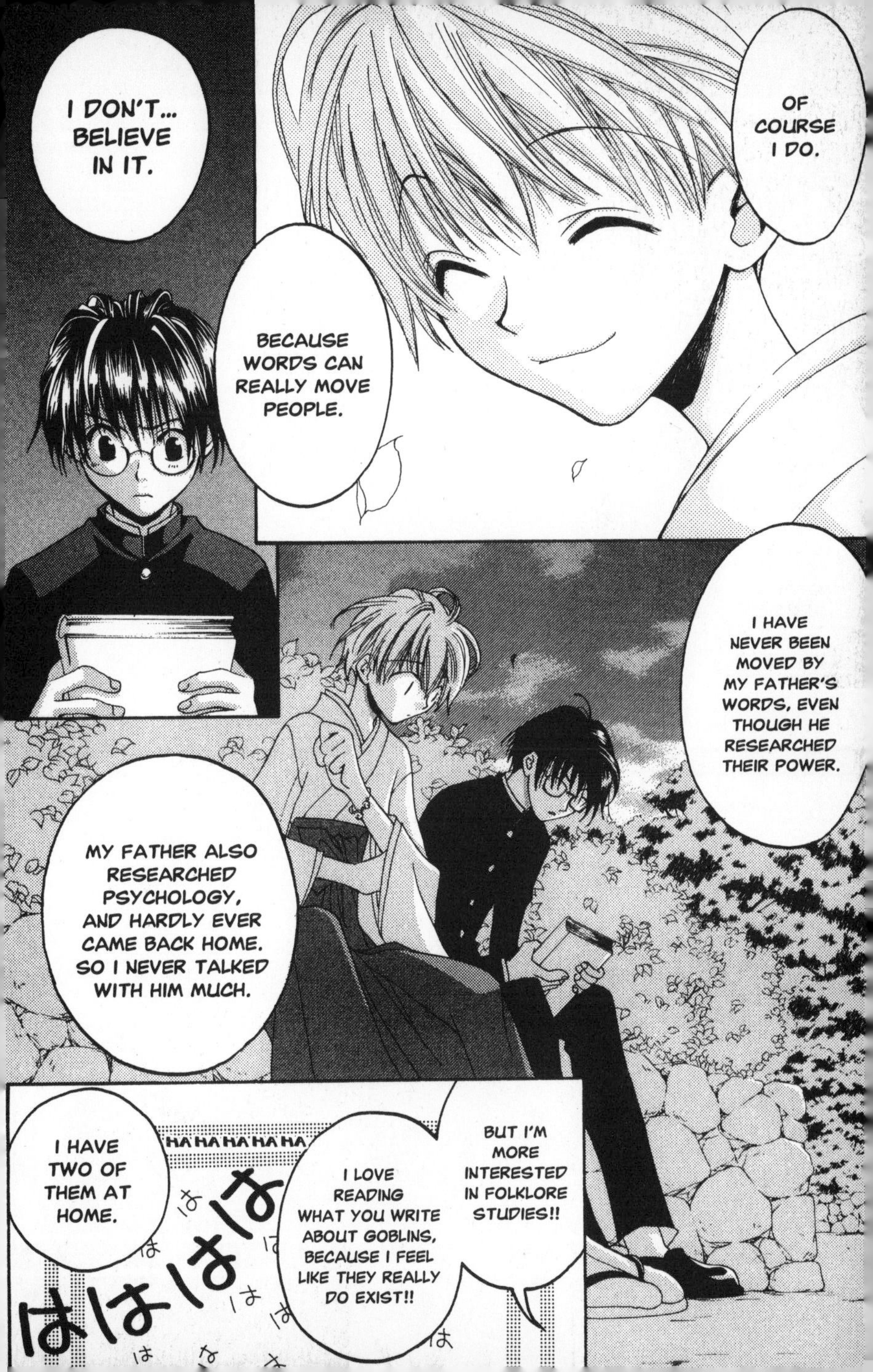
OF COURSE I DO.
BECAUSE WORDS CAN REALLY MOVE PEOPLE.
I DON'T... BELIEVE IN IT.
I HAVE NEVER BEEN MOVED BY MY FATHER'S WORDS, EVEN THOUGH HE RESEARCHED THEIR POWER.
MY FATHER ALSO RESEARCHED PSYCHOLOGY, AND HARDLY EVER CAME BACK HOME. SO I NEVER TALKED WITH HIM MUCH.
BUT I'M MORE INTERESTED IN FOLKLORE STUDIES!!
I LOVE READING WHAT YOU WRITE ABOUT GOBLINS, BECAUSE I FEEL LIKE THEY REALLY DO EXIST!!
HA HA HA HA HA HA
はははは
I HAVE TWO OF THEM AT HOME.

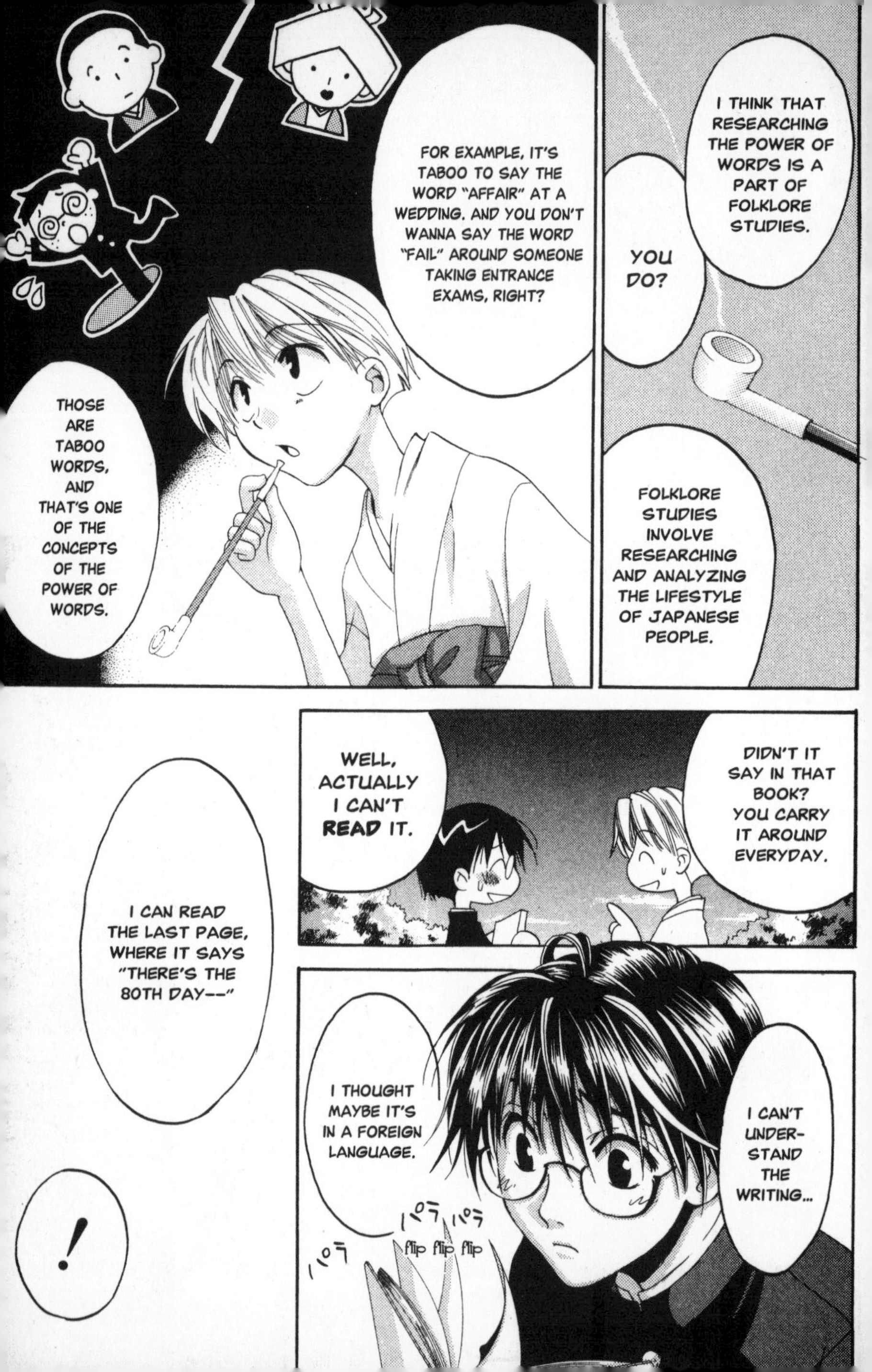
I THINK THAT RESEARCHING THE POWER OF WORDS IS A PART OF FOLKLORE STUDIES.
YOU DO?
FOLKLORE STUDIES INVOLVE RESEARCHING AND ANALYZING THE LIFESTYLE OF JAPANESE PEOPLE.
FOR EXAMPLE, IT'S TABOO TO SAY THE WORD "AFFAIR" AT A WEDDING. AND YOU DON'T WANNA SAY THE WORD "FAIL" AROUND SOMEONE TAKING ENTRANCE EXAMS, RIGHT?
THOSE ARE TABOO WORDS, AND THAT'S ONE OF THE CONCEPTS OF THE POWER OF WORDS.
DIDN'T IT SAY IN THAT BOOK? YOU CARRY IT AROUND EVERYDAY.
WELL, ACTUALLY I CAN'T **READ** IT.
I CAN'T UNDER-STAND THE WRITING...
I THOUGHT MAYBE IT'S IN A FOREIGN LANGUAGE.
パラ パラ パラ
flip flip flip
I CAN READ THE LAST PAGE, WHERE IT SAYS "THERE'S THE 80TH DAY--"
!

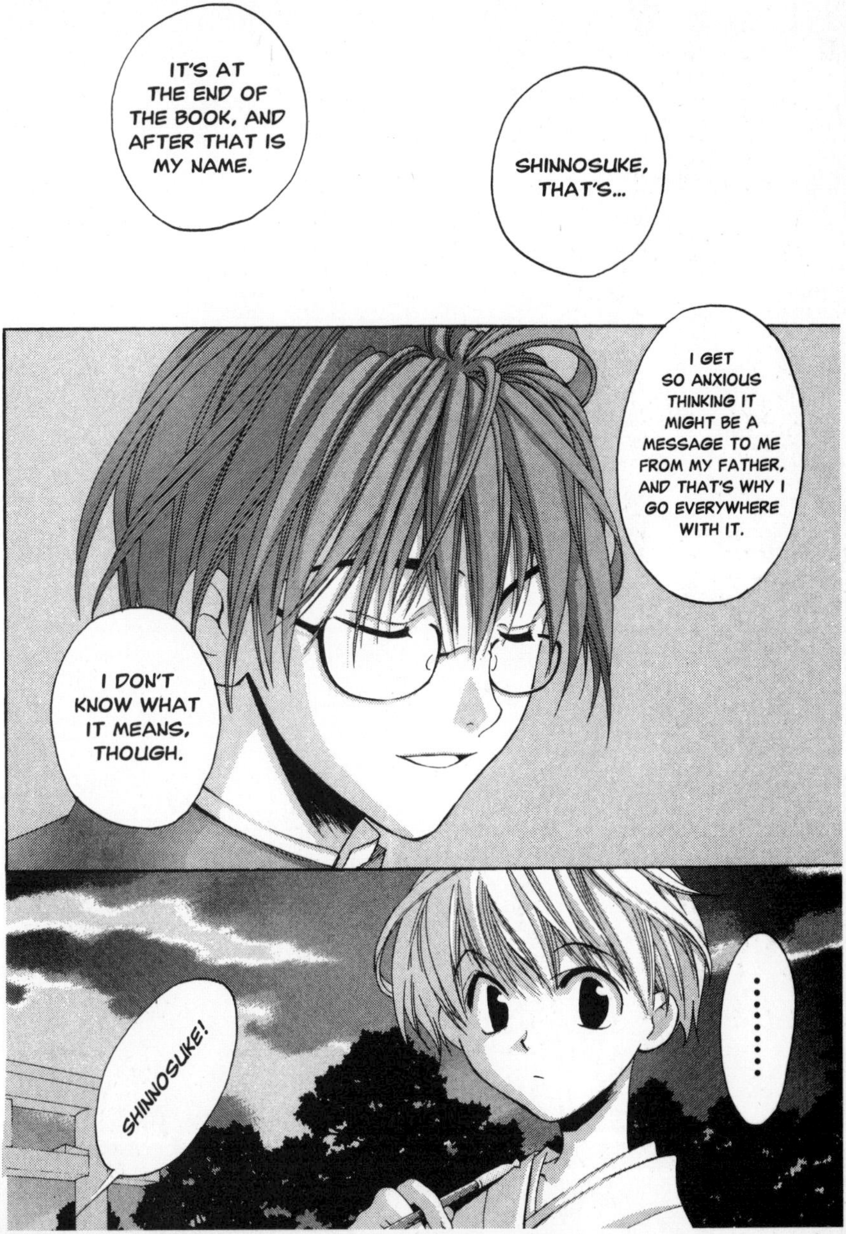
IT'S AT THE END OF THE BOOK, AND AFTER THAT IS MY NAME.
SHINNOSUKE, THAT'S...
I GET SO ANXIOUS THINKING IT MIGHT BE A MESSAGE TO ME FROM MY FATHER, AND THAT'S WHY I GO EVERYWHERE WITH IT.
I DON'T KNOW WHAT IT MEANS, THOUGH.
......
SHINNOSUKE!

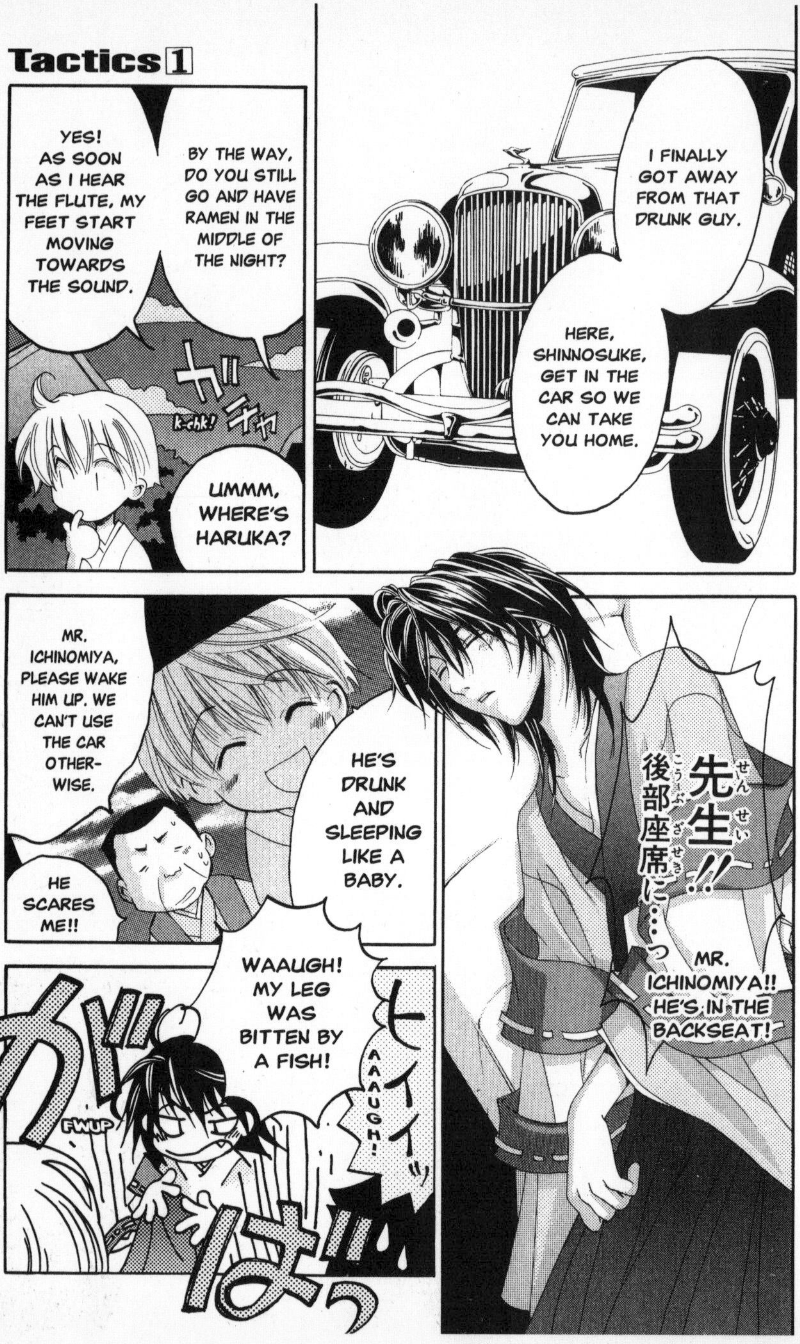
I FINALLY GOT AWAY FROM THAT DRUNK GUY.
HERE, SHINNOSUKE, GET IN THE CAR SO WE CAN TAKE YOU HOME.
BY THE WAY, DO YOU STILL GO AND HAVE RAMEN IN THE MIDDLE OF THE NIGHT?
YES! AS SOON AS I HEAR THE FLUTE, MY FEET START MOVING TOWARDS THE SOUND.
ガチャ
K-CHK!
UMMM, WHERE'S HARUKA?
先生!! 後部座席に…っ
MR. ICHINOMIYA!! HE'S IN THE BACKSEAT!
HE'S DRUNK AND SLEEPING LIKE A BABY.
MR. ICHINOMIYA, PLEASE WAKE HIM UP. WE CAN'T USE THE CAR OTHER-WISE.
HE SCARES ME!!
WAAUGH! MY LEG WAS BITTEN BY A FISH!
ヒィーッ
AAAUGH!
ガ
FWUP
ばっ

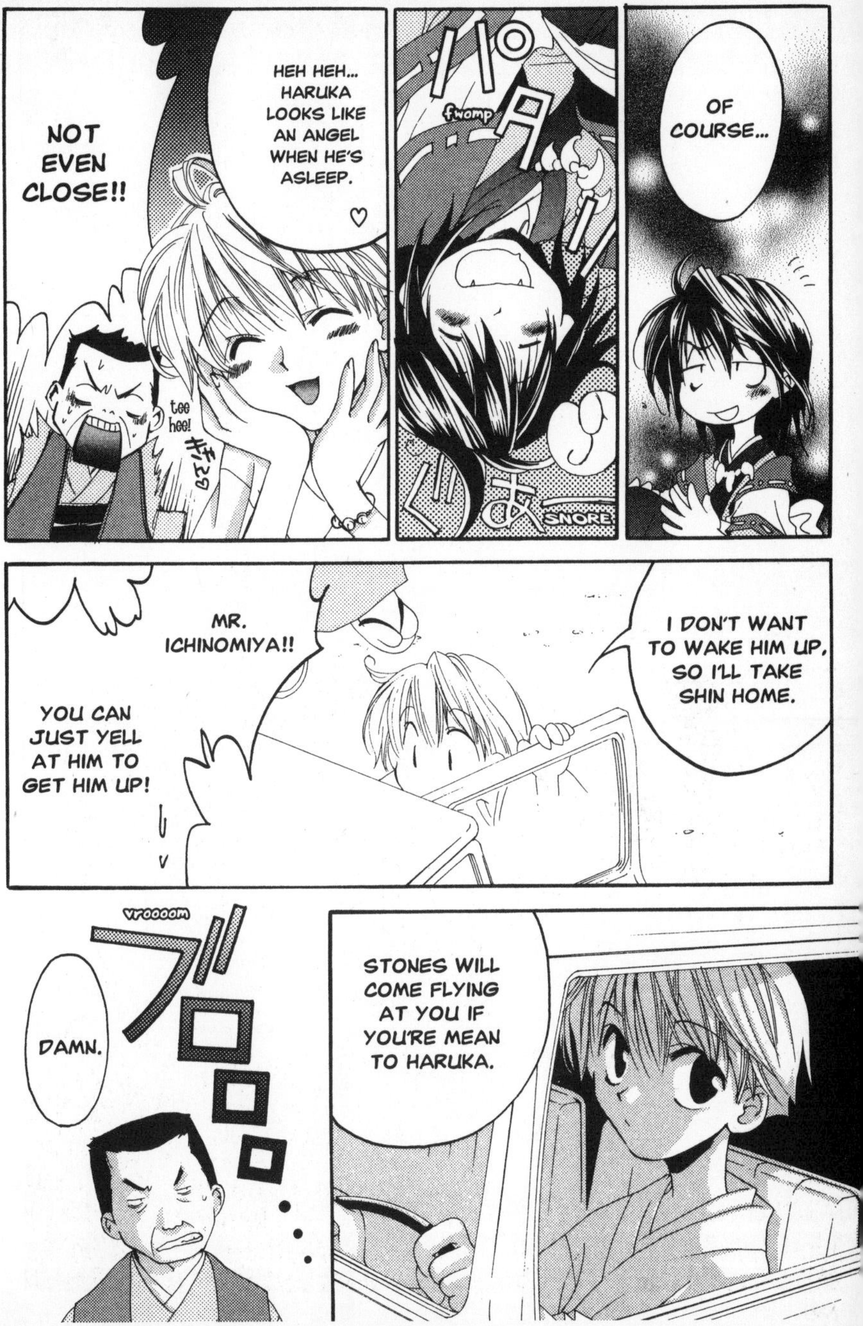
OF COURSE...
fwomp
SNORE
HEH HEH... HARUKA LOOKS LIKE AN ANGEL WHEN HE'S ASLEEP. ♡
NOT EVEN CLOSE!!
tee hee!
I DON'T WANT TO WAKE HIM UP, SO I'LL TAKE SHIN HOME.
MR. ICHINOMIYA!!
YOU CAN JUST YELL AT HIM TO GET HIM UP!
STONES WILL COME FLYING AT YOU IF YOU'RE MEAN TO HARUKA.
vroooom
ブロロロ
DAMN.

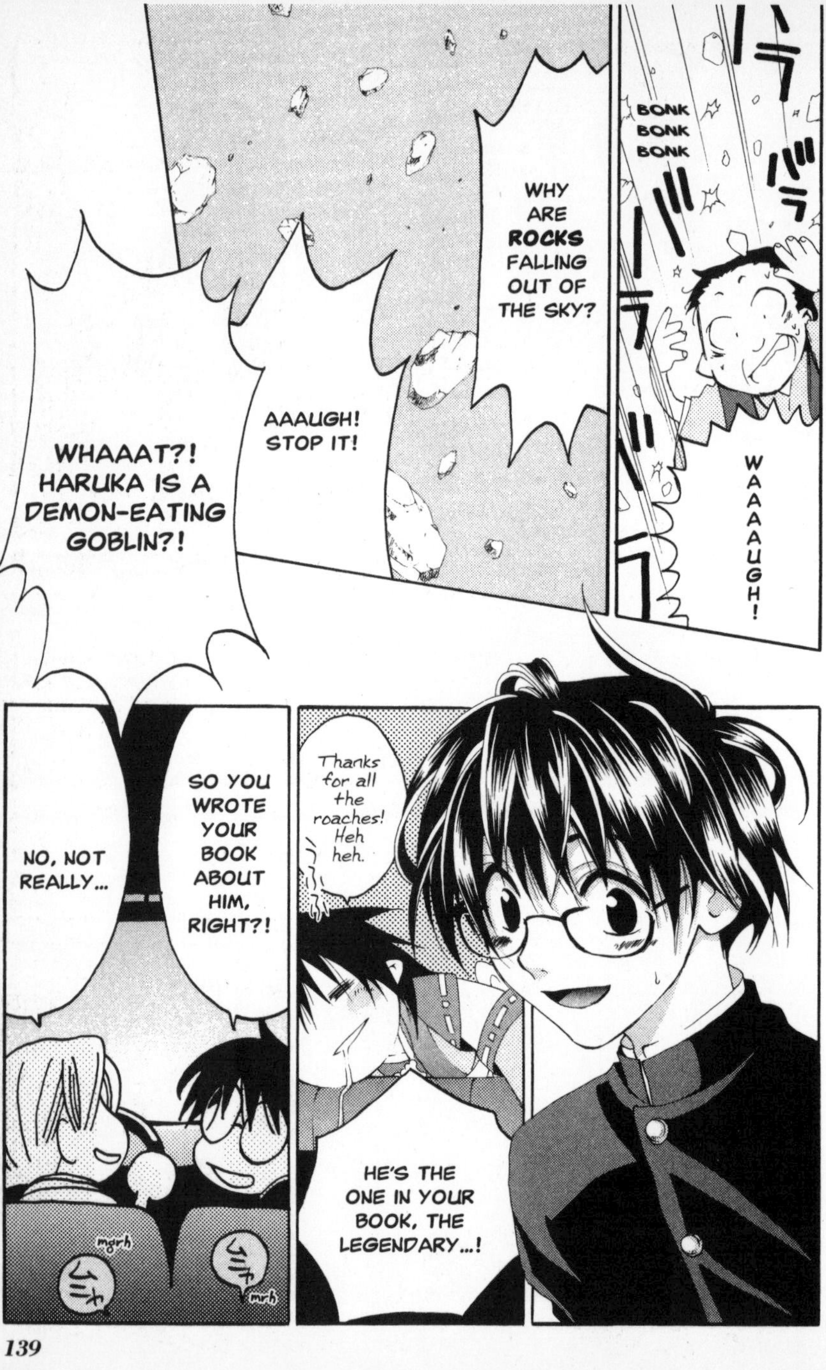
BONK
BONK
BONK
WAAAAAUGH!
WHY ARE ROCKS FALLING OUT OF THE SKY?
AAAUGH! STOP IT!
WHAAAT?! HARUKA IS A DEMON-EATING GOBLIN?!
Thanks for all the roaches! Heh heh.
HE'S THE ONE IN YOUR BOOK, THE LEGENDARY...!
SO YOU WROTE YOUR BOOK ABOUT HIM, RIGHT?!
NO, NOT REALLY...
mgrh
mrh

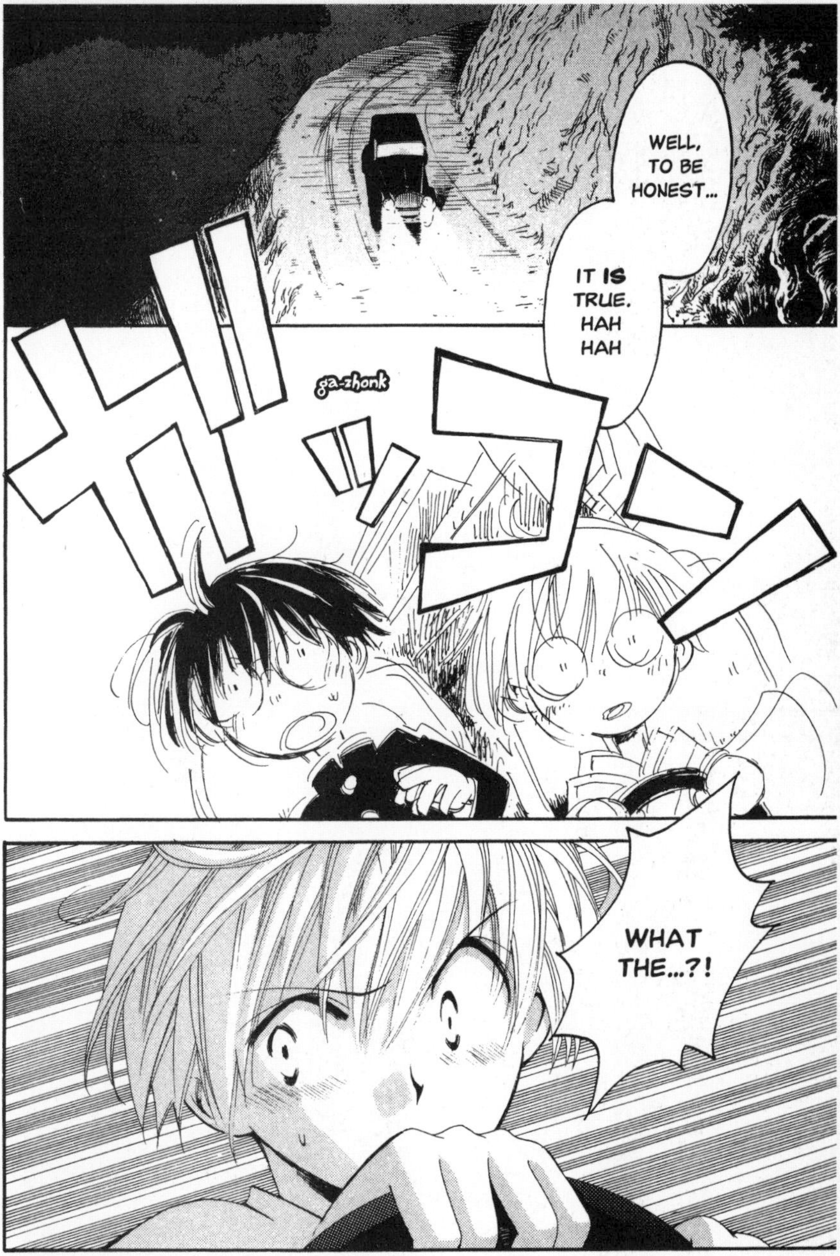
WELL, TO BE HONEST...
IT IS TRUE. HAH HAH
ga-zhonk
WHAT THE...?!

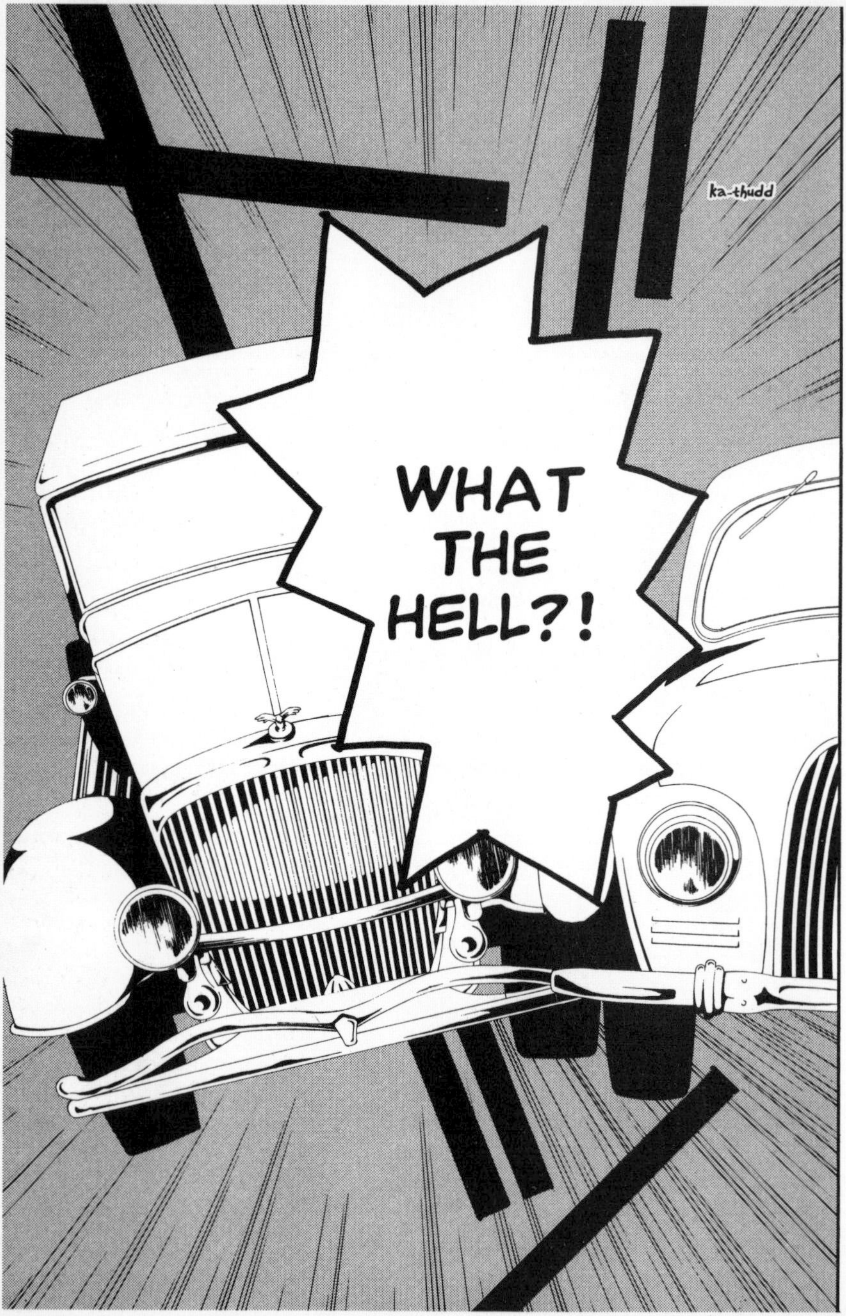
ka-thudd
WHAT THE HELL?!

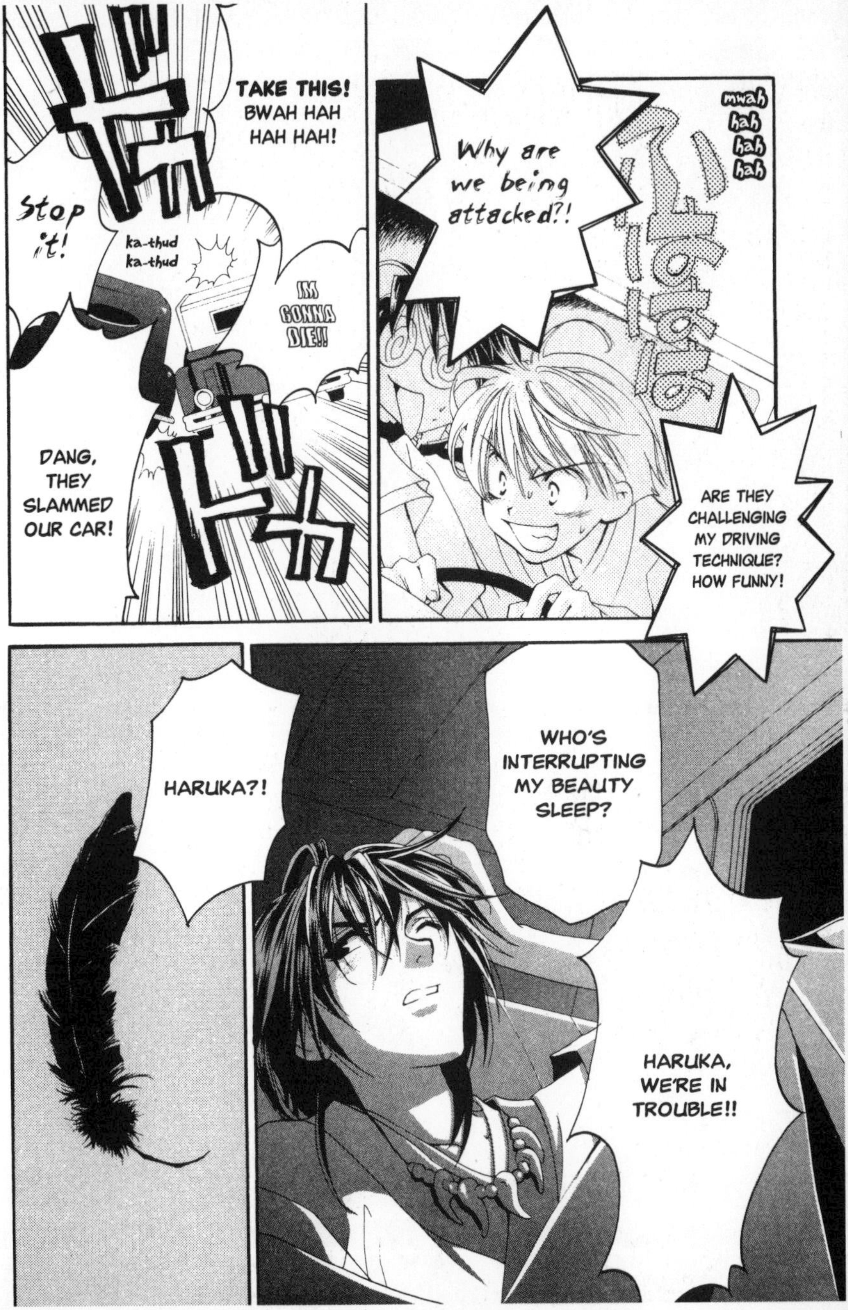
mwah hah hah hah
Why are we being attacked?!
ARE THEY CHALLENGING MY DRIVING TECHNIQUE? HOW FUNNY!
TAKE THIS! BWAH HAH HAH HAH!
IM GONNA DIE!!
Stop it!
ka-thud ka-thud
DANG, THEY SLAMMED OUR CAR!
WHO'S INTERRUPTING MY BEAUTY SLEEP?
HARUKA?!
HARUKA, WE'RE IN TROUBLE!!

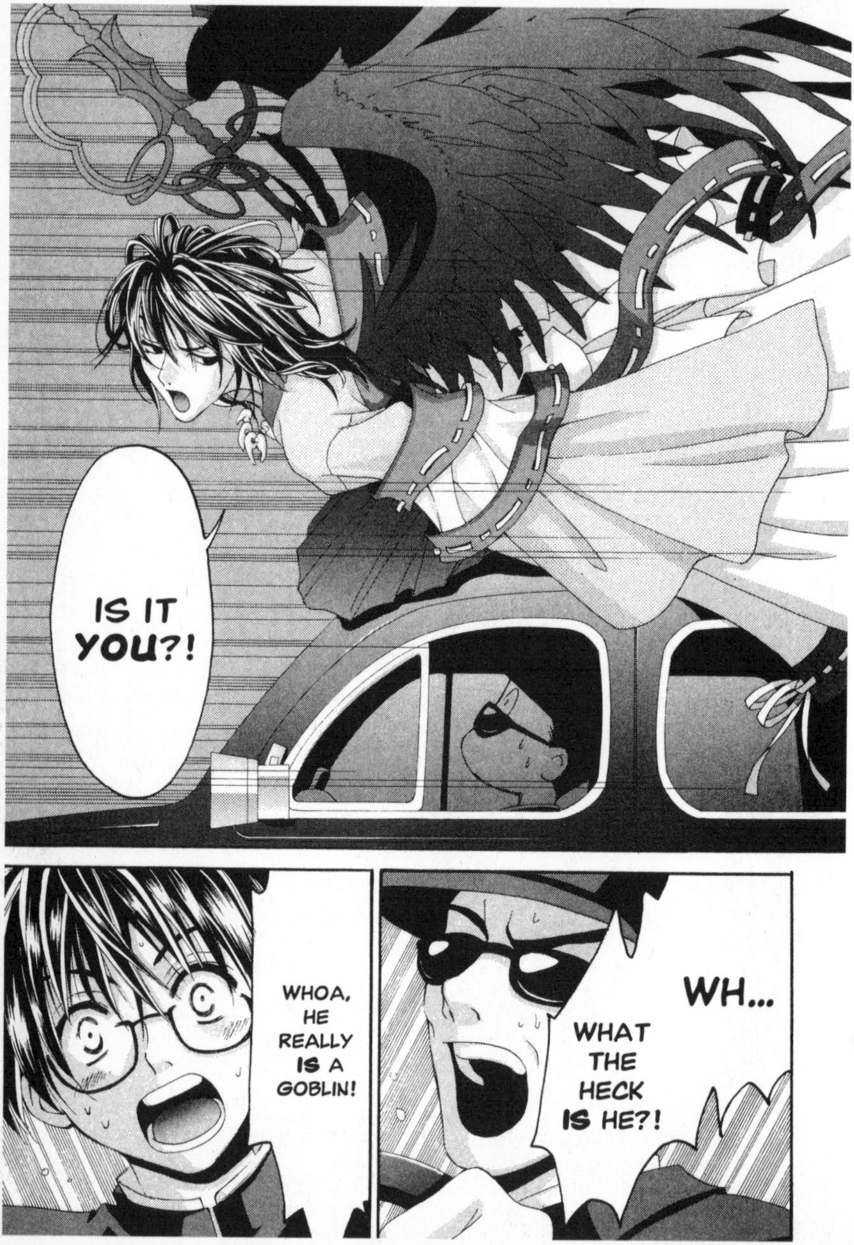
IS IT YOU?!
WH...
WHAT THE HECK IS HE?!
WHOA, HE REALLY IS A GOBLIN!

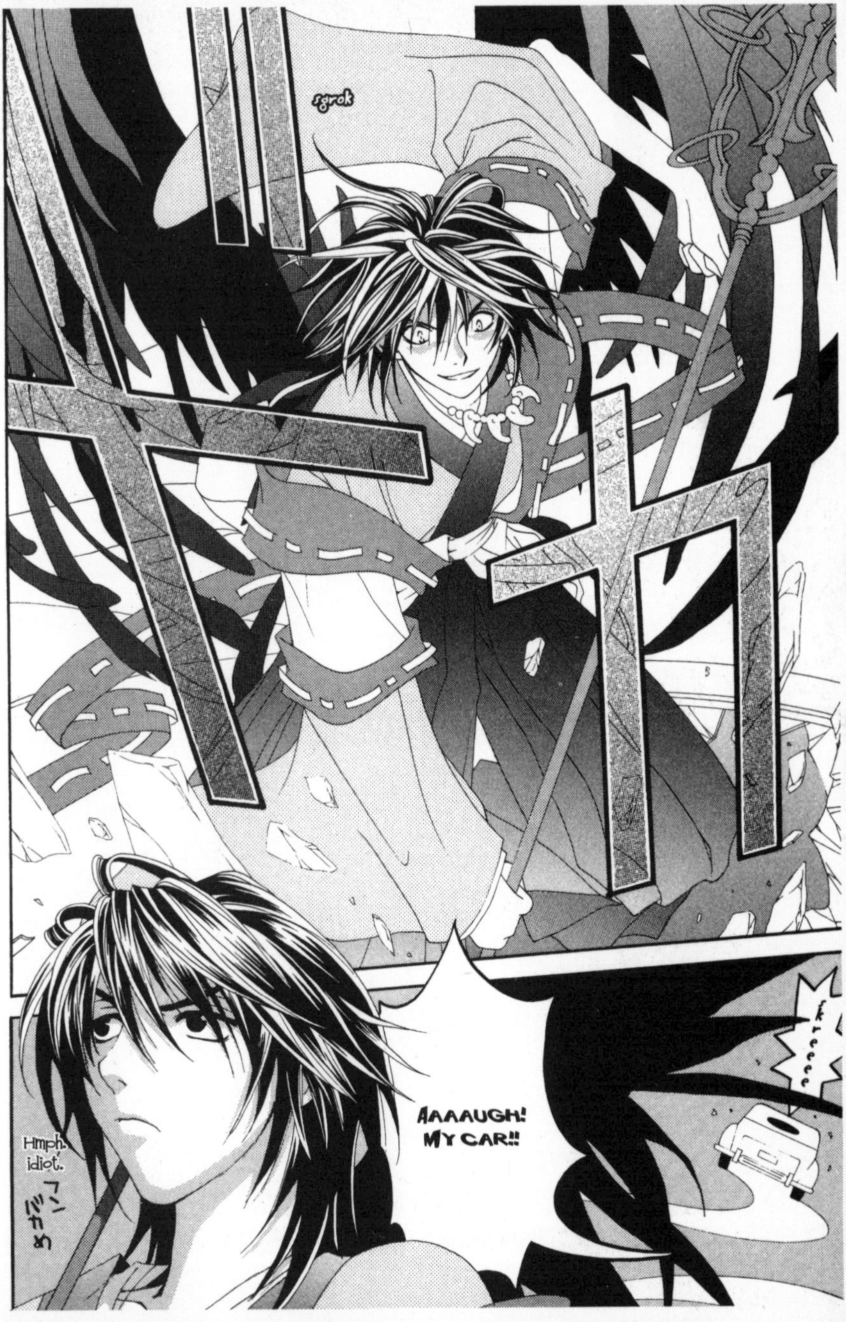
sgrok
skreeee
AAAAUGH! MY CAR!!
Hmph. idiot.
フン バカめ

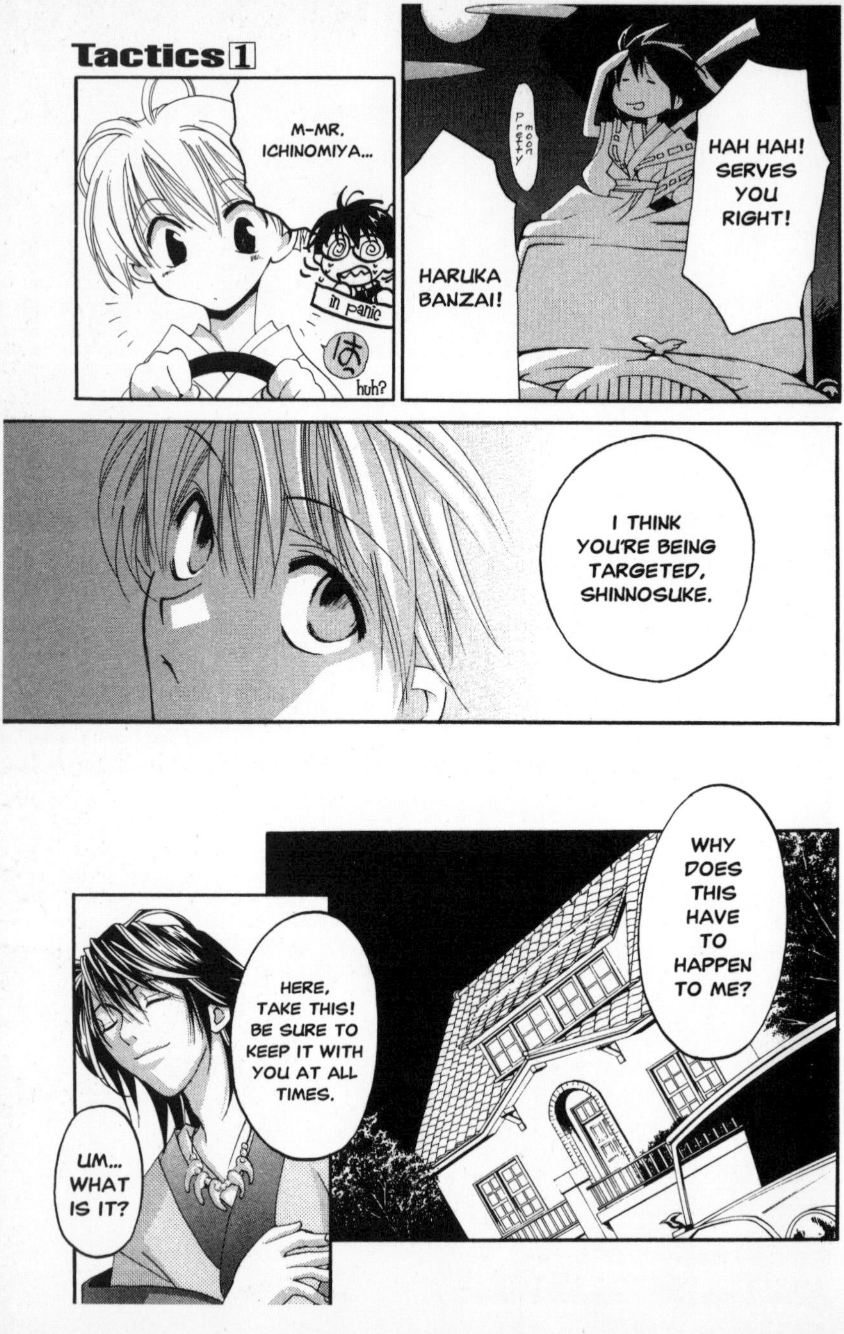
Pretty moon
HAH HAH! SERVES YOU RIGHT!
HARUKA BANZAI!
M-MR. ICHINOMIYA...
in panic
は
huh?
I THINK YOU'RE BEING TARGETED, SHINNOSUKE.
WHY DOES THIS HAVE TO HAPPEN TO ME?
HERE, TAKE THIS! BE SURE TO KEEP IT WITH YOU AT ALL TIMES.
UM... WHAT IS IT?

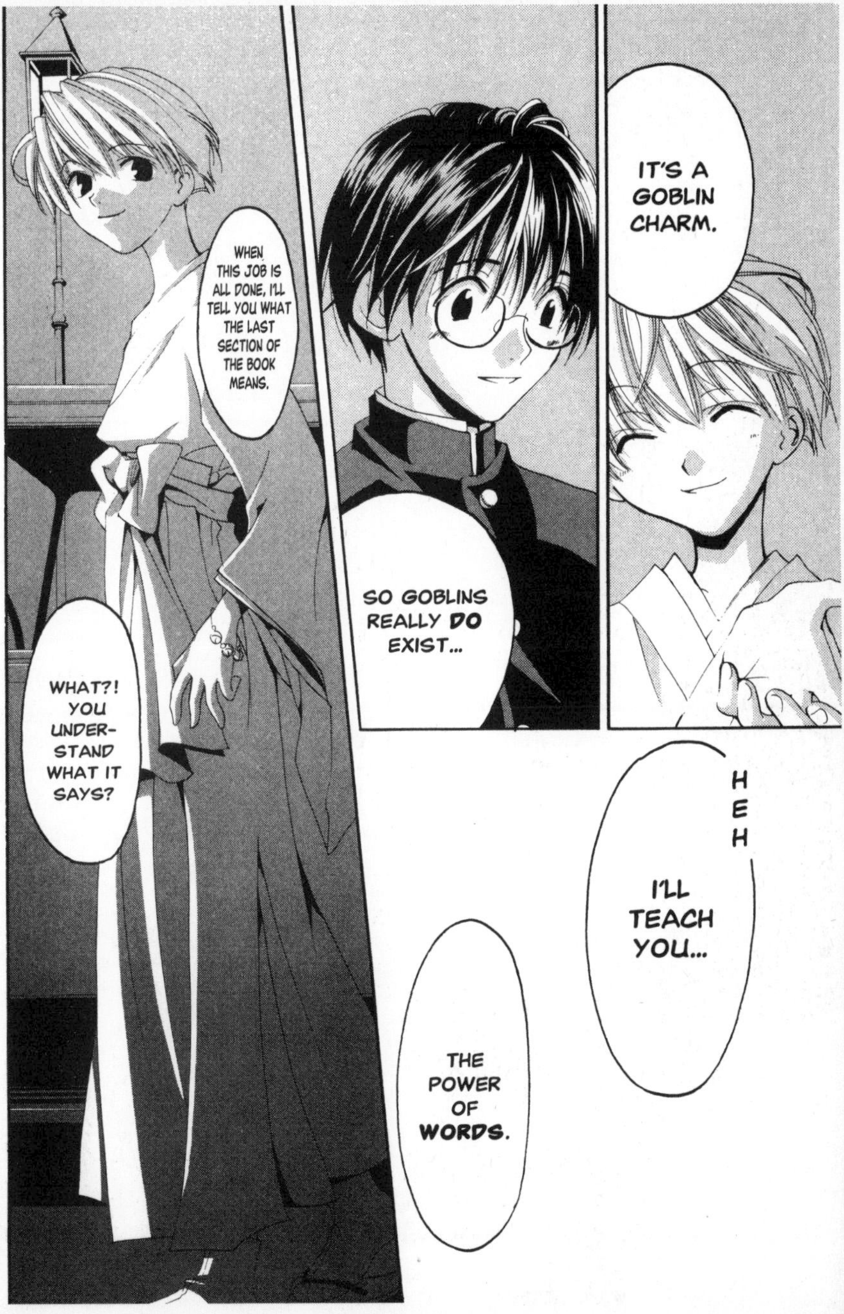
IT'S A GOBLIN CHARM.
SO GOBLINS REALLY DO EXIST...
WHEN THIS JOB IS ALL DONE, I'LL TELL YOU WHAT THE LAST SECTION OF THE BOOK MEANS.
WHAT?! YOU UNDER-STAND WHAT IT SAYS?
HEH
I'LL TEACH YOU...
THE POWER OF WORDS.

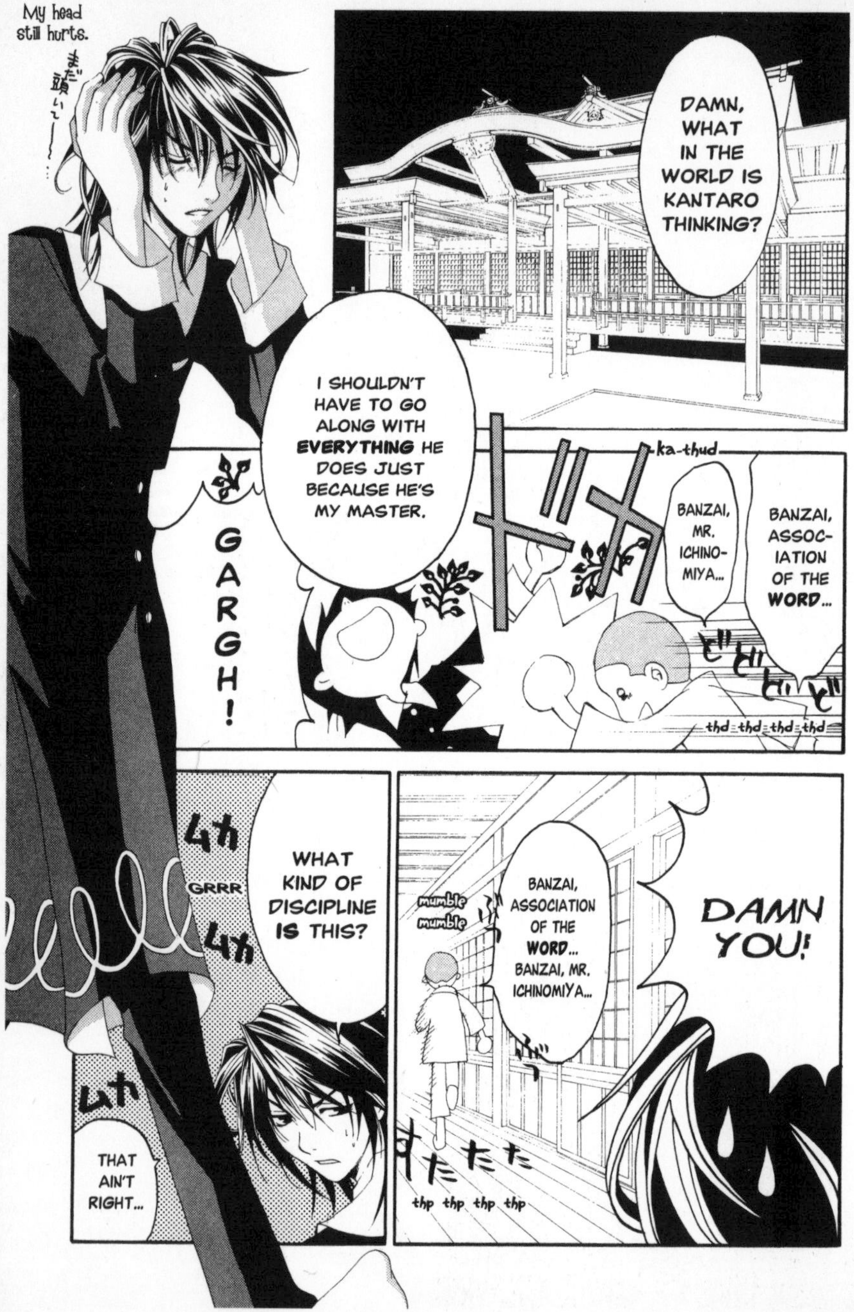
DAMN, WHAT IN THE WORLD IS KANTARO THINKING?
My head still hurts.
まだ頭いて〜〜…
I SHOULDN'T HAVE TO GO ALONG WITH EVERYTHING HE DOES JUST BECAUSE HE'S MY MASTER.
ka-thud
BANZAI, ASSOCIATION OF THE WORD...
BANZAI, MR. ICHINOMIYA...
thd thd thd thd
GARGH!
DAMN YOU!
BANZAI, ASSOCIATION OF THE WORD... BANZAI, MR. ICHINOMIYA...
mumble mumble
thp thp thp thp
WHAT KIND OF DISCIPLINE IS THIS?
GRRR
THAT AIN'T RIGHT...

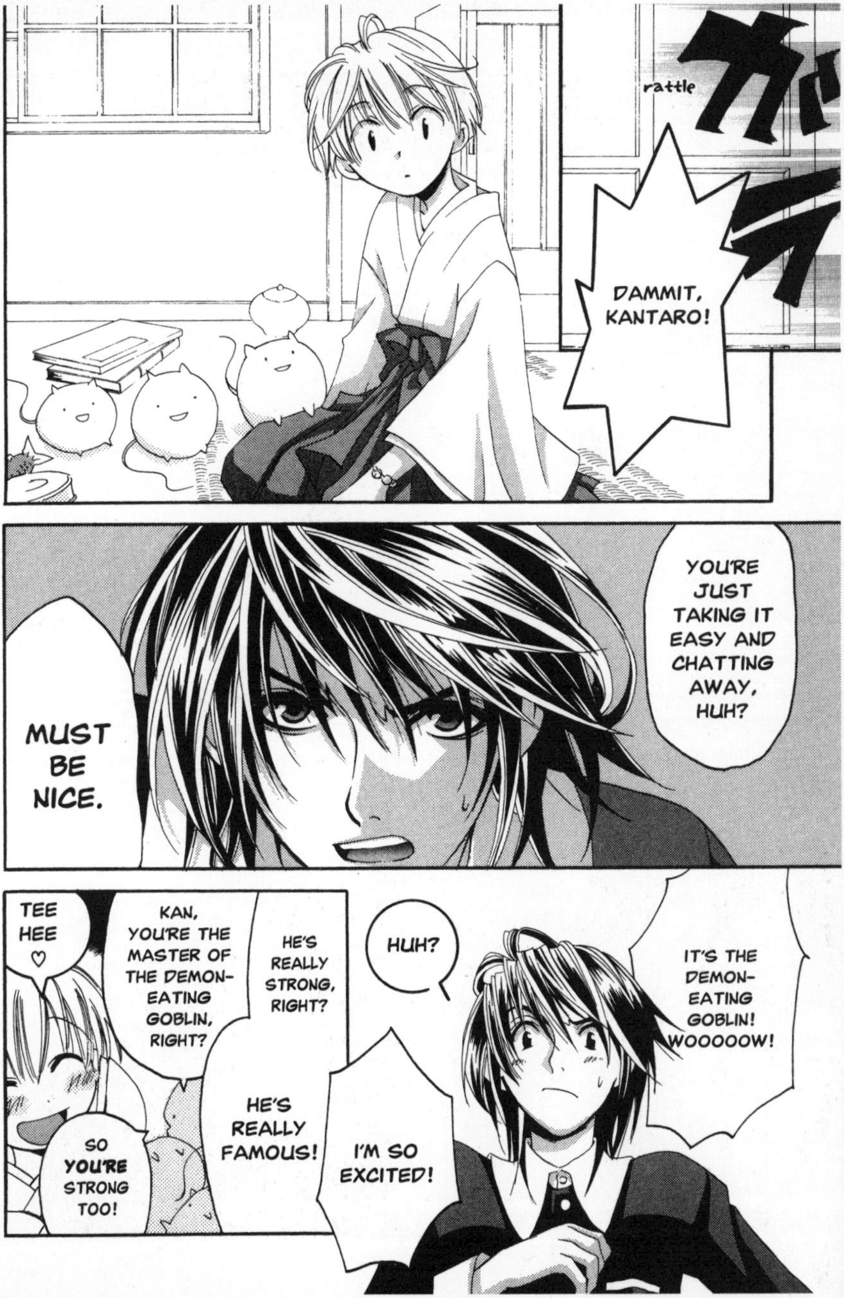
rattle
DAMMIT, KANTARO!
YOU'RE JUST TAKING IT EASY AND CHATTING AWAY, HUH?
MUST BE NICE.
IT'S THE DEMON-EATING GOBLIN! WOOOOOW!
HUH?
I'M SO EXCITED!
HE'S REALLY STRONG, RIGHT?
HE'S REALLY FAMOUS!
KAN, YOU'RE THE MASTER OF THE DEMON-EATING GOBLIN, RIGHT?
TEE HEE ♡
SO **YOU'RE** STRONG TOO!

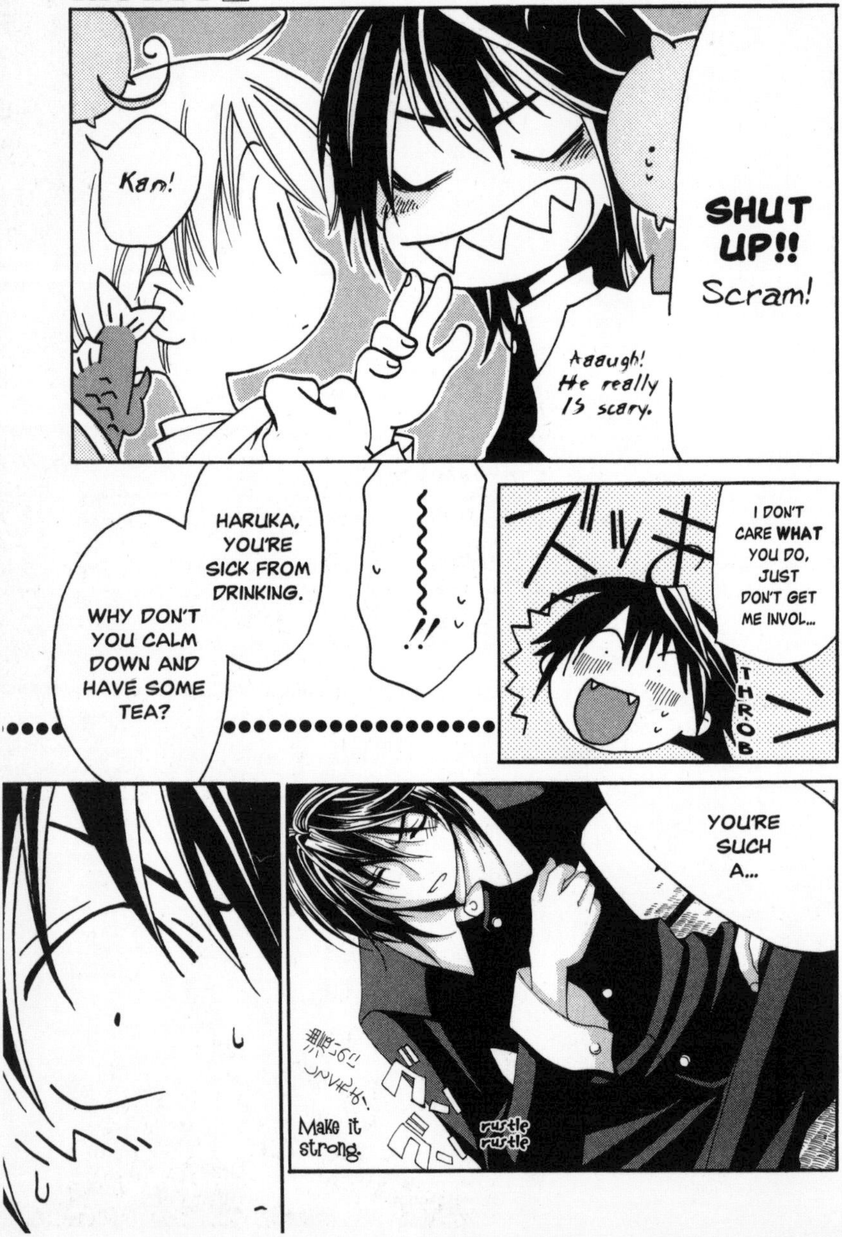
SHUT UP!! Scram!
Aaaugh! He really IS scary.
Kan!
ズッキ
I DON'T CARE WHAT YOU DO, JUST DON'T GET ME INVOL...
THROB
!!
HARUKA, YOU'RE SICK FROM DRINKING.
WHY DON'T YOU CALM DOWN AND HAVE SOME TEA?
YOU'RE SUCH A...
rustle rustle
Make it strong.

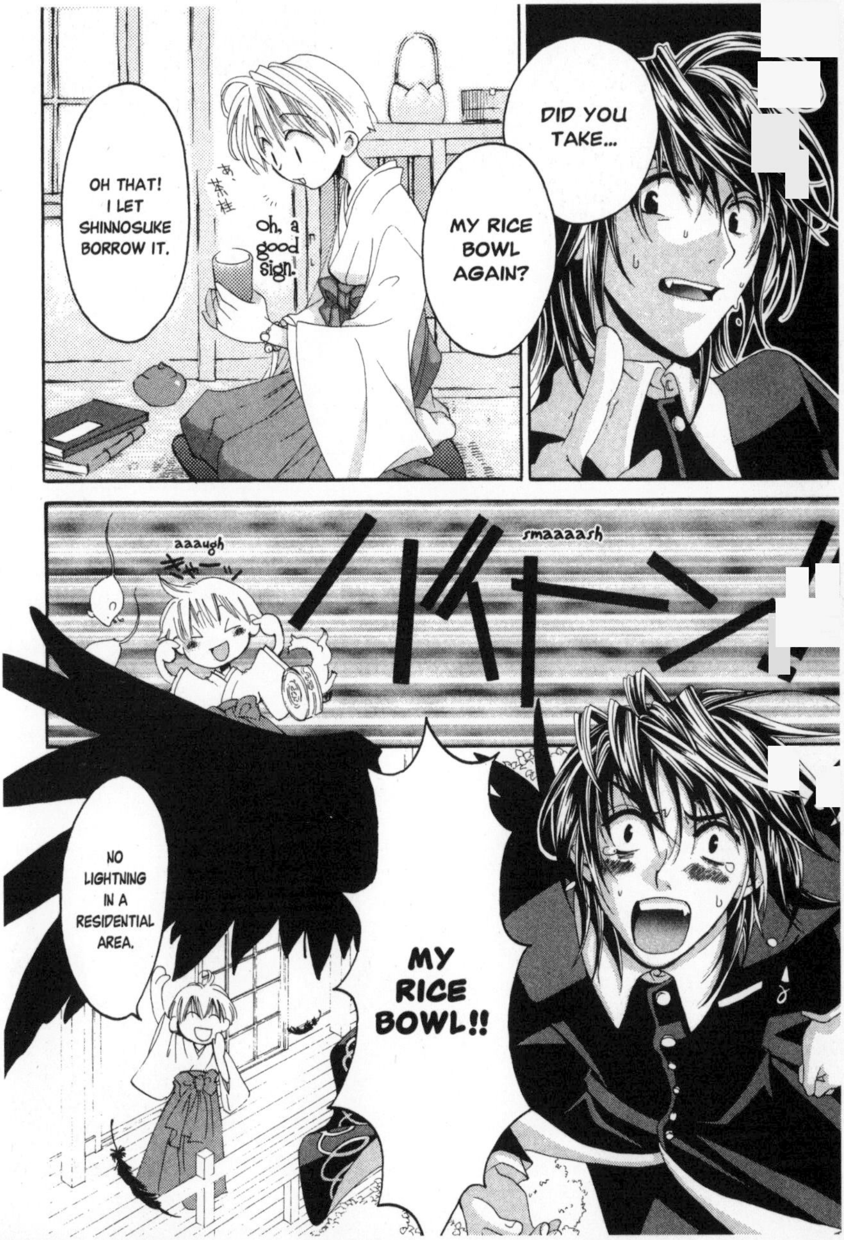
DID YOU TAKE...
MY RICE BOWL AGAIN?
OH THAT! I LET SHINNOSUKE BORROW IT.
あ、茶柱
oh, a good sign.
smaaaash
aaaugh
MY RICE BOWL!!
NO LIGHTNING IN A RESIDENTIAL AREA.

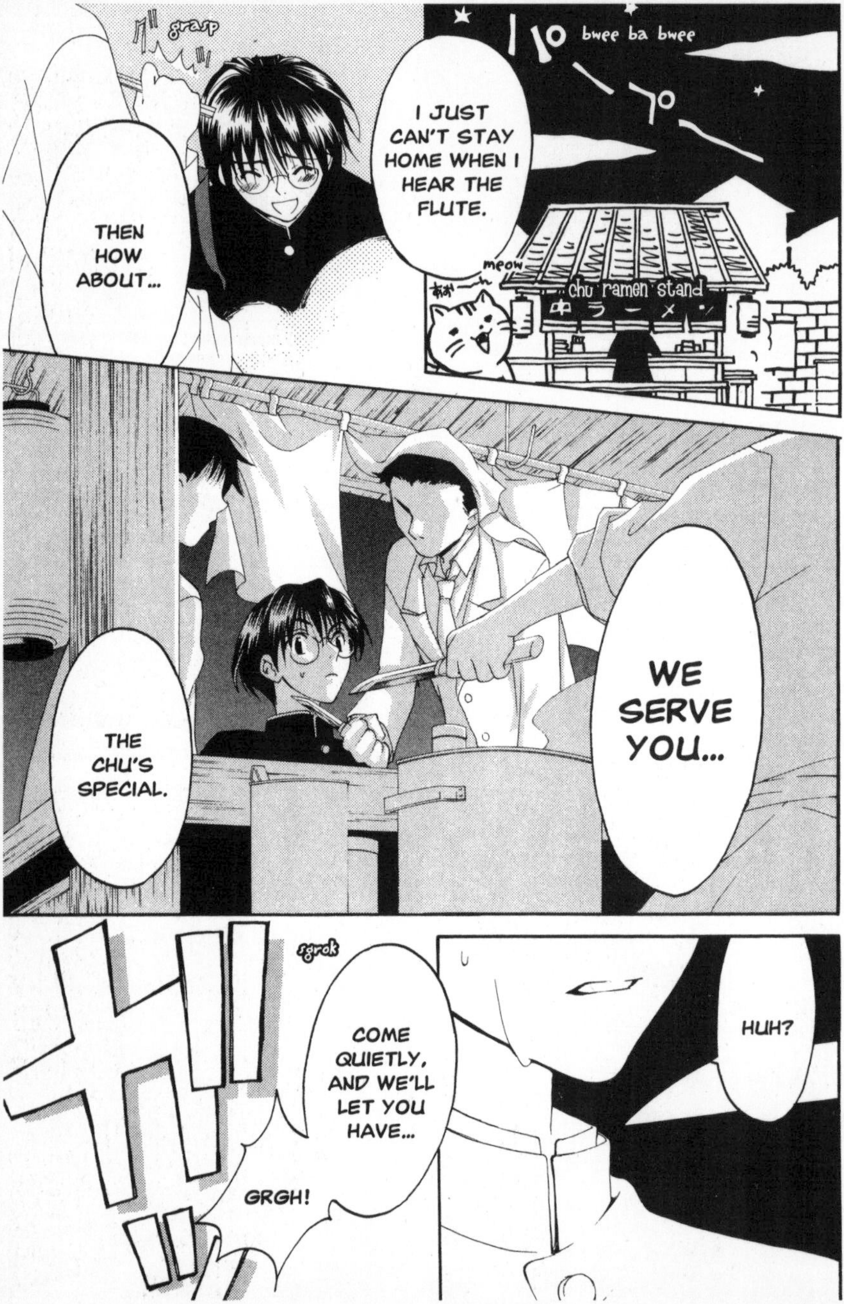
bwee ba bwee
I JUST CAN'T STAY HOME WHEN I HEAR THE FLUTE.
meow
chu ramen stand
grasp
THEN HOW ABOUT...
WE SERVE YOU...
THE CHU'S SPECIAL.
HUH?
sgrok
COME QUIETLY, AND WE'LL LET YOU HAVE...
GRGH!

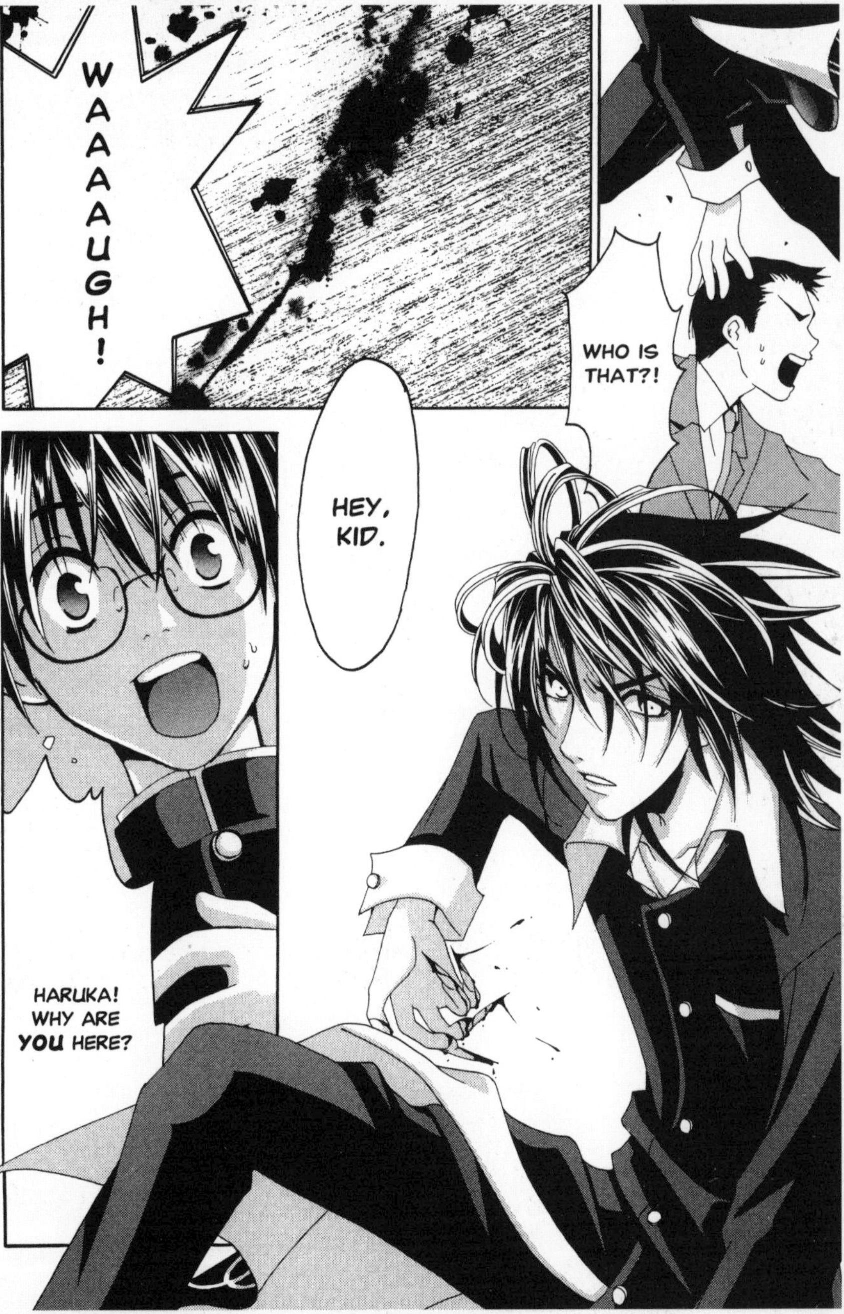
WHO IS THAT?!
WAAAAUGH!
HEY, KID.
HARUKA! WHY ARE YOU HERE?

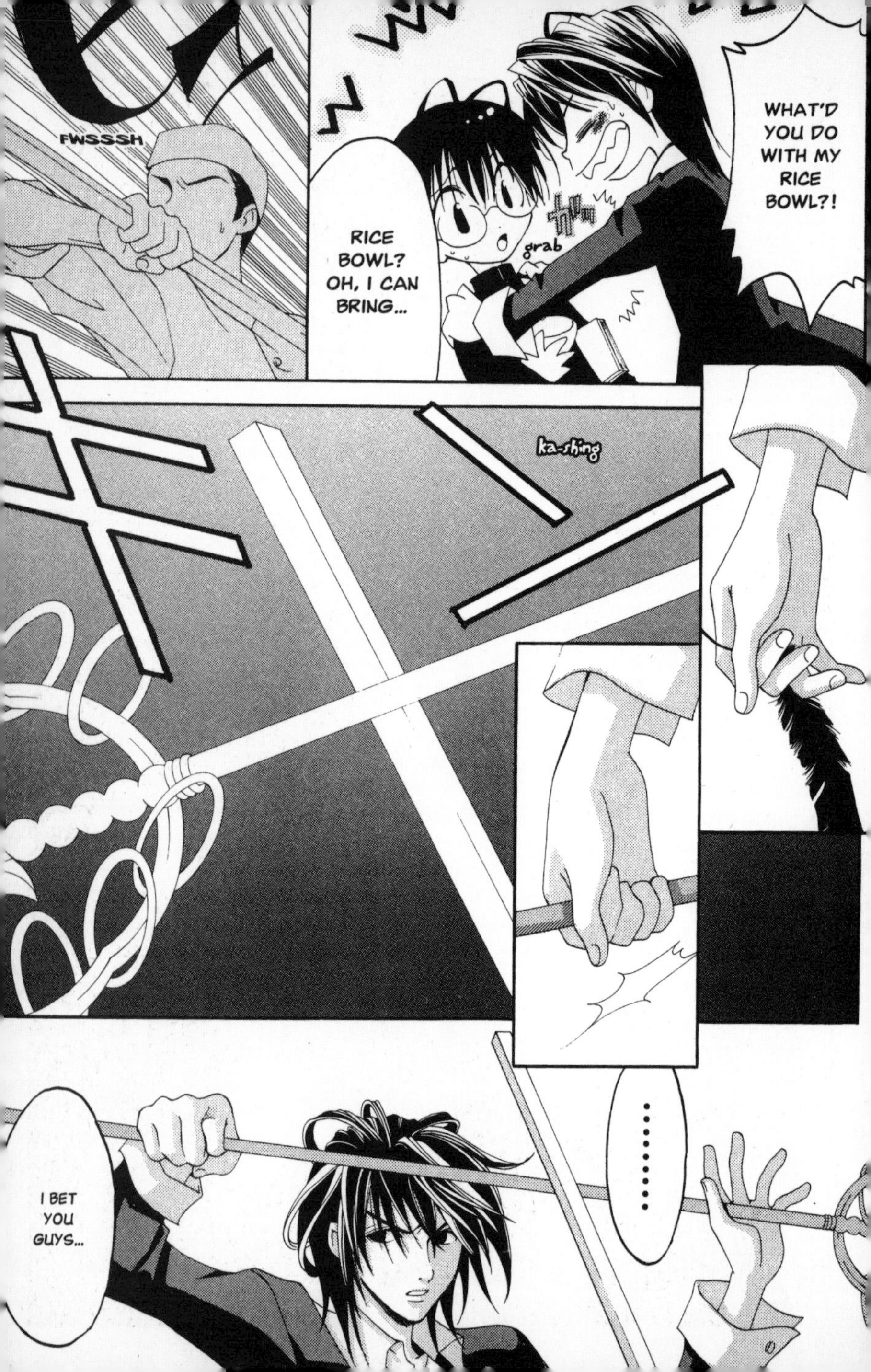
WHAT'D YOU DO WITH MY RICE BOWL?!
grab
RICE BOWL? OH, I CAN BRING...
FWSSSH
ka-shing
....
I BET YOU GUYS...

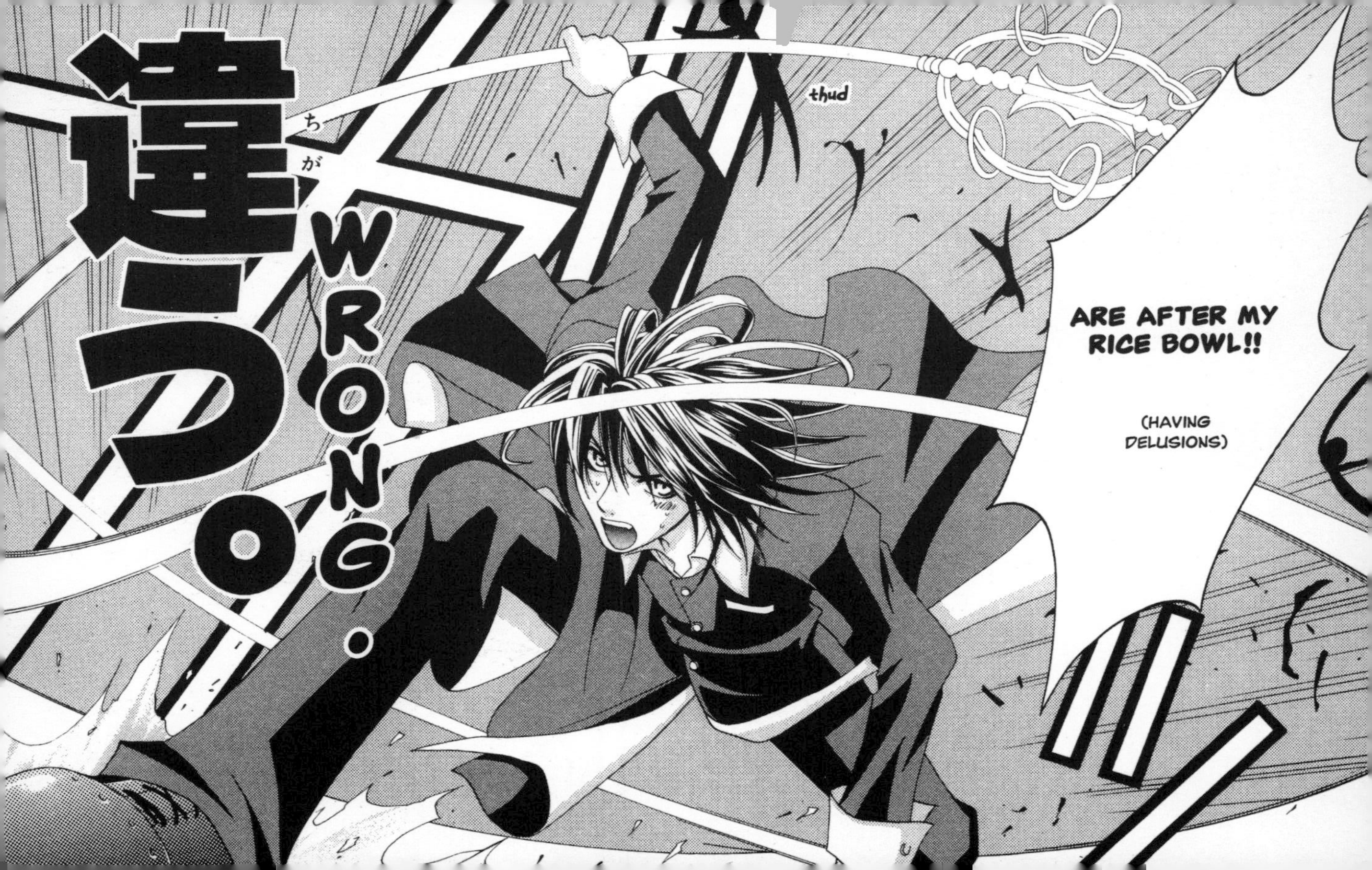
ARE AFTER MY RICE BOWL!!
(HAVING DELUSIONS)
thud
違う。
WRONG.

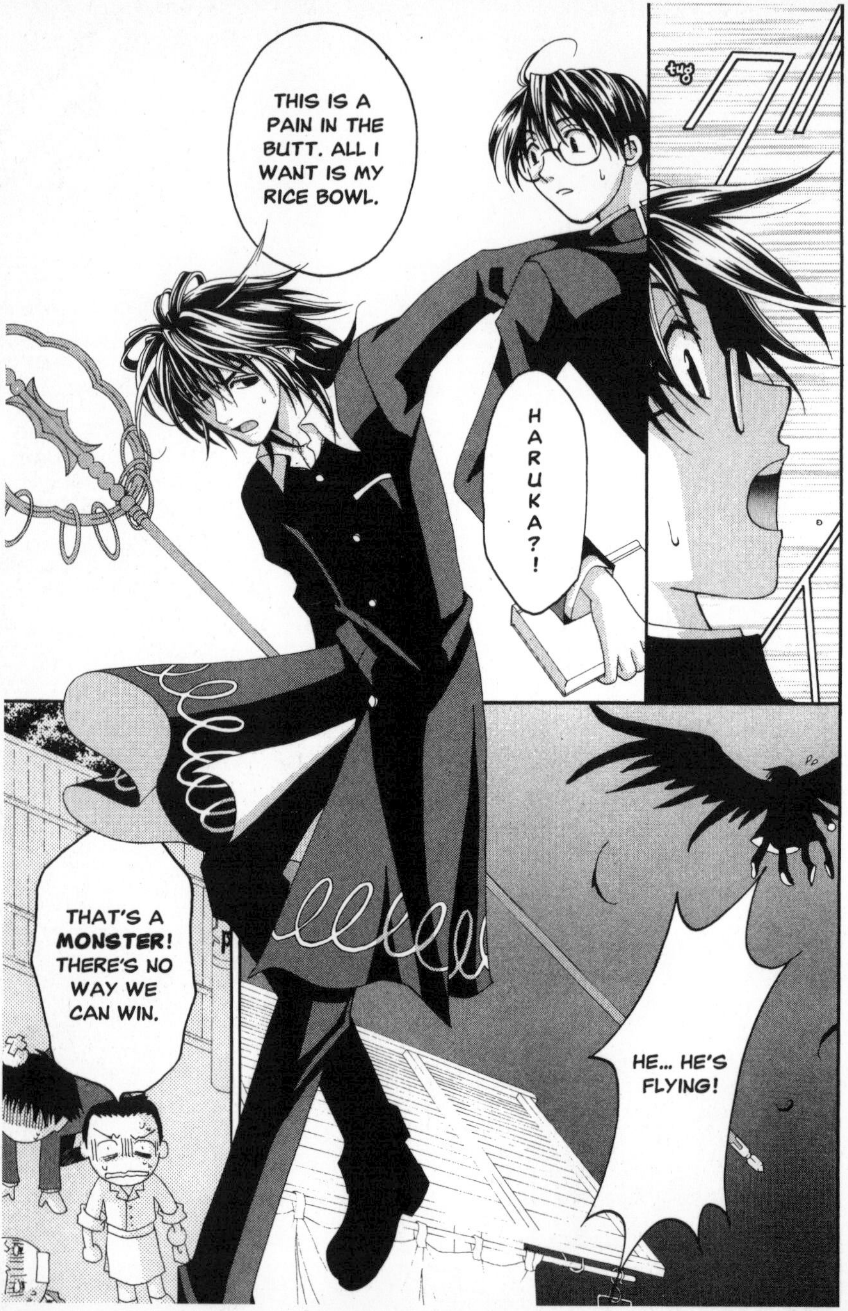
tug
HARUKA?!
THIS IS A PAIN IN THE BUTT. ALL I WANT IS MY RICE BOWL.
HE... HE'S FLYING!
THAT'S A **MONSTER**! THERE'S NO WAY WE CAN WIN.

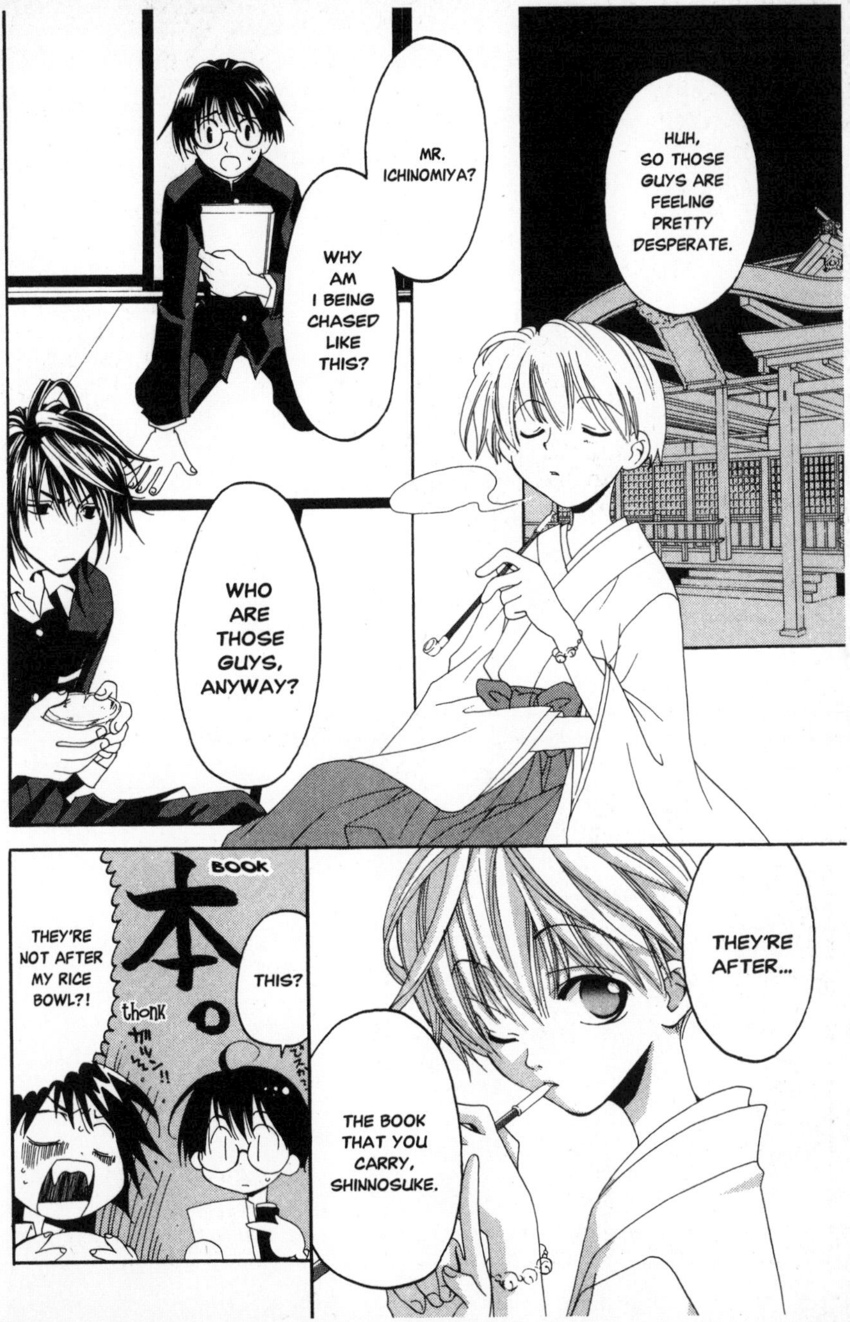
HUH, SO THOSE GUYS ARE FEELING PRETTY DESPERATE.
MR. ICHINOMIYA?
WHY AM I BEING CHASED LIKE THIS?
WHO ARE THOSE GUYS, ANYWAY?
THEY'RE AFTER...
THE BOOK THAT YOU CARRY, SHINNOSUKE.
BOOK
THIS?
THEY'RE NOT AFTER MY RICE BOWL?!
thonk

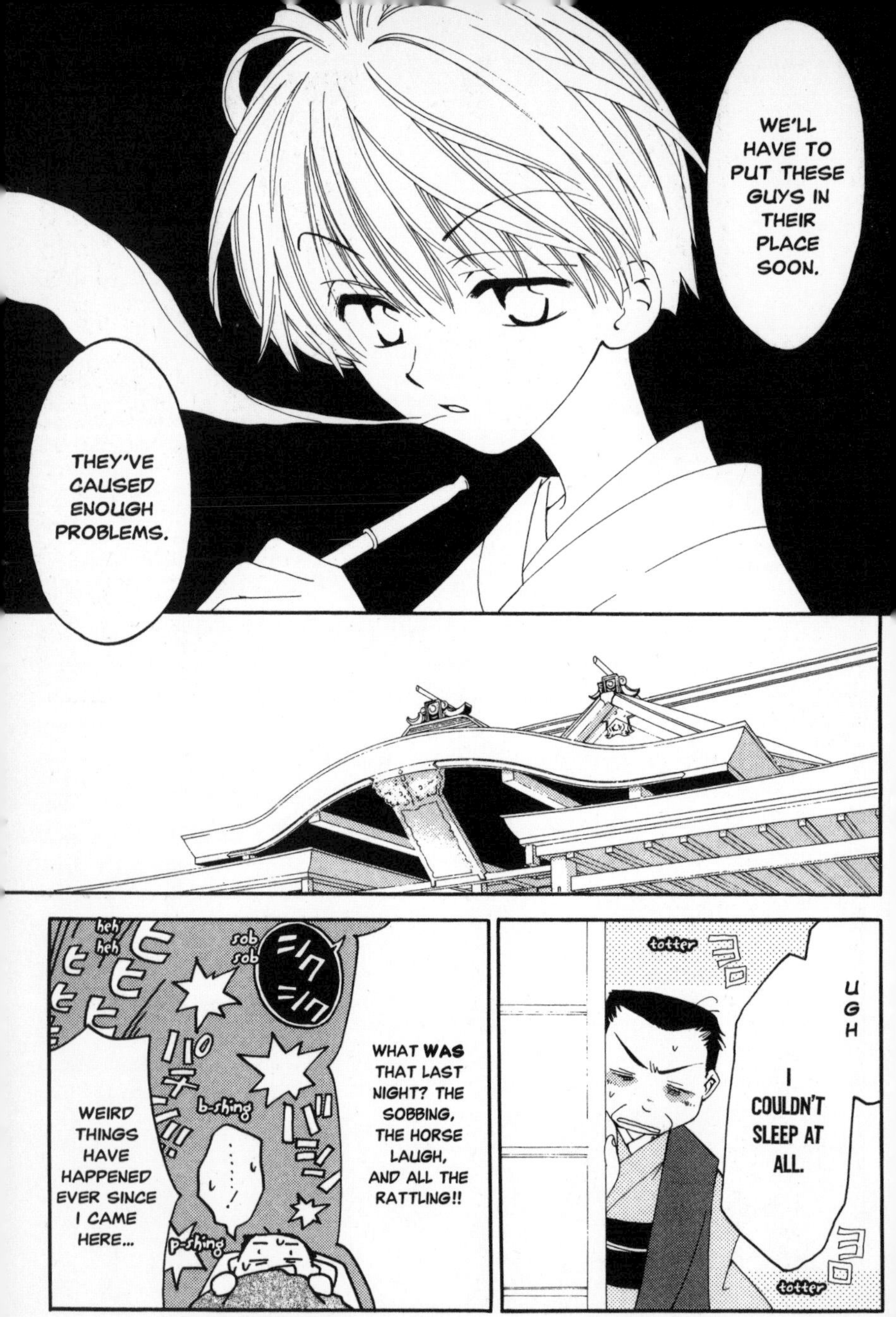
WE'LL HAVE TO PUT THESE GUYS IN THEIR PLACE SOON.
THEY'VE CAUSED ENOUGH PROBLEMS.
totter
UGH
I COULDN'T SLEEP AT ALL.
totter
heh heh
sob sob
b-shing
WHAT WAS THAT LAST NIGHT? THE SOBBING, THE HORSE LAUGH, AND ALL THE RATTLING!!
WEIRD THINGS HAVE HAPPENED EVER SINCE I CAME HERE...
p-shing

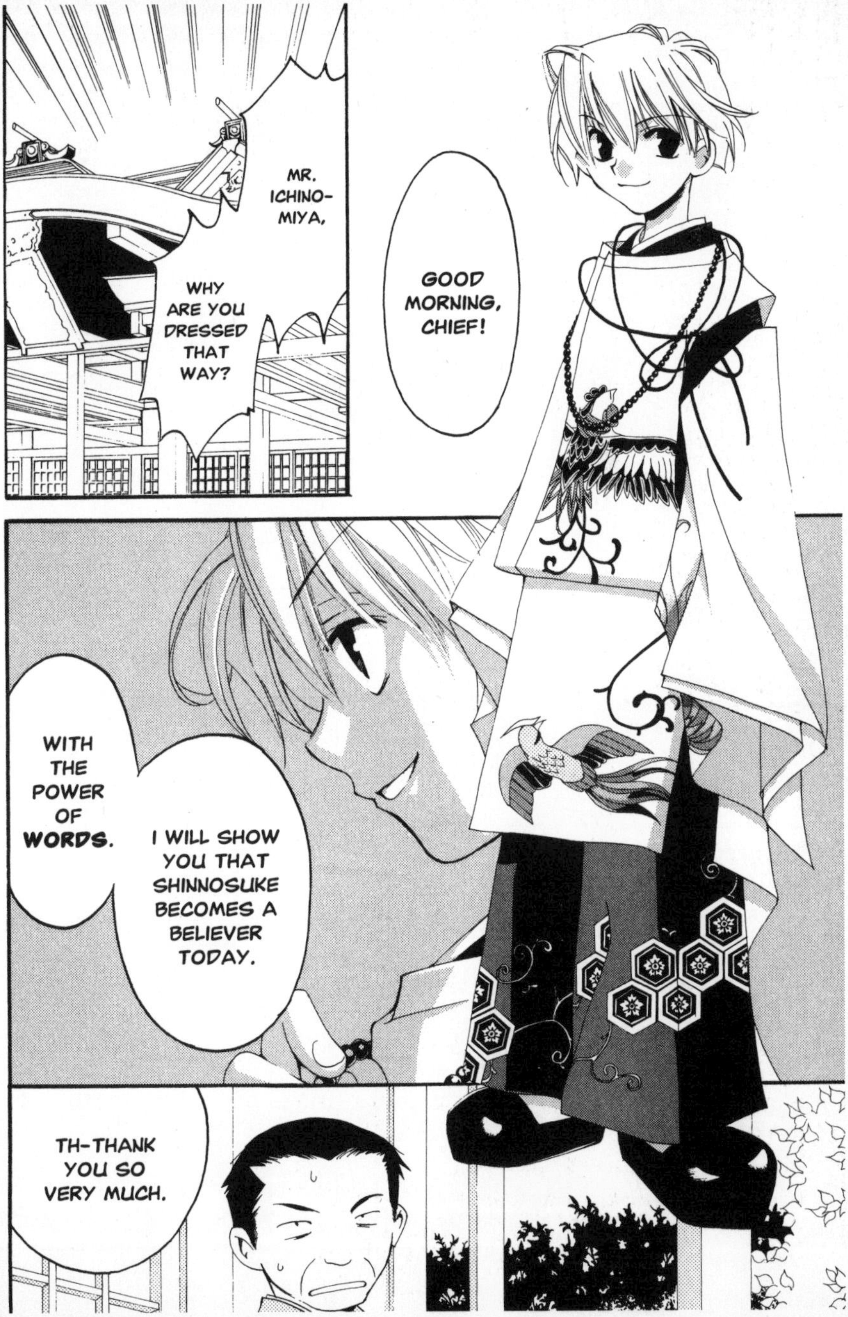
GOOD MORNING, CHIEF!
MR. ICHINO-MIYA,
WHY ARE YOU DRESSED THAT WAY?
I WILL SHOW YOU THAT SHINNOSUKE BECOMES A BELIEVER TODAY.
WITH THE POWER OF **WORDS**.
TH-THANK YOU SO VERY MUCH.

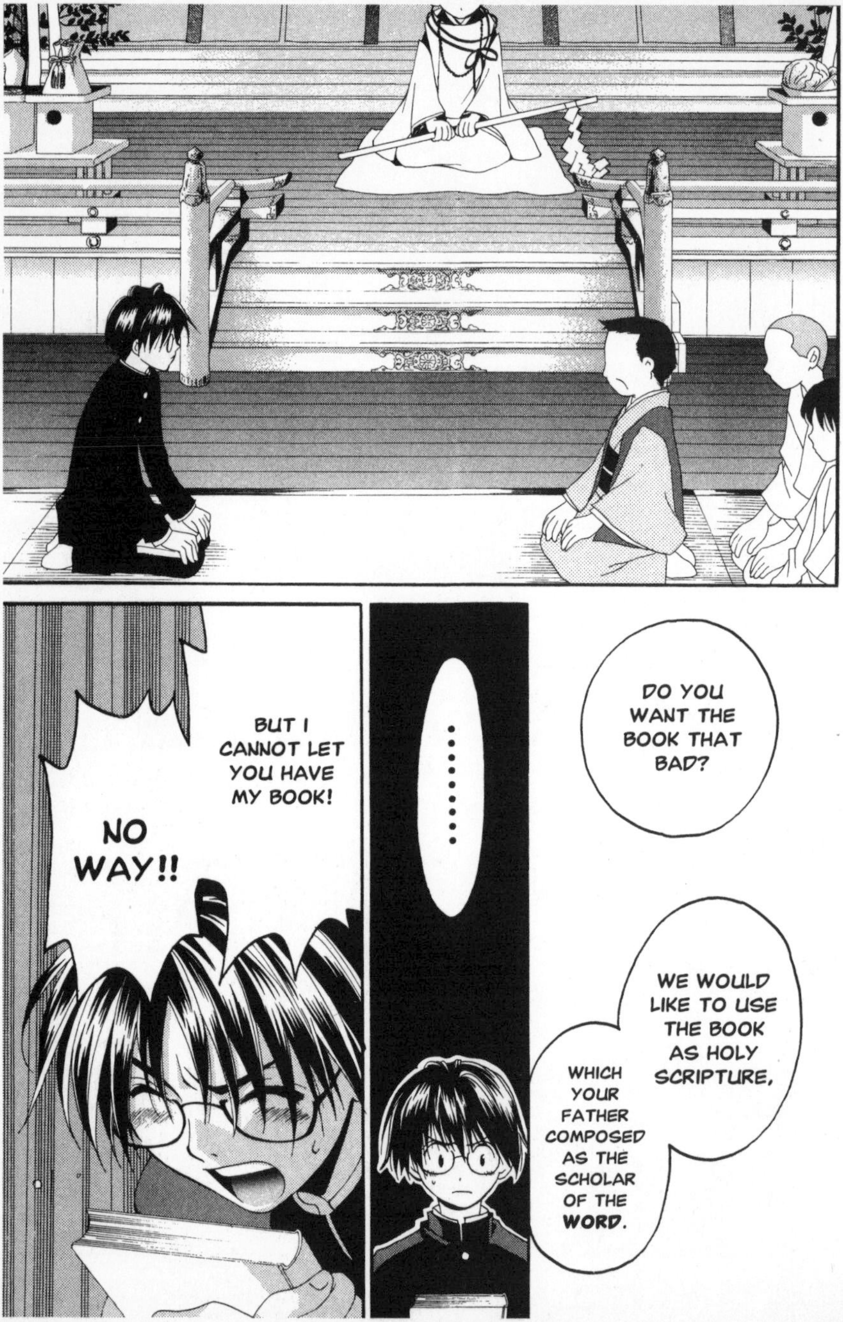
DO YOU WANT THE BOOK THAT BAD?
WE WOULD LIKE TO USE THE BOOK AS HOLY SCRIPTURE,
WHICH YOUR FATHER COMPOSED AS THE SCHOLAR OF THE **WORD**.
....
BUT I CANNOT LET YOU HAVE MY BOOK!
NO WAY!!

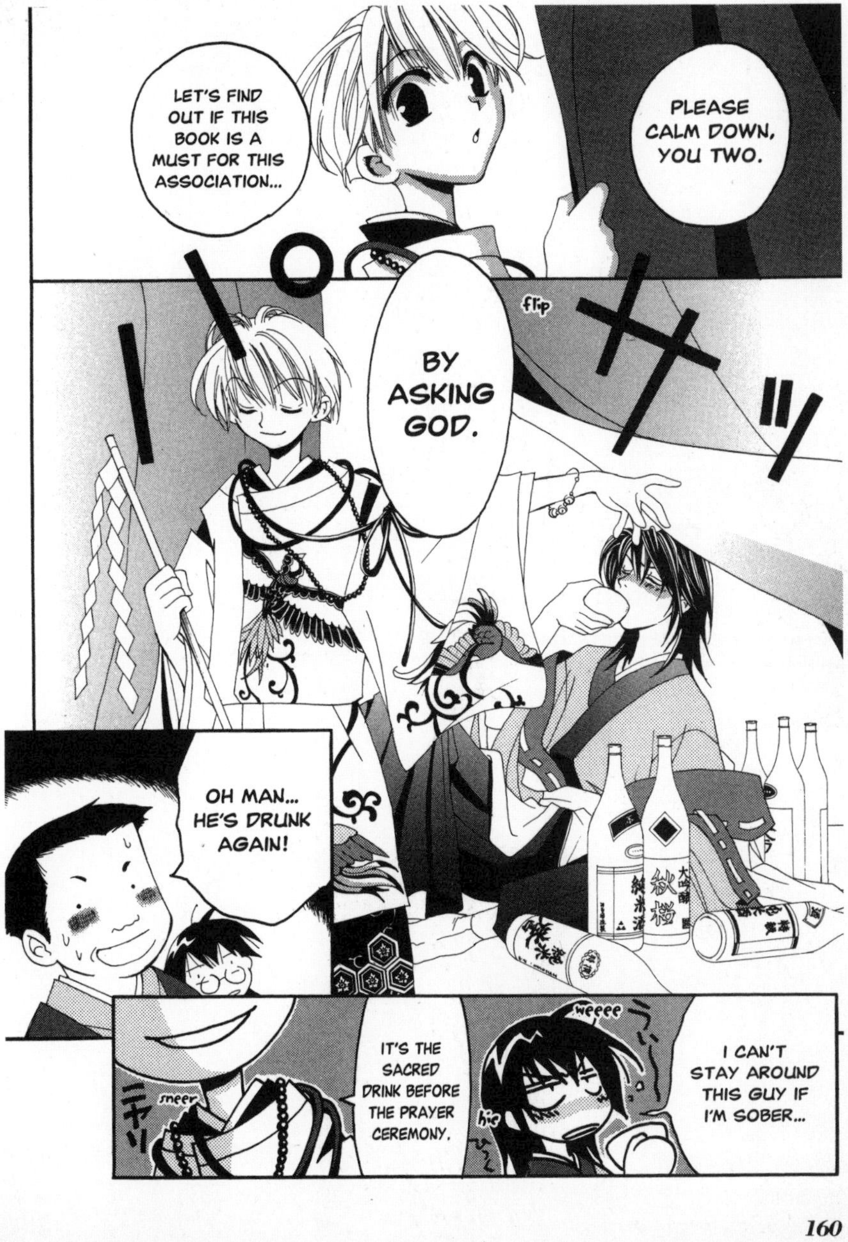
PLEASE CALM DOWN, YOU TWO.
LET'S FIND OUT IF THIS BOOK IS A MUST FOR THIS ASSOCIATION...
flip
BY ASKING GOD.
OH MAN... HE'S DRUNK AGAIN!
weeee
I CAN'T STAY AROUND THIS GUY IF I'M SOBER...
hic
IT'S THE SACRED DRINK BEFORE THE PRAYER CEREMONY.
sneer

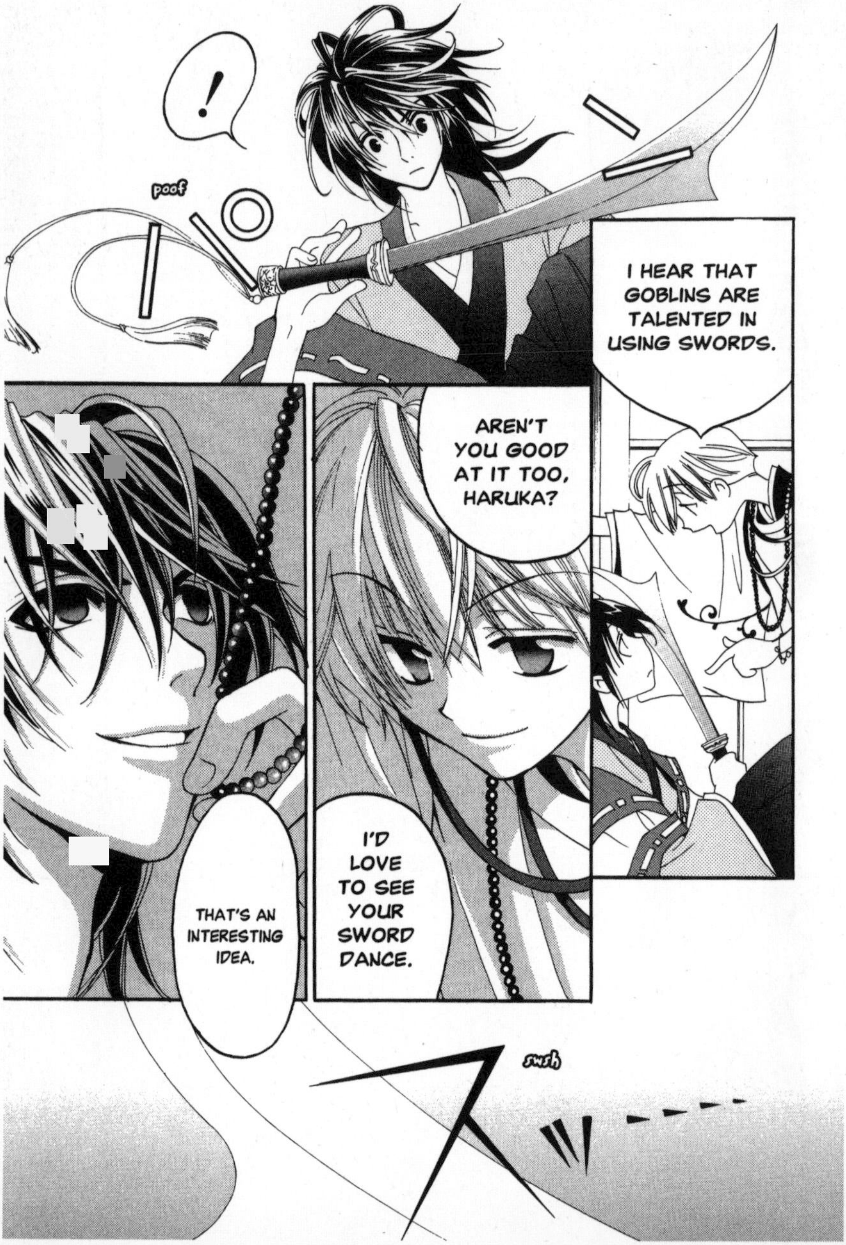
!
poof
I HEAR THAT GOBLINS ARE TALENTED IN USING SWORDS.
AREN'T YOU GOOD AT IT TOO, HARUKA?
I'D LOVE TO SEE YOUR SWORD DANCE.
THAT'S AN INTERESTING IDEA.
swsh

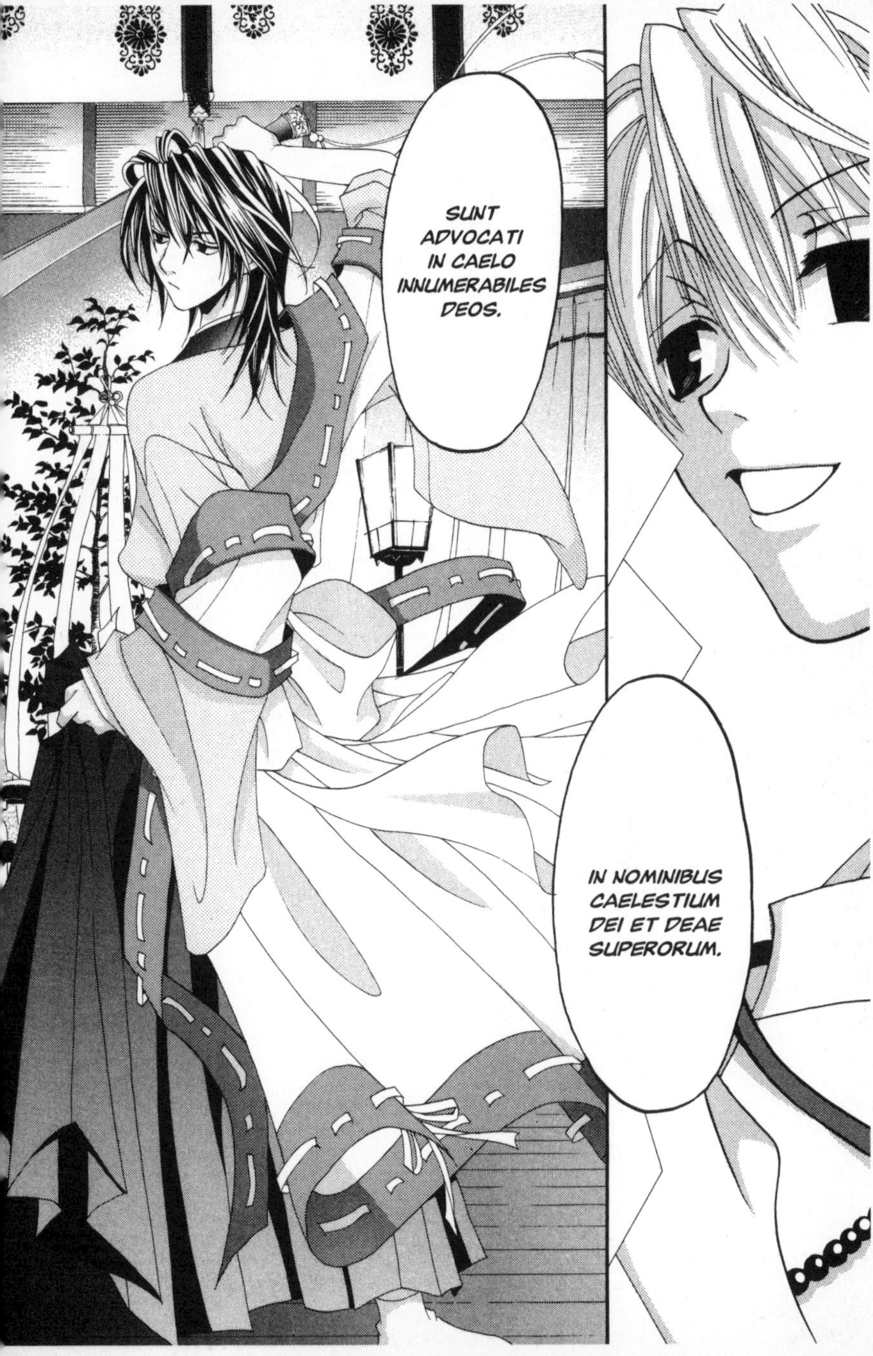
SUNT ADVOCATI IN CAELO INNUMERABILES DEOS.
IN NOMINIBUS CAELESTIUM DEI ET DEAE SUPERORUM.

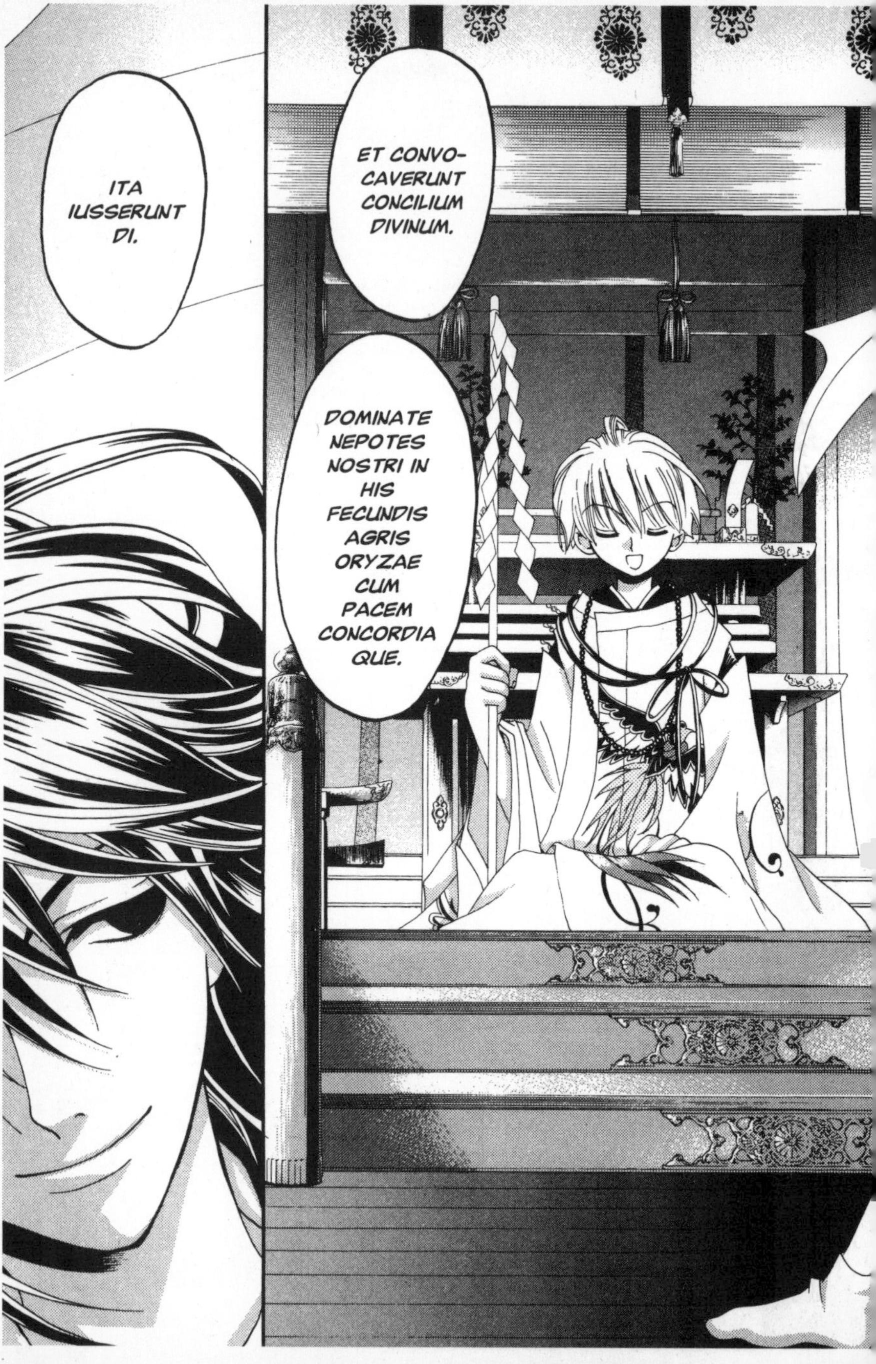
ET CONVO-CAVERUNT CONCILIUM DIVINUM.
DOMINATE NEPOTES NOSTRI IN HIS FECUNDIS AGRIS ORYZAE CUM PACEM CONCORDIAQUE.
ITA IUSSERUNT DI.

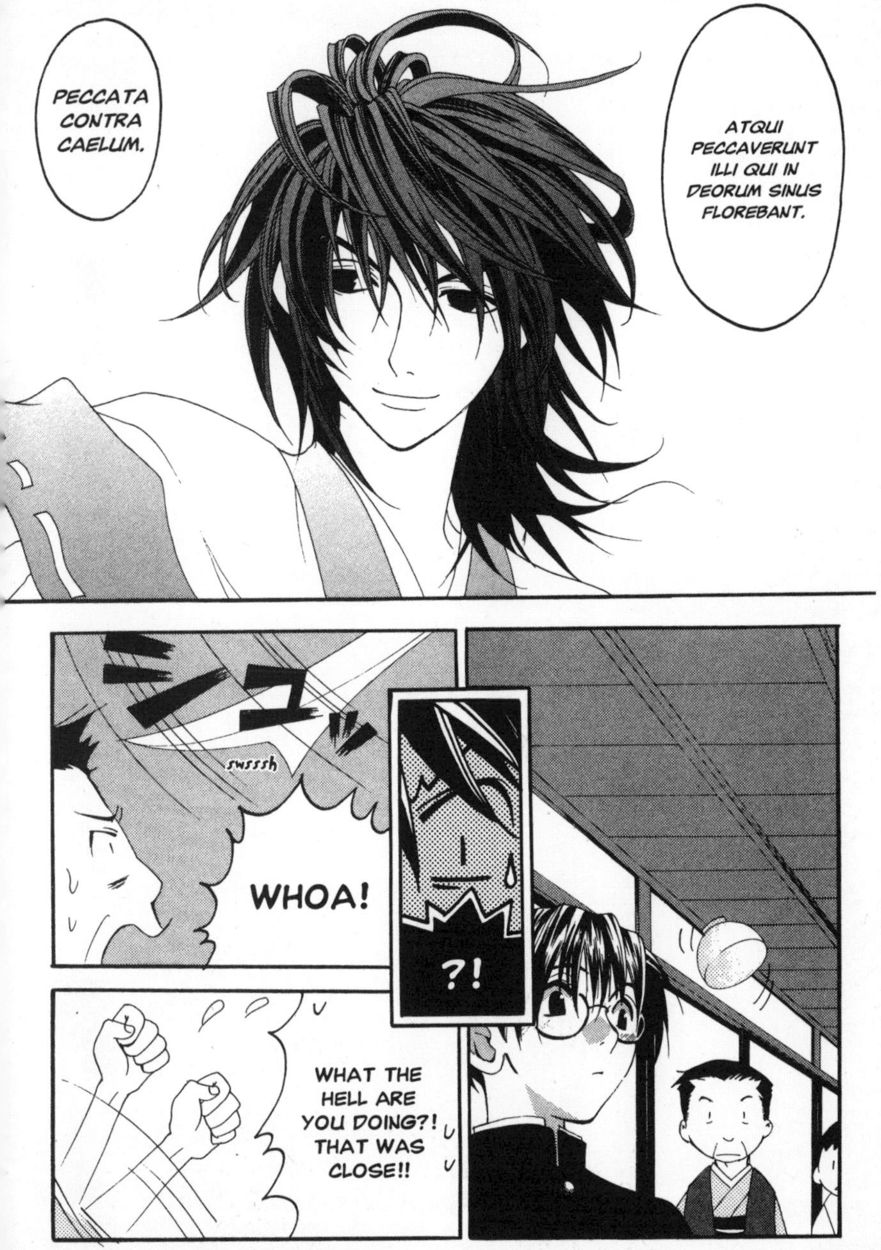
ATQUI PECCAVERUNT ILLI QUI IN DEORUM SINUS FLOREBANT.
PECCATA CONTRA CAELUM.
?!
シュッ
swsssh
WHOA!
WHAT THE HELL ARE YOU DOING?! THAT WAS CLOSE!!

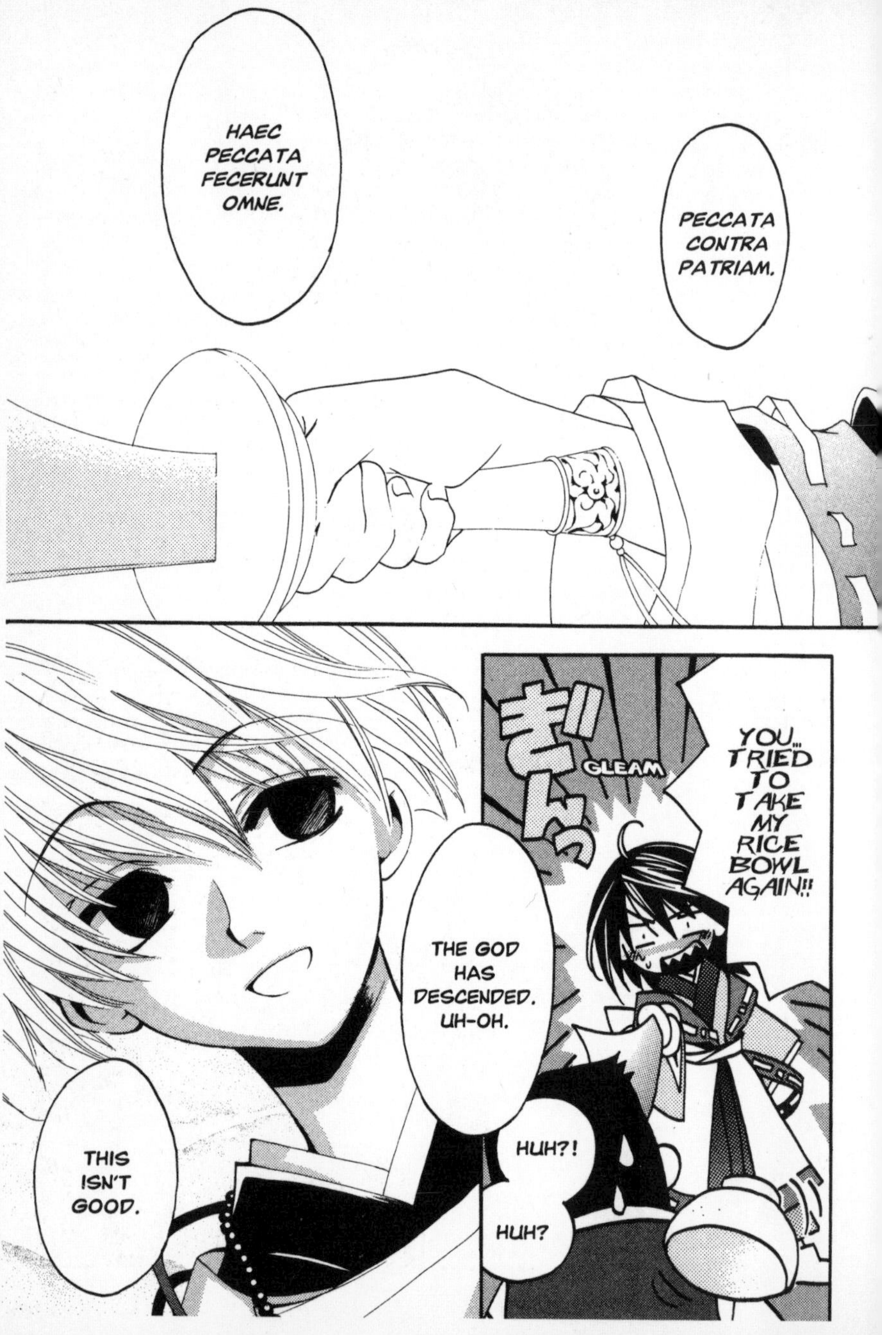
PECCATA CONTRA PATRIAM.
HAEC PECCATA FECERUNT OMNE.
YOU... TRIED TO TAKE MY RICE BOWL AGAIN!!
ぎんっ
GLEAM
HUH?!
HUH?
THE GOD HAS DESCENDED. UH-OH.
THIS ISN'T GOOD.

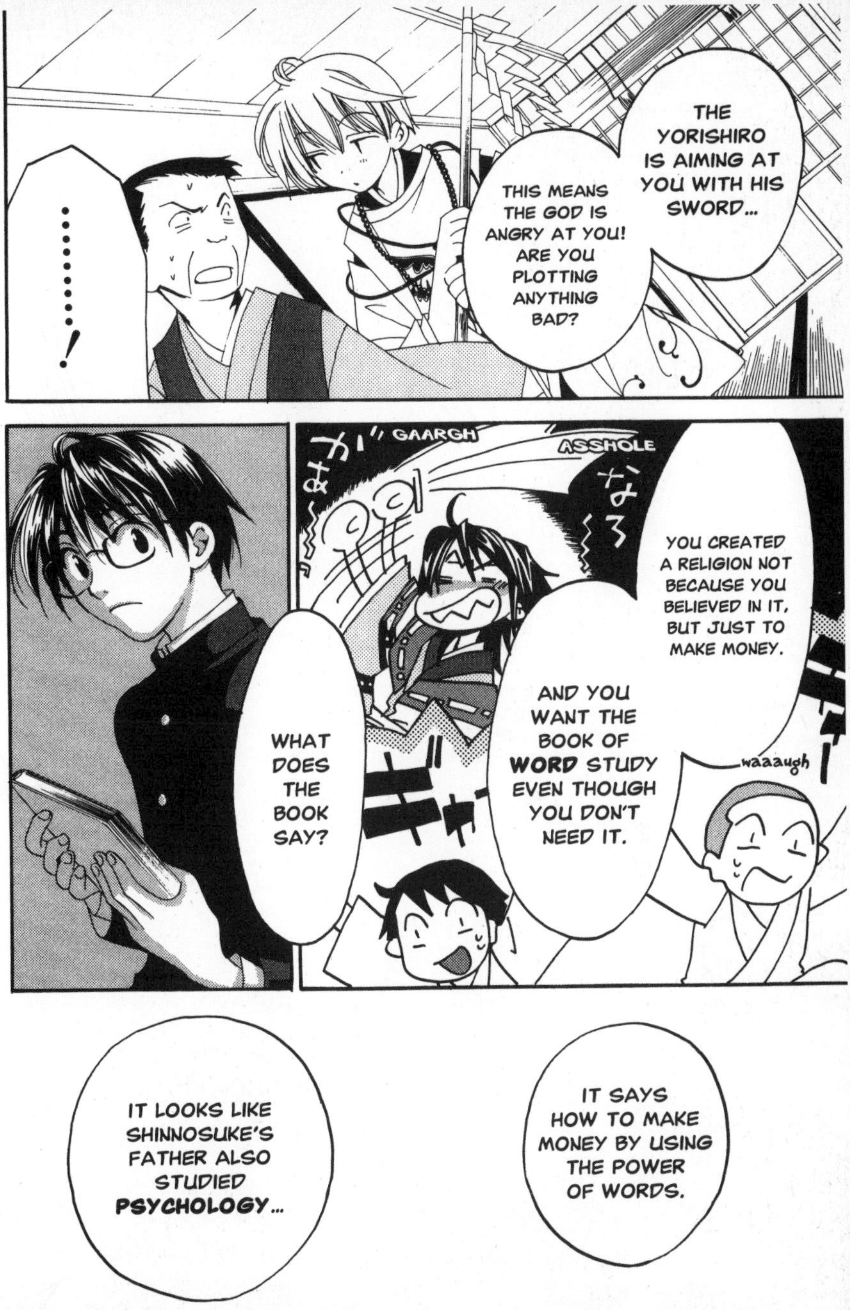
THE YORISHIRO IS AIMING AT YOU WITH HIS SWORD...
THIS MEANS THE GOD IS ANGRY AT YOU! ARE YOU PLOTTING ANYTHING BAD?
.........!
YOU CREATED A RELIGION NOT BECAUSE YOU BELIEVED IN IT, BUT JUST TO MAKE MONEY.
ASSHOLE
AND YOU WANT THE BOOK OF **WORD** STUDY EVEN THOUGH YOU DON'T NEED IT.
GAARGH
waaaugh
WHAT DOES THE BOOK SAY?
IT SAYS HOW TO MAKE MONEY BY USING THE POWER OF WORDS.
IT LOOKS LIKE SHINNOSUKE'S FATHER ALSO STUDIED **PSYCHOLOGY**...

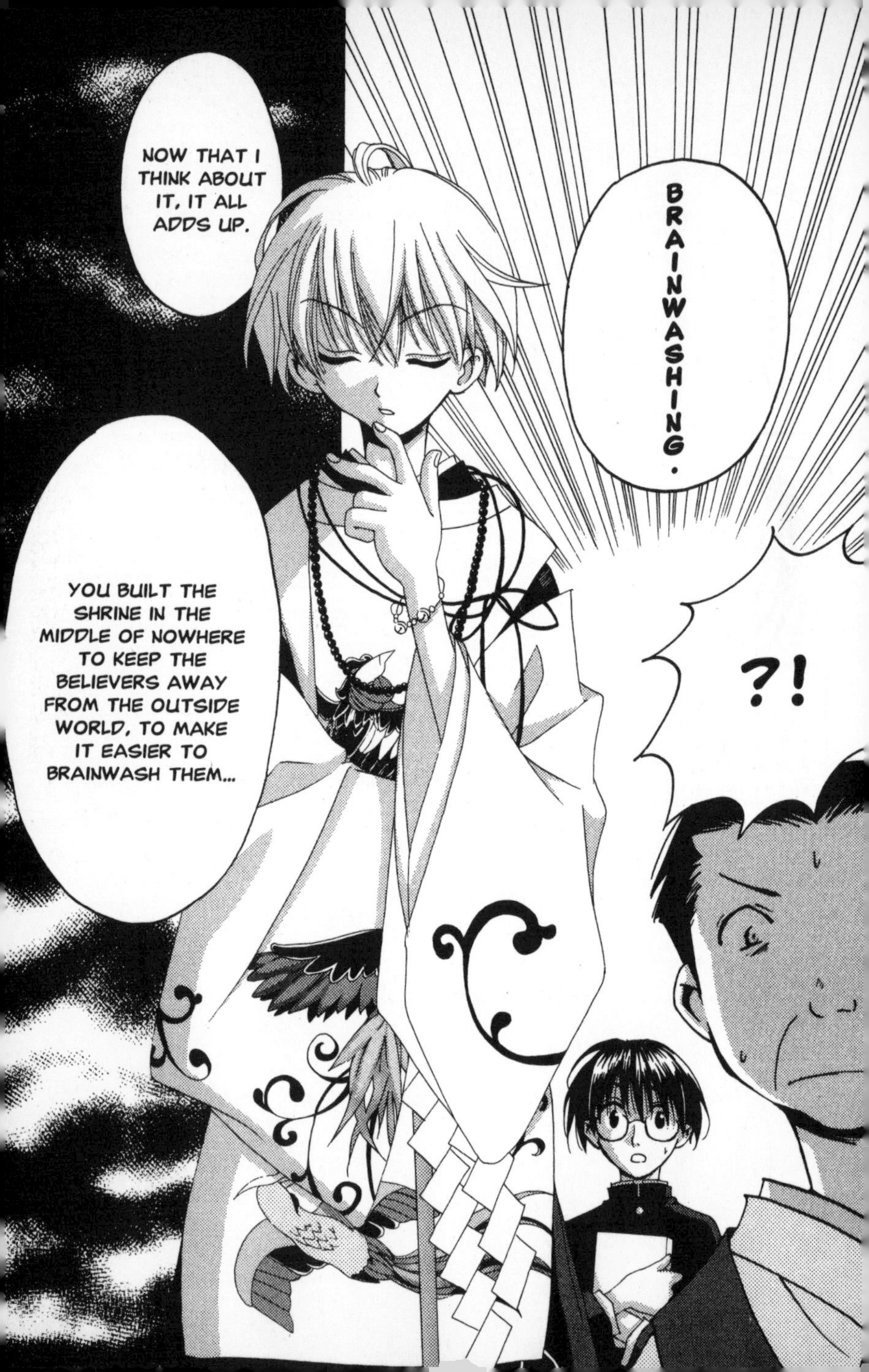
BRAINWASHING.
NOW THAT I THINK ABOUT IT, IT ALL ADDS UP.
?!
YOU BUILT THE SHRINE IN THE MIDDLE OF NOWHERE TO KEEP THE BELIEVERS AWAY FROM THE OUTSIDE WORLD, TO MAKE IT EASIER TO BRAINWASH THEM...

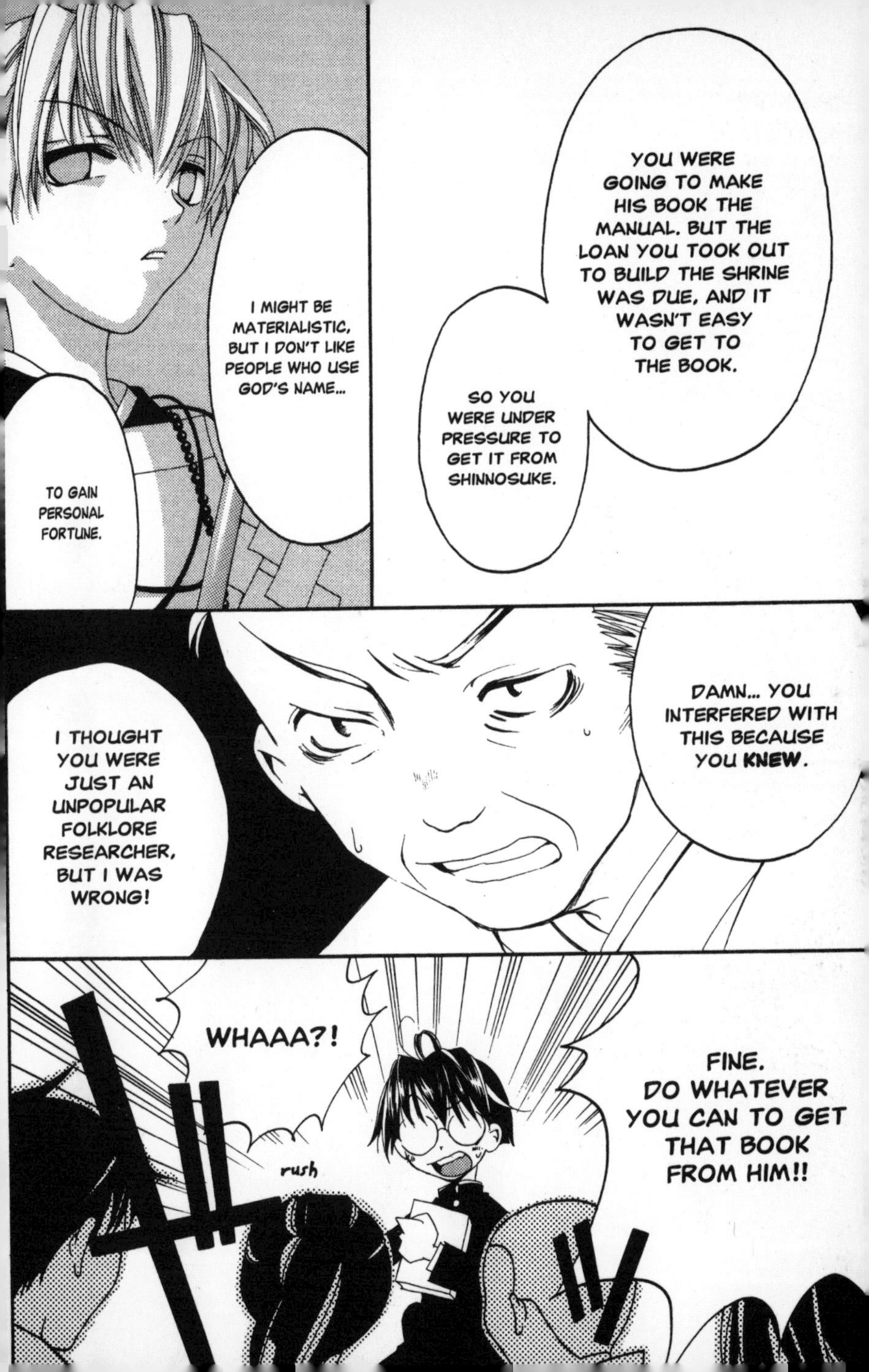
YOU WERE GOING TO MAKE HIS BOOK THE MANUAL. BUT THE LOAN YOU TOOK OUT TO BUILD THE SHRINE WAS DUE, AND IT WASN'T EASY TO GET TO THE BOOK.
SO YOU WERE UNDER PRESSURE TO GET IT FROM SHINNOSUKE.
I MIGHT BE MATERIALISTIC, BUT I DON'T LIKE PEOPLE WHO USE GOD'S NAME...
TO GAIN PERSONAL FORTUNE.
DAMN... YOU INTERFERED WITH THIS BECAUSE YOU **KNEW**.
I THOUGHT YOU WERE JUST AN UNPOPULAR FOLKLORE RESEARCHER, BUT I WAS WRONG!
FINE. DO WHATEVER YOU CAN TO GET THAT BOOK FROM HIM!!
WHAAA?!
rush

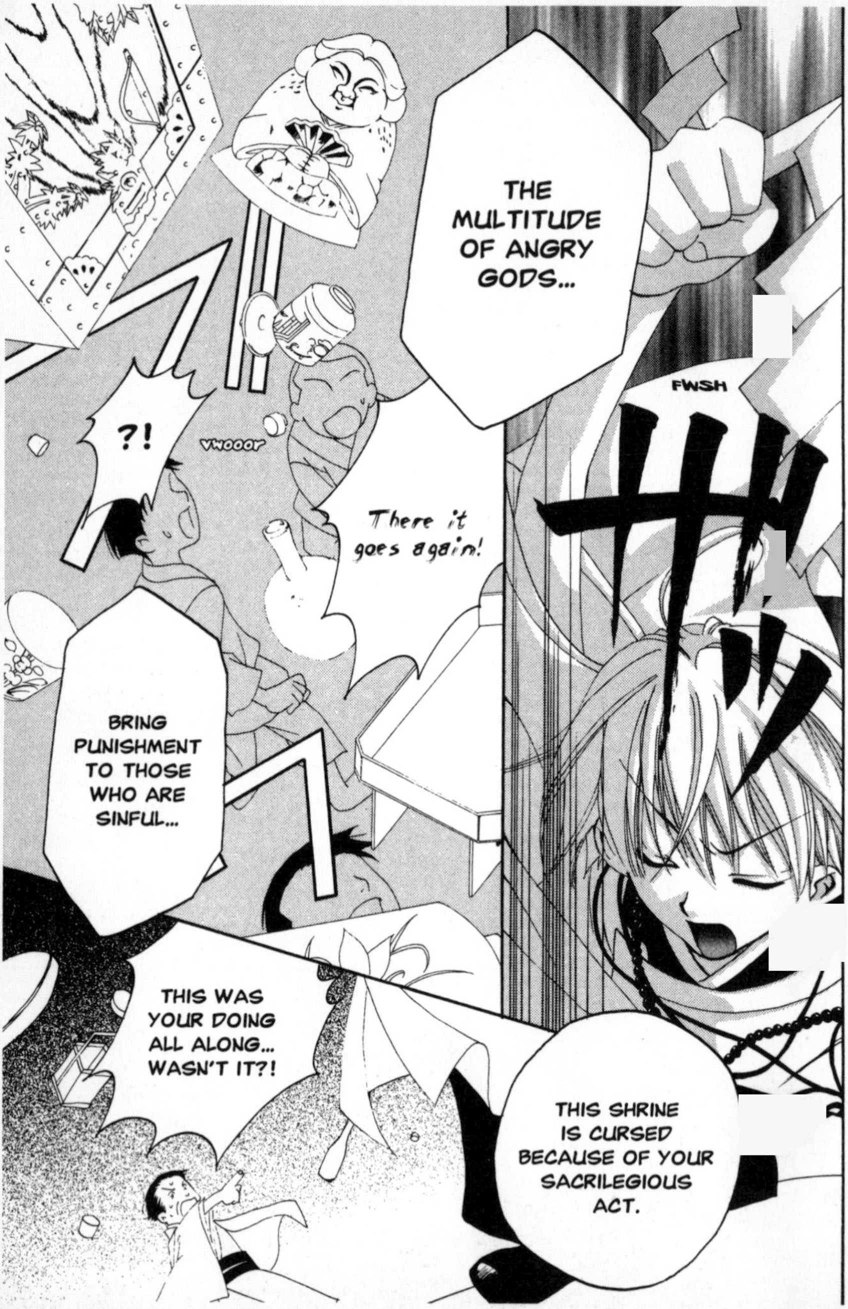
THE MULTITUDE OF ANGRY GODS...
FWSH
サッ
?!
vwooor
There it goes again!
BRING PUNISHMENT TO THOSE WHO ARE SINFUL...
THIS SHRINE IS CURSED BECAUSE OF YOUR SACRILEGIOUS ACT.
THIS WAS YOUR DOING ALL ALONG... WASN'T IT?!

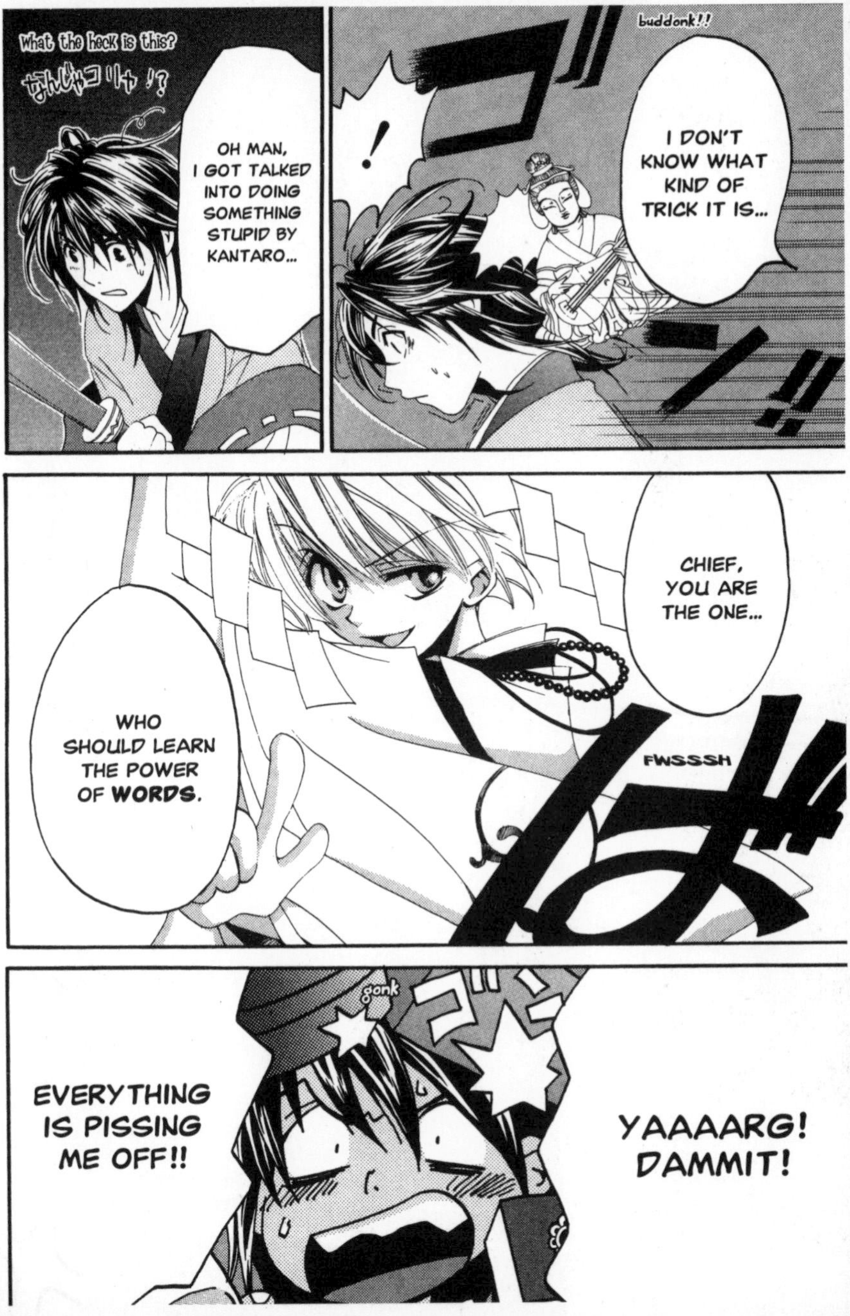

buddonk!!
I DON'T KNOW WHAT KIND OF TRICK IT IS...
What the heck is this?
なんじゃコリャ!?
OH MAN, I GOT TALKED INTO DOING SOMETHING STUPID BY KANTARO...
CHIEF, YOU ARE THE ONE...
WHO SHOULD LEARN THE POWER OF **WORDS**.
FWSSSH
gonk
YAAAARG! DAMMIT!
EVERYTHING IS PISSING ME OFF!!

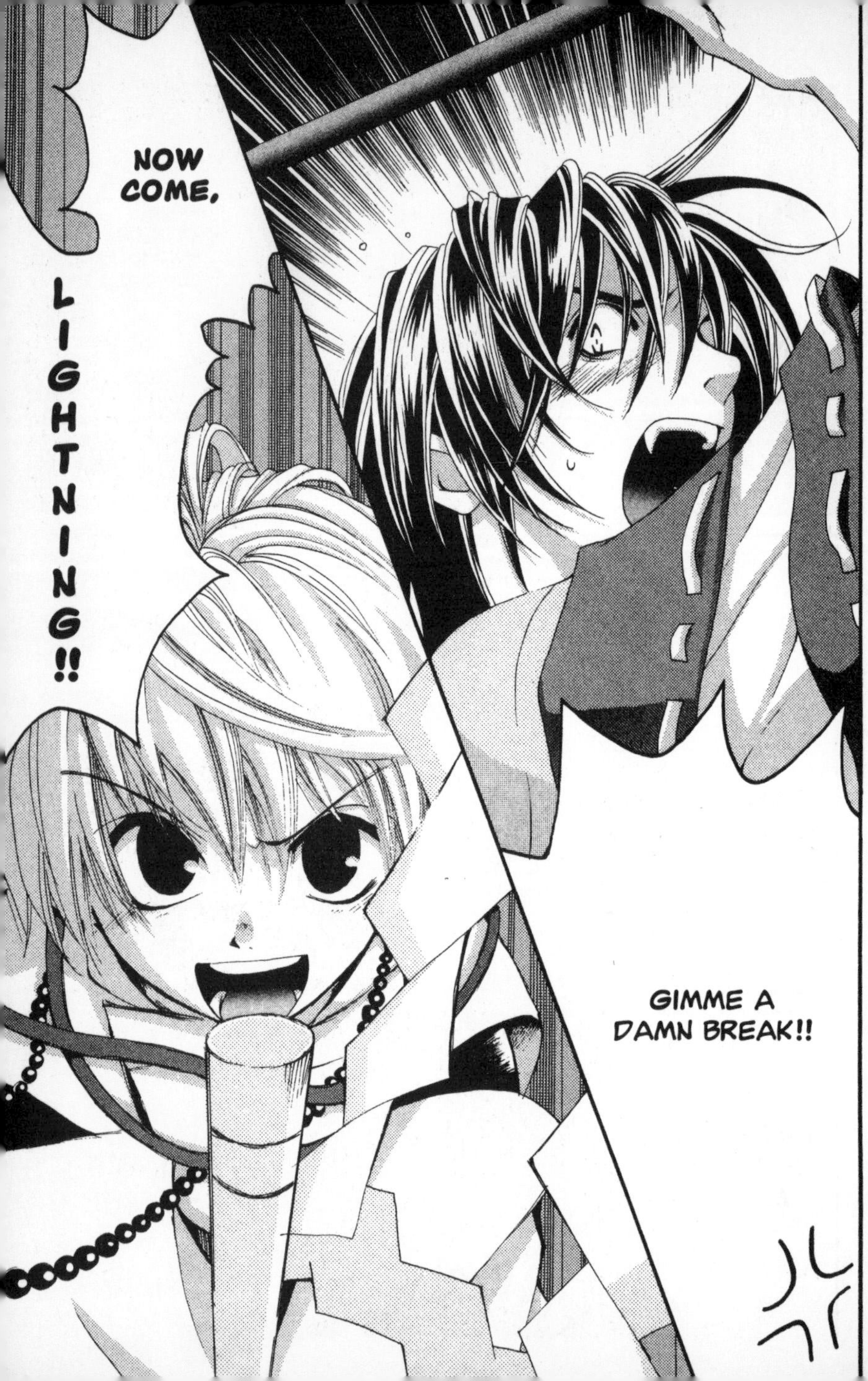
GIMME A DAMN BREAK!!
NOW COME,
LIGHTNING!!

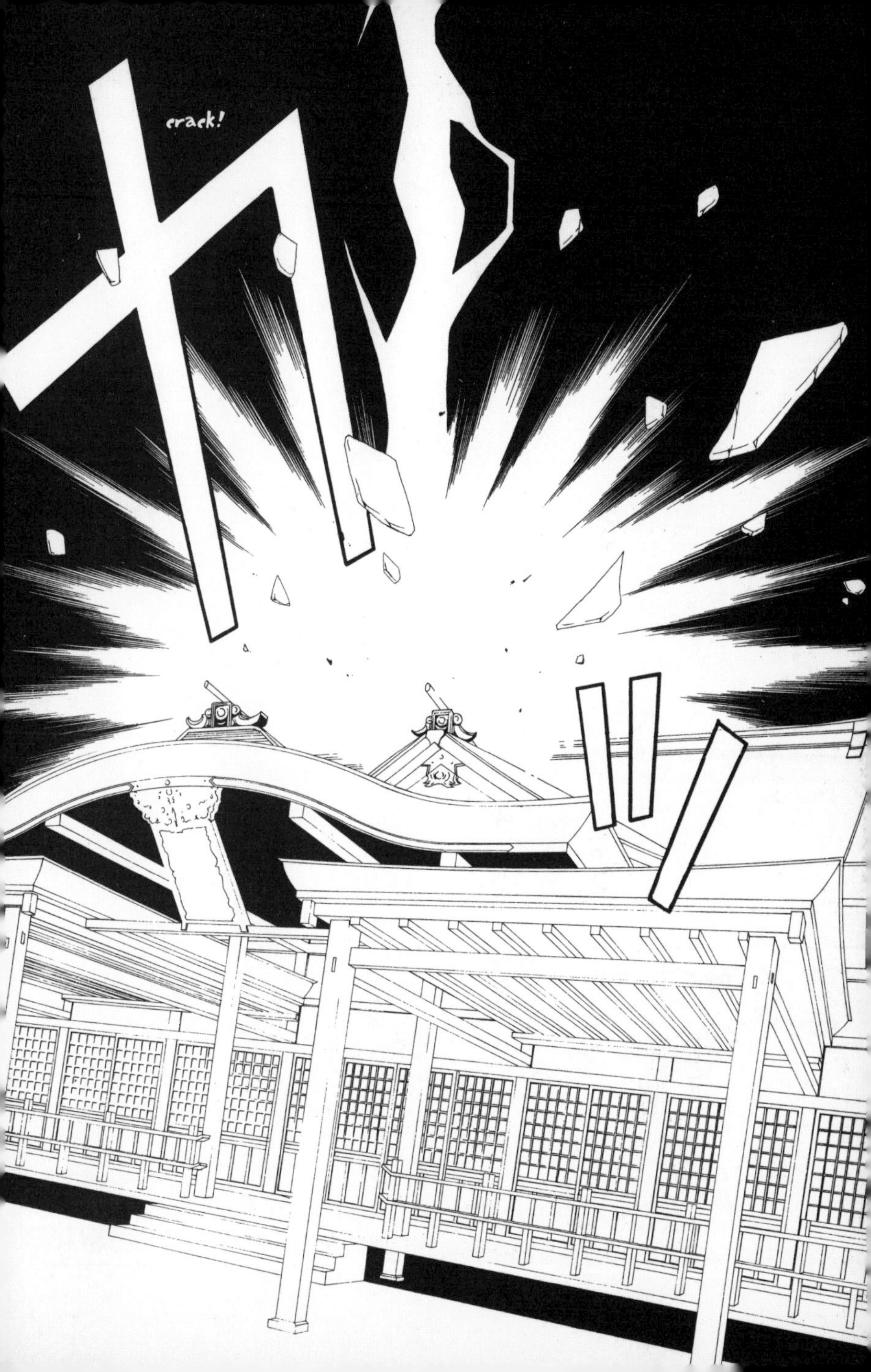
crack!

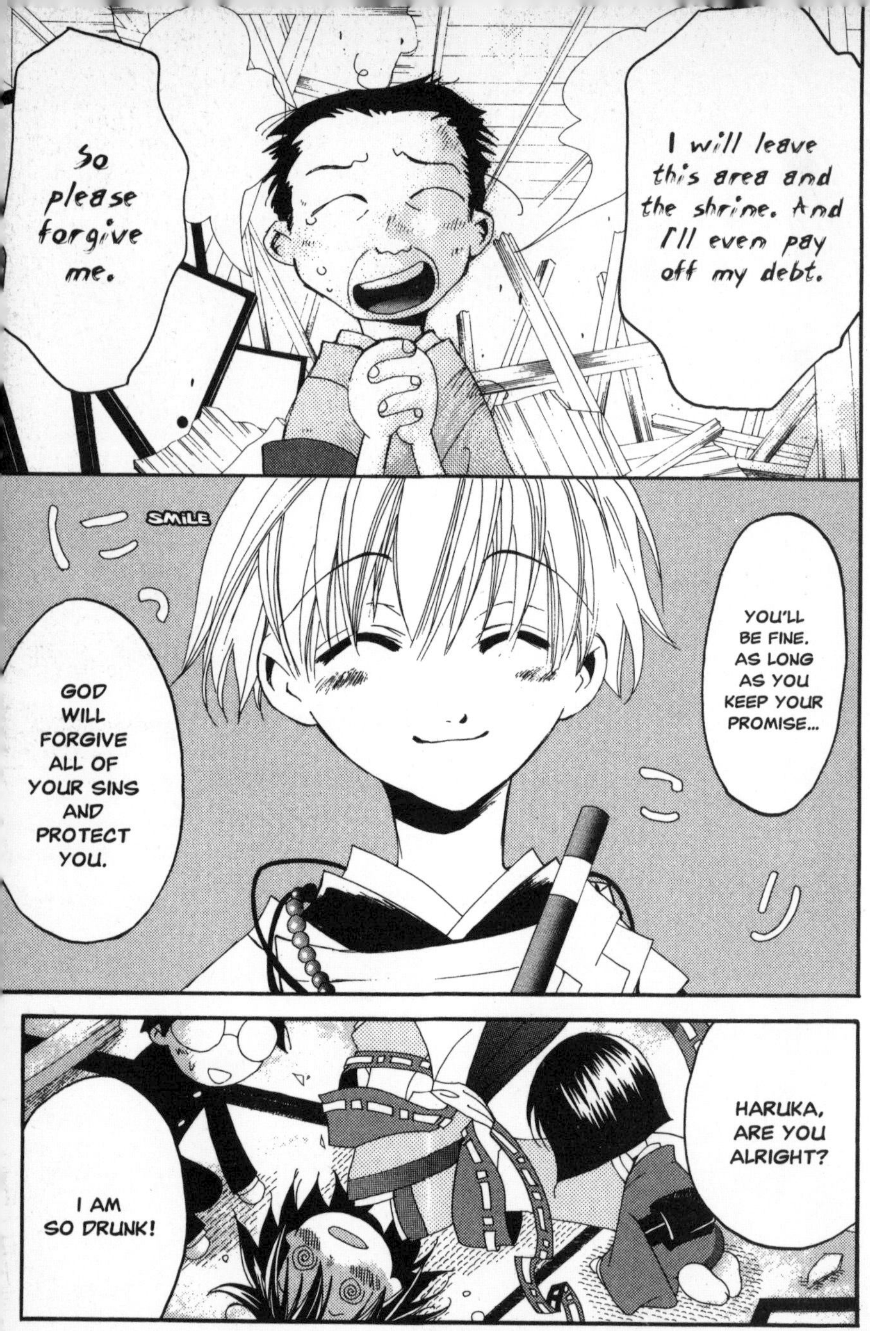
I will leave this area and the shrine. And I'll even pay off my debt.
So please forgive me.
YOU'LL BE FINE. AS LONG AS YOU KEEP YOUR PROMISE...
SMILE
GOD WILL FORGIVE ALL OF YOUR SINS AND PROTECT YOU.
HARUKA, ARE YOU ALRIGHT?
I AM SO DRUNK!

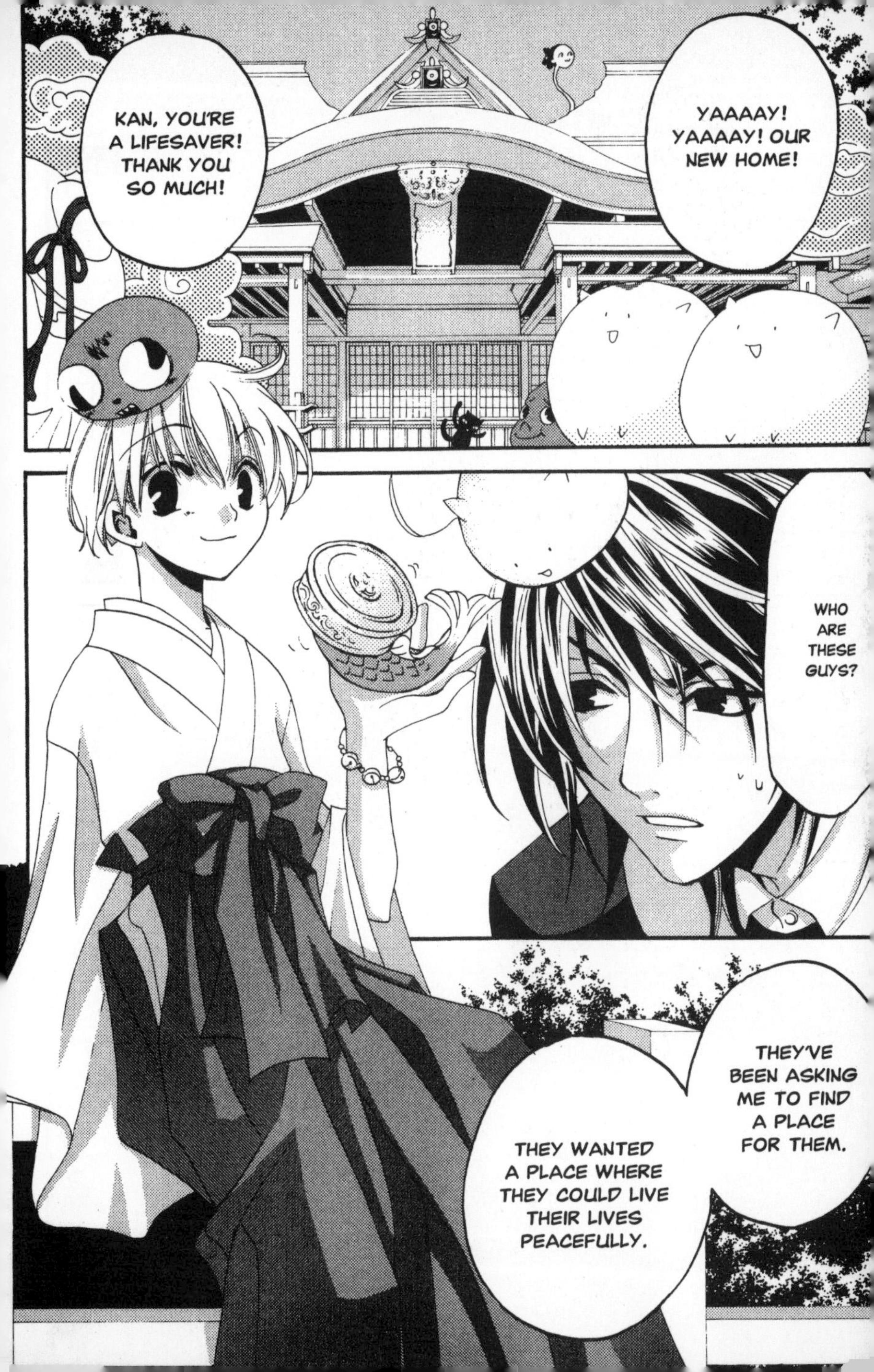
YAAAAY! YAAAAY! OUR NEW HOME!
KAN, YOU'RE A LIFESAVER! THANK YOU SO MUCH!
WHO ARE THESE GUYS?
THEY'VE BEEN ASKING ME TO FIND A PLACE FOR THEM.
THEY WANTED A PLACE WHERE THEY COULD LIVE THEIR LIVES PEACEFULLY.

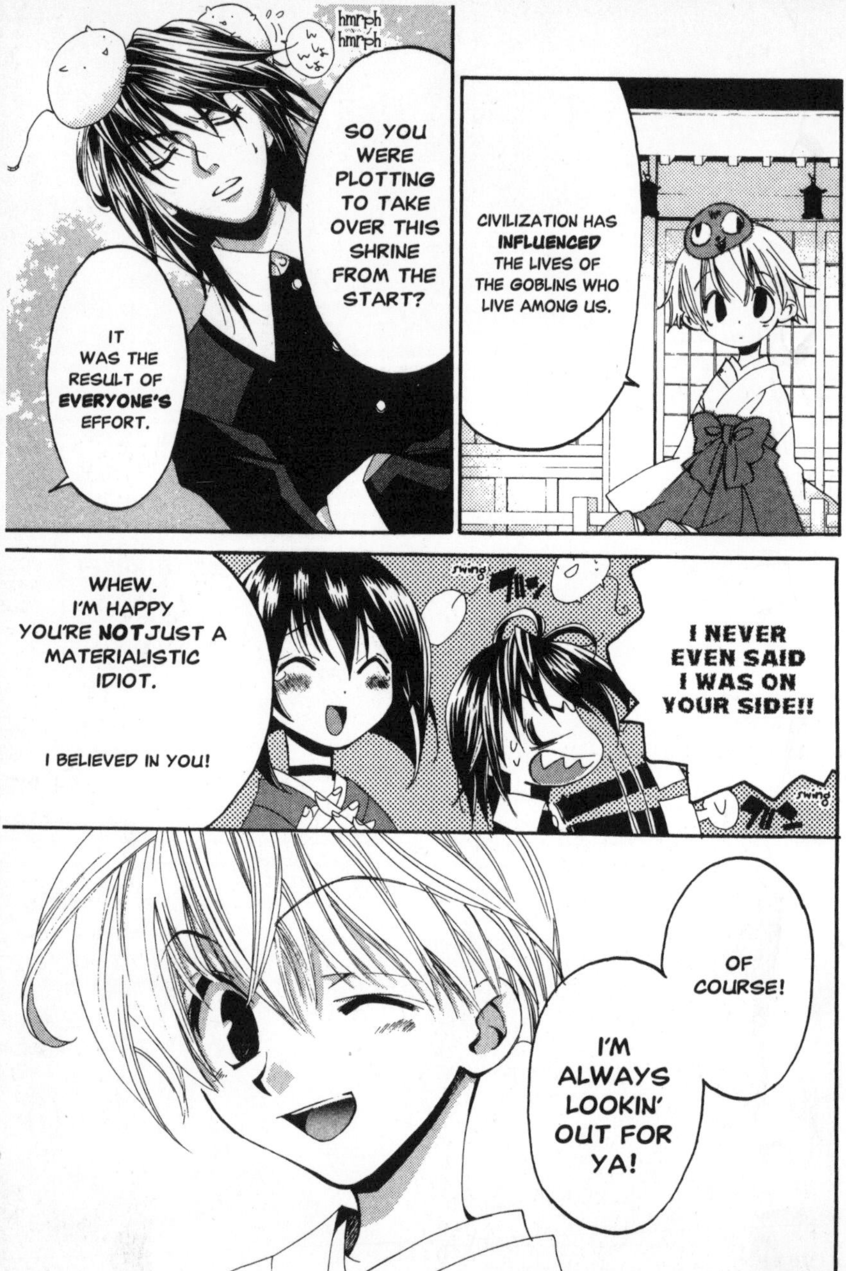
CIVILIZATION HAS INFLUENCED THE LIVES OF THE GOBLINS WHO LIVE AMONG US.
hmrph hmrph
SO YOU WERE PLOTTING TO TAKE OVER THIS SHRINE FROM THE START?
IT WAS THE RESULT OF EVERYONE'S EFFORT.
swing
I NEVER EVEN SAID I WAS ON YOUR SIDE!!
swing
WHEW. I'M HAPPY YOU'RE NOT JUST A MATERIALISTIC IDIOT.
I BELIEVED IN YOU!
OF COURSE!
I'M ALWAYS LOOKIN' OUT FOR YA!

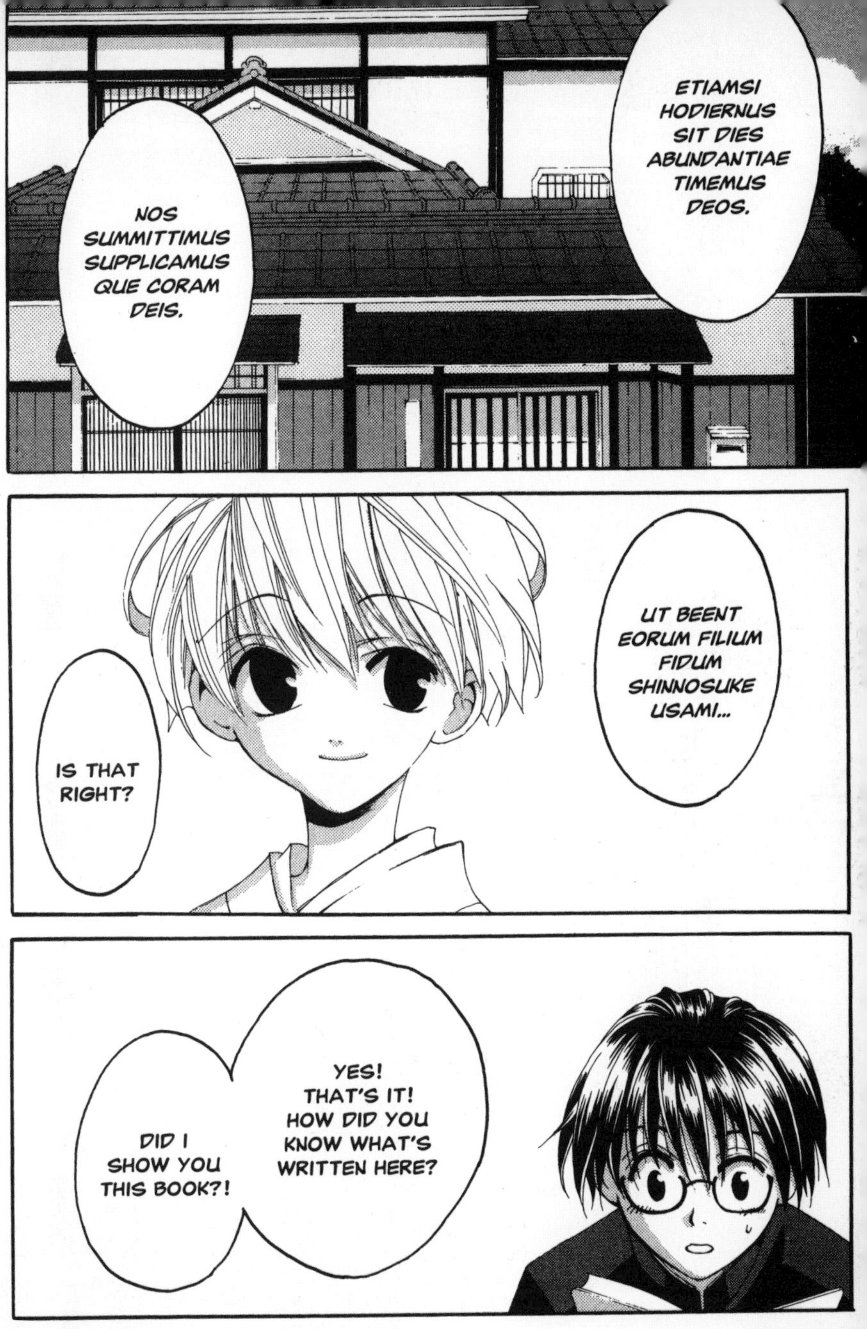
ETIAMSI HODIERNUS SIT DIES ABUNDANTIAE TIMEMUS DEOS.
NOS SUMMITTIMUS SUPPLICAMUS QUE CORAM DEIS.
UT BEENT EORUM FILIUM FIDUM SHINNOSUKE USAMI...
IS THAT RIGHT?
YES! THAT'S IT! HOW DID YOU KNOW WHAT'S WRITTEN HERE?
DID I SHOW YOU THIS BOOK?!

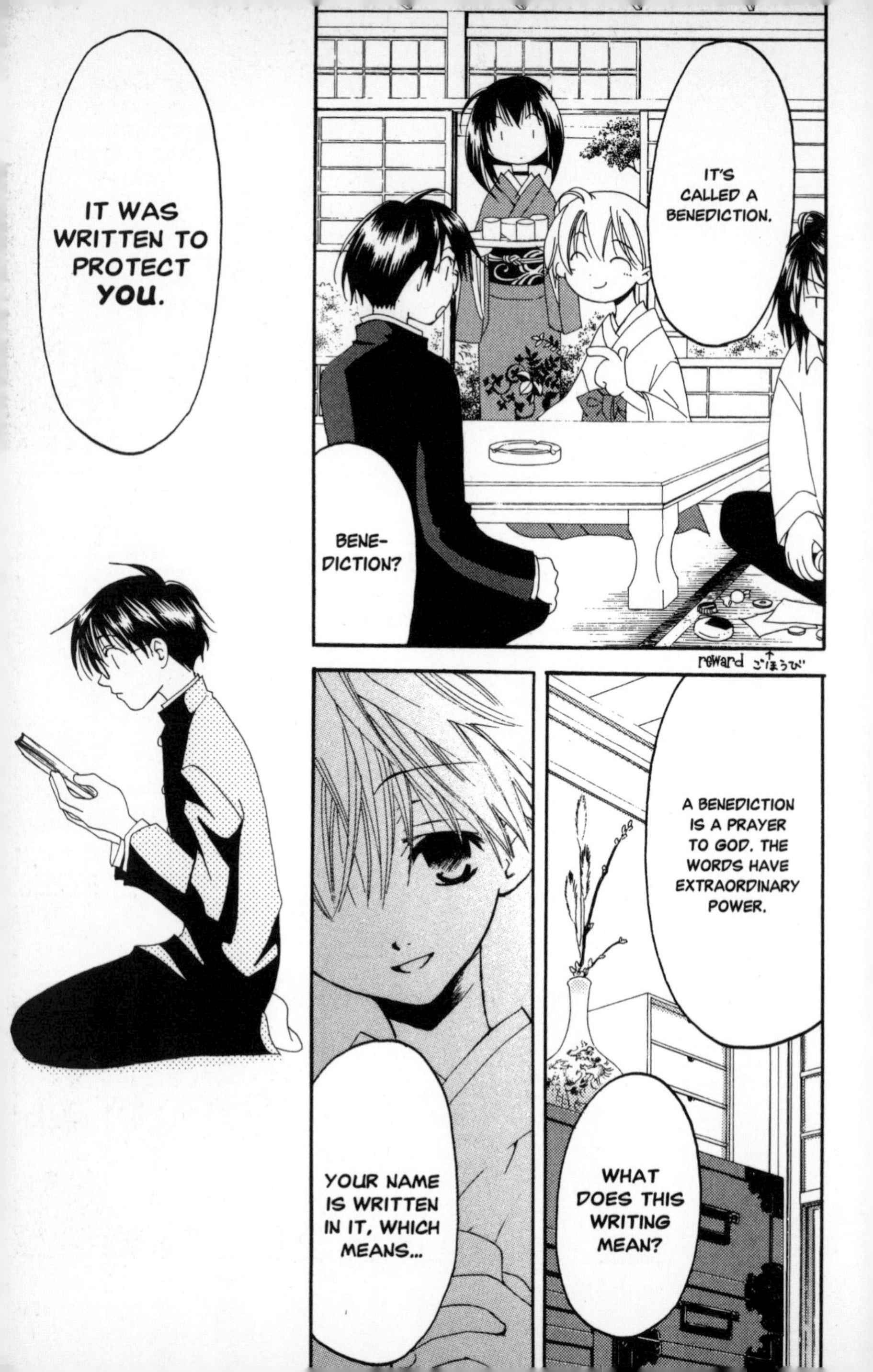
IT'S CALLED A BENEDICTION.
BENE-DICTION?
reward ごほうび
A BENEDICTION IS A PRAYER TO GOD. THE WORDS HAVE EXTRAORDINARY POWER.
WHAT DOES THIS WRITING MEAN?
YOUR NAME IS WRITTEN IN IT, WHICH MEANS...
IT WAS WRITTEN TO PROTECT YOU.

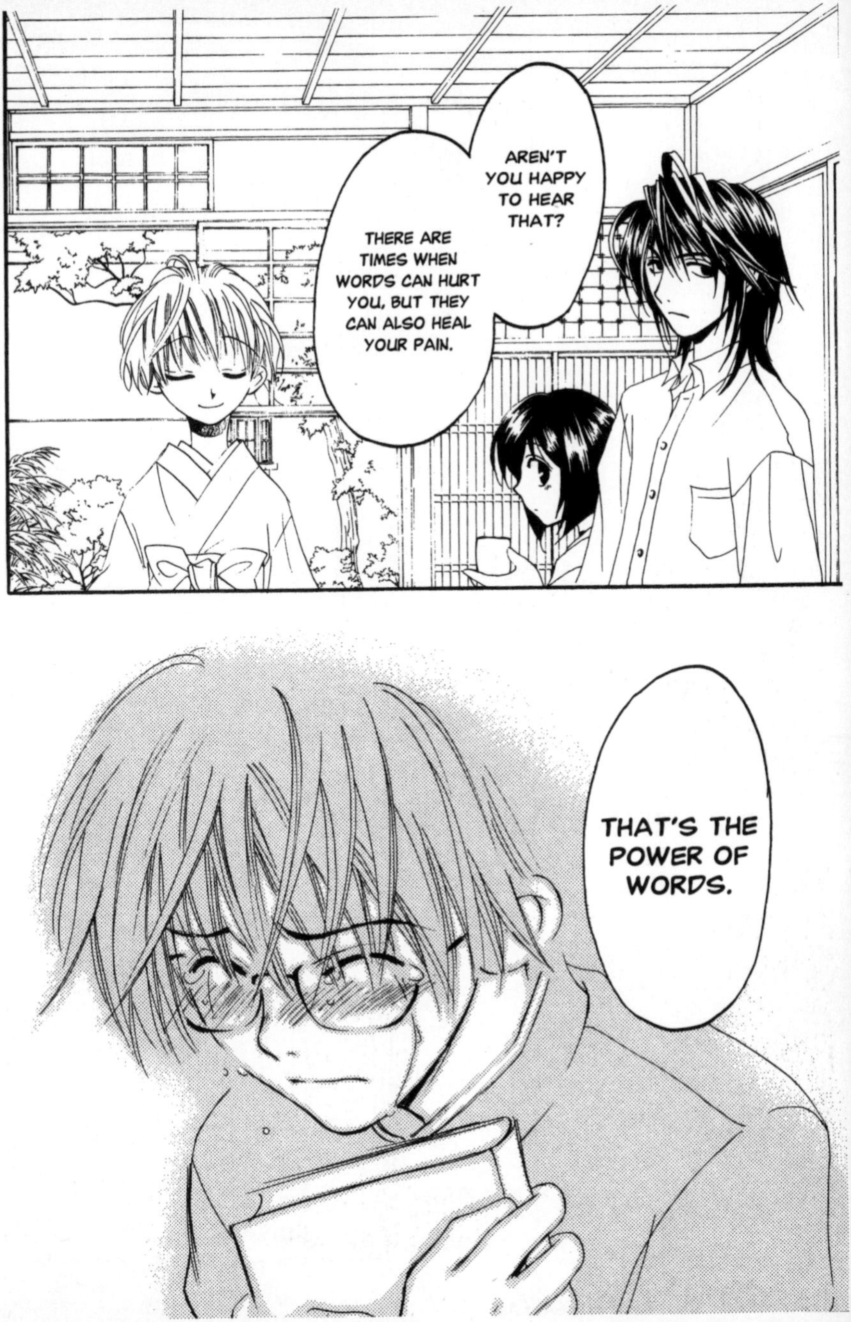
AREN'T YOU HAPPY TO HEAR THAT?
THERE ARE TIMES WHEN WORDS CAN HURT YOU, BUT THEY CAN ALSO HEAL YOUR PAIN.
THAT'S THE POWER OF WORDS.

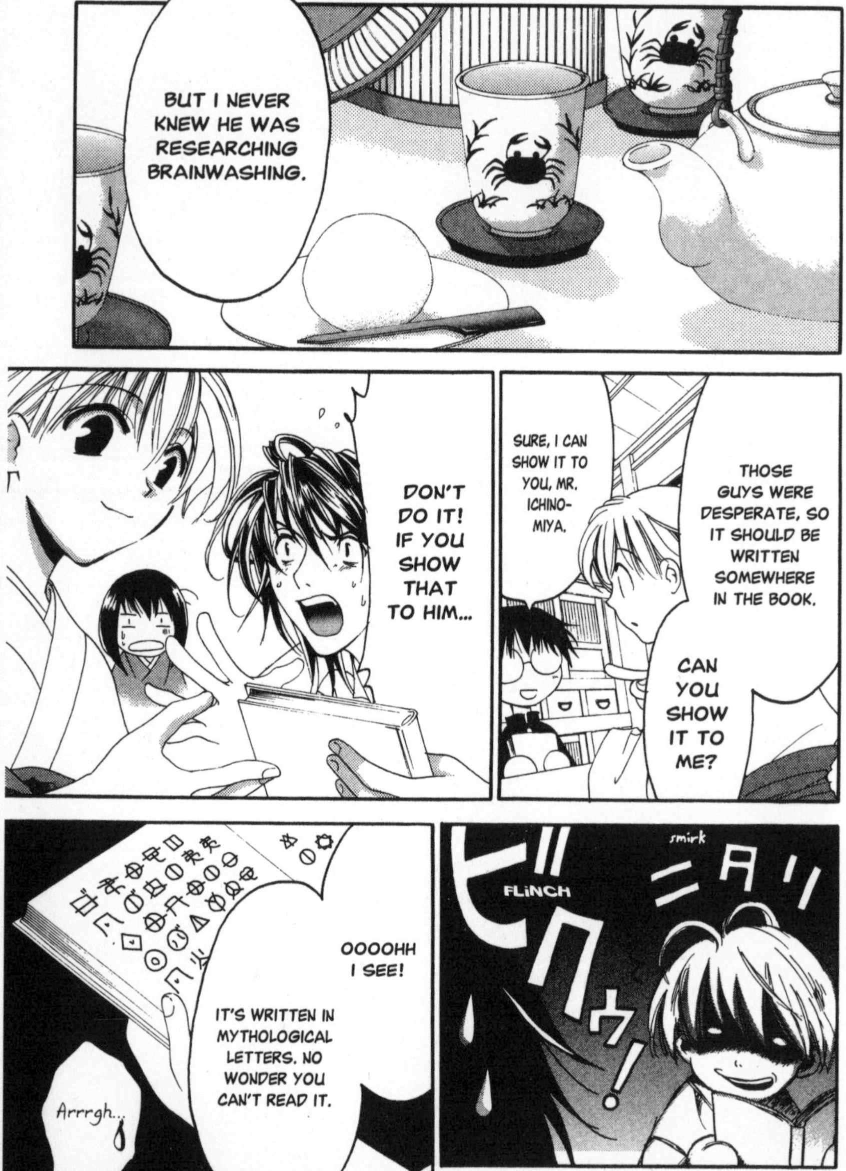
BUT I NEVER KNEW HE WAS RESEARCHING BRAINWASHING.
THOSE GUYS WERE DESPERATE, SO IT SHOULD BE WRITTEN SOMEWHERE IN THE BOOK.
CAN YOU SHOW IT TO ME?
SURE, I CAN SHOW IT TO YOU, MR. ICHINO-MIYA.
DON'T DO IT! IF YOU SHOW THAT TO HIM...
smirk
ニタリ
ビクゥ!
FLiNCH
OOOOHH I SEE!
IT'S WRITTEN IN MYTHOLOGICAL LETTERS. NO WONDER YOU CAN'T READ IT.
Arrrgh...

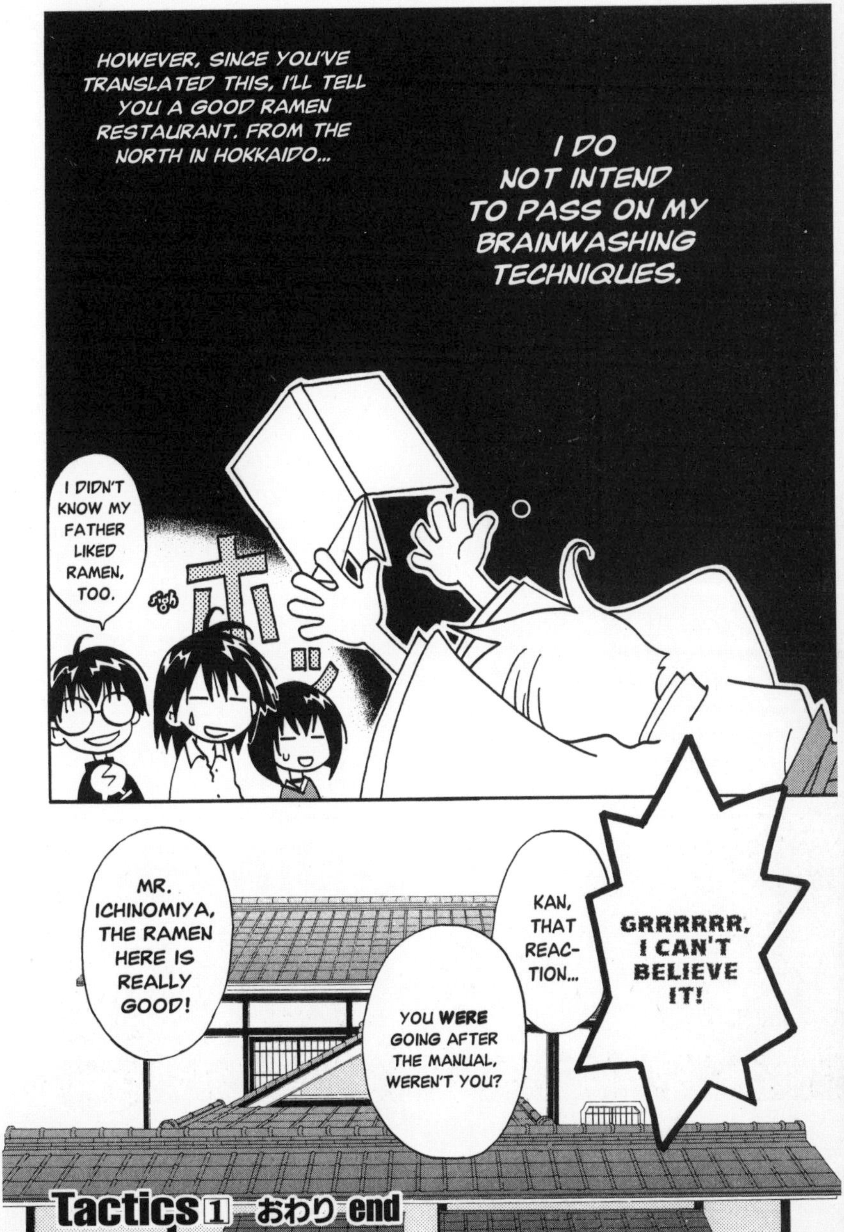
I DO NOT INTEND TO PASS ON MY BRAINWASHING TECHNIQUES.
HOWEVER, SINCE YOU'VE TRANSLATED THIS, I'LL TELL YOU A GOOD RAMEN RESTAURANT. FROM THE NORTH IN HOKKAIDO...
sigh
I DIDN'T KNOW MY FATHER LIKED RAMEN, TOO.
GRRRRRR, I CAN'T BELIEVE IT!
KAN, THAT REAC-TION...
YOU WERE GOING AFTER THE MANUAL, WEREN'T YOU?
MR. ICHINOMIYA, THE RAMEN HERE IS REALLY GOOD!
Tactics 1 おわり end

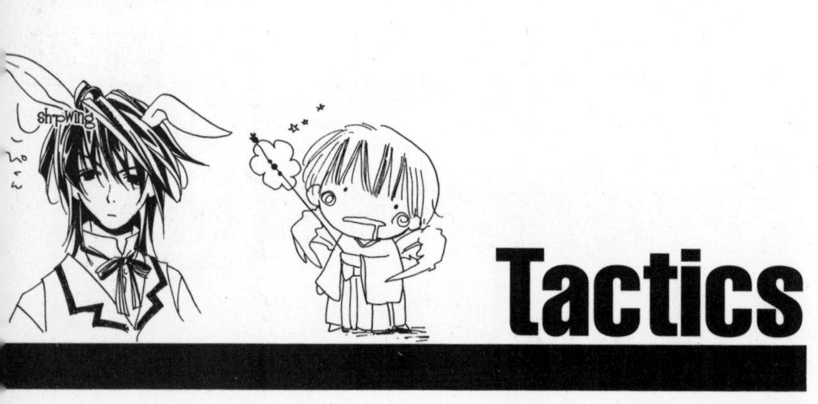
sh-pwing

Tactics

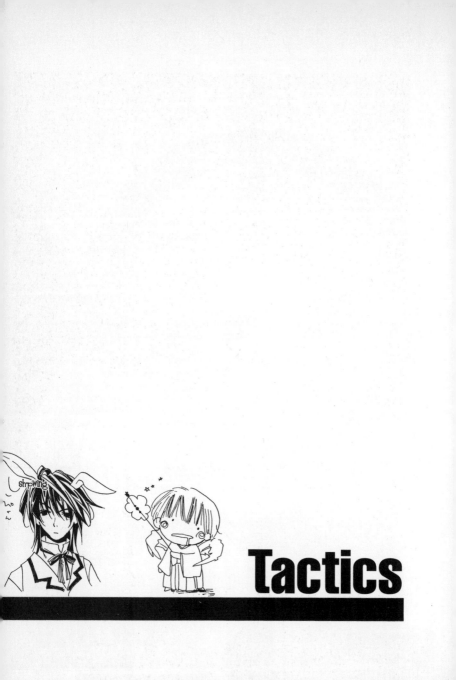

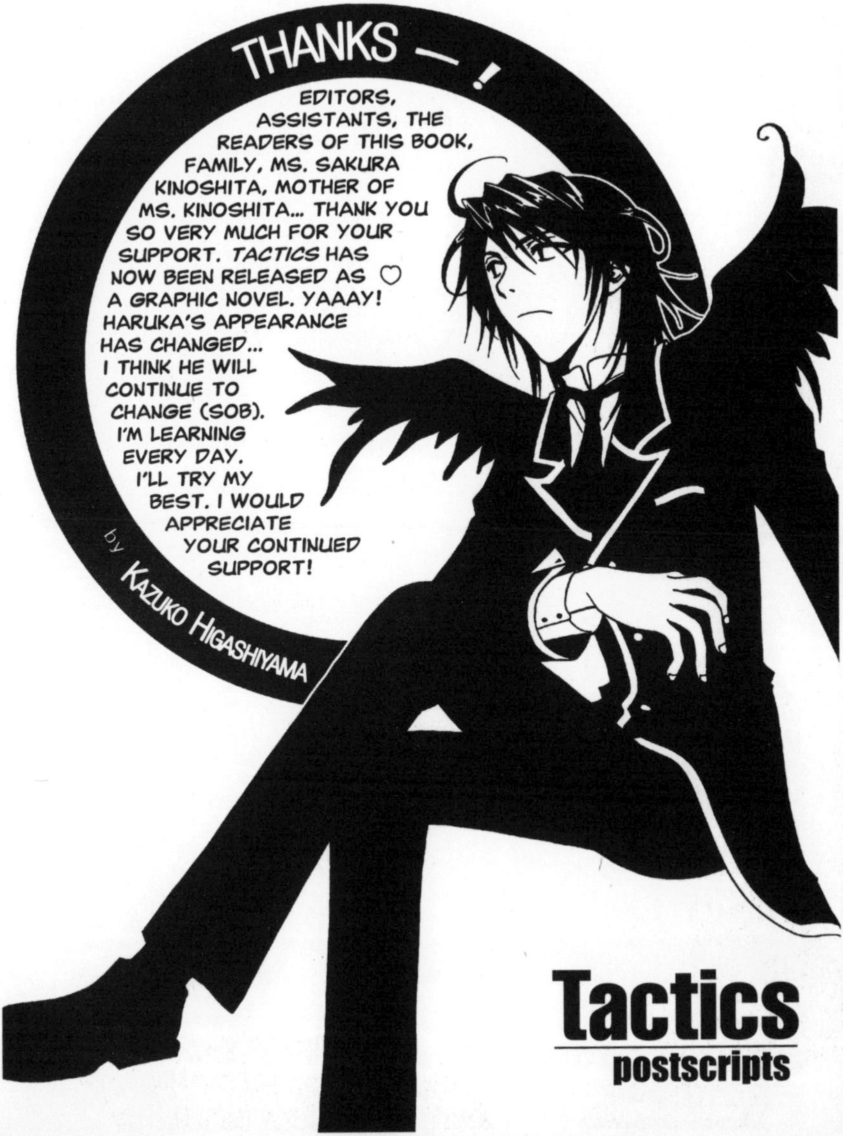
THANKS —!
EDITORS, ASSISTANTS, THE READERS OF THIS BOOK, FAMILY, MS. SAKURA KINOSHITA, MOTHER OF MS. KINOSHITA... THANK YOU SO VERY MUCH FOR YOUR SUPPORT. *TACTICS* HAS NOW BEEN RELEASED AS ♡ A GRAPHIC NOVEL. YAAAY! HARUKA'S APPEARANCE HAS CHANGED... I THINK HE WILL CONTINUE TO CHANGE (SOB). I'M LEARNING EVERY DAY. I'LL TRY MY BEST. I WOULD APPRECIATE YOUR CONTINUED SUPPORT!
by KAZUKO HIGASHIYAMA

Tactics
postscripts

Tactics
postscripts

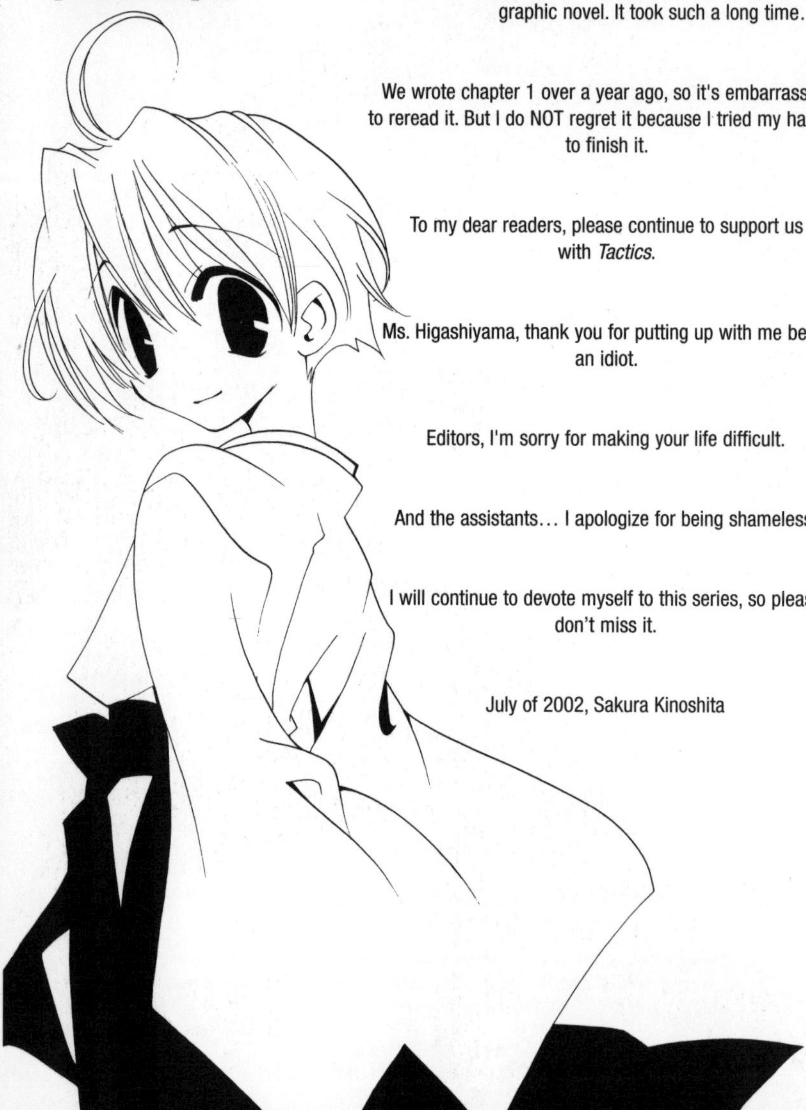

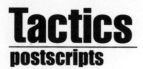

Hello and how do you do? I'm Sakura Kinoshita.

Thank you for purchasing *Tactics* 1. It finally came out as a graphic novel. It took such a long time...

We wrote chapter 1 over a year ago, so it's embarrassing to reread it. But I do NOT regret it because I tried my hardest to finish it.

To my dear readers, please continue to support us with *Tactics*.

Ms. Higashiyama, thank you for putting up with me being an idiot.

Editors, I'm sorry for making your life difficult.

And the assistants... I apologize for being shameless.

I will continue to devote myself to this series, so please don't miss it.

July of 2002, Sakura Kinoshita

Tactics vol.1

© Sakura Kinoshita / Kazuko Higashiyama 2002
All rights reserved.
First published in 2002 by MAG Garden Corporation.
English translation rights arranged with MAG Garden Corporation.

Translator	**MADOKA MOROE**
Lead Translator/Translation Dept. Supervisor	**JAVIER LOPEZ**
ADV Manga Translation Staff	**KAY BERTRAND, AMY FORSYTH, HARUKA KANEKO-SMITH, EIKO McGREGOR, BRENDAN FRAYNE & JOSH COLE**

Print Production/ Art Studio Manager	**LISA PUCKETT**
Pre-press Manager	**KLYS REEDYK**
Art Production Manager	**RYAN MASON**
Sr. Designer/Creative Manager	**JORGE ALVARADO**
Graphic Designer/Group Leader	**SHANNON RASPBERRY**
Graphic Designer	**SHANNA JENSCHKE**
Graphic Intern	**MARK MEZA**

Publishing Editor	**SUSAN ITIN**
Assistant Editor	**MARGARET SCHAROLD**
Editorial Assistant	**VARSHA BHUCHAR**
Proofreaders	**SHERIDAN JACOBS & STEVEN REED**
Editorial Intern	**JENNIFER VACCA**

Research/ Traffic Coordinator	**MARSHA ARNOLD**

Executive VP, CFO, COO	**KEVIN CORCORAN**

President, CEO & Publisher	**JOHN LEDFORD**

Email: editor@adv-manga.com
www.adv-manga.com
www.advfilms.com

For sales and distribution inquiries, please call 1.800.282.7202

ADV MANGA is a division of A.D. Vision, Inc.
10114 W. Sam Houston Parkway, Suite 200, Houston, Texas 77099

English text © 2004 published by A.D. Vision, Inc. under exclusive license.
ADV MANGA is a trademark of A.D. Vision, Inc.

ISBN: 1-4139-0178-6
First printing, October 2004
10 9 8 7 6 5 4 3 2 1
Printed in Canada

the adventure continues in

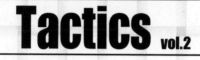

Tactics vol.2

When concerned parents beg help for their troubled son,
it's Kantaro and company to the rescue! With a little
investigation and a whole lotta family therapy, he might be
able to reunite a confused mom and dad with their lonely little
goblin son. And when children suddenly disappear from a village
ruled by the fearsome Sugino, only Kantaro has the wits and
willpower to tackle a negotiation of monstrous proportions. With
a talent for diplomacy and a goblin at his side, Kantaro is
unearthing peace and harmony between the ogres and
bogeymen of both worlds in *Tactics* vol.2!

coming soon from ADV Manga!

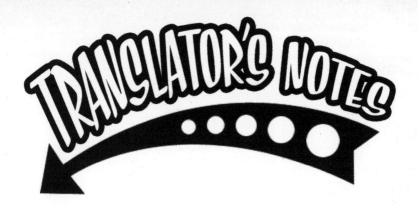

TRANSLATOR'S NOTES

 Haruka

While Haruka is an actual Japanese name, it's also used in a different sense to mean "by far." Thus, Kantaro is making a pun, in giving the demon-eating goblin a name that shows he is "by far" stronger than other demons.

 Kansai and Kanto

Kansai is an area in western Japan that is home to cities such as Osaka and Kyoto, whereas Kanto includes Tokyo and the surrounding prefectures.

 Yoko

In Japanese, *yoko* can refer to a kind of fox spirit. Kantaro is again using this name as a pun, in that Yoko is also a girl's name (though written with different kanji characters).

 Tenko vs. Tenko

The villagers misread *tenko* in Japanese as "heavenly fox" because the character for ten is the same in both words, and the *ko* only slightly different.

 Haruka

The kanji characters shown here are commonly used in girls' names, hence Haruka's embarrassment.

 Rain boy

This odd little creature (called *amefuri kozou* in Japanese) works for Rain God of China. As we saw, he has the ability to call forth rain, and is usually depicted with an umbrella stuck to his head and a lantern in his hand.

 Nine word chant

The actual name for this chant, which is used against evil spirits, is *kuji* ("nine letters"). The chant is read *rin-pyou-tou-sha-kai-jin-retsu-zai-zen*, and means something like "Form a line, soldiers about to battle and glancing at the field before you."

Tanuki

Often described as a "raccoon dog," is a real animal and a member of the dog family. In Japanese folklore, however, it tends to stand upright, and is capable of changing its appearance.

 Proverb

In Japanese, the proverb that corresponds to "Don't count your chickens before they're hatched" is *Toranu tanuki no kawazanyou*, or "Don't count your tanuki fur as sold until you've caught the tanuki first."

 Yorishiro

God was believed to work through a *yorishiro*, a medium or symbol for the spirit of god. Things such as jade balls, stones, trees, boughs, rocks, animals, mirrors, and swords are famous as yorishiro.

p. 129 **(1) Udon**

Japanese-style noodles made with wheat and a touch of salt. They're usually served in hot clear soup, typically topped with some vegetables, slices of meat and egg.

(2) Ramen

If your only exposure to this dish has been the instant variety then you don't know what you're missing. Ramen is an incredibly tasty dish that is big business in Japan—famous restaurants will have customers lined up around the block, waiting for over an hour to sit down and have a bowl of those hot, delicious noodles. For a glimpse of the breadth and appeal of ramen, www.worldramen.net is an absolute must-visit.

 Ramen stand

Ramen stands (or carts) may not be as prevalent as they once were, but they're still out there. Drivers of ramen carts usually have a distinctive bell or horn they sound when they come around.

 Norito / Shukuji

Haruka is dancing to what Japanese people call *shukuji* (or *norito* in old Japanese), a benediction read in celebratory ceremonies. The Japanese is very old, and so we decided to use Latin to illustrate the age, religiousness, and the mysteriousness of what the author is trying to convey. Below is the English translation of the norito:

High in the heavens live the God and Goddess,
the holiest of Holies /And they did summon a heavenly host of Gods
"Our grandchildren shall rule over these bountiful fields of rice, peace and harmony"
Thus did the Gods command/But those who prosper in the bosom of heaven have
sinned Sins against heaven/Sins against country/All these sins do they commit

 Norito

Below is the English translation of the norito:

Even on this joyous day of plenty do we fear the Gods
Bowing in their great presence we do humbly pray
That they may bless their loyal son Shinnosuke Usami...

Special thanks to Jack Wiedrick for the translation of old Japanese to Latin, Japanese to 16th-century English, and all the definitions provided for each phrase of the *Norito*! Thanks Jack, you're awesome!

Mythical Detective LOKI Ragnarok

vol. 1

The **strange** cases of a boy **detective** who may just be a **god**!

from Sakura Kinoshita, who brought you *Tactics*!

Loki is no normal 10-year-old boy! For one thing, he is a mythical detective. He is also the father of Fenrir the Dog and Yamino. And he may just be the Norse god of mischief! These are the strange cases of the world's strangest detective. In his first case, Loki must help a mute girl he names Spica. Spica has been cursed by Odin—who hates Loki. But does Spica have some other connection with Loki that has been disguised?

In his second case, Fenrir has been kidnapped. Loki is aided in his search by the prophetess Skuld the Norn. But Skuld has her own reasons for separating Loki from his son!

Volume 1 available in October 2004!

www.adv-manga.com

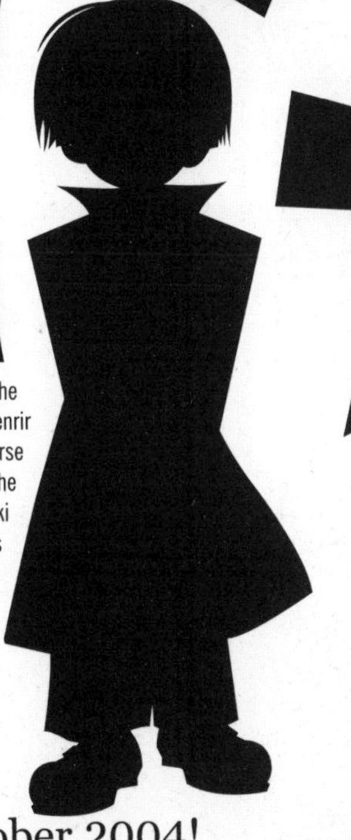

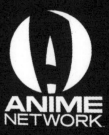

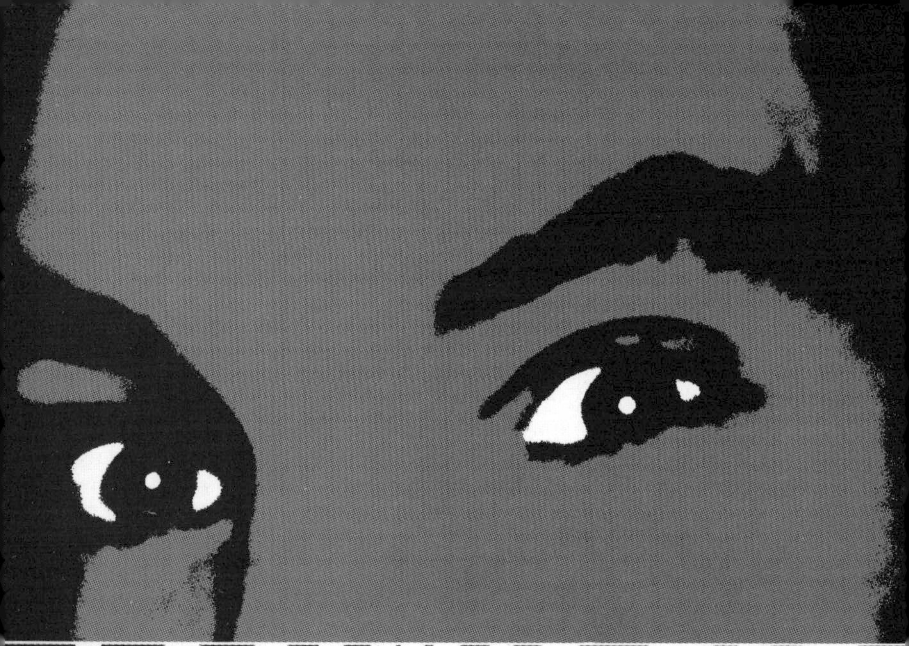

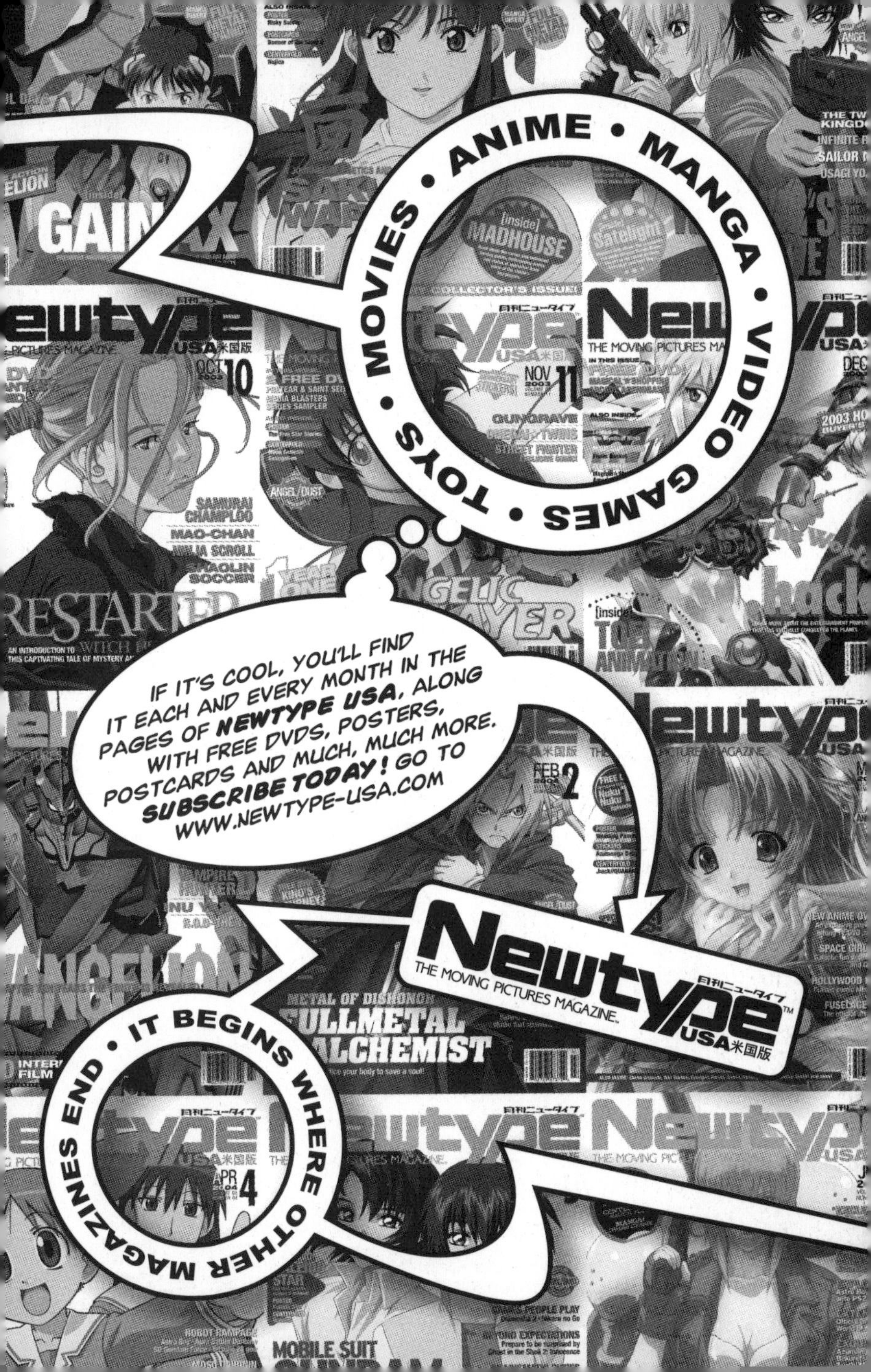

ANIME • MANGA • VIDEO GAMES • TOYS • MOVIES •
IF IT'S COOL, YOU'LL FIND IT EACH AND EVERY MONTH IN THE PAGES OF NEWTYPE USA, ALONG WITH FREE DVDS, POSTERS, POSTCARDS AND MUCH, MUCH MORE. SUBSCRIBE TODAY! GO TO WWW.NEWTYPE-USA.COM
Newtype™ THE MOVING PICTURES MAGAZINE. 月刊ニュータイプ USA 米国版
IT BEGINS WHERE OTHER MAGAZINES END •

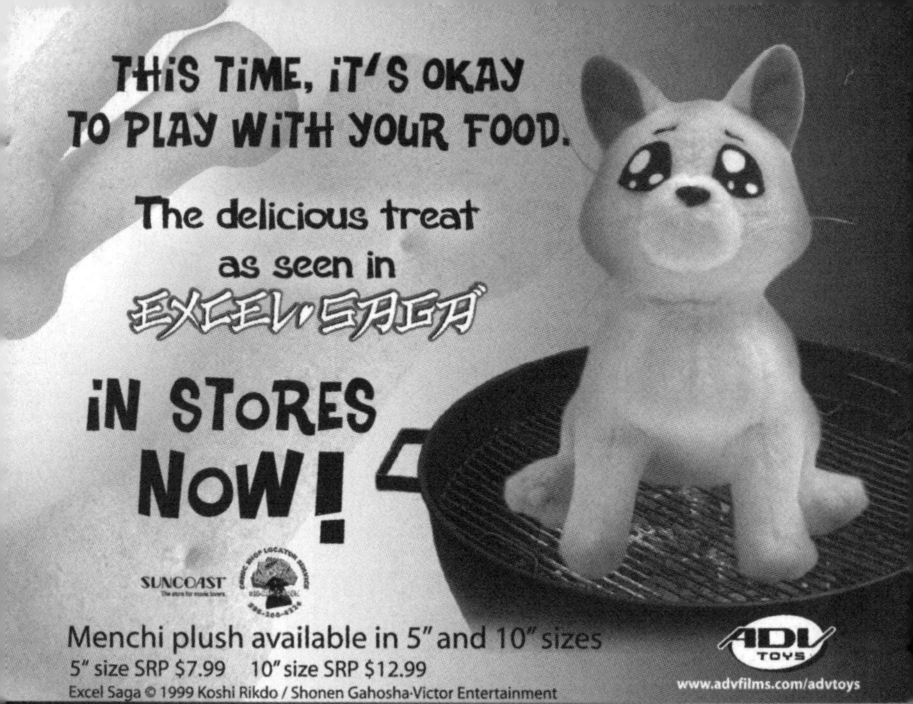
THIS TIME, IT'S OKAY
TO PLAY WITH YOUR FOOD.
The delicious treat
as seen in
EXCEL SAGA
IN STORES
NOW!
SUNCOAST
Menchi plush available in 5" and 10" sizes
5" size SRP $7.99 10" size SRP $12.99
Excel Saga © 1999 Koshi Rikdo / Shonen Gahosha-Victor Entertainment
ADV TOYS
www.advfilms.com/advtoys

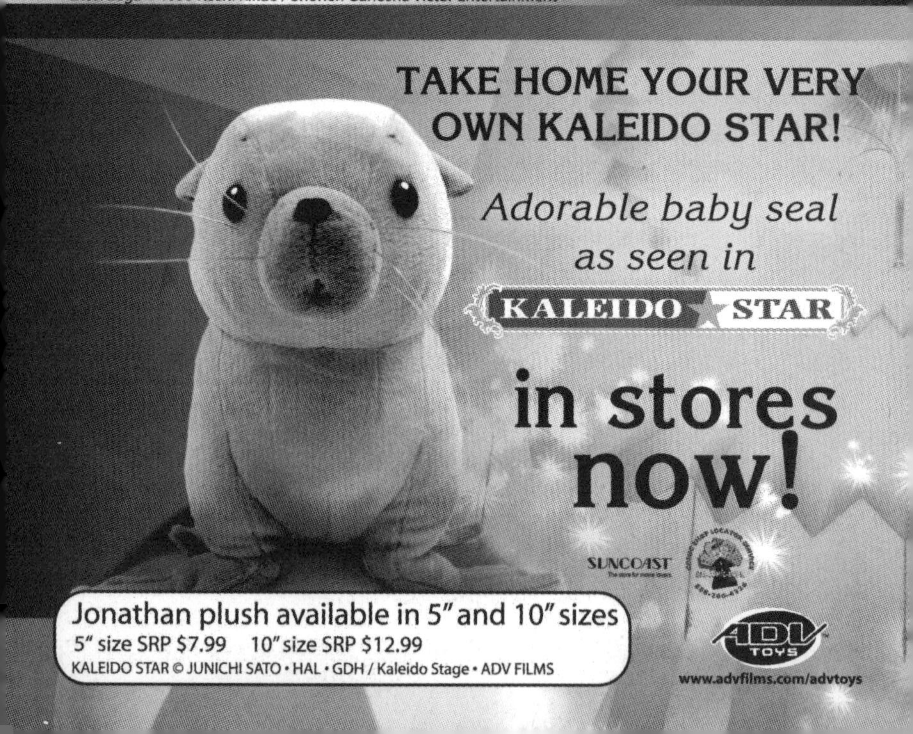
TAKE HOME YOUR VERY
OWN KALEIDO STAR!
Adorable baby seal
as seen in
KALEIDO STAR
in stores
now!
SUNCOAST
Jonathan plush available in 5" and 10" sizes
5" size SRP $7.99 10" size SRP $12.99
KALEIDO STAR © JUNICHI SATO • HAL • GDH / Kaleido Stage • ADV FILMS
ADV TOYS
www.advfilms.com/advtoys

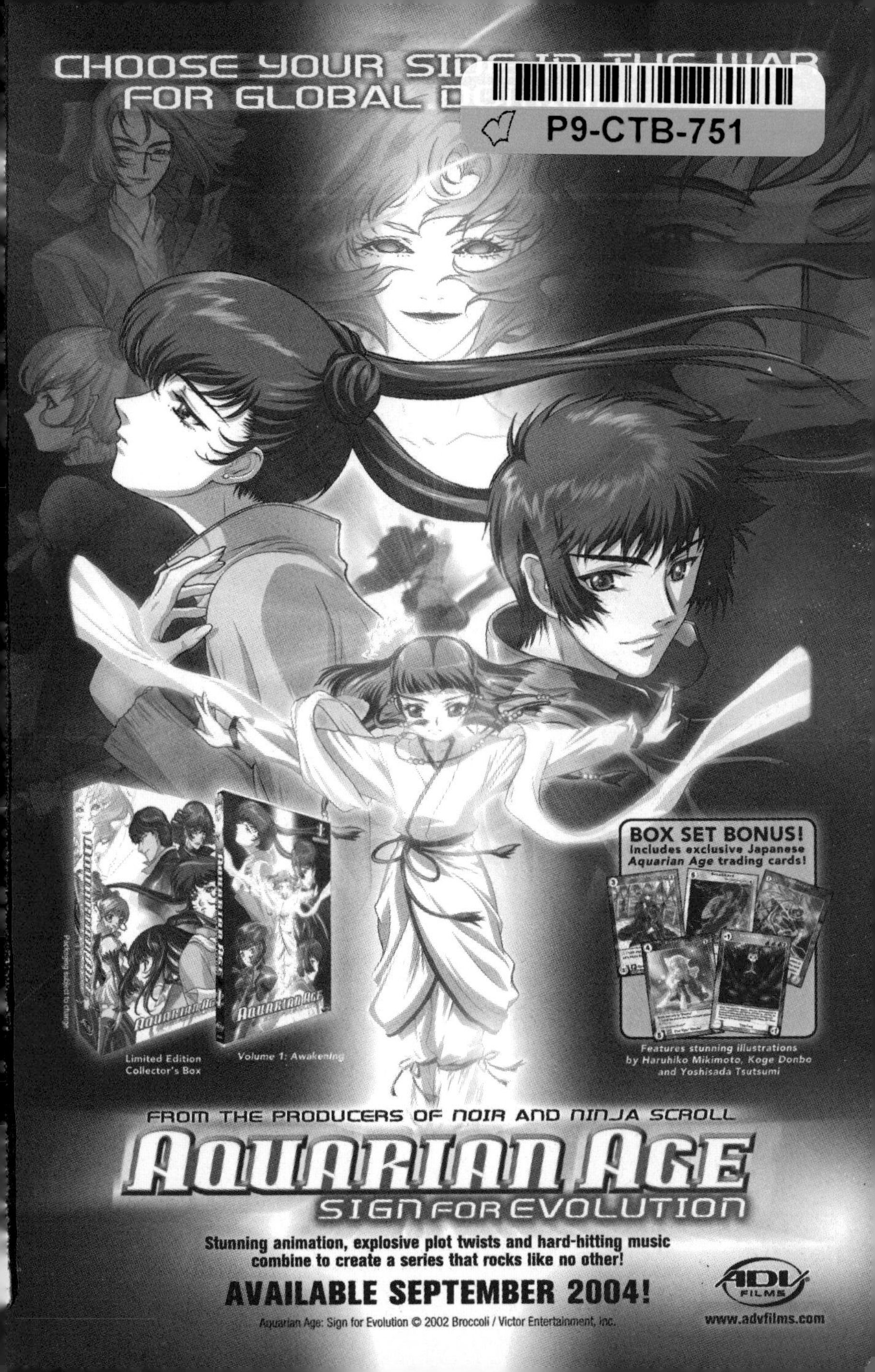
CHOOSE YOUR SID
FOR GLOBAL D
P9-CTB-751
BOX SET BONUS!
Includes exclusive Japanese Aquarian Age trading cards!
Limited Edition Collector's Box
Volume 1: Awakening
Features stunning illustrations by Haruhiko Mikimoto, Koge Donbo and Yoshisada Tsutsumi
FROM THE PRODUCERS OF NOIR AND NINJA SCROLL
AQUARIAN AGE
SIGN FOR EVOLUTION
Stunning animation, explosive plot twists and hard-hitting music combine to create a series that rocks like no other!
AVAILABLE SEPTEMBER 2004!
ADV FILMS
Aquarian Age: Sign for Evolution © 2002 Broccoli / Victor Entertainment, Inc.
www.advfilms.com